The DEATH of STALIN

The DEATH of STALIN

Georges Bortoli

Translated by Raymond Rosenthal

PRAEGER PUBLISHERS · NEW YORK

Published in the United States of America in 1975
by Praeger Publishers, Inc.
111 Fourth Avenue, New York, N.Y. 10003

Originally published in France
under the title *Mort de Staline*
by Editions Robert Laffont, S.A.

© Editions Robert Laffont, S.A., 1973
English translation © 1975 by Praeger Publishers, Inc.

Library of Congress Cataloging in Publication Data

Bortoli, Georges.
    Death of Stalin.

    Translation of Mort de Staline.
    Bibliography: p.
    Includes index.
    1.   Stalin, Iosif, 1879–1953. 2.   Russia—Politics and
government—1936–1953.   I.   Title.
DK268.S85B613   947.084′2′0924   73-19434
ISBN 0-275-10120

Printed in the United States of America

Contents

Sections of illustrations follow pp. 56 and 152.

Preface

On March 5, 1953, a great many things changed for all of us because an old man died on the outskirts of Moscow. A week after his burial the world already felt that it was no longer the same place.

Whether or not he was the product òf his epoch, he had become an epoch in himself. There was Stalin, and then there was post-Stalin. There was an immense dominion, a glorious, brilliant leader with boundless powers, the fear and love he inspired, the superhuman genius with which he was invested. Then, from one day to the next, there was an abyss of oblivion and guarded whispers. His most zealous disciples pretended to forget their master. At one time, they even denounced his crimes. And then, once again—silence. His compatriots would even reach the point where to avoid mentioning his name they would describe his rule by a shy circumlocution: "The epoch of the personality cult."

Nobody had ever disguised himself with such genius. He made a myth of his person, a kind of Plato's cave of his sovereignty—shadows on the wall. His reign lasted twenty years, but it is one of the most poorly known in history.

I have tried to rediscover him. Above all I wanted to describe this transition from one period of time—his—to another. To follow step by step Stalin's last days and the first days of the new era. I looked through the documents and listened to witnesses, all kinds of witnesses. People who met him. People who chopped wood in Siberia and were there because of his orders.

With all my heart I thank all those who helped me draw closer to him, who have nourished this book with the flesh and blood of their own harsh experiences.

I have had to respect the anonymity of some of my informants. A law that is still in existence forbids Soviet citizens from "furnishing information" to a foreigner, so that any story told in confidence becomes a crime. I can only hope that this survival of former times will finally disappear, together with all the prison cells which still exist —and that some day a reissue of this book can name, without fear of harming them, all those who have let me share their memories.

Moscow-Paris
1968–73

part I
SUMMER

1

The Motorcade

*One day I was walking down the Arbat
When God passed by in five automobiles.*
— Boris Slutsky

July, 1952

Approaching at a furious speed, headlights swept down the middle of the avenue. Not the usual white headlights of Moscow cars. Bright yellow searchlights. At the same time, a raucous, nasal, almost animal wail of horns and sirens filled the air. Taut with emotion on the sidewalk, you found yourself overtaken, passed, surrounded, in a split second, by scores of policemen who suddenly appeared from nowhere. You had just enough time to catch a glimpse of five black limousines flashing by, their drivers riveted to their steering wheels and curtains hiding the back seats. You have just been grazed by legend and history. The All-Powerful, the terrible and wise leader who holds each minute of your life in his hands, was there for an instant.

The Arbat, with its old Arab name, is one of Moscow's liveliest streets. It slows down as night falls, but even then there is an endless parade of old women in gray dresses and headshawls on their way home with the eternal shopping bags, and couples strolling out of the Art Cinema on the square and walking unhurriedly to the nearby Metro station, where a large red M flares out brightly.

A signal from the Kremlin had shattered this quiet routine. All traffic lights on Arbat and, farther ahead, on the Bolshoye Dorogomiloskiye and Mozhaisk were switched to red. Militiamen blocked the intersections and the side streets so that the route was completely clear.

3

Security guards in uniform and plainclothes lined the edge of the sidewalks, while passersby huddled against the walls. Shutters closed. Then, racing from the Kremlin through the Borovitsky gate, the big black limousines tore through the city at breakneck speed.

Stalin was going to his house in the country.

In a car with thick bullet-proof glass and an armor-plated body, he was hidden from view by the curtains in the back seat. All of the cars in his escort were identical and none had license plates. It was impossible to distinguish Stalin's car from the rest; and the drivers, true virtuosos, continually passed each other, weaving in and out and changing places in the motorcade, in a strange sort of ballet.

In the quarter of a century that Stalin had wielded absolute power, nobody had even heard of a shot being fired at him. Nevertheless, year after year, the security with which he surrounded himself was being constantly perfected.

Three thousand agents of the MGB—the Ministry of State Security —watched the twelve-mile route from the Kremlin to Stalin's dacha. Everyone living along the route was the object of special surveillance, and all newcomers were carefully screened.

"If you got a *propiska*, a residence permit to live on the Arbat, in those days, it was like getting a certificate for super-citizenship," a Muscovite said.

The whole world thought that Stalin lived in the Kremlin. But this had not been true for about twenty years. His real home was his country house near Kuntsevo, southwest of Moscow, though press, poets, films, and an obsessive iconography continued to associate his name and image with the ancient red-walled citadel—a worthier place for a hero than a suburban villa. On that July night, as always, a window in the Kremlin's great governmental building remained lit until dawn. Anyone walking on Red Square could see it. And late passersby could respectfully gaze up at the splotch of light above the arrow-shaped crenelations on the rampart and unconsciously repeat the phrase used on the radio, "He lives, thinks, and works for us."

But people accustomed to seeing the five cars pass beneath their windows guessed the truth. From Stalin's comings and goings, they might even have concluded that as he grew older he was spending less and less time in the office. But why concern oneself with such awesome mysteries? Why mention this State secret and run the risk of terrible punishments? Merely to hint at Stalin's whereabouts amounted to endangering his safety and made one a bad citizen. The entire country, then, submissively continued to see its leader where he was not. And Western correspondents weren't any better.

A cloud hid Stalin from his people's eyes, turning him into this dim figure speeding through the night, preceded by the wail of sirens. The man whose face was everywhere but whose real face nobody knew.

In the faint gleam from the dashboard, or whenever he switched on a light to glance at his pocket watch, the little seventy-two-year-old man huddled in the back seat of the ZIS 101 looked very gray. The dense brush of mustache, which *Pravda*'s retouchers always darkened with black, was gray. His thinning hair, even the thick hairs low on his forehead, which painters dared not imagine as anything but full and black as at the time of the Civil War, or, at the most, sprinkled with a few silvery threads, was almost completely white.

In paintings and on film, he was always shown huge and majestic, his head lifted above those of his comrades-in-arms, above the surge of the assembled populace reaching up toward him. Gerasimov, the illustrious pontiff of official painting, portrayed him among the Kremlin's towers, dominating Moscow with his huge athletic stature. A Georgian painter even succeeded, toying a bit with the laws of perspective, in making him larger than the palm trees on the seaside boulevard at Sukhumi.

But behind the auto's closed curtains there was only a frail, old, pot-bellied man, whose neck formed a thick fold on the stiff collar of his jacket.

Thousands of poets and writers, some of them great and famous, have celebrated him in a hundred different languages.

In his own country, he was called "our beloved father," "our dear guide and teacher," "our dear and well-beloved Stalin," "the greatest leader of all times and of all peoples." Thousands of metaphors clustered around his venerated name. In the entire Soviet Union, there was never published a single book, brochure, pamphlet, or thesis in chemistry, astronomy, botany, or philology, no matter what, which did not contain several references to his thought and teachings. Every single family festivity, be it a wedding or anniversary, was certain to propose a toast to him—generally the first toast. The cult was part of daily life. When a rise in the norms of production was announced,* the workers would sigh but say: "Stalin knows." And when sausage was not to be found in the stores, the housewives would murmur: "If Stalin only knew."

In most apartments, one came across his photograph or some kind of plaster bust—a copy of the effigies which welcomed you in administrative offices and at the entrances to subway stations, in classrooms and savings banks, in factories and movie theaters (where his

* Since all workers were paid on a piece-work basis, the "norm" was the amount of production that they must furnish for a given salary.

silhouette appeared to the left of the screen and Lenin's to the right, each accompanied by a quotation culled from his writings).

An engineer passing through Moscow to his new assignment in Siberia counted 101 portraits and busts of Stalin in the Kazan station alone. His statues rose in clearings in the forest and on the tops of mountains. His inflexible, just stare followed you from dawn to dusk, even into your most secret, intimate privacy. He was invisible, and his appearances were as infrequent as miracles. But he was also omnipresent, the eye that saw everywhere.

Alexis, the patriarch of all the Russias, proclaimed him the chosen son of Providence, just as in the past the Tsar had been the Lord's anointed. And for quite a long time, Soviet poets habitually endowed him with supernatural powers:

> He orders the sun of the enemies to set.
> He speaks—and the East reddens for his friends.
> If he tells the coal to turn white
> It will be as Stalin wishes.[1]

Music cannot lag behind poetry, and so more than 2,000 chants and hymns celebrating Stalin's human and superhuman gifts were registered. In the summer of 1952, the Young Guard publishing house sent to press a new collection in which, among others, one found the *Stalin Cantata* by A. V. Aleksandrov, founder of the Red Army Chorus, and the famous *Stalin Song* with music by Khachaturian.

A Soviet citizen who was twenty-five in 1952, not very conformist by nature, told me: "I did not believe a word that our newspapers printed. But as for *him*—that was another matter. He was beyond all the words. He was in the depths of us, too strong to be fought against."

I have rediscovered a small book with a red binding which is entitled *Rodina Schastlivykh*—the *Nation of the Happy*.[2] About sixty poems, some of them signed with well-known names. Stalin is everywhere. Often these are psalms, pure and simple, such as these litanies on *his* name:

> In this word there is strength, health, happiness.
> From the earth to the sun
> Above the glory of our people
> This word rises like a rainbow with seven bands.
>
> It rises like a song above the gardens,
> Up there where the peaks glitter in the light.
> Leaving the eagles behind without wings . . .

This word, this great word is Stalin!
The soul, flesh, and blood of the people.

On the opposite page, a dedication indicates that this small book was offered on May 21, 1938, to student Tanya A., as a reward for her scholarly successes.

If Tanya A. has survived the war, she is about fifty years old today. What does she think of the hero of her youth? Can a person destroy such conditioning? Can one forget that kind of love?

It was quite simply a god who appeared in the sky of Moscow on holiday evenings: An immense portrait of Stalin, tied to a captive balloon, swayed gently in the wind from twilight to dawn, lit up from the ground by the spreading rays of searchlights.

In fact, it was an all-powerful father whom the little Russians worshiped when they repeated the sentence they were taught in school: "Thanks to Comrade Stalin for our happy childhood!"

Invisible, the divinity rolled past in his motorcade of ZIS cars, the auto that bore his name, since ZIS are the initials for *Zavod Imeni Stalina* or "Factory Named After Stalin."

Where Moscow's last buildings end, the motorcade left the Mozhaisk highway. It turned left and followed a road that a red disk striped with yellow announced as forbidden to all other cars. This was the governmental route—the route used by only one man. Nobody could travel over it except Stalin himself, his guests, and the people who served and guarded him.

It was only ten minutes since Stalin left the Kremlin and already the forest surrounded him, a forest thickened by the night. A sharp turn to the left, in the direction of the Lenin hills. A turn to the right. A slight climb. Not a person in sight, but two barriers opened as if by themselves. In its turn a high wooden portal opened without delaying the progress of the ZIS, which followed a long avenue and then finally stopped in front of a very simple building in the middle of a thick wood.

2

Kuntsevo

It was here that Stalin had spent his sleepless nights for at least twenty years, working, all alone, his telephones at his side, or receiving his ministers at two o'clock in the morning, or dining until dawn with his close collaborators. Everything, from Berlin to the Pacific, converged on this house hidden among the trees, at a place called Volynskoye, near Kuntsevo.

The lords of the international Communist movement knew this house. In the winter of 1949, Mao was sumptuously welcomed here in the large room on the second floor. Tito, when he still belonged to the family, spent a whole night defending himself against the alcohol and arguments of the master of the house, who, being a Georgian, liked to get other people drunk in order to wrest their secrets from them.

Since the war, the chief members of the Politburo gathered there almost every evening, seated around a long table laden with a profusion of hors-d'oeuvres and dishes of meat resting on hotplates. The food was spicy—and so was the conversation. Wines and vodka flowed in torrents. More than one guest rolled under the table amid coarse, tumultuous gaiety.

Such dinners became rarer. Corroded by arteriosclerosis, Stalin began to take care of himself. The closest of his intimates spoke guardedly about a stroke he had had but which he had overcome. Often at night, he remained alone in the silence of the dacha, protected by a host of invisible guards.

Most of the house's rooms were furnished in precisely the same way—sober and ugly. A large table, chairs, a few armchairs, a sideboard. All of it anonymous and without style. Here and there a beautiful rug, a reminder that the owner really did come from the Caucasus. Almost everywhere couches, on which he stretched out to read or dream. And many fireplaces—he liked to poke at a fire.

In the official banquet rooms, one could admire his portraits. Some of them showed him in his dress uniform, loaded down with gold braid and decorations, which he never actually wore. He left these frills and ornaments to his marshals, and even when he dressed up in the role of Generalissimo, he preferred ordinary combat attire, like Napoleon.

When he went to sleep, he left the large room and shut himself up in a small, low-ceilinged room which held only a narrow bed and a night table. Except for the dark oak paneling on the walls, everything here was severe and bare, as in the consultation room of a public dispensary.

Molotov, the son of middle-class parents, played the Western gentleman, sporting beautiful pajamas and impeccable bathrobes when he got out of bed. Stalin scoffed at this. He often wore a combination of day and night linen, sometimes even going to sleep fully dressed under a blanket, removing only his boots. Except for his taste for good food, which was always simple and countrified, he was a man of Spartan, rather uncouth habits. His only luxury was power.

The man stretched out on his hard bed in this monastic chamber was the eternal victor, the man who always won. The poor and humiliated child from the poor district of Gori, the pock-marked narrow-shouldered seminarian, the small Georgian agitator, the obscure revolutionary eclipsed by all the big guns of the Party, now ruled over close to a billion people. His rise to power was not the trajectory of a cannonball, not Alexander the Great's or Napoleon's sudden, brilliant breakthrough to fame, but rather a slow progression, step by step, with gritted teeth. When Joseph Vissarionovich Dzhugashvili * chose a long time ago the name of Stalin—the man of steel—he did not realize how well he was putting it: the man who never takes off his armor. Always ready, always on the alert. And always alone.

He had no friends. He had dispersed his early comrades, slaughtering most of them, preserving only a few prostrated associates, some of whom he also exterminated when he felt like it.

He had no family. He himself had blurred the tracks, organized a void. Concerning his father, the shoemaker Vissarion Dzhugashvili, who died when Stalin was a child, it was merely said that he was a

* Russian names are composed of three elements: given name (Joseph or Iosif), patronymic (Vissarionovich: the son of Vissarion), and surname (Dzhugashvili).

poor and brutal drunkard. Opponents used to insinuate—when people still dared to insinuate—that he might not have been the real father.

His mother, the strong and pious Catherine Geladze, was a little better known. Having managed by dint of sewing and laundering to get him into the seminary where his politics veered from black to red, she lived long enough to see him at the pinnacle of power. She died at about eighty in a palace which he had requisitioned for her and where he visited her only three times in fifteen years. She occupied only one small room furnished with an iron bed. Here, at last, we find a family characteristic, the Spartan spirit.

But our discoveries end there. No sisters or brothers—all of them died at an early age. And, during the entire course of this illustrious existence, not a single trace of a Dzhugashvili cousin, a Geladze uncle, a relative, even a distant one, on either the maternal or paternal side.

A willed solitude which had also been imposed on the historians. God did not have relatives. Nevertheless, it was an astonishing solitude when one thinks of the overflowing Georgian families, so rich in generous, demonstrative and encumbering relatives. Was this Dzugashvili a true Georgian? Many saw him endowed with a strong dose of Ossetian blood. The Ossetians, a small people living in the mountains, are the Georgians' neighbors, but do not have their culture or great traditions. Around 1840, travelers described them as pilfering bandits, never without their rifles, which they propped on a forked stick, in order to aim accurately. They were also renowned for having supplied the Tsars with a large contingent of prison guards. At any rate, Stalin, having destroyed the documents and liquidated the witnesses, remodeled his childhood to suit himself, whenever he felt like it.

When it came to women, there was the same vacuum. His first wife, Catherine, died of tuberculosis after three years of marriage; his second, Nadezhda, after about fifteen years and tragically. Attempts were made to substantiate a story about an unsuccessful operation, but the suicide story surfaced irresistibly. For a long time, however, people preferred to believe that he had murdered her, just as Ivan the Terrible and Peter the Great had murdered their sons, and Catherine the Great had let her husband be killed. On the other hand, whether she held the revolver herself or he helped her, what difference did it make? It certainly was he who made going on impossible for her.

And what about 1952? The Western newspapers were full of stories about a certain Rosa Kaganovich, to whom Stalin was supposedly married. There were plenty of details: Rosa Kaganovich, of Jewish extraction, was a physician, with strong legs and burning black eyes. She was the sister (or, according to some, the niece) of Lazar Kaganovich, one of the principal members of the Politburo. A number of widely distributed newspapers had published her photograph. Several years later, Stalin's daughter would openly declare that Rosa Kaganovich never existed.

And yet she was not invented by the press alone. In 1952, all of the Soviet Union, from the Baltic to the Ussuri, believed in her existence. People who considered themselves well-informed would smile discreetly and refer to Lazar Kaganovich as "the brother-in-law." Even when terrorized, people do not easily deprive themselves of the romance of history.

But Stalin wanted to appear disincarnate. To the rare guests who had access to him, he presented the image of a lonely man. He vacationed alone in the south and entertained alone at his dacha. Those invited to these long dinners always talked about purely male evenings.

Yet nobody believed that he could have lived for twenty years without female companions. Nadezhda died in 1932. The next year, Isaac Babel, a well-informed writer with good connections in the hierarchy, confided to Parisian friends: "They are looking for a mistress for the Secretary-General." The Secretary-General sent Babel to gossip in the netherworld, but those who were close to him before he became a god knew him to have a fiery temperament and brutal appetites. His tastes were no secret. He had a holy horror of intellectual women and preferred fleshy, opulent beauties. On meeting Lyubov Orlova, the movie star of the thirties, he had half-jokingly threatened her husband:

"You will have to deal with me if Lyubov Petrovna gets any thinner."

Docilely, the Soviet cinema began to be thronged with robust milkmaids.

"The level of his demands on women was . . . simpler," his daughter wrote; and she added: "I think that the round-faced, pug-nosed Valechka, who was his housekeeper his last eighteen years, completely fitted his ideal of a woman in a home: She was corpulent, neat, served at table deftly, and never joined in any conversations." [1]

So what then? Some discreet secretaries? Some buxom housekeepers? Stalin was the master of his secrets. He had hidden itineraries, and his private trains stopped at deserted stations. Whenever he thought it convenient, he ordered the destruction of archives that might embarrass him—his own and those of the State. All of his servants, right down to the last kitchen helper, were members of the State Security services and sworn to silence. Above all, there was the fear which tied all tongues.

That was how he concealed his mistresses when he was a full-blooded, robust, and brutal fifty-year-old man. Now that he was old and sick, the need for a woman was the least of his worries.

Yakov, his first son, had died in captivity in Germany. Stalin had not lifted a finger to save him. He did not like prisoners of war; he felt that they were either traitors or deserters. After the victory, he had all such persons tried and for the most part thrown into concentration camps—Russian camps after the German ones.

His second son, Vasily, had a marvelous career as his father's favorite: at twenty-three, he became a general in the Air Force. But Stalin was told that he was an alcoholic misfit and he hardly ever saw him any more.

Svetlana, his daughter, had the same experience. She was only allowed to see him at long intervals, and then it was more an audience than a family visit. Yet it is true that he had loved her. When she was ten years old, he used to write her very tender letters; he called her "my little sparrow," "my delight." But later on, he was irritated by her passionate attachment to a Jewish film-maker, her brief love affairs and two divorces. Yet her second husband was almost the perfect match: the son of Andrei Zhdanov, who, until his death, was one of the Leader's closest comrades. He was a serious young man, a functionary in the Scientific Department of the Central Committee. When he picked up his pen, it was to put in their places the "subjectivist" scholars and to express the necessary reservations about Einstein's suspect theories.[2] Svetlana should never have left such a proper husband.

Stalin had eight grandchildren. But he allowed only three of them to be introduced to him—and summarily at that. He had never felt the need to meet the others. In a country where the child is king, this absence of tenderness was almost unprecedented.

He made up for this solitude by becoming the universal grandfather at ceremonies and in the official iconography; tiny Pioneers wearing red kerchiefs, little girls with blond braids and dainty pinafores would rush up to him, their arms laden with flowers. Then a broad smile would lift the heavy mustache.

Stalin had gotten rid of his two wives' families. He had ordered two brothers-in-law shot and his four sisters-in-law thrown into prison (two were still in prison and two died there). A third brother-in-law, a general, opportunely died of a heart attack when he arrived at his office and found that all his colleagues had been arrested.

By 1952, Stalin had only political ties, the relations that exist between a master and his subordinates. These were the only relationships that interested him.

His solitary existence was not without mobility. Everywhere there were villas, State properties set aside for his personal use. His permanent residence was at Kuntsevo. But not many miles away, Lipki and Semonovskoye, with their woods and melancholy ponds, were fully staffed and always ready for his arrival all year long. He could go to the vicinity of Great Novgorod in the Valdai mountains, or to the Crimea, where he had only to choose among ancient imperial palaces and new state dachas. But as a rule he preferred his native Caucasus. He had had villas built near Sochi, Adler, and Gagra, all in sight of the snow-covered mountain ranges. Merzhanov, his official architect, endowed them with a sober style and green roofs which blended into the violent vegetation of the Abkhazis. Then he ordered Merzhanov's arrest, but more villas were built for him by Sukhumi—on Lake Ritsa in the region of Kutaisi, higher in the mountains.

At the end of each summer, he migrated. Following the sun, he would spend two months in the south, while the leaves on the slopes of the Caucasus turned gold and scarlet. In the autumn of 1951 he had also stopped off at Borzhomi. He stayed in a charming summer pavilion of pink stone built for the Grand Duke Michael, brother of Nicholas II. It was filled with the refinements of the old Tsarist court: antique rosewood furniture, handsome Dutch fireplaces, a malachite table which came, people said, from the Malmaison. But he had his bedroom set up on the ground floor to avoid climbing stairs, which he found arduous, and furnished it with the sort of well-varnished, anonymous, factory-made furniture that was dear to the European middle class in 1930.

His portraits were hung almost everywhere. And facing his desk was a large portrait of Lenin.

Borzhomi's climate slightly disconcerted him. It was quite rainy for the Caucasus. Lonely in the room with two beds, Stalin burned logs, dipping into the woodbox prepared at his request. It is not known whether he ever used the large Russian billiard table left behind by the previous occupant, the brother of the executed Tsar.

Those sojourns in the Caucasus were recommended for his health. Now and then, he managed to go take the waters at the Tskhaltubo thermal station, where a bath house as high as a two-story building had been built just for him. Small and lonely in the midst of slightly demented luxury, he would sit on the marble throne at the end of an immense marble bathtub and wait for the water to rise and cover his shoulders.

But this year for the first time he had no desire to leave for the south. He wanted to strike a heavy political blow while he still had the strength to carry it off. In the autumn, he would call a Party congress (something he had not done for thirteen years) and make some changes in the hierarchy. So he would not be able to go anywhere.

Besides, travel was beginning to weigh heavily on his old body. He felt better at Kuntsevo where, without leaving Moscow, he could satisfy his two needs: solitude and nature.

This man, so insensitive to the interiors which surrounded him as to cover the walls with bad reproductions cut out of newspapers when he could take whatever he liked from any Soviet museum, had a physical love for this Podmoskovye countryside, this wild, free nature at Moscow's very gates. His dacha was set in a real forest of black pine trees and white birches, woods with a sharp, tangy smell around which swarmed an intoxicated population of wasps. It was a dense, natural forest, despite the clearings made near the house for flower beds, despite the tall fence which imprisoned him.

For cold days, the house was shielded on three sides by large glass panels similar to closed-in porches, and on such days, Stalin would go from one to the next, following the course of the sun, like a sickly old plant in its greenhouse. But during the summer, when it was hot, as soon as he woke in the morning, his devoted servant Valechka brought him breakfast in the garden. He had always had the habit of reversing the order of night and day, and morning started for him around midday, sometimes later.

At this point, some of his collaborators would join him under an arbor with their documents. And, while martlets flashed across the sky, he would sign documents, lay down the law, spare one man, condemn another, displace whole populations, build and rebuild his gigantic, bloody edifice. Sometime in the afternoon, he would go back to the Kremlin. Sometimes he would simply decide to stay at Kuntsevo.

At ease in this balmy heat, he would make a few good-natured remarks about the weather or the caterpillars to a gardener. He often flaunted a slightly demagogic benevolence toward his more humble servants. It was with his close associates that he was imperious, caustic, at times even foul-mouthed.

He usually wore a rather worn "safari" jacket—the garment without insignias but of a military cut and with four capacious pockets, which he adopted after the revolution. He exchanged it for the full-dress uniform of the Generalissimo only on specific public occasions. His trousers were stuffed casually into soft leather boots.

In the morning, well rested, he still walked with a lively step. But, apart from that, he was an old man with a sallow, rough complexion. His sparse hair was gray, but he did not bother to have it dyed, like Budenny or Mikoyan. He did not depend on the barbers for rejuvenation, but on the painters—and solely for the sake of history.

Despite the ravages of old age, he had the profile of an intelligent wild beast, a curved profile with a low forehead which sloped down into the large nose with flaring nostrils. When he was seen full face, one was struck by his eyes, yellow like those of a tiger, lying in ambush behind heavy lids. He had a coarse face with gross, massive cheekbones and skin, pitted with smallpox, that was greasy. Nadezhda Mandelstam called him "the man with the grubby fingers" because they left stains on books. He was once a small Georgian, black as a raven and as well tempered as a blade. Now his rounded shape made him look shorter than his five feet ten inches. The tailors skillfully padded his uniforms, but when he wore his old "safari," one could see his narrow, drooping shoulders. His left arm was a bit stiff and bent, due to an early accident (which got him an exemption from military service in 1916), and when, from time to time, he took little strolls, he would rest it casually against his hip.

The delicacy of his finely shaped hands contrasted with his heavy face, splotched with freckles. They were the hands of an old man, and he would join them, clasp them, like an old seminarian. Sometimes he would absentmindedly slip his right hand into the front of his tunic, as the heir of another great revolution once did. He liked to affect a certain slowness, letting his words fall unhurriedly, like maxims or riddles. But beneath this calm was a tenseness, a holding oneself in check. When he was young, he was capable of flinging a stool at a comrade's head in the middle of a political meeting. Even today, despite old age, he would occasionally burst into raucous fits of rage. Or he made boisterous jokes. He had an acrid, insistent sense of humor, and, when he wanted to be, he could even be charming.

Forced by the state of his health to stop smoking, he still flourished his pipe, which for so long a time had been an integral part of his personality and which he carried in his trouser pocket. He took care of himself in a rather anarchic fashion. For a while, he was interested in Bogomolets's studies on rejuvenation, and the laboratories of the Ukrainian professor were inundated with rubles. But, being suspicious, he put himself into doctors' hands as little as possible. Like many old people from that era, he thought he could treat his illnesses by swallowing a few drops of tincture of iodine in a glass of water.

He would like to have had a very long life. After all, the Caucasus is the land of centenarians, and his work was not yet finished. But he knew that his body was betraying him. With his intimates, he enjoyed talking about his death—partly to watch their reactions and partly to hear them cry out in protest and reassure him. For protection against the iciness of old age, he went to his dacha at Kuntsevo, to make contact with the earth and the air of the pine trees. Here he found the sort of active leisure which he valued more than anything else. He took it easy; sometimes he played chess. He read a lot, but he was never fond of fat volumes through which one picked one's way slowly, elbows on the table. He preferred leafing through a book or a magazine, half reclining.

The dacha was also his fortress, the voluntary prison in which he shut himself away to defy both the living and the dead—those millions of dead. He was obsessed by distrust and suspicion. Visitors summoned to his receptions were all searched. Before entering his office, those on a more intimate footing had to hand their briefcases to the officer on duty. A few hundred yards from the dacha, within the park's enclosure, the guards' building could lodge more than one hundred men. It was a squat, hexagonal construction, with windows on all sides that reached almost to the ground. Thus, at the first alarm, soldiers could rush out simultaneously from all sides. They were equipped with the best weapons, an abundance of vehicles, and searchlights that could penetrate into every nook and cranny of the park, which was strewn with traps and mines. On the outside, beyond the tall green barrier, other detachments were patrolling with their dogs.

The part of the dacha where Stalin slept was an inner sanctum even more effectively concealed, more mysterious, and better protected than the rest of the house. Only carefully screened servants had access to it. All the same, certain indiscretions made it possible to evaluate the complexity of the devices set up to protect Stalin against any attempts at assassination. There was talk of armored doors bolted from the inside, some activated by remote control. There was talk of rooms without windows or windows blocked by slabs of reinforced concrete. There were descriptions of a whole network of bells and buttons that allowed Stalin to call for help at any moment. Two witnesses, while drawing a picture of the austere bedroom with its narrow cot, added: "Actually, there was not just one room, but rather four identical rooms. He chose one of them each night—at the last moment." Everything was planned to foil the crime which was never attempted, perhaps never even imagined. Stalin personally oversaw each detail and made sure that new devices and methods were added to protect him. No, it was not yet time for him to die.

All great rulers usually lose touch with the men they rule over. But Stalin cut himself off deliberately, deliberately restricted himself only to contacts with his courtiers, who also, imitating his example, were locked up in their small dungeons. When, by chance, he emerged from his closed world, it was only to plunge into another abstract world, a solemn banquet in the Hall of Columns, a commemorative evening at the Bolshoi, a drab succession of speeches. Sometimes, sitting deep in his box, he attended the performance of an opera. In 1947, he bestowed upon the cruiser *Molotov* the honor of pacing her bridge while she was in the Black Sea. But he never visited the workers in their factories or the peasants on their collective farms, just as during the war nobody ever saw him inspecting the soldiers at the front. His powerful mind divined everything at a distance.

Two or three times a year, the people who had been assembled to march caught a glimpse of his vague silhouette high on a reviewing stand. Occasionally, a bewildered school child was ordered to climb all the way up to the stand and embrace him.

This way of being invisible, of being up there, high above everyone, nourished the legend and the cult. Physical fear and intelligent calculation joined hands to turn the recluse of Kuntsevo into a deity ensconced on his cloud. But sometimes God picked up the telephone.

Boris Pasternak, Ilya Ehrenburg, and a few others all heard one evening the coarse Georgian voice in their receiver. On those rare occasions, Stalin's secretary would call the chosen person: "Dial such and such a number." At the other end of the line would be Stalin in person. For some mysterious reason, Stalin had decided to take an interest in one's personal case. After the conversation, the number would became inoperative.

3

The Celebration

July 23–27, 1952

At dawn on this summer Sunday, floods of humanity converged on Tushino, a small airport on the near outskirts of Moscow. Subways, streetcars, and buses were stormed by a dense, silent crowd, a crowd that was ebbing and flowing like the sea, shoving forward unhurriedly, on the verge of suffocation, like a patient, deaf ram. Whether they had come voluntarily or had been officially chosen, they all exhibited the special transportation pass they had been given the day before at their factory, enterprise, or office, or, as is said in the U.S.S.R., their "collective."

It was "Aviation Day," a great holiday. So great that it was customary for Stalin to show up in person as he did on the First of May. This year, the celebration was doubly important. As Levitan, a speaker for special occasions, pointed out, at that very moment, a thousand miles from Moscow, the Volga-Don Canal, "the great construction of the Stalin era," "first-born among the great constructions of Communism," the main link in "the Stalin plan for the transformation of nature," was being inaugurated. From the height of the loudspeakers installed along the streets leading to Tushino, the inspired commentary crashed down on the crowd with all the force of its many decibels.

The populace swarmed all around the airport like patient ants. Men in shirt sleeves, women in cotton dresses. Groups of young boys and girls forged ahead, singing to the sound of an accordion. Here and there an early drinker brandished his *pollitra*—his pint of vodka—

amid general, good-natured tolerance. Members of the Komsomol, *druzhinniki*, benevolent cops in civilian clothes, red armbands on their sleeves, helped the militia to channel this turbulent flood.

For the trip to Tushino, men and women workers had piled into factory trucks—Molotov trucks, similar to the American GMCs. Driven by official chauffeurs the "Pobedas"—which according to *Pravda* could "easily outdistance both the Opel and the Mercedes"— arrived with factory managers, administrative cadres, and officers accompanied by their wives in light silk dresses and picture hats.

The long black ZISes of the dignitaries did not appear until after midday. By then the air field was already invaded by an immense crowd spilling over onto the banks of the Moskva river. The sun had dried out the rich, greasy clay. People sat on the grass, their heads protected by newspapers. All eyes stared fixedly at the official reviewing stand draped with red bunting and covered with flowers, flanked by gigantic portraits of Stalin and his "comrades-in-arms." But, at this point, let us yield the floor to the reporters of *Pravda* of July 29, 1952:

"Two o'clock in the afternoon. Comrade J. V. Stalin ascends the governmental rostrum, hailed by cheers which for a long time refuse to abate. The Soviet people welcome the appearance of the wise leader, the great educator, the inspired strategist. Comrade Stalin cordially salutes the crowd. The ovation grows stronger, expressing the unlimited devotion and ardent love of the Soviet people for Joseph Vissarionovich Stalin.

"From one end to the other of the vast field resound these words which come from the very heart, the depths of the soul: 'Glory to our great Stalin!'

"Hundreds of thousands of people greet Stalin in a transport of enthusiasm. In a tumultuous ovation, the workers express their gratitude to the founder of Soviet aviation, the best friend of the pilots, the great guide and teacher of the Soviet people. Under Comrade Stalin's leadership, the Soviet people have built their admirable air fleet, the Stalin *Falcons* have mercilessly crushed the enemy in the air, on the sea, and on land. With this name, Stalin, our country advances with assurance toward Communism."

The celebration began. First an airplane pulled through the sky an enormous red banner painted with Stalin's portrait. Then a group of about sixty planes, almost wing to wing, spelled out the words: "Glory to Stalin"—"tracing in the sky," *Pravda* remarked, "the acclamation which the whole world cries out to honor the wise leader and teacher."

Next came aerobatics executed by pilots of the Pan-Soviet Society of Volunteers, the para-military organization, and the focal point, the heart of the celebration: the Air Force review. A flyby under the command of the young, alcoholic general who had had such an atonishing career, General Vasily Stalin, the leader's son.

At his post of command stood a small, thin man with the body of an undernourished adolescent, a hatchet face, and black, slightly gypsy eyes inherited from his mother (Nadezhda had gypsy blood). Nervous, almost feverish, he chain smoked and could in a moment become rude and unpleasant. He was surrounded by an atmosphere of adulation. During the war, Pouyade,* on a visit to his command post, was surprised to see heavily decorated officers respectfully picking up the cigarette butts this spoiled brat threw on the floor. But this servility was understandable. With a single word, Vasily could make or destroy a career, wreck a life. Shortly after the victory, Air Marshal Novikov, who had displeased him, disappeared as if through a trapdoor. In January, 1953, a group of deportees would find traces of Novikov at the transit prison of Chelyabinsk in Siberia. One of the prison barbers would boast to newcomers of having shaved the eminent old Marshal's head.

With his huge dacha, his horses, and his dogs, Vasily was one of the most typical of Moscow's gilded youth, among whom were included the children of high officials, actresses, stage directors, and famous athletes. Unfortunately, he had a dubious reputation, compromised by all sorts of ambiguous activities—shady deals involving soccer and hockey and the construction of stadiums and swimming pools, which, though never completed, cost the state a fortune. Shockingly brutal, he beat up women and police officers. It was even said—though never officially confirmed—that he killed the husband of one of his mistresses. Above all, he was habitually drunk. At the age of thirty-one, he could no longer pilot a plane and most of the time seemed incapable of giving a reasonable order.

His father, tired of his idiotic indiscretions, was about to strip him of his rank as chief officer of Moscow's Regional Air Command, to which he had ordered him appointed. This flyby on July 27, 1952, would be Vasily Stalin's last day of glory.

Here in the sky of Tushino were the MIG-15s, the very same planes which at this very moment were fighting under Chinese colors in Korea against American fighters. Aerial combat had actually entered the jet age less than two years ago. On that day, over the Yalu River, American F-80 Shooting Stars met for the first time adver-

---

* At that time a colonel and the commander of the famous French Fighter Squadron, the "Normandie-Niemen," which fought with the Russians.

saries worthy of them: MIGs piloted by God knows whom—Russians? Chinese?

The word MIG is a contraction of Mikoyan and Gurevich, the names of the plane's designers. Artem Mikoyan was the brother of that other Mikoyan, the famous political leader who on this day could be seen on the official reviewing stand, not far from Stalin. Family feeling being one of the virtues of good Soviet society, this phase of the aviation show was being directed by Lieutenant-Colonel of the Guard A. A. Mikoyan, son and nephew of the aforementioned personages.

Now it was the turn of the YAK fighters, conceived by Yakovlev, Stalin's favorite airplane designer. Since the beginning of the war, Yakovlev had been showered with honors. It was just at the time when Tupolev was getting out of prison, a "special prison," of course, one of those *charachki* where imprisoned engineers were put to work. Tupolev had designed projects of such excellence that he was given his freedom. But even more than Tupolev, more than Ilyushin, Yakovlev remained the favorite. He was even authorized to publish his memoirs of the Leader, whose foremost quality he somberly defined: "Stalin is exceptionally modest."

Bombers, massive parachute jumps, flights of heavy helicopters, this aerial review was proof of the absolute priority which Stalin accorded to defense problems. It was also proof of his people's deep-seated passion for flying. The preoccupation with "Russian priority" —the slogan of this era—undoubtedly carried the commentators a trifle too far when they asserted that "the world's first airplane" was built by the Russian inventor A. F. Mozhaisky (*Pravda*, July 28, 1952). But it was also true that even in the thirties, when it was a weak, shaky country, when its first assembly lines were just beginning to turn out its first bad trucks, the Soviet Union was already proudly exhibiting to the world its great airplane, the *Maksim Gorky*.

Thousands of miles to the south, equally festive and ecstatic crowds were at this very moment gathered near the first lock of the Volga-Don canal.

In the front row of the audience stood Pietro Nenni, who had just been awarded the Stalin Peace Prize at the Kremlin and headed a delegation of the Italian Left.

The howl of the sirens, the blare of the brass bands, the cheers issuing from tens of thousands of throats shattered the air. The ship *Joseph Stalin* glided toward the first lock, flaunting a banner with the words "Glory to the Great Stalin" inscribed on it in gigantic gold letters.

A colossal statue of Stalin, thirty-six feet high, dominated the scene. He himself had personally signed a decree releasing thirty-three tons of copper to erect this monument to himself. On each of the statue's epaulettes, two men could lie down comfortably to sleep. And this shape could be seen from across the flat steppe beyond Stalingrad, about fifteen miles away. In the July 12, 1952, issue of *Izvestia,* a well-intentioned poet saluted this mountain of bronze in verse:

> Coming from Stalingrad
> And the Don
> We see beyond the boat
> Above the Volga, the monument
> Of the Leader,
> The father, the friend of all peoples.

> . . . On the banks of the Volga Stalin has appeared,
> Looking into the distance.
> He has removed his cap.

> The water plays, full of reflections,
> The eagles circle below the clouds.
> From the five seas the boats
> Salute him with their sirens.

> He opens the way of the canal,
> And the entire world sees that it is
> The fulfillment of the promise
> He gave to Lenin.

Khrushchev would later speak mockingly of the millions spent to build this gigantic statue, "while ever since the war the people of this region have lived in huts."

The canal was called the V. I. Lenin Canal. Stalin blended the cults, associating himself with the glory of his dead predecessor. His *Abridged Biography,* copies of which were distributed by the thousands, proclaimed once and for all: "Stalin is the Lenin of today."

Nevertheless, on film—the authentic film kept in the archives—the "closest disciple" never appeared near the master. All through the Revolution and the Civil War, Stalin was absent, a blank. The newsreels of the time always showed a Trotsky or a Zinoviev at Lenin's side. Therefore, they were locked away to gather dust in the cinema collections. One had to be content with a few photographs. A photograph was of course quite malleable; with a pot of glue and a pair of scissors, one could make a group of people who were never together.

For weeks and weeks, in every factory, every workshop, every office, every meeting, every youth assembly, orators praised the canal. It was almost as if the Soviet people depended on it for their lives, just as the Egyptians rely on the Nile for theirs. Just a canal, and yet much more than a canal. The transformation of nature means the accelerated transition from Socialism to Communism. Stalin was the demiurge who turned the world upside down so as to make a gift of it to all mankind. The great postwar projects would bend the elements to the needs and pleasures of the workers.

Step by step, cameramen followed each stage of the canal's excavation. Their film was lyrical: A whole village was moved away on platforms; hills were turned into valleys; a sea rose. The Don Cossacks celebrated their unification with the population of the Volga with huge cavalcades. A kolkhoz offered a gigantic banquet to the builders: pink hams, great pyramids of luscious fruit. Stalin's cinema adored rustic revels. In reality, the villages didn't even have enough bread.

The camera lingered on the loyal gaze of the workers, etched their virile, angular profiles below large, slightly tilted caps, and waxed discreetly sentimental over the women mechanics with their long blond tresses. But it ignored the thousands of prisoners employed to build the canal and its dam under the black, persuasive eyes of the tommy guns. Yet, a few weeks later, the name of Sergei Nikiforovich Kruglov, Minister of the Interior and chief overseer of the concentration camps, appeared on a list of people who had been decorated with the Order of Lenin: "For the completion of the canal on schedule," [1] as the communiqué stated.

From Sholokhov to Olga Berggolts, all the famous names were called upon to celebrate the canal. The press reached the very height of lyricism: "The century-old dream of our people. . . . The great Stalin plan aimed at uniting all the seas of the European part of the U.S.S.R. with a single system of waterways is accomplished. . . . Moscow, the capital of our Fatherland, has become the port of five seas."

As to the strategic importance of the canal, not a single word, despite the fact that Stalin not so long ago had explained it in Djilas's presence.[2] This would have struck a jarring note in the predetermined lyrical chorus.

On the morrow of the great day—doubly great because of the opening of the canal and Stalin at the Tushino airport—*Pravda* offered its readers a commemorative issue. Only four pages—but in these four pages Stalin's name appeared 123 times.

4

Comrades-in-Arms

At Tushino, the crowd acclaimed the master, but it did not forget the disciples lined up on either side of him.

On Stalin's right were several marshals and admirals, glittering with stars and gold braid, but despite the bulk and importance of their 175 divisions, their influence was limited. The only one with any real standing was Bulganin, the political marshal, a handsome man with cold blue eyes. It was from the Party that the army took its orders. Popular military figures, from Tukhachevsky to Zhukov, had been shot or removed by the Secretary-General, who, after the war, to prevent any misunderstanding, awarded himself the supreme rank of Generalissimo.

The truly illustrious persons were the civilians on Stalin's left. People in the crowd who, by straining their eyes, caught a glimpse of them from afar could see that they were divided into two schools of dress: those who, like the skinny Suslov and the plump Malenkov, remained faithful to the military blouse and the semi-military caps of the Civil War period; and those who, like Aleksei N. Kosygin, rising star of the new generation, dressed in civilian style, with a tie and a soft felt hat.

More casual, the ebullient Nikita Khrushchev wore a tie, but braved the July sun with a bare head.

Legendary heroes, small shapes on this high reviewing stand, these were the *soratniki,* the "comrades-in-arms." To be a top-level figure in 1952, it was important that the *Great Soviet Encyclopedia,* at the very beginning of the article concerning you, characterize you as "a close comrade-in-arms of J. V. Stalin." The addition "faithful disciple of Lenin" did not hurt, but that was a matter of some gener-

25

ations back. Only those who had known the living Lenin were entitled to it.

The most illustrious of the *soratniki* was Vyacheslav Mikhailovich Molotov, the most faithful of the faithful.

His real name was Skryabin, like the famous composer Scriabin, but they were not related. From a middle-class family in northern Russia, he had had a fairly polished upbringing, with violin and dancing lessons, and enrollment in the St. Petersburg Polytechnical Institute. But, before long, he plunged into revolutionary activities. In 1909, at the age of nineteen, he was deported. The failed 1905 Revolution with its legendary events—the revolt on the battleship *Potemkin,* the barricades in Moscow—had just taken place. Molotov, who was the least romantic and the least imaginative of men, the most frigid and formal, nevertheless went along with the lyrical current of the period. He exchanged the name Skryabin for his clandestine pseudonym, which derives from *molot* or "hammer," a tool whose qualities of obstinacy, heaviness and monotony he shared. In 1912 he was one of the founders of *Pravda,* the newspaper of the future.

Before long, the hammer was in the hands of the master. Molotov backed Stalin in the Party struggles without reservation. He helped him to rise above his rivals, fighting Trotskyists, then Zinovievists and Bukharinites with meticulous tenacity. He was one of the small group to whom Stalin owed everything. In 1930, the Secretary-General rewarded him by making him President of the Council (then called "Council of the People's Commissars"; the less fraternal but more "proper" "Council of Ministers" reappeared only after the war).

It was Molotov who received Ribbentrop at the Foreign Office in 1939 to sign the German-Soviet Pact. It was he who announced the news to the people over the radio when German tanks were unleashed on Russia. On the Committee of Defense, during bad times, he was Stalin's close adviser and right arm. At Teheran, Yalta, and Potsdam, the West discovered him at his chief's side, and at the U.N. he was called "Mr. Nyet." He had a slight stutter, but his Western colleagues were awed by his merciless logic, his patience, and his obstinacy. Chakovsky, a very official writer, described him in 1940 in Berlin confronting Hitler—countering the Chancellor's lyrical furors with his old pedantry, his stern schoolmaster's tone.[1]

He wore the bureaucrat's pince-nez and had the diligent air of a good student. Churchill considered him "the perfect modern robot." Voroshilov called him, more simply, "stone-ass." Djilas, who observed him from close up, declared: "One should not underestimate Molotov's role. Stalin and he complement each other."

In 1949, he was relieved of his post in the Ministry of Foreign Affairs, but for everybody he remained number two. The city of Perm was renamed Molotov in his honor. His name was also given to eleven other towns and villages, to a district in Moscow, one of the highest peaks of the Pamir range, a cape in the Arctic Ocean, dozens of enterprises, kolkhozy, sovkhozy, a home for young people, culture parks, and war and merchant ships, not to mention the country's largest auto factory. Half of the trucks in the U.S.S.R. rolled by with a highly visible "Molotov" stamped on their hoods.

The great cult was nourished by seemingly small facts. A dignitary's importance was measured by the number of cities, communities, and industrial and agricultural enterprises that bore his name. When the dignitary fell, the names changed. "This is Kossior-Radio." Kossior was the chief Party secretary in the Ukraine. When the radio station dropped the first part of its name, Ukrainians knew that Kossior was going to be shot.

In 1952, it had been three years since Molotov's wife had been arrested. She had been one of Moscow's most prominent hostesses, giving receptions, taking the waters at Karlsbad, living in grand style like the aristocratic ladies of bygone times. As a rule, the wives of highly placed men in the U.S.S.R. tried to remain in the background, but Polina Zhemchuzhina-Molotova, former factory worker turned prominent militant, pursued a personal career. She received all sorts of titles and awards: member of the Central Committee, Minister of Fisheries, jury member of the high fashion committee. She was chiefly known, however, as being responsible for the Soviet perfume industry. Thanks to her, elegant women could use cosmetics and the heavy, expensive perfumes "Red Moscow" and "Queen of Spades."

Being Jewish, she found herself involved in the many "Zionist conspiracies" which began to blossom in 1948. The Central Committee met in order to strip her of all her functions in the Party. Rumor had it that, contrary to custom, the vote was not unanimous. With a reckless show of courage, Molotov abstained. But Polina was handed over to the prosecutors.

Her disappearance was not much noticed by the diplomatic corps. The postwar repression was remarkably discreet. It was as though a trap door had suddenly opened. There were no great trials, as in 1937, no articles in the newspapers. Even the person's replacement in office was generally not announced. Those who knew kept their mouths shut.

Polina Molotova was sent to a camp in North Kazakhstan. Her husband did not know where she was, or even if she was still alive.

But he continued to appear at official ceremonies, stone-faced, at Stalin's side.

Besides, there was no reason to take offense. Stalin made a habit of arresting his closest collaborators' wives. The wife of Kalinin, the head of the Soviet State, was tortured and thrown into jail for years. Nevertheless, the old, bearded president continued to receive the accreditation letters of foreign ambassadors and to pin on decorations with his shaking hands. He died in 1946, covered with honors. During his final months, his wife had been returned to him.

The wife of Poskrebyshev was also arrested. Poskrebyshev, the head of Stalin's personal secretariat for almost twenty years, knew all the secrets. He could speak casually, even rudely to any dignitary. But he did not protest. How could he? His wife was the sister-in-law of one of Trotsky's sons. Stalin liked these stains on his collaboators' records. They made it easier to keep them in line. No, the fact that your wife was in prison did not mean that your career had been shattered.

Molotov's case was different. He was personally under fire and he knew it. Stalin no longer consulted him, no longer invited him to his dacha. He had even publicly suggested that his old associate might be an English spy—another instance of the eternal prestige of the British Intelligence Service. Molotov knew that the worst was suspended over his heavy, scholarly head. Would it come in a month, in a year? Arrests were already sweeping away his old colleagues.

Stiff and reserved, in his proper dress and with his hair smoothed down and neatly parted, he looked like an aged child who was being punished. The rebuffs he received made him suffer as much as the fear of death. He worshiped his dreadful master.*

A Bolshevik from the age of sixteen, he could not conceive of life outside the Party. And the Party was Stalin. While President of the Council, Molotov signed all the terror decrees of the 1930's. While a member of the Politburo, he approved the long lists of Communist leaders condemned to death. Probably, if he had been faced by the executioner, he, too, would have shouted "Long live Stalin," as did all those old militants he had sent to be shot.

"Humility," Stalin said, "is the Bolshevik's ornament." In practice, it was in relation to their chief that the Party's cadres had to display this particular quality. He gave them power, privileges, and honors,

---

* And he always would worship him. Sixteen years later, in 1968, the old pensioner Molotov, while working at the Lenin Library in Moscow, happened to sit next to a French student. Noticing that the young woman looked at him with curiosity, unsure of recognizing him, he slipped her a piece of paper, proudly introducing himself: "Molotov, Stalin's right arm—of old." He never repudiated the man who wanted him to die.

but not a sense of security. Day in, day out, they lived in fear for their positions and their very lives. Healthy uncertainty.

Stalin first eliminated his opponents, then the lukewarm who had vaguely lent an ear to his opponents. After this, he went to work on his original collaborators, all those who had unswervingly helped his ascent. It would not be good for anyone to be able to ask, "Who made you king?" An old comrade like Molotov was already just a vestige of the past.

Periodically, the old cadres in all the leading official bodies, above all in the police, were swept away to make room for younger people. Stalin liked newcomers who owed him everything and looked up to him with fervid devotion. The old-timers were also respectful, but habit made their respect a trifle mechanical. There were days when their eyes showed a glimmer of fatigue, the shadow of a second thought.

Besides, this turnover in trusted aides allowed him to use one of the oldest tricks of power: Those on their way out were blamed for the sins of the regime. Stalin excelled at making his associates endure anything. He would assign them the most impossible, most bloody tasks and then, with a single word, repudiate them, throwing them to the mob. And the mob was delighted to see that the great leader had been secretly on their side all along.

Marshal Voroshilov, a friend from time immemorial, his comrade at the defense of Tsaritsyn, was just about to be transformed into a foreign agent.

Brave and stupid, a good soldier and a bad strategist, this former noncommissioned officer had clung to Stalin's coattails since the Civil War. He had helped purge the Red Army of most of its leading cadres. He had acquiesced in Tukhachevsky's execution, applauded that of Yakir, and subscribed to the decision to throw their families, including fourteen-year-old children, into jail.* He had ordered thousands of division, regimental, and battalion commanders shot or deported, leaving an anemic army to face the German onslaught. Stalin made him Commissar of Military and Naval Affairs, which he then directed through him. He put on a public display of crude affection: "You're an idiot, but an old friend. I love and respect you." He didn't even take him to task too severely for the tall stories he told in 1941 about the army's condition.

Kliment Yefremovich Voroshilov was now in semi-retirement, but he was still deluged with honors, luxurious dachas, and riding horses. His imposing nose, his small mustache, and his handsome cavalry-

---

* Note especially the details given by Aleksandr Shelepin at the Twenty-second Congress.

man's bearing made him a favorite subject of the official painters, and Voroshilov's "March" was one of the bravura pieces of the parade bands.

But it had occurred to Stalin that he, too, must be a British spy, and the State Security Agency had installed a sophisticated listening device in his home.

On the other hand, Anastas Mikoyan was suspected of being not a British but a Turkish spy.

This exotic nuance was obviously due to his Armenian origin. The inventor of "Socialism in a single country" abhorred everything that smacked of the cosmopolitan. It displeased him that Soviet Armenians, huddled on the rocky slopes of their Caucasus mountains, should have close cousins, Turkish Armenians, on the other side of the border. It displeased him that they should have in common one religion, one language, and a great past. It displeased him that their spiritual leader, the Patriarch Catholicos, lived in the U.S.S.R., while the place of their greatest sentimental attachment, Mount Ararat, was close by, but in Turkey.

Of course, between these two communities was the Soviet frontier, bordered by a wide strip of plowed land which was carefully examined each day for possible footprints. Yet one never knew. When an American archaeologist announced that he intended to search for Noah's Ark on Mount Ararat, the official poet Mikhalkov bared his fangs:

> But our frontier sentinel does not sleep.
> Keep that in mind, 'archaeologist' Smith.[2]

And that is why Anastas Ivanovich Mikoyan was a Turkish agent. The accusation was absurd. Mikoyan was so completely Russified that when, as required by protocol, he went to Yerevan to present his candidacy for the Supreme Soviet, he found it very difficult to slip a few Armenian words into his Russian speech.

Small, ugly, with a sharp profile, very black eyes, and very dark skin, Mikoyan, like Stalin, came to politics by way of the seminary. If he had survived so long it was thanks to his legendary astuteness. Foreign commerce was his domain, and he occupied a high place in the *soratniki* hierarchy.

In the summer of 1952, Engineer V.M. settled down in his new office in Kharkov and noticed with satisfaction that it was adorned by a portrait of Mikoyan. Portraits were also distributed according to rank: The director was entitled to Lenin, the chief engineer to Stalin, and his assistant to Molotov.

"Mikoyan," V.M. thought. "No doubt about it, this means a nice fat promotion."

Immediately to the left of Stalin on the Tushino grandstand was stocky, round-shouldered Lavrenty Pavlovich Beria, contemplating the airplanes through his pince-nez.

When the NKVD (People's Commissariat for Domestic Affairs) was entrusted to him in 1938, nobody thought that he would stay alive very long. His two predecessors had just come to a tragic end. The first, Yagoda, had made a spectacular exit, as one of the accused in the great purge trials. The second, Yezhov, had disappeared on tiptoe. (All Moscow had looked for him, some claiming that he was in a lunatic asylum, others that he was living in great secrecy in a small house near Koltso. Actually, he was about to be shot.)

After the purges, Stalin loosened the vise slightly by repudiating Yezhov, who had only followed his orders. So Beria released several thousand of the several million people arrested by his predecessor and earned the reputation of a liberal.

His career in his native Caucasus, however, was horrifying. He was a bloodthirsty adventurer, an expert in the use of police intervention.

As a courtier, he was a genius. He seduced Stalin with the maniacal zeal he affected in order to insure his own safety. He knew how to remain alive while working his way up to the summits of the Politburo. He was marshal of the police. But he did not wear the uniform, preferring instead a brick-colored overcoat and a felt hat pulled down over his eyes, which gave him the appearance of one of his inspectors. Behind the rimless spectacles, his gaze was blank and opaque.

Fat and heavily built, he had little resemblance to the official portrait which lengthened his face and endowed him with a fine broad, intellectual brow. He loved wine and was, according to Svetlana Alliluyeva, inevitably drunk at the end of an evening.

A man with a greenish complexion and damp hands, he was driven by an uncontrollable passion for beautiful women. Two young girls were specially raised for him in Moscow so that he could take them to his private apartment or his dacha. Women who pleased him were showered with splendid gifts; even a dacha on the Black Sea was not too grand; but those who annoyed or irritated him were in trouble. The story of one such woman, a pretty young actress, whom for discretion's sake I shall call L., circulated for a long time in Moscow's small theater and movie colony.

One day, Beria invited L. to have dinner with him in his apartment. When she arrived, the young actress was unpleasantly surprised to find that she was the only guest. As soon as dessert was served, Beria became so insistent and ugly that L. ran out of the room and into the street before anyone thought of stopping her. Downstairs, awaiting her, was a chauffeur who could see that all had not gone well that evening, but who impassively handed her a bouquet of flowers—Beria's usual gallantry after a rendezvous.

Somewhat at a loss, L. looked back and saw Beria's pince-nez gleaming in the night as he watched her from the balcony of his apartment. Then, a thick, lugubrious voice with a Georgian accent descended into the street: *"Eto ne buket, a venok."*—"It's not a bouquet but a wreath."

A few days later, L. was arrested.

In July, 1952, Beria had deadly worries. He had always maintained absolute control over the MGB * (Ministry of State Security), and had arranged for his protégé Abakumov to be placed at its head. Now his police empire was slipping out of his grasp. Abakumov was about to be demoted, and the hunt for Beria's men, in all departments, was at hand. In his native Georgia, his supporters had been decimated as a result of the "Mingrelian affair"—another "pro-Turkish" conspiracy. Stalin also reproached him for the delays in building the H-bomb, which he thought should have been ready long ago. (This sector of atomic research had been entrusted to Beria.) In short, Beria, despite his fifty-three years, was now part of the old generation, which would take the blame and thus clear the way for a new generation of *apparatchiki*.

But, after all, Stalin was old and sick. Nobody in his entourage was sacrilegious enough to hope for the god's death, but Beria was cynical enough to think that his disappearance could save him as the bell saves a boxer on the ropes.

While waiting, he was extremely careful. He was not, like Molotov, a martyr ready to put his head on the block. Nor was he one of those old Bolsheviks who were willing to confess to any outlandish crimes, if they thought the honor of the Party demanded it. Unencumbered by faith of any sort, Beria would fight back. Beneath the apartment where he entertained the ladies there were cellars filled with tunnels that branched out to mysterious places.

---

* One of the two ministries that resulted from the breakup of the old NKVD after the war.

5

The Young Manager

The ninth person to the left of Stalin on the Tushino reviewing stand was Aleksei Kosygin, a man with a pale, slightly melancholy face under a wide-brimmed felt hat. Forty-eight years old, this economic and financial expert belonged to a much different generation from the Molotovs and Mikoyans. But, though he was a wholly original type when compared to his elders, he was, just like them, a survivor. He had escaped the postwar purge: the purge of Leningrad.

Kosygin was born in Leningrad, in 1904, when the city was still St. Petersburg, the capital of Russia. He became mayor of the city when he was thirty-four. Two years later, Stalin appointed him Vice-President of the Council. By 1952, he had held this title, which he shared with Mikoyan, Beria, Voroshilov, and a few others, for twelve uninterrupted years. His career was all the more striking since there seemed to be nothing at all striking about the man, and all the more rapid since it started so late and so low on the hierarchical ladder.

From the very beginning, Aleksei Nikolayevich Kosygin's biography seemed typical of that of a young Bolshevik. A worker's son, he enlisted in the Red Army at the age of fifteen and became a member of the Party when he was twenty-one. But he did not take the royal road, the career of a Communist Party functionary. He preferred dirty workshops to the comforts of an office, the techniques of production to the techniques of politics. At the age of thirty, he finished his education, receiving a degree in textile engineering. At this point, he was only an insignificant technician. Two years later, however, he was the manager of one of Leningrad's largest factories. Then, suddenly, he took off for the summits.

33

It is, of course, easy to discern in this sudden acceleration the magnetic pull of the void. At all posts of responsibility, the purges left behind empty spaces which definitely had to be filled as quickly as possible. But in Kosygin's case one also has the feeling of a sense of integrity about his job, a taste for precise solutions.

Stalin saw in him a technician and, besides the vice-presidency of the government, which was chiefly an honorific title, burdened him with many concrete responsibilities. First, the portfolio of the Ministry of the Textile Industry. Then, after an interlude at Finance, the leadership of the Ministry for Light Industry. This industry was a stepchild, the least popular of all. Accepting responsibility for it required a bit of humility and a lot of pride.

To Stalin, who thought only in terms of tons of steel, dressing the Soviet people and supplying them with consumer goods were futile occupations. In principle, these were Kosygin's jobs, and they were supposed to exclude him from the serious concerns: those of national defense. Yet, in 1947, when Stalin visited the Black Sea fleet, the only civilian at his side, amid the glitter of military epaulettes, was Kosygin in his modest gray suit.

Indeed, in a country where the ministry of agricultural machinery produced radar parts, nothing was certain. Institutionalized camouflage made it rather difficult to determine just who was responsible for what.

About one aspect of the situation, however, there was absolutely no need for speculation: Kosygin had risen very high. In 1950, pamphlets celebrating the Great Leader's seventieth birthday were spread all over the planet. It goes without saying that not just anyone was allowed to render such homage. From Khrushchev (*Stalinist Friendship Among the Peoples, Gauge of Our Country's Invincibility*) to Malenkov (*Comrade Stalin, the Leader of Progressive Humanity*), through Beria, Bulganin, Kaganovich, and Shvernik, only the great could appear among the authors. Kosygin was one of them. His, *We Owe Our Success to the Great Stalin*, was distributed throughout the world in several languages.

Kosygin's rise in the government naturally kept pace with his progress in the Party. On the Central Committee since 1939, he was admitted to the inner sanctum—the Politburo—as a candidate in 1946, and as a full member in 1948. Yet he remained a production man, not an ideologue. Marxism was his tool. Marxism put the gigantic machine of State economy in his hands.

He appeared soft, and his handshake was hesitant, but he was as tough as leather. He was nailed to his desk for fourteen hours a day, and he enjoyed it. In another era, he would have been a great businessman or merchant. The cold blue eyes in his very pale face, always ravaged by anxiety, demanded precise answers; he knew all the documents and insisted that others know them.

Kosygin was not a liberal. He believed that his compatriots needed a fist to guide them. In the 1950's, during a private conversation with a visitor who expressed the hope that the regime would relax somewhat, Kosygin replied indignantly: "You are mad! Our Russians would be at each other's throats."

He preferred real power to the mere appearances of power and was content to remain in the background leaving the spotlight to others. So much zeal combined with prudently measured ambition was bound to attract Stalin, and the Great Leader had done much to push the cautious young man with a crew cut.

It was unfortunate for Kosygin, however, that he had been born in Leningrad and had started his career there. Leningrad belonged to Zhdanov, a turbulent figure who overshadowed Malenkov, who always regarded himself as the only possible successor to Stalin. When Zhdanov died, in 1948, Malenkov, often with the support of Beria and doubtless that of Suslov, began to persecute his entourage. Stalin, feeling that the time had come for renewed severity after the relative laxness the cadres had enjoyed in the euphoria of victory, had given his blessing to the purge. Besides, he had never liked Leningrad. It was in this beautiful city of stone and water, this door flung open to the winds from Europe and the high seas, that revolutions were born. And Stalin never forgot that.

Ninety per cent of Leningrad's Party apparatus disappeared, as well as thousands of officers, functionaries, administrators, and teachers. The atmosphere of 1936 sprang up again, with its arrests at dawn and the silence of the survivors, pretending not to notice the gaps in their ranks.

Kosygin had worked with Zhdanov during the siege of Leningrad. After the war, though by then he could rely on his own wings to bear him aloft, he remained vaguely within Zhdanov's orbit. Furthermore, it was obvious that he was from Leningrad. He had the accent and the citified air which so clearly distinguish the Leningrader from the warmer but coarser Muscovite. How could he help but be an embarrassment when he was so patently the very prototype of the upstarts who disconcerted their elders with unprecedented technical competence? In short, he was a perfect target.

Working hard and lying low, too solitary to become deeply involved in any intrigue or to let himself be trapped in one, he managed to escape death, but not disfavor. Though still at his post, he could feel the void opening up beneath him. Prudence counseled a retreat.

Calmly and tenaciously, he let the storm pass in that extremely personal way of his, which always expected the worst but never resigned itself to it. His face clearly showed the marks of anxiety —and always would. But, like an iceberg, he was unsinkable.

6

A Summer in the Fields

Harvest time was at hand. Wheat was ripening in the fields of the Ukraine, the Kuban, Central Russia, the Altai.

On the front pages of newspapers, "Letters to Stalin" from members of the kolkhozes sang of love and happiness.

They began with an act of adoration:

Dear Joseph Vissarionovich:
    We, the workers of the fields, men and women of the kolkhozes, workers of the MTSes,* of the sovkhozes, the forestry cooperatives, and agricultural specialists of the Ryazan region, send you, our wise leader, teacher, and friend, brilliant inspirer and organizer of the victories of Communism in our country, our ardent salute and our warmest wishes for many long years of life and health for the good and happiness of the Soviet people and of all of progressive mankind fighting for peace in the world.[1]

Then came an account of their activities:

Joseph Vissarionovich, following your directions with regard to the development of agriculture in the region of Ryazan and thanks to the constant attention and the immense material and technical aid afforded them by the Party, the government—and also by you personally, Comrade Stalin—along the guidelines of Socialist competition for the fulfillment of the commitments made to you in 1951, the men and women of the kolkhozes, the workers of the MTSes and sovkhozes have achieved further progress.

This was followed by a triumphant avalanche of statistics filling eight long columns. Quintals, tons or poods of wheat, beets, potatoes,

* Machinery and tractor stations.

37

onions, cabbages, hay, milk, butter, figures on livestock reproduction and on the thousands of acres of plains reclaimed or fallow land cleared off, the dozens of electrified villages: the picture of a rich land bursting with crops.

And the commitments for the future—"we shall do even better." Again, figures, figures, figures. Special promises were made to Comrade Stalin by each district, even the Khrushchev kolkhoz, to produce more *makhorka*—the coarse tobacco peasants roll into cigarettes.

An infectious, warm-hearted lyricism. And yet, upon closer scrutiny, the statistics were disquieting. One found either a skillful vagueness, with triumphant but unverifiable percentages, or alarming modesty. The workers of the kolkhozes solemnly promised eighty poods of grain per hectare. A proud resolve; but it amounted to little more than one metric ton, or 2,204.6 pounds per hectare. Inspired by Michurinist genetics, the cows were expected to yield from 2,500 to 4,000 quarts of milk each year. Even assuming that the commitment was kept, where was the record?

Every summer for twenty years, one had read the same unfulfilled promises. Prosperity was always just around the corner.

That summer, a young Soviet factory worker and several of his co-workers were chosen to work in the fields. It was the custom. Year after year, industry, the army, and the student corps had to supply labor for the harvest. There were never enough peasants. The reason for this shortage was hard to determine, for, from the vantage point of postwar Europe, the Soviet Union seemed to have one of the largest rural populations.

When the young man arrived at the kolkhoz in Central Russia where he was to work, he found a village of three hundred "souls," straight out of Gogol. Log izbas, huts, lined both sides of a dirt road, which was either swamped in mud or buried in white dust. The izbas were collapsing from old age, and the beautiful carved wood casements framing the windows had not been painted in decades. The brilliantly plumaged ducks, once the pride of the Russian countryside, no longer splashed about on the pond, now encumbered with weeds.

Nor were there any men, or at best very few. The twenty or so that were there held such positions as president of the kolkhoz, accountant, secretary, or mechanic, positions that required the exercise of authority or technical ability. Everything else rested on the shoulders of the *babi*, the female workers, who were fifteen times more numerous than the males.

The factory worker—who twenty years later still remembers how astonished he was on that first day—recounted his rural experience:

> My comrades and I were assigned to a peasant who would be responsible for lodging and feeding us. The food was always the same. Every day our hostess would pour water, milk, flour, and potatoes (especially the peels) into a pot. She would add bits of fish if the kids had poached some in the morning from the river. The pot was put on a large stove of fireproof brick—the Russian stove that heats the izba in the winter and on which one can sleep—where it would remain for hours on end. When it came out, its contents would have become a sort of gluey starch with no particular taste. After about fifteen days of this diet, I had to be taken to the nearest hospital for an enema.
>
> We were also entitled to bread. But the kolkhoz's "planning administrator" cheated on the "norms." He stole flour and added more water. On the outside, the bread was very black and hard, but, when the knife cut through to the inside, water would trickle out. As a supplement, small bits of straw would show up among the crumbs.
>
> When we complained, the peasants looked at us with jealousy and disdain: "You lads from the city are delicate eaters."
>
> In the izba, there were a few old miserable sticks of furniture, a few chests, and no electric light. But, in the street, loudspeakers connected with the village's collective receiving set retransmitted the programs from Radio Moscow. Propaganda always came first.
>
> I was assigned to winnowing the grain. This was still done in the old-fashioned way. Using a long wooden shovel, I would fling the grain in the air, and it would dance in the sun like a July snowstorm. The wind would do the rest; the bran and wheat would fall into two separate piles. After this, I worked at the deliveries. There trucks spread a generous trail of wheat grains behind them on the highway, but this didn't seem to bother anyone. On the other hand, we had to be on guard against theft, especially since the silo had not yet signed the voucher of receipt. All night, from dusk to dawn, I would guard the large pile of wheat, with a rifle on my shoulder. I kept close to the pile. If thieves had stolen that wheat, I couldn't have gotten away with less than ten years in the camps. I was eighteen years old.

The Russian nights of those years were full of such black shapes shouldering rifles, keeping watch at the railroad stations, protecting the wheat against pillagers.

Gleaning was forbidden. Gathering sprigs of scattered wheat constituted "embezzlement of Socialist property." The price: six to ten years in prison.

"In the morning," our witness recalled, "the leaders of the team would come and hammer on the doors of the izbas: 'Marfa, Yevdokia, and Malania, report to work!' The women would start

shrieking, inventing a litany of illnesses. If they managed to get out
of work, they headed for the woods and picked red and brown
berries which they could sell in town. They could then buy city bread,
which was more digestible than the bread at the kolkhoz."

All the memories of this summer of 1952 reveal the same stark
misery. A young girl from Novosibirsk, a student in her last year
of school, was also sent to work in the fields. Loyal, enthusiastic,
and something of a tomboy, she was happy to have a chance to
see the countryside, to be useful. But, in her letters to her family,
she admitted that she was hungry. "I have a great desire for sugar.
Could you please send me a few packets of candy, which will do
instead." Returning home at the end of a month, she devoured
her family's entire supply of sugar without saying a word. The
family commented: "Nevertheless, the kolkhozes do as much as
possible for the students; they give them milk to drink."

The villages to which city workers were sent were the most
presentable. In other places, people lived worse than in the concentration camps. In January, 1953, fifty recently freed political prisoners
arrived at a Siberian kolkhoz in the district of Kazakhinskoye. They
had served their sentences, but, according to the custom of the
period, they had to remain in enforced residence.* They had been
picked to work here.

They stared at each other, dumfounded. "In the camp we at least
had huts to sleep in and soup every day." The villagers formed a
circle around the new arrivals, who were dressed in filthy prisoners'
rags. "You see, these are good clothes. That's how people should
be dressed." And they kept trying to buy the prisoners' boots.

The next morning, Ignace Szenfeld, a deportee of Polish origin,
appeared before the authorities. "Send me back to prison. Sentence
me, give me another ten years again. I won't stay here. This kolkhoz
is death."

In Moldavia at Kubu, where the soil was richer, people did not
live as badly. But no peasant lived comfortably. Besides, as a rule,
the kolkhozians did not receive a kopek of pay.

The kolkhoz—a cooperative of producers—sells its harvest to the
State and theoretically distributes the income from the sale among
its members. In practice, the prices set were so low and the costs
so high that there was no profit and nothing to be shared. In a village
of the Middle Volga, the peasants received no money in 1949, 1950,

_____

* In this situation, one was no longer a *zaklyuchenny*, a prisoner, but a *soslanny*,
a deportee.

and 1951. In 1952, the accountant granted them an "advance" of a few rubles.* "For the time being, that's the best we can do." Only the "big shots" in the kolkhoz, the president, the police, the overseers, etc., were paid regularly.

The muzhiks grumbled a bit, as a matter of form. The serfs, their ancestors, had cultivated the owners' lands until 1861. Then they tilled the land of the *mir*—the peasant community corporation. At the beginning of the century, the shrewdest among them got the chance to buy a few hectares of land. But after that, collectivization took back everything. Nothing in the history of these peasants had prepared them for ownership or the experience of freedom. For long centuries, they had been accustomed to welcoming misfortune like a brother.

In default of payment in money, they received payment in kind. Once a year, the kolkhoz gave them a little grain, a few dozen pounds, in return for their year's "work-days," on which their allowances were reckoned and which the accountant inscribed carefully in their registers. They exchanged the wheat for a little flour or ate it right off, after boiling it.†

In fact, the peasants survived only because of their private truck gardens. Each family used the patch of land it had received from the kolkhoz to plant potatoes or raise a cow. A cow was the equivalent of a lease on life, for it could provide milk, manure for the plot of ground, even a calf. The richer peasants would also buy a pig, which they would care for like their own child. Remembering the family pig, L.S., a deportee who lived with Siberian peasants in 1952, said: "He kept warm with the rest of us next to the stove. He would ask leave to go out to see to his needs. He was terribly polite and well-mannered."

The peasants tried to earn the rubles which the cooperatives did not pay them at the kolkhoz market—the officially tolerated free market. There they sold at the highest possible prices the products of their truck gardens, together with a little milk, the mushrooms they gathered in the fields, and various crude handicraft objects they made on winter evenings. In Siberia, the old women offered shawls woven out of goat hair or rabbit fur. The money they collected was almost entirely spent on buying bread. If they wished

---

* This was the old ruble, before the monetary reform of 1961. This old ruble, which was worth about a tenth of the present ruble, represented approximately fifteen cents in 1973.

† The kolkhozians now receive a wage in money with a guaranteed minimum—of course, very small—in contrast to the practice in Stalin's time.

to forget their misery, there was *samogon*, rotgut, made at home by distilling frozen potatoes.

On collectivized lands, the peasants sowed the seed and harvested out of fear of the police. If the assigned quantities were not harvested, there would be a deluge of punishments. This system of constraint was economically disastrous. Under it, a Russian peasant produced just enough to feed four people, whereas an American farmer could feed more than twenty.

Stalin's last contact with the peasants was in 1928, when he took a three-week trip through Siberia to inspect the wheat deliveries. Since then, he had never again been seen in a village.

In 1928, the land had not yet been collectivized. The peasants were to a great extent the masters of their production, and they found themselves in sharp conflict with the State. The supply of wheat to the cities was inadequate. Historians have given numerous reasons for this crisis in deliveries: a breakdown in confidence, a deteriorated economy, the price of wheat fixed too low.

At that time, Soviet farmers had the misfortune to find themselves confronted by a narrow-minded man. Stalin, the inspired tactician, was the exact opposite of an economic wizard with a free, inventive intelligence. He disliked embracing a situation in its complexity; he preferred the simple knife-thrust. Faced with the need of re-creating the country's agriculture after the NEP interlude, he used the only method he had faith in: force.

In 1929, he decreed that the collectivization of the land would be speeded up either by consent or by force. Four years later, there was no longer any private exploitation of the land worth mentioning.

Lenin, who had foreseen that the operation would require one or two decades and had advised against herding the peasants into the kolkhozes like cattle, was manifestly surpassed by the trenchant genius of his successor. Stalin was praised to the skies. In 1952, twenty years later, the "Stalinist statute of the agricultural trust" remained the golden rule.

But the peasants remembered that it had been imposed by terror and bloodshed. They remembered that the police, the army, all the forces at the disposal of the State had been unleashed against the countryside. People had been shot, cut down by swords, hanged, and drowned. Millions of people, whole families and villages, had been deported—and few had returned. The designated enemy was the "kulak," the rich peasant. But the ordinary peasants, even the poor ones, were struck down, too, for they were equally stubborn.

In the spring of 1933, Stalin declared that, since the dispute had been settled, it was time for clemency. A secret order which he and Molotov signed declared: "As the result of our success in the countryside, the moment has come when there is no longer any need for massive repressions."

He demanded an end to the "bacchanal of arrests." He set strict quotas for deportations to Siberia: 2,000 families in the Ukraine, 1,000 in the North Caucasus, 1,000 in the Middle Volga, etc. Prisons were ordered "disencumbered," and he reduced the number of inmates from 800,000 to 400,000. He even ordered that the prisons fight exanthematous typhus.[2]

It was all a little too late. Famine had worked faster than the troops of repression. In the Ukraine, in the spring of 1933, peasants died of hunger in the tens of thousands. The army had to come to bring in the harvest, burn the corpses, and disinfect the cottages.*

Official Soviet sources put the number of dead or deported "kulaks" at five million. But one evening when he was being confidential, Stalin told Churchill that during the collectivization period he had clashed with 10 million adversaries. And we know what he usually did with adversaries.[3]

As one can imagine, all this created bitter resentment. With the arrival of the Germans in the Ukraine in 1941, it exploded in an outburst of hideous retaliation. It was from among the kulak or pseudo-kulak families who had been martyred at the beginning of the 1930's that the worst of the German collaborators were recruited.

In the summer of 1952, order reigned once again. The harvest was a ceremony, a ritual, which painting and film vied with one another to celebrate: They showed squads of combine harvesters, with red flags raised above them, diving into a golden sea of wheat, and beautiful young kolkhoz girls, with scarves tied around their heads, radiant with self-assurance and strength.

The results did not live up to this forced lyricism. Despite the symbol of the new regime, the Tractor (which, to tell the truth, was wholly inadequate both quantitatively and qualitatively), the land never yielded enough wheat. For Soviet housewives, flour remained a rare article which appeared in the stores once or twice a year, before the holidays. The rest of the time, it could be found only on the black market. As for meat or milk, the situation was worse.

---

* The "anti-kulak" repression and the famine of 1932–33 were the two best-hidden events of the 1930's. A Ukrainian doctor explained to me that the hospitals were absolutely forbidden to report cases of death from malnutrition. The doctor had to register them as deaths from some ordinary disease.

Thirty years later, Soviet writers, notably, Mikhail Alekseyev, V. Tendryiakov (published in Russia), and Vasily Grossman (published in the West), began to write about the great famine with an almost intolerable wealth of detail.

There was less livestock per thousand inhabitants than in 1916, the last year of Tsarist Russia's death agony.* The countryside had to be bled dry in order to send a pitiful supply of meat to the cities. Famine had struck during the winter of 1946–47. In the Ukraine and Belorussia, devastated by the war, there was a great drought, and again there were the dying with enormous eyes, their bellies swollen by hunger. And, in 1933, repulsive stories of cannibalism began to circulate.

Stalin didn't want to know anything about this. During the summer of 1946, on his way to one of his dachas in the south, he received delegations of Ukrainian notables who had come to present him with juicy melons, rich watermelons, and sheaves of grain with enormous ears. The countryside must be rich, for that is what people told him.

The films he saw in the Kremlin depicted this abundance in detail. Djilas, who sat next to him to watch films on happiness in the kolkhozes, noted that he reacted to the screen "like an uneducated man who confuses artistic truth with reality."

Stalin loved stories about heroic cowgirls and robust field hands. In a period when few movies were made in Russia, he ordered Soviet studios to devote at least one large production each year to these heroes. He particularly enjoyed Pyryev's *Cossacks of the Kuban,* in which one could see the usual purple passage: a village festival depicted as opulent as a Flemish wedding feast.

According to the unwritten history of Soviet cinema, two trucks loaded with food were requisitioned and sent on location to film this sequence, on express orders from the Kremlin. Driven wild by splendors the likes of which they had never seen before, children, dogs, and cats in the village almost spoiled the production. They would rush out from nowhere to pinch turkeys and hams each time the scene was set and the director shouted, "Shoot!" Pyryev, a movie director famous for his rages, had to deal harshly with them. For a long time after, his colleagues in Moscow described how he even went so far as to strangle two cats with his own hands.

If Stalin loved operetta peasants, he distrusted real peasants, whom he considered shifty, elusive and disorderly. He never tired of having them lectured, scolded, and called to order. The very same newspapers which drew a grandiose picture of agricultural successes branded the kolkhozians lazy and backward. *Pravda* of August 18, 1952, went on endlessly about the gigantic mess in the Altai, combine harvesters immobilized because of a lack of parts, grain left to rot in the fields, wheat waiting for trucks, trucks waiting for drivers, drivers waiting

* See above all the facts presented by Khrushchev a year later, in September, 1953, to the Central Committee.

for orders. It went into detail about the behavior of a certain Kuligin, the director of an MTS, who got drunk for days on end instead of going to work, and allowed the machines to lie idle in their sheds.

Stalin's mind was busy. With its individual houses, its individual plots of land, the kolkhoz was a bastard organism, a half-way stop on the road to true socialization. The real future lay with the sovkhoz. There, in the service of a veritable State farm, the peasants became workers like those in the mines and in the foundries. Not a trace of private initiative.

Unfortunately, the not very numerous sovkhozes showed no tendency to grow and multiply. As always, Stalin dreamed of imposing what was not done willingly. The end of the summer of 1952 saw the publication of a pamphlet in which he announced that the end of the kolkhozian phase was in sight: "It is a question of liquidating the contradictions by progressively transforming kolkhozian property into national property." [4]

In the meantime, the kolkhozes were regrouped in more extensive farms in order to organize them more effectively and to provide them with a more rigorous bureaucracy. The apostle of this regroupment was a short, fat man with shrewd eyes whose career did not arouse much interest among Kremlinologists. His name was Nikita Sergeyevich Khrushchev. Very interested in agricultural problems, godfather to numerous farm collectives which bore his name, he had invented the "agro-cities." It was a matter of concentrating the farmers in vast, urban-style agglomerations. As they often did, Malenkov and Beria joined forces to block the path of this rather petulant and imaginative fellow. The projects for agro-cities had a tendency to return to the files.

What else could be done? Increase the kolkhozians' taxes.

The half-starved peasant was also an overtaxed peasant. The great annual terror was the visit each autumn of the "inspector of finances," whose small vehicle could traverse any sort of terrain. Sent to collect the *naturnalog*, the tax in kind, he seized the best products from the individual plots, the few chickens and vegetables to be found. Inability to pay the tax meant confiscation of a peasant's cow and plot of land, the only things that provided a meagre subsistence for his family.

Where were the men? city people who visited the farms often wondered. They saw almost no one but women, widows and deserted wives, and children who raced about all summer barefooted.

Many men had not returned from the war. But those who were left had run off to the cities and the factories, where a person could live better. Theoretically, this rural exodus should have been prevented by the passport system that Stalin established in 1932. Without an internal passport, a peasant could not settle in a city unless the authorities allowed him to—and the general tendency was not to give him such permission. But human ingenuity is great, and peasant stubbornness infinite. There were many tricky ways of getting a passport, the precious document which transformed a man of the soil into a city dweller. Some of the methods were even picaresque. Near Tula, one determined fellow kept on punching the secretary of his kolkhoz with his fists until the police came and arrested him. For the certificate of freedom at the end of a jail term could, if one knew how to use it, pave the way to a passport.

It was military service, above all, which emptied the countryside. The factories, which also lacked labor power, recruited the demobilized soldiers as they came out of the barracks, offering them places in their dormitories, with the passport as a kind of incentive. Still barely literate, these laborers did not form a very effective work force. Of course some of them were quickly trained.

Women could not be drafted into the army so it was more difficult for them to get away from the country. The best solution for them was to marry a city man, the bearer of a passport. It was the kolkhozian version of the old story of the shepherdess who married a prince. In a Siberian kolkhoz, sixteen-year-old peasant girls offered themselves to white-haired prisoners: "Marry me. Some day they will give you a passport. Then you can leave and take me with you."

Another witness saw gatherings in the evening of young girls in a Russian village in 1952:

> The girls came to meet two or three young boys, who had not yet left for military service, and took them off to dance on the threshing floor. They wore the traditional long, embroidered dresses with old soldiers' boots on their feet, which one could hear hammering the soil till late into the night.
>
> They sang very old, naïve, and licentious *chastushki*.
>
> They sounded sad. The girls knew that the boys, at the end of their three or four years of service,[*] would do anything not to return.
>
> One day I asked a woman: "Why do you live so badly here?" She replied, "Oh, if my son who is in the army could tell Stalin that we have a bad kolkhoz president, a bad secretary, I am sure our leader would do something for us."

[*] The official duration of military service, variable according to the branch, frequently includes some "unofficial extensions" (for example, six months more to work in the fields, etc.).

A Visitor to the Kremlin

On August 22, 1952, just before ten o'clock in the evening, a Renault "Petrel" carrying a tricolor pennant appeared at the Kremlin's Borovitsky gate. Louis Joxe, France's new ambassador to Moscow, was being received by Stalin.

It was an unusual event. Since the beginning of the year, the head of the Soviet Government had seen only three foreign visitors: a faithful ally, Chou En-lai; a "fellow traveler," Pietro Nenni; and a neutralist, the Indian Radhakrishnan. He was not in the habit of talking with Western diplomats. His last meeting with a French ambassador was in 1949.

Louis Joxe had presented his credentials to Shvernik, President of the Presidium of the Supreme Soviet, on August 17. Up to that point, everything had been normal. But five days later, with the greatest secrecy, the Russian protocol service alerted the French Embassy, one of the handsomest embassies in Moscow with its *osobnyak* of pink stone on Bolshaya Yakimanka Street.* Comrade Stalin wanted to see the ambassador. Hurried telephone calls were exchanged throughout the day, in an atmosphere of mystery and confusion. At last, the meeting was arranged; it could take place that very evening.

At this period, the Kremlin was a forbidden fortress. The Russian people were not permitted to see the treasures of art and history contained within its crenelated walls. Only those who had the onerous privilege of working there, and the rare invited guests, were even allowed inside.

A pilot auto met the French car and led it through the night past the empty office buildings and deserted cathedrals. The windows were lit up in the administrative offices, as they were in all the

* Today rebaptized Dimitrov Street.

Moscow ministries. Each night till dawn, Stalin's insomnia kept tens of thousands of functionaries awake waiting for his orders.

Then, Kazakov's Senate House. Some generals and colonels waited. Stalin stood on the first landing. He was dressed with ostentatious simplicity in his gray-blue "safari."

Stalin and his guest went into a large room with walls panelled in dark wood almost to a man's height. The furniture was even simpler. At the back of the room was Stalin's office, long, banal, and without style. In a corner, a large, white-tiled Russian stove rose to the ceiling. Italian-style shutters framed by dark, heavy curtains concealed half the length of the windows that looked out on the Kremlin's inner courtyards. On the walls, Lenin's portrait rubbed elbows with those of two of the Tsars' generals: Suvorov, the butcher of Poland, and Kutuzov, Napoleon's adversary. There was nothing special about the carpets and chandeliers. One could find the same sort in hundreds of copies in Moscow's hotels and restaurants.

Not a single personal object or sign of comfort. The master here obviously had no use for armchairs. But a couch was hidden away in an adjoining room. The only important piece of furniture in this half-empty space was a huge conference table, surrounded by a throng of chairs. Only six people were seated around it: Stalin, his Minister of Foreign Affairs Vyshinsky, Louis Joxe and his aide Broinval, and two interpreters, the Kremlin's and the ambassador's.

Stalin seemed old and tired. His face was sallow, his general appearance sickly. He looked older than his seventy-two years. As he accompanied his guest, he stayed close to the large table, walking next to it as though afraid of not having some sort of support at hand.

His mind was still supple, still alert. In his manner of carrying on a conversation, courteously but in sudden bursts, there was a note of contained fury, of a leap that was being curbed. Two or three times, the claws were unsheathed, but retracted. He complained bitterly about the German rearmament and demanded clarification as to NATO's activity. The French Ambassador parried as best he could, assuring him that the Atlantic Pact was not a threat to anyone. Stalin listened attentively, using a red pencil to cover a sheet of paper with large vertical strokes. Then he spoke quietly to Vyshinsky, who was dumbfounded.

"If NATO is as Monsieur the Ambassador says, why don't we join it?"

He continued the interview, playing at cat and mouse. In the crease of his eyebrows, in the deep lines that descended obliquely from his nose to his mustache, there was an irony which seemed to be perpetually repressed. Rather good-naturedly, he let it be known that he was aware of his interlocutor's habit of walking around Moscow. Then suddenly and without much reason, he became aggressive. He was in the middle of comparing London's subway (which he saw in 1907) to Moscow's, an eminently anodyne and agreeable topic of conversation, when suddenly his voice became louder: "Yes, this country had a great deal of backwardness compared to the West. But just look, since then it has caught up with the West." And that took care of that. Now the atmosphere was more relaxed.

This sensitivity about backwardness did not last too long. Soon he became sentimental, speaking with rather obvious emphasis about the French aviators who fought on the Russian front. "I liked those fellows, my Normandie-Niemen boys."

Nothing concrete was presented, neither a proposition nor even an attempt to feel the ambassador out on a particular point. Stalin was beating around the bush. From time to time, his yellow eyes, with lower lids raised like those of a bird, would stare at his interlocutor with harsh, distrustful attention. Then he would lower them again to his sheet of paper, which he slashed with red marks.

Andrei Vyshinsky seemed a bit abstracted, not at all excited by this unusual interview. This man who, before becoming Minister of Foreign Affairs, was the judge-executioner of the great purge trials, this man who called the accused rats or vipers, who kept demanding blood and more blood, proved to be affable and to have excellent manners. He spoke French quite well, a fact which betrayed his bourgeois origins, and unlike Molotov, who was always fascinated by his chief, he seemed not at all in awe of Stalin. He was a well-armored monster.

After half an hour, the interview suddenly ended. Sensitive to the real importance of various personalities, Stalin had not forgotten to inquire about General de Gaulle, who, however, had been out of public office for more than six years.

The next morning the Soviet papers announced the meeting in four lines. It made a great impression. In the streets, Muscovites saluted the ambassador's car, recognizable because of its tricolor flag (at this period, the heads of diplomatic missions to Moscow were required to fly their colors at all times). But press comments in the United States and West Germany were rather somber. Did Monsieur Pinay's government intend to double-cross its Western allies? Such questions would create an atmosphere of distrust and suspicion for some weeks.

The important thing was obviously not what was said but that the inteview actually took place, that the head of the Soviet Government singled out the French Ambassador for attention, while he had never met with either the American or the British ambassador. Stalin knew that France was fearful and divided over German rearmament and the European Defense Community. By meeting with Louis Joxe, he had made a date, just in case.

Nineteen hundred and fifty-two was the year of Soviet diplomacy's last attempt to prevent Bonn from rearming. To the Germans, it sketched the outlines of a deal: reunification of the country in exchange for its neutralization. As for the French, it was not a bad idea to blow a little on the ashes of the great anti-Nazi alliance.

Perhaps Stalin also wanted to prove that he was still there, that, despite his age, everything must still pass through him. He still had the talent for those small, ambiguous gestures which made people think and worry.

This was the period of the cold war. The period of the great fear of atomic war. The most traumatic magazine cover of the times was one on *Collier's*—a photographic montage showing a soldier of the U.N. occupying the U.S.S.R. On its side, the Soviet press flayed the Americans with maddening litanies of abuse. An editorial in *Pravda* on December 17, 1952, represented the usual tone: "There is no limit to the crimes of the American aggressors in Korea. . . . The American aggressors have torn a baby from its mother's arms, have killed it, gouged out its eyes, and tried to force the unfortunate mother to eat them."

The U.N. was the forum in which the adversaries challenged each other. The Truman administration, which was reaching the end of its term, improved the system of alliances and military bases surrounding the U.S.S.R. And General Eisenhower, the Republican candidate for President, was already being attacked by *Pravda* for "hysterical boasting."

"Drink a glass of cold water, Ike, and calm down," the paper wrote on August 29, 1952. "General Eisenhower can frighten the crows away from the kitchen gardens if he likes the politics of intimidation so much."

A Russian officer told Svetlana Stalin in confidence: "Now's the time to begin, to fight and to conquer, while your father is alive. At present, we can win!" [1] A foolish statement: American atomic superiority was unmistakable. Nevertheless, the Soviet army had more than four million men under arms.

Withdrawn into itself, the U.S.S.R. had willingly practiced the politics of absence. Yet in July and August of 1952, its athletes participated for the first time in Olympic games—the ones held in Helsinki. Soviet journalists immediately reached an even more flagrant pitch of chauvinism than their Western colleagues. Flag-waving frantically at each and every national victory, they granted only a few lines to the repeated triumphs of the Czech Zapotek, who was nevertheless a citizen of a loyal socialist country.

The Peace Movement was born from the fear of atomic war. But it was not a spontaneous creation. It was invented by Stalin, who understood the support he could muster in the West by a profound protest against the impending holocaust. The Communist Parties kept a tight rein on the movement, but various Catholics and liberals cooperated with it. There was no doubt about the sincerity of these intellectuals' emotions. They signed hundreds of petitions and organized meeting after meeting to denounce Adenauer as a man thirsting for revenge. In France, the war in Indochina was another reason for union among the "fellow-travelers." Jean-Paul Sartre himself, though slandered by *L'Humanité,* went to the Elysée Palace to present a petition to Vincent Auriol demanding the release of Henri Martin, the Communist quartermaster jailed for having fought against the "filthy war."

In Korea, all was quiet. The front was immobile, the armistice talks stalled. But suddenly Communist radios throughout the world began making a din about a new American crime. Bubonic plague germs had been spread over North Korea and China. Certain scientists in the West, for example Joliot-Curie, the Nobel Prize winner, supported the accusation.

The Soviet citizens believed it. The accusation of criminal sabotage was one of Stalinism's techniques. For twenty years, the press in the U.S.S.R. had been talking about imperialist agents who threw nails in machines and broken glass in flour. Just this year potato bugs had cruelly ravaged the Russian and Belorussian potato crops. The kolkhozians looked up; some of them had heard airplanes pass overhead the night before. Those potato bugs were surely American.

One was either for the Soviet Union or against it. One was either for or against Stalin, with love or with fiery hatred.

The Other Planet

Who knew Stalin's country? The iron curtain allowed only hand-picked groups of travelers past its barriers. Even Western Communist militants were denied entry to the U.S.S.R. except in special cases.

Thus, we had only a one-way window to the Soviet Union, and almost nonexistent statistics. The largest country in the world was steeped in mystery. One did not know, one thought one knew. *Figaro*, a conservative French newspaper, thought it possible that Moscow was preparing for the institution of free bread. But this was a fairy tale. The fact that "bread included" had at times been the practice in restaurants in Moscow gave substance to these rumors. But the lines continued to grow longer in front of the bakeries; people waited to buy bread just as black and expensive as ever. Wheat production was still desperately inadequate. But none of this mattered. "Free bread" set the West dreaming. The Soviet Union was the country of dreams.

Who, except apologists, could describe the U.S.S.R. of 1952? The few Western correspondents in Moscow lived like plague-carriers of luxury, carefully isolated from all sources. They had to fish up their information from the pages of *Pravda* because the population gave them a wide berth. And not without reason: Article 58, paragraph 4 of the Criminal Code provided the harshest punishments for those who "collaborated with the international bourgeoisie." If necessary, this could be applied to a Soviet citizen who gave directions to an American on the street.

Quite simply, the law prohibited foreign journalists from gathering information by speaking to Soviet citizens. Information could be obtained only through the government or under its control. Even if one wanted to interview a soccer player, the political authority had the right to organize the interview and to be present when it took place. Confronted by wooden faces, interviewees who gave you the slip, and reticent silence, the correspondent lived in a slippery, fugitive world at the edge of a dark forest whose depths he could barely glimpse.

The government gave a visitor's permit to those it liked, took it away from those who displeased it. Of the four French correspondents admitted to Moscow in 1952, three were Communists. Americans were entitled to four non-Communist journalists, but three of them were in a difficult personal situation and subjected to the worst sort of pressure. They were married to Soviet women. Stalinist law did not recognize mixed marriages, and if the correspondents were expelled —and this was a constant threat—their wives and children could not possibly follow them.

What's more, all dispatches were subjected to the most ferocious censorship. If you telephoned, you had to stick to the text that had been approved in advance; if, inadvertently, you put back a word struck out by the censor, the communication was cut off. Telegrams had to be left in the gloomy gray building of the Central Telegraph Agency, in the hands of even gloomier functionaries. You never knew whether they would be sent or in what state. One day, an American correspondent, anxious to add the "human touch," thought it would be a good idea to begin a political commentary with this observation: "Spring is early this year in Moscow." The next morning, his editor-in-chief cabled to ask him what the devil had happened. This opening sentence was the only one that had passed the censors.

On January 16, 1952, the Soviet government imposed new limitations on the movement of foreign diplomats. Out of 1,500 Soviet cities and towns, only about twenty remained accessible—provided, of course, that one took steps in advance to be certain that the trip was completely authorized. All the rest were excluded once and for all: Towns situated about forty miles from their embassies were as remote and unattainable as the moon. Certain retaliatory measures were taken by fourteen of the NATO governments.

It was during this period that the American Ambassador George F. Kennan forgot himself and made this striking statement: "I have been interned by the Nazis at Berlin. The only difference in Moscow is that—provided I do not speak to anyone I meet—I can walk through the streets." Soviet authorities declared him "persona non grata," and from October, 1952, the United States Embassy would be without an ambassador for several months.

Besides, this American Embassy was irksome because of its location; its windows looked out on the Kremlin—at a respectful distance, it is true—just like those of the British Embassy. Both were asked to move.* Did Stalin consider them too close? Did he fear indiscreet observation? Had he yielded to his obsession of rifles equipped with telescopic sights? A trifle farther away from the Kremlin but located on the route of the five black cars, the Indian Embassy was also asked to move.

The few delegations of Communists and their sympathizers permitted to make study-tours of the U.S.S.R. traveled in a vacuum, jealously protected from contacts with individuals. Invited to admire Soviet achievements, they were astonished that the directors of the "Stalin" factory refused to divulge their production statistics. The directors of the "Red October" plant would not even tell them the number of workers employed there. This information was classified, a state secret. And these were show-factories, the ones always chosen to receive such visits. Advanced industry and research were surrounded by barbed wire, lookout posts, and police dogs. Research institutes did not have addresses but numbers, like the military postal sectors.

In order to pierce this thick wad of mystery, the Western intelligence services did not neglect even the smallest means. In Soviet camps in East Germany, their agents dug through the garbage. A soldier would sometimes use a letter from home for hygienic purposes; and, despite appeals for prudence, despite censorship, a small concrete fact might sometimes slip through. In a region of Belorussia, the livestock had foot-and-mouth disease. In Kiev, people were complaining about a renewed outbreak of sexual crimes. After being duly disinfected, the letters and their modest secrets would go to build up the dossiers of the experts. Espionage has no smell.

In Stalin's Russia, one remained silent when a relative was arrested. A woman whose husband died in a camp pretended she was divorced. Another woman, whose brother was in the Kolyma camp, claimed that she was an only child. Even the bravest people refrained from

---

* In fact, the American Embassy has moved. Its old address on Karl Marx Avenue now houses the executive offices of Intourist. The English Embassy has remained in the same place it occupied at the time of Stalin, that is, on Maurice Thorez Plaza.

mentioning lost relatives except among close friends. Besides, what could they say? One would have to have lived in a camp to understand what it was like. And prisoners rarely came back. Those who did never talked about it.

It was the silence of fear. Fear of new repressions: Anyone who talked freely was guilty. Fear of everyday difficulties: Your fellow tenant and your colleagues would turn their backs on you if they discovered that you were a close relative of an "enemy of the people." So one camouflaged as much as possible.

The incessant pounding of the propaganda machine had borne fruit. With very few exceptions, the great majority of Soviet citizens wanted to believe in the monstrous conspiracies. They found comfort in the proverb—where there is smoke there is fire. So many people would not be arrested for no reason. If one had nothing to be reproached with, there was nothing to fear. Besides, Stalin was good. He limited the repression to what was absolutely necessary. He did only what had to be done for the security of the revolution which, after thirty-five years, still had to be protected.

People actually believed in the menace of imperialist agents, Trotskyists, and Zionists. They believed in the virtues of the police— the "glorious Chekists," and, when the Chekists came to arrest a son, a husband, or a brother, those involved would say: "This time it's a mistake, a slip. But usually they're right." People were ashamed and frightened to see their relatives mixed up with scoundrels. And they remained silent and sent them packages on the sly.

If mouths had talked, the repression would have been seen in its true dimensions. But they did not until 1956, after the Twentieth Congress. In 1952, concentration camps were the dark side of the Soviet planet. Soviet citizens, with all the force of instinct, clung to the sunlit side.

Yet the dark side was never far away. Prisoners were to be found not only in Siberia but also in Moscow and the large cities. You could touch them with your hand.

They were the workers on the large construction sites, the men wielding trowels and pickaxes. Moscow's new university, with its shiny new tower, 787 feet high, was undoubtedly built in part by volunteers from the Komsomol, the Communist youth organization. rounded by armed guards? For a long time, people in the camps told the story of a prisoner who worked on the construction site of the But behind them, how many hundreds of prisoners were there suruniversity. One evening he made wings of plywood, attached them

to his shoulders, and flung himself from the top of the huge skyscraper, hoping to glide down to the opposite bank of the Moskva
river and escape. The story ended badly. The Icarus of the camps
was crushed on the ground.

Columns of prisoners being led to work, surrounded by guards
and dogs, were met early in the morning by citizens on their way to
work. Sometimes women threw bread to the convicts. A detachment
of prisoners was even installed for a while alongside Red Square to
work on a construction job not far from GUM, the government-run
department store. Only a fence separated them from passersby.

The top floor of School No. 150 in Moscow, not far from the
Dynamo Stadium, provided an overhead view of a small camp of
about 200 men. Students and teachers could follow their routine:
assembly, departure for work, return . . .

The television studios were installed at No. 53 Shabolovka Street,
still in the heart of Moscow. In 1952, it broadcast only three or four
hours a day, but its staff began to grow hugely. Engineers, musicians,
cameramen, set-designers, whole corps of technicians crossed paths
at the entrance to the studios. On fine summer days, the announcers
preferred to reread their copy in the sunny garden at the foot of the
broadcasting tower. To one side, lightmen would play a meditative
game of checkers until it was time for the cameras to begin rolling.

And the world of the concentration camp? It was right across the
way. At No. 46, to be precise. A small alleyway between two
apartment buildings, like so many others in this Moscow full of rear
courtyards and small gardens. A high enclosure invisible from the
street, guarded by an armed guard. Behind the enclosure was the
"Colony for Re-education Through Work No. 1," which belonged to
the "Direction of Camps and Colonies of Work of the Office of the
Ministry of the Interior for the Moscow Region." In the official documents, a series of initials: "I.T.K. no. 1 U.I.T.L.I.K.U.M.V.D.M.O."
Police language has a genius for bewildering acronyms.

Six hundred prisoners worked in a factory making couplings and
joints. They were "short-timers"—three to seven years. "Politicals"
mixed up with "common law criminals," which was contrary to the
trend of the times.

With them in the factory were also free workers. A prisoner speaking to such a worker had to address him as "citizen boss." He was
forbidden to call him by name and strictly forbidden to use the expression "comrade." When free workers went home in the evening,
they avoided saying anything to their wives about the strange fellow-

workers. The prisoners, however, remained in the colony, about 200 men to a hut, plus the bedbugs.*

People bumping into a column of prisoners on the street would reassure themselves by saying, "They are thieves." This was not necessarily untrue. "Common criminals" were better treated than enemies of the people and they often showed up among the convicts assigned to construction sites in large cities. These were the best construction jobs. The climate was less deadly than just below the North Pole and one could get packages from home, sometimes even visits from one's family. On these jobs, one was also less likely to meet the prisoner who, having come to the end of his rope, was slowly dying from hunger and exhaustion. Moscow's prisoners were a privileged lot. Their only fear was being sent to die in the gold mines of Kolyma.

Many free citizens preferred not to know what was going on, not to be too interested in the enormous stormcloud forever swelling over their heads. Without even thinking about it, passersby on the other side of the street would readily look away.

A decent camouflage helped them do this. One day a group of prisoners working on the Shirokovskaya dam in the Urals were given ordinary clothing and filmed. Months later at the Saturday movie show (one of the benefits dispensed by the "cultural and educational sections" of the camps), they recognized themselves on the screen. They had been transformed into "enthusiastic Komsomols, volunteers for the great work of construction."

Trains full of passengers leaving or returning to Moscow passed through the Potma railroad station, which was no more than 280 miles away. Not far from the station, in the middle of dense forests, was a camp of medium importance—about fifty thousand prisoners.†

Teams of prisoners were frequently brought to the stations to unload the trains, but the Potma camp had been placed under a "special regime." Consequently, its inmates—mostly "politicals"—were obliged to wear large, very conspicuous numbers on their caps, sleeves and right knees. One day the appearance of these numbered men at the station caused an uproar.

"A train stopped near us," an old prisoner recalled. "The passengers

---

* In a "colony" the prisoners lived at their place of work, while in a "camp" the areas of habitation and work were separated.

† A large camp still exists at Potma. Among its recent guests were the writers Sinyavsky and Daniel, and the young writer Yury Galanskov, who died in 1972.

rushed to the windows to look at us, shouting: 'Who are these men? Who are you?' 'Prisoners,' we replied. 'Silence!' shouted the guards. Conversation was forbidden.

"A tall, elegant, white-haired man stepped off the train onto the platform, took off his hat, and bowing deeply, his hand touching the ground, greeted us in the old Russian style. Then, sobbing, he got back on the train."

This incident taught the authorities a lesson. From then on, when prisoners were sent to the station, they were given different clothes. Without any numbers. The trains would go by, whistling peacefully, and their passengers, snug in their compartments, would vaguely look at the busy workers outside, whose guards were not too visible.

Officially, the largest industrial projects and the most spectacular building jobs were in the hands of the Ministry of the Interior. When appropriately deciphered, this meant that the largest tasks rested on the shoulders of the inmates of the concentration camps. But who, in 1952, knew how to decipher?

Who knew the dark side of the planet? On August 12, 1952, somewhere in the U.S.S.R., twenty-five Jewish writers and intellectuals of high repute were shot. For years, they had been tortured and left to go hungry in prisons and camps. They were not anti-Communists— many of them were not even anti-Stalinists. They had committed the simple crime of remaining faithful to Jewish culture and the Yiddish language.

No one, not even their families, was told of their execution. Esther Markish, the widow of the brilliant poet Perets Markish, one of the executed men, continued to shuttle across Moscow from prison to ministry, as she had done for the past three years, trying to find out what had happened to her husband. The officials continued to tell her nothing. If they did reply, they would only say: "The examination of his case is still in progress."

So week after week, Esther Markish continued sending small packages through the mail, in the hope that prison authorities would give them to her husband.

part II
AUTUMN

The Congress

The hall was austere, a long expanse of bare walls divided by Corinthian pillars. Where the coronation throne of Nicholas II used to stand, a large Lenin in white marble looked down upon the 1,192 delegates of the Nineteenth Congress of the Communist Party of the U.S.S.R. On this Sunday, October 5, 1952, they had come for the inaugural session in what used to be called the Halls of Saint Andrew and Saint Alexander in the Tsar's great palace. The two halls had been combined to form this immense cube.

It was ten o'clock at night. Faithful to his habits, Stalin had preferred to begin with an evening session. The sixteen members of the Presidium filed onto the podium one after another and at very long intervals. Each had enough time to receive his share of applause. Since they followed each other in alphabetical order Stalin was only the fourteenth in line.

Delirium greeted him. Experienced cheer leaders directed an explosion of hurrahs.

"To Comrade Stalin . . ."

"Hurrah!"

"For our dear, beloved Stalin . . ."

"Hurrah!"

"For our wise leader . . ."

"Hurrah!"

All this broke out in waves against a crackling backdrop of applause and above the deep roar of pounding feet. Blue-eyed Russians, massive Ukrainians, Uzbeks wearing embroidered skullcaps, Kirgiz with high cheekbones—everybody standing up, yelling and screaming. It was all very visceral and very well organized.

The object of all this fervor sat down modestly with the other members of the Presidium at the very end of a row of chairs.

This was his custom. He was a master in the art of making people search for him. The contrast between his simple pose and the admiration rising up to him made a deep impression on Auguste Lecoeur, a member of the French delegation. "His behavior," Lecoeur wrote in his book *Le Partisan*, "seemed to me the very essence of modesty and only increased my admiration."

In fact, as his intimates noticed, Stalin found it more and more difficult to stand the crowd. When he had to face a large assembly, he became tense and restless. As he grew older, it got worse, and he sank deep into the group of his comrades as if into a cocoon.

Contrary to his usual practice, he decided not to make the report on Party activity and entrusted the job to Malenkov. As a result, Malenkov was greeted by everyone with the deference due a hereditary prince. Had Stalin decided that he was not immortal? Had he publicly chosen his successor, made out his last will and testament?

With him nothing was simple. Exactly two days before the Congress, his new work, *Economic Problems of Socialism in the U.S.S.R.*, had appeared. First printing: 1,500,000 copies; complete reproduction of the book in the magazine *Bolshevik* and in *Pravda*. It was still Stalin, not Malenkov, who made news. Malenkov gave the report, but Stalin actually had written it.

On the opening day of the Congress it was not the Congress that *Pravda* saluted but Stalin and his essay. "The great leader of science," Aleksei Surkov wrote, "the inspired architect of Communism, Comrade Stalin, in his new work of enormous theoretical and practical importance, points out to us the road to the complete victory of Communism. . . . Stalin's genius has discovered the fundamental law of socialism." In the same issue, three academicians, Oparin, Dubinin, and Vinogradov,* went into a trance: "Comrade Stalin's inspired work opens unlimited perspectives to a new efflorescence of science in our country."

The tone had been set. All that remained for the orators at the Congress to do was to praise, one after the other, "the magnificent gift" given them by their leader.

For months, *Economic Problems* remained the most important concern, the pillar of all political and cultural activity. The Academy of Sciences of the U.S.S.R., Moscow University, and the universities in the provinces devoted special meetings to it. Foreign Communist

---

* V. V. Vinogradov, a linguist, who should not be confused with V. N. Vinogradov, future star of the "men in white" trial.

parties supplemented the effort by assuring its circulation throughout the world.

Stalin was never satisfied with being just the boss. He wanted the laurels of the theoretician without which he could not live up to his biography's image of him as the true "Lenin of today."

This was the basis of his cult. He was the man who knew. By the sheer force of his powers of reason he could read the future. It was rational magic. The newspapers constantly repeated it: "Stalin's strength lies in his gift for scientific foresight." A new Newton, he had discovered the laws of gravitation that control societies. Armed with this method, he could never be wrong.

His adversaries always found this picture of Stalin the thinker hilarious. Trotsky called him "our party's most eminent mediocrity." Bukharin asserted: "Stalin's first quality is cold indifference." And, in an open meeting, the old Marxist scholar Ryazanov had told him: "Now stop that, Koba,* you are making yourself ridiculous. Everybody knows that theory is not your field." But for a long time now all the laughers had been silenced forever.

On the middle levels, his intelligence was clear. It was when he tried to scale the summits that he began to puff and pant. *The Economic Problems of Socialism* claimed to retouch Marx, substituting for his law of "standardization of the rate of profit" an uncertain "law of maximum profit." Had Stalin really read *Das Kapital?* When it came into contact with the hard crystal of ideas, his crafty mind became blunt.

Nevertheless, he was a good vulgarizer. Simple and convincing, he had a feeling for the textbook, for the catechism, if you like. The seminary had left its mark on him. He excelled at the edifying aphorism—for example, "blows forge steel and break glass."

Some people said that he had little to do with the writing of his books. But they ignored the evidence: There was a Stalin style. There was no doubt that a group of collaborators prepared the material for his books; and it was proven that sometimes he appropriated other people's property, copying the ideas or phrases of Plekhanov or Chernyshevsky without deigning to give them credit. But it was he who gave these writings their definitive form.

Solzhenitsyn, who depicted him suffering at night over a blank white page, was surely close to the truth. He recognized a colleague.

Stalin's style was heavy, stuck together with such cumbersome phrases as *we go on, it follows that,* and such lazy ones as *it is clear*

* One of Joseph Dzhugashvili's first pseudonyms, when he was not yet called Stalin.

that, history shows that, which exempt one from showing anything. Accumulation and repetition were constant procedures. One of the masterpieces of the genre was the triumphal speech of January 18, 1933, with its paragraphs endlessly balanced by the cadence of "We do not have . . . we now have . . . we do not have . . . We now have. . . ." Religious litanies in the oath to Lenin: "We swear to you . . . we swear to you . . . we swear to you. . . ." Logical litanies in the *History of the Communist Party:* "We continue . . . as a result . . . We continue . . . as a result. . . ." The mind was benumbed, fascinated. The author's remarkable aura did the rest. In a French edition of *Dialectical Materialism and Historical Materialism,* the preface declares quite simply: "The text of this work which we present to the public has been translated for the first time into French in 1937, three centuries after the appearance in 1637 of Diderot's *Discourse on Method.* These are two monuments to the same effort, two works of the same stature." [1]

The Descartes of the Kremlin had a wide range of tones. He conversed with Heraclitus, but he was also the man of common sense, the good, sturdy fellow with his feet planted firmly on the ground. "But what about the seeds, Comrade?" he asked the delegate from the kolkhoz, who was lost in the clouds of his own eloquence. Stalin was the universal spirit and mind, capable of embracing everything.

Did he believe it? What did he believe? It was hard to imagine the thin adolescent who in 1894 entered a seminary in Tiflis surrounded by the pomp of the Nineteenth Congress. Had he accepted what the priests taught him only to discard it later? Had he even used the scowl of faith to mask profound indifference? And when he converted to Marxism, what part was played by ardent conviction and what by vengeance, motivated by the need to conquer?

In his pamphlet *Marxism and the National Question,* written in 1933, he seemed at moments to have expressed himself fully. In the supple play of ideas there was something close to felicity in both the writing and the understanding. Perhaps it was because, being a Georgian, he felt deeply involved in this study of the colonial question. Perhaps it was also because Lenin, who actually bent over him at this period, irrigated his cold, dry spirit.

Since then, however, doubts were no longer possible. For forty years, ideas had been for him only tools, good only for their utility. When he published a theoretical text, it was only to justify certain practical measures. His articles, essays, treatises, and programmatic speeches were tactical acts aimed at ruining his adversaries, so as to establish his power more effectively. His writing followed the course of his politics without fear of contradicting either himself or the announced policy. *Economic Problems of Socialism* was simply the portrait of the U.S.S.R. of tomorrow, a tomorrow which Stalin intended to impose on it.

It was a chilling portrait. Despite certain contradictions, one thought was quite clear: More would be demanded of the Russian workers and peasants, who were already at the last gasp. More and more steel, and then even more: The priority of heavy industry was reaffirmed again and again with crushing insistence. Consumers' goods could wait—the time for abundance was pushed far into the future.

The rural areas would have to bleed themselves even more. They would have to purge themselves of the last traces of economic freedom—what Stalin called "market production" and "the circulation of market goods."

These additional sacrifices were demanded of a country that had already been bled white and aspired with all its being to a little prosperity in the new era of peace. Thirty-five years after the revolution, "the engineer of the locomotive of history" announced that the end of the tunnel was not yet in sight.

At the beginning of the book, it was true, Stalin presented his readers with a surprising and pleasant novelty. No, it was not certain that the capitalist world was preparing to pounce on the U.S.S.R. It was possible that the capitalist countries would fight among themselves, since they were torn by all sorts of imperialist ambitions. Warned in time, the exegetes adjusted without delay their former commentaries on the dogma of the "inevitability of wars."

This apocalyptic appreciation of the bitter conflicts among Western countries was rather amusing. In fact, Stalin was playing a classic diplomatic game. By receiving Louis Joxe in Moscow and sending such an important person as Gromyko to be the ambassador in London, he flattered French and British pride, while hardening his attitude towards Washington.

The vision of a less threatened U.S.S.R. contrasted with the highly regimented economic program of the "Communism of War" type. In *Economic Problems,* Stalin seemed in his most coercive mood. His problem seemed to be to make his authority felt as heavily as possible, perhaps from fear that it had become soft with the passage of the years and the new habits that had taken over. The turn of the screw announced for industry and agriculture was only part of a vast program to bring the people to heel.

It was in the midst of the storm that he would be seen as the providential leader. So once again he was working to gather the dark clouds.

Before the Congress, the parties of the republics—that is, the parties of the sixteen republics which made up the Soviet Union—held separate meetings. From Georgia to the Baltic regions, a wind of purge had blown everywhere, right across the land. Everywhere, the press had uncovered shortcomings—in industry, commerce, agriculture, and in the political machinery. Shortcomings were the last stage before sabotage, treason, and conspiracy.

The Congress opened in a heavy, charged atmosphere. The delegates needed that dose of optimism characteristic of all political personages not to recall their predecessors of the prestigious "Congress of conquerors"—the Seventeenth Congress in 1934. In the three years that followed the Congress, more than half of those conquerors, 1,108 out of 1,970, were arrested, deported, or massacred.

The very convocation of the 1952 Congress was a warning. It was obvious that Stalin had not called it to carry out the Party's statutes, which provided for a Congress at least every four years. The statutes had been violated for so long that nobody even thought of them any more (the last Congress had been held in 1939). Nor was it a matter of solemnly launching a Five-Year Plan before this great assembly, as was the custom for a long time. The Fifth Plan had already been in progress for more than two years.

Even the least subtle among the delegates felt that a big political operation was being planned. And, under Stalin, a political operation always meant a slaughter.

Once the Congress had opened and he had received his tribute of acclamations, Stalin disappeared. For eight days the interminable sessions took place without him, with one speech after another, all of which sounded alike. Each speech began and ended with a dithyrambic homage to the absent hero and returned to a few of his special merits as it progressed.

As was foreseen, Malenkov started the ball rolling with his report on activity. Khrushchev replied by presenting the new statutes, about which each speaker pretended to be very excited, while knowing full well that the only statute that counted was Stalin's mood. In passing, Malenkov was not above taking a swipe at Khrushchev, attacking him, without naming him, on his own terrain—agriculture. Khrushchev counterattacked by criticizing the management of the Party, an eminently Malenkovian domain. A discreet clash between two rotund men, one quite soft, the other brawny. The soft rotundity got all the attention.

Georgy Maksmilianovich Malenkov was a man of memorandums and dossiers. He was exactly fifty years old; but a long time ago he had entered Stalin's secretariat, where he was initiated into the most formidable mysteries. He knew everything about everybody.

Sunk in fat, his features had a feminine touch, and his enemies derisively called him *Malania,* the nickname for a simple, good-natured woman. He compensated for his unmasculine physique with extremely crude language. Perhaps he picked up the habit from the Cossacks of Orenburg, among whom he spent his childhood, unless he acquired it from Stalin, a great indulger in obscenities. In any event, he had a rather fine mind. Official sources were discreet about his origins, but it is thought that they were not overly proletarian. A diplomat recalled him at this period as "the only cultivated man in the ruling group." "He was," he added, "even able to talk about Shakespeare."

Since Shakespeare was one of Stalin's known favorites, it was useful, in a well-planned career, to be able to quote him. But what was more surprising, Malenkov could also talk about Proust, Gide and Montherlant. Aside from that, he imitated his master. Like him, he wore a high-collared blouse and covered his slick black head of hair with a military-looking cap, when almost all the other high officials of the Party had abandoned this attire of the Civil War days.

He was as prudent and as wary as a big cat. A native of the Urals, he combined finesse with composure and a great deal of circumspection. Djilas, who met him some years later, wrote of him: "He gave the impression, of being a secretive man, cautious and ill at ease. It seemed that beneath the folds and layers of fat lived another man, lively and clever, with black, intelligent, piercing eyes."

He was very adept at intrigue. When Zhdanov, his old rival, had the good sense to die, Malenkov lashed out at his supporters and at Leningrad, his vindictiveness heightened by the brilliance of his victims. Against Voznesensky, a famous economist and political figure with a great future, he was especially violent, until a weary Stalin gave him the economist's head on a platter. It was Malenkov who invented "file cards for the cadres," with detailed biographies of all Party members. He did not hesitate to use them for police purposes.

During the war, with Stalin and Molotov, he played a considerable role on the "State Committee for Defense," with responsibilities in the field of armaments, above all in airplane construction. Before entering political life, he had had time to get a degree in engineering.

He was a good aide, a skilled performer, and an adviser who knew how to prepare precious overall reports. But, used to remaining in the background, he had little prestige. His was the temperament of a confidant, a man of the council chamber and the corridors. He was handicapped by never having been in a position of command on a large scale. And Beria's rather conspicuous control over him did not help his status.

The sudden investiture that giving the report on Party activity represented certainly conferred new stature on him. But he still had to assert himself.

Khrushchev, the boss of the Ukraine before and after the war, had had more opportunity to show his temperament ,and authority. During the dark years, Lieutenant General Khrushchev spent more time with the staff officers at the front than in the Kremlin. This provincialism kept him removed from the summits of power, but it allowed him to assert himself as a boss and to build up an apparatus.

For the moment, he was a man of relatively modest renown, and the new statutes he was presenting would handily put him in the limelight. Their most striking innovation was of a formal nature: Frow now on one would say "Communist Party" instead of "Communist Bolshevik Party." The vanished adjective recalled the heroic times, and Stalin execrated the "old Bolsheviks," those old veterans of the revolution who imagined they had rights over him. Besides, the modifier, which evoked the old Party split in 1903 between Bolsheviks and Mensheviks, no longer had any practical value. After all, the last Mensheviks had long since gone down the drain. Some particularly hardy members of this moribund species could still be found, clinging to a shred of life in the camps in Siberia. Those who joined the conquerors while there was still time to do so had been forced to behave with all the passion of neophytes—such as the zealous prosecutor Vyshinsky—in an attempt to wipe out their original sin.

Apart from that, the statutes showed the same tendencies as the other documents of 1952: strengthening of discipline and reinforcement of Moscow's control of the countryside.

If the report was gray, the man who read it was quite colorful. To begin with, he was the only leader of the Stalinist generation who occasionally expressed himself simply. But not when he put on his eyeglasses and read his speech. Then, dreary and stammering, he succumbed to the law of the genre whose keynote was boredom.

But when he let himself go and improvised—which in itself was an anomaly—he was direct and petulant, calling a spade a spade, and, because he was a real man of the people, using even worse language, right down to profanity. When speaking to a meeting of workers and peasants, he took obvious delight in ditching the usual rhetoric and using the vulgar joke and the old proverb.

Instead of staying cooped up in his office like his colleagues, he loved to get his hands dirty. He was a ball of fiery energy rolling in all directions, impelled by the need for action. When he was in charge of the construction of the Moscow subway in 1935, he trotted enthusiastically through the tunnels, which ressembled somewhat the mines in which he had worked in his youth. First Secretary in the Ukraine, he splashed and waded in the black soil, giving long speeches to stupefied kolkhozians on the gastronomic merits of rabbit.

Among Soviet dignitaries, all of whom were polished by their immersion in dialectical materialism, he was almost a political illiterate. Theory bored him. He had the faith of a coal miner, a little man awed at having risen so high thanks to a regime which could only be excellent since he, Khrushchev, owed it everything. A very concrete sort of man, he loved the heat of stables and blast furnaces with their flow of molten steel, and sought contact with others, either to lash them with abuse or to smother them with sentimentality.

He had neither the time nor the inclination to concentrate. Like the insect whose name he bore—in the Ukraine a *khrushch* is a May bug —he was always humming with activity.

Despite his southern name and his long career between the Donets and Dnieper, he was not considered a true Ukrainian. Born in the gubernia of Kursk on Russian soil, he talked like a Russian peasant, without a single trace of that Ukrainian accent which makes g's explode in a guttural roll never heard in Muscovite throats.

In the Ukraine, he had proved to be a man loyal to the central power, a man who had come to discipline the richest republic in the Union, where the population was as large as that of France and was always ready to rebel against Moscow. Sent by Stalin to Kiev in 1938 to carry out the great purges, he displayed a zeal in shedding blood that made him famous. At the time, the *Pravda* of the Ukraine wrote: "The merciless extirpation of the enemies of the people—Trotskyists, Bukharinites, bourgeois nationalists and all the other pigs of spies— only began when the Central Committee of the All-Union Communist Party sent the unshakable Bolshevik and Stalinist Nikita Sergeyevich Khrushchev to the Ukraine." The sort of praise that makes one shiver.

Yet the heavy head with its small, piercing eyes and the massive jaw, with its widely spaced teeth reinforced by a steel bridgeplate, spoke with anger and brutality more than with systematic and persevering nastiness. He was cruel when riled and his immediate entourage feared his rages, his shouts, his whims. Khrushchev was no termite. He was a dangerous carnivore when aroused.

Nobody knew how many deaths and deportations he had on his conscience in the Ukraine. On the other hand, it was said to his credit that in the postwar purges it was Malenkov and not he who directed the slaughter. Called back to Moscow at the end of 1949, he became a member of the small circle of Stalin's intimates but did not take part in the murderous "Leningrad affair," which was then far from being over. Some people saw this as a result of his natural good nature, while others put it down to his more prosaic desire to oppose Malenkov.

In any case, he was as crafty as a horse trader, with sudden spurts of happy improvisation and a habit of erecting a whole scheme in one minute and tearing it down the next. A theatrical temperament, which fear of the boss did not permit him to deploy in its full splendor. A thunderous temperament. Among all these frigid functionaries, he astonished people by laughing uproariously and becoming boisterously sentimental.

These outbursts were aided by alcohol. Khrushchev drank like a sponge and ate like an ogre, gulping down food without too much discernment. His capacity for absorption amazed everyone at Stalin's nocturnal feasts. He had the thick lips of the sensualist and sometimes the frailties of the sentimentalist. When he visited a factory, the presence of a pretty girl could lower his capacity for attention.

Nina Petrovna, his second wife, a militant who was prudently blind, helped him and supported him in his work. From his two marriages he had five children, which was a lot in a Russia that had become population conscious.

He had risen very high, but a greater future had been denied him. He was not serious enough. He was already fifty-eight, and the official photographs added white hair to his seriously balding head.

He was pragmatic, not cynical. Even corrupted by power, he remained a man of the people, a man of the Russian people which, half worker, half peasant, believed in the Revolution as in Christ.

10

Be Patriots

The Communist world had passed in review on the speakers' platform. Thorez the Frenchman, Liu Shao-Ch'i the Chinese, Gottwald the Czech, and Hoxha the Albanian. Almost a hundred orators had spoken, from old Marshal Voroshilov to blond, fresh Yekaterina Furtseva, Khrushchev's energetic assistant at the Moscow Gorkom— the Committee of the Party in the city. Muratov the Tatar had saluted Stalin as "the best friend of the Tatar people," the people he dispersed and exterminated. Fadeyev, great patron of the writers—with the light blue eyes of the fanatic—had beaten his chest with his hand: "We have not known how to apply in literature the inspired work of Comrade Stalin as expressed in his work on Marxism in linguistics."

Malenkov, associated with Stalin by many of the speakers, exhaled a thick cloud of incense. Korneichuk, the Ukrainian writer, praised him for having "made a great contribution to Marxist esthetics in his report." Leonid Brezhnev, first secretary of Moldavia, linked the leader and his successor in the same homage: "Comrade Malenkov . . . has brilliantly shown the victories of the Soviet people won under the inspired leadership of Comrade Stalin." Mikoyan had gone even one better: "As Comrade Malenkov has well said, the wheat problem has been definitively solved." Thousands of Soviet citizens would then complain to the Party, asking why, under these conditions, there was still no bread in certain places.

On the evening of the tenth day, Stalin reappeared and mounted the speakers' platform.

He had always liked slowness, it gave him his best effects. A magisterial slowness which signified: Listen carefully, my every syllable counts. Now the fatigue of old age added to his slowness. But he still looked solid. "A robust peasant," said Roger Garaudy who, from the seats of the French delegation, watched with a pounding heart that tanned, squat shape.

Stalin was not dressed in his uniform with its brilliant epaulettes but in an austere gray, rather shabby blouse. He was not the commander in chief but the militant, the leader of all the proletarians. On his chest, he wore a single gold star, the insignia of the Heroes of Socialist Labor.

At past congresses, his speeches would last an entire day. This one took less than ten minutes. The weariness of an old man afraid to test himself with a long speech gave him an air of sobriety and good-naturedness. Choosing the familiar approach, he spoke without notes, groping a bit for words. With his monotone voice, his awkward attitude, and his meager vocabulary, he had never been a firebrand. But this evening he was the grandfather of the people, recalling his youthful struggles, measuring the road he had traveled: "Now the struggle of our party has become easier and work itself is done with more gaiety." The hall melted with tenderness.

He was an immobile orator, but in his marked Georgian accent there was the gesticulation of southern lands. He knew Russian, but he had made something different of it. This language, which he had learned late in school, was not his real tongue, and he had profoundly transformed its music, its internal rhythm, drawing from it sounds that were both sharper and softer. At moments, one lost the thread of his discourse because of a bizarrely articulated word.

On this October 14, his diction seemed even more shaky than usual. Some people in the hall thought fleetingly about the persistent rumors concerning his health.

But only a handful entertained these anxieties. Swept by enthusiasm, the Congress exploded in an ovation which lasted longer than the speech. Hordes of men in black and women in gray raised outstretched arms toward the prophet.

Stalin's remarks were especially addressed to the delegations of the "brother parties," which were more numerous than usual. Above all, the Communists of the West, the followers of Thorez and Togliatti—mentioned by name—all those who were not in power.

He said to them: Be patriots.

"The bourgeoisie sells the rights and independence of nations for dollars. The flag of national independence and national sovereignty is thrown overboard. There is not the slightest doubt that this flag is held by you, representatives of the Communist and democratic parties, who must lift it again and carry it forward, if you want to be patriots, if you want to be the leading force of the nation."

In passing, one admired the abrasive humor: This man shedding a tear for national independence was the same man who set in motion the machinery to establish order in the satellite countries by slaughtering the most glorious Communist militants. But the interesting thing about the appeal was that it established for Western Communists a definite direction: the direction of national fronts. They were to seek alliances on the Right so as to oppose American influence, NATO, and the beginnings of a united Europe. The mission which Stalin had assigned to them was once again much less that of making a revolution than of serving his own planetary diplomacy.

These allies, whom he drafted for front-line positions in the cold war, were entitled to all honors at the close of the Congress. It was they who were the heroes of the great final banquet the next night in St. George's Hall, the gayest, most beautiful of all the rooms in the Kremlin.

11

A Pleasant and Happy Companion

Voroshilov presided. He was the *tamada,* as the Georgians put it, the toastmaster. He toasted each of the forty-four Communist Parties and workers present, which meant emptying to the last drop that many small glasses of *pertsovka,* or vodka with pepper. The worthy marshal acquitted himself of this task without much visible damage.

Stalin was being careful and spared himself. He didn't drink vodka but only wine, and not very much at that. At each toast, he got up, carrying with him his own bottle and glass, and went to drink with the head of the delegation that was being toasted. He exchanged a few words with him and then returned to the table of honor, always carrying his bottle and glass.

Since the wine in his bottle scarcely changed, everyone present could measure his sobriety. But there was even more praise for his simplicity. This *mukuzani,* this wine of the Caucasus, which he carried from table to table, with the look of a big, good-hearted bear, what a lesson! He was the exact opposite of Hitler and Mussolini. No triumphal processions as at Nuremburg, no balcony as at the Palazzo Venezia. He was the most modest of great men. It never occurred to anyone that in this business of carrying his wine with him, there might be a strong element of distrust. Yet in the great purge trials there were quite a few memorable stories of poisonings.

Changeable, as old men usually are, he seemed to have recovered from his illnesses of August. He gave evidence of excellent physical condition. Jovial and relaxed, he did not neglect the tables laden with meats and baskets of sumptuous fruits brought in from Moldavia and the Caucasus expressly for the Kremlin. Each bunch of grapes represented at least a day's pay for a worker. From his pocket, Stalin exhumed the pipe which the doctors had advised against, but which went so well with the part of a tranquil papa, blowing smoke up into the crystals and flowers, squinting like an old peasant. Then he became lively, throwing out a few pleasantries and laughing loudly. From his seat, he was heard shouting to the musicians to play his favorite pieces, folk songs. When the music really pleased him, he moved his hands to beat the time, applauded boisterously, and even sang in accompaniment to the musicians. A little rowdy, but a very pleasant and happy companion with a sonorous voice, he was enchanted by his little party and determined to enjoy himself.

Russian warmth and Caucasian exuberance seemed to combine. The hall was plunged into euphoria. The musicians in uniforms or long robes and the marbles with the gold inscriptions of the names of regiments and officers decorated by the Tsar with the Order of St. George furnished the indispensable note of reassuring respectability. Monumental Gottwald, old Wilhelm Pieck, the small Hungarian Rakosi—all these leaders bowed down with craftiness and mortal worries called to each other from one table to the next amid huge shouts of laughter. Heirs of the old world, they had the right to be gay. Besides, since Stalin was gay, tomorrow did not exist.

12

The Brother Parties

While his boss Gottwald caroused in Moscow, Arthur London was in prison in Prague.

For twenty months now, this ex-Minister of Foreign Affairs for the Czech government had been under arrest. Twenty months of interrogations. By dint of sleepless nights, blows, insults, threats, extorted depositions, physical tortures, moral trickery and false casuistry, the "judges" had prevailed against his will. On this October 15, he was very busy learning by heart the "confessions" which had been dictated to him. He had to recite them without a mistake at his trial, which was supposed to take place the coming month.

In nearby cells, thirteen other prisoners of importance were also doing their homework. Among them, the ex-Minister of Foreign Affairs Clementis and, especially, Rudolph Slansky, the former number two man in the regime. All of them had practically always been Communists. Several among them had also mercilessly persecuted and harassed deviationists of all kinds. But on the day of the trial they had to present themselves as "Trotskyist-Titoist traitors, Zionists, bourgeois nationalists, enemies of the Czech people, of the People's Democratic Republic, and of socialism." [1]

They had to admit that they had sold their country's secrets to Western powers, notably to the French Ambassador Dejean.

Twelve of them would be hanged, three others sentenced to life imprisonment. All of them, both the living and the dead, would later be rehabilitated. Arthur London, one of three survivors, would write *The Confession* in order to explain how one can force a faithful, fanatical militant to accuse himself of imaginary infamies.

For the People's Democracies, the hour of the purges struck in

76

1948. Tito, the most famous of the East European leaders, was breaking with Stalin. And Stalin, in order to avoid all danger of further contamination, had recourse to his customary methods. In 1949, the Hungarian Minister of Foreign Affairs Rajk, the Bulgarian Vice-Prime Minister Kostov, and the Albanian Vice-President Xoxe were all executed, together with big batches of supposed Titoists, in the midst of a concert of savage imprecations. Hundreds of small, medium, and large leaders were thrown into prison—Gomulka in Poland, Kadar in Hungary, Husak in Czechoslovakia. Behind these well-known figures stood innumerable faceless crowds. From the Balkans to the Baltic, policemen and prosecutors had run amok. Teams of Soviet advisers were on the spot to supervise them, instruct them, and show them how to set up proper trials.

To a certain extent, Tito was a self-made man, a man who had seized power with rifles and partisans instead of waiting for Stalin and the Red Army. The Yugoslavs wanted to be independent because they felt they deserved it. The lesson was not lost. In all "brother countries," all those who bore arms for Communism instead of remaining in the school for cadres in Moscow had been hunted down. Most suspect were the old leaders of the International Brigades. Besides their glorious past, which made them rather disturbing, in Spain they had made certain impermissible contacts with Trotskyists and anarchists. Stalin had them slaughtered, as he had already done ten years before to the Russians who had distinguished themselves in Madrid and Guadalajara. He also clamped down on the so-called cosmopolites, that is, the Jews. Out of fourteen people sentenced in the Slansky-London trial, nine were Jews. The Romanian Ana Pauker, a Jew and a Stalinist purer in her faith than Stalin himself, was in disgrace. On the other hand, Rakosi, also a Jew, was President of the Council at Budapest. He had been very zealous. The Hungarian prisons were packed with all sorts of prisoners. Among them was even a fine pianist, Gyorgy Cziffra, whom Europe would discover a number of years later. At that moment, he felt that both his life and career were worth very little.

In a strenuous attempt to remain abreast of events, the French Communist Party also carried out a purge. On September 16, *L'Humanité* suddenly denounced the "factional work" of André Marty and Charles Tillon (one a member of the Secretariat, the other of the Political Bureau). Veterans of the International Brigades, these important men had led partisans and guerrillas and, like Rajk and London, belonged to a combative breed of men with backbone that Stalin especially disliked. Marty, a controversial but illustrious figure, the leader of the Black Sea mutiny and the only living

Frenchman mentioned in the *History of the Communist Party (Bolshevik)*, became for his old comrades "the policeman Marty." The factory named for him in the U.S.S.R. was rebaptized. On December 10, 1952, *Pravda* commented: "Marty and Tillon had the tendency to underestimate the role of the Soviet Union in the liberation of France." Certain aspects of their condemnation were less dramatic; they were allowed to go into bitter but peaceful retirement.

The severely shaken French party was without its leader, Maurice Thorez, who had been under treatment in the U.S.S.R. since his stroke two years before. The absence of this strong personality, willingly transformed by propaganda into a providential hero, was deeply felt, even if emissaries shuttled back and forth between Paris and the Caucasus. The news that he had reappeared in Moscow to speak at the Congress was greeted with tremendous enthusiasm.

Of all the "brother parties," the one that gave Moscow the greatest satisfaction was the Chinese Party. One of the themes most often exalted by the Soviet press of 1952 was the "great friendship."

But the euphoria was artificial. Stalin had always felt that these friends would some day become rivals, and, at the end of the war, he had signed a treaty of alliance with Chiang Kai-shek. The Chinese Communists had conquered a country of about 600 million inhabitants with great difficulty and with weak and reluctant Soviet help.

Since about 1950, Stalin, to support the victory, had sent thousands of advisers and technicians to the young People's Republic, contributing about 300 million dollars to building up its technology. In Soviet papers, this technical cooperation took on splendid colors. "The Chinese people," one read in *Pravda* of February 7, 1952, "raise their eyes with enormous gratitude to their great friend, the Soviet Union. . . . The success of the Soviet people is the star which lights the road to follow." A Chinese journalist wrote in *Pravda* on November 6, 1952, "Thank you, older brother." And Chou En-lai himself expressed humble thanks for "the cordial and patient way in which Soviet comrades have transmitted their knowledge to us." This appeared in *Pravda* on January 1, 1953, on the occasion of the restitution of the railroad in Manchuria which the Russians had taken at the end of the war. (Control of Port Arthur, however, remained in Russian hands for another two years.)

Fortified with a good conscience, the older brother regarded the younger brother with friendly condescension, not thinking that he too perhaps had a great longing to become an adult.

Ilya Ehrenburg tells the story of a factory built by the Russians in China during that period. The machines proved to be much taller than the average height of the Chinese workers. "That doesn't matter," said the tall, stout Russians, "we'll build platforms for you in front of the machines to lift your workers up." All smiles, the little Chinese asked them politely not to do anything; they would take care of the problem themselves. After great efforts, they decreased the height of the machines by sinking their bases into the ground. "Apparently," Ehrenburg adds, "they considered the idea of the platforms somewhat insulting." [2]

13

On the Tomb

We have lived in the hand of God.
In his hand, right at his side.
He did not live in the blue of the skies.
Sometimes we could see him
Living. On the tomb.
He was not more wicked or more wise
Than that other fellow—named Jehovah.
—BORIS SLUTSKY

November 7, 1952

Thirty-fifth anniversary of the Revolution. Just before eleven o'clock, Stalin came out of the Kremlin to preside over a great parade on Red Square.

This was an annual ceremony, but Stalin's presence was unusual. As a rule, he spent November in the Caucasus and saved himself for the parade on May Day. According to his daughter, he did not like these festivals of the Revolution because it was at the close of one that his second wife tragically died twenty years earlier.

But this autumn the Nineteenth Congress had kept him in Moscow. He had worn his military uniform with the epaulettes of a generalissimo—the rank he created for himself. Thus togged out, he seemed rejuvenated, even taller. His shoemaker was an expert at making him gain an inch or so. The important people who could see him from close by considered him in good physical condition—despite what was for him a very early hour. He scaled the stairs to the reviewing stand on Lenin's tomb quickly, with the light step of a mountaineer.

80

Inspired by the tomb of Xerxes, Stalin had this monument of granite and porphyry built so that people could come and worship the founder of the Soviet Union. It was he who arranged for this high place, this reviewer's stand which would allow the heir to be associated with the cult of the master. Opposite him, like a reflection of their double presence, he could see their two giant pictures nailed to the wall of GUM, the large State department store.

Soviet chroniclers were considerably annoyed by this commercial building facing the regime's most hallowed spot. But in their accounts of ceremonies commemorating the Revolution they dared not call the store by name. So they resorted to a circumlocution: "The large building across from the tomb."

For the parade, this utilitarian, overdecorated building was smothered in bunting, blazons, and slogans written in golden letters on a scarlet background. Regiments of soldiers marched by on the immense square between the red bulk of the historic Museum of History and the multicolored cupolas of Basil the Blessed. Before Stalin, they executed an impeccable "eyes right." The booming sound of the brass bands and the rumbling of the tanks rose up around Stalin like incense. He was the *veliky polkovodets,* the great strategist. Among all the titles he had bestowed on himself, this was perhaps the one of which he was most proud. It was also the one which might be the most debatable.

His first efforts in military art during the Polish campaign and in the Civil War were mediocre, full of bitter disputes with better strategists such as Trotsky or Tukhachevsky (the same man he later remembered to kill). He showed no sign of the petulant imagination which attracted attention to a certain Captain Bonaparte. He saw things slowly, and not very correctly.

In 1941, he did not prepare the Soviet armies for the obviously imminent invasion by Germany—in order not to irritate Hitler. As a result, the Germans had the pleasure of confronting half-finished fortifications, uncamouflaged airfields, headquarters staffs without instructions, and divisions which had just been alerted. But later, when thousands of ordinary soldiers and young lieutenants fell shouting "for country and for Stalin," their sacrifice turned him into a God of War, the banner of a people. In the bloodshed, in the hardships and sufferings, in the final victory, Soviet citizens wanted to see in him the very image of their homeland.

After the army, the people marched past, shouting up to him. A million Muscovites passed by beneath his feet. Each of Moscow's twelve districts had formed its own column. The management of each enterprise and each factory had selected members of the personnel to take part in the parade, and had ordered banners, posters, models. Rising above this human sea were graphs glorifying the latest successes of the Five-Year Plan, naïvely realistic pictures representing a new subway station or the capital's latest skyscraper. The delegation of the "Sovetsky" district distinguished itself by carrying a huge book in which one could read in letters of gold: *J. Stalin. Economic Problems of Socialism in the U.S.S.R.* Thousands of banners sang the praises of the party of Lenin-Stalin and reproduced the directives of its last Congress. Thousands of portraits much larger than life strode along above the heads of the people. First of all, Stalin's portrait. Then the portraits of Marx, Engels, Lenin, those of the *soratniki* and those of the foreign Communist leaders. A gallery of heads assembled according to the fashion prevailing at each purge. He did not change: In the enormous effigies of which the little old man, high up there, was only a remote replica, he was always forty years old, with smooth features and a head of black hair.

These portraits of leaders were mass-produced by a special workshop. The technique was simple: The appropriately embellished features of the personage to be portrayed would be projected on a large white cloth. The painter would follow the contours of this image, emphasizing the shadows and highlights with a little black paint. This was called "painting with a dry brush."

Then the cloth was shifted, and the image projected would fall three yards farther ahead. The picture-making would then begin again. An expert could knock out five Berias or Molotovs a day. This was a good source of money for young, impecunious artists.

Beneath this floor of red flags paraded about one out of every seven Muscovites. (In the small or medium-sized provincial towns, the entire active population had to parade on this day.) All the professions were represented, metalworkers and academicians, doctors and post office employees, railway workers and masons, office clerks and draughtsmen. There was no mixing of the various professions; the people wearing fur coats were separated from those wearing flannel. It was all orderly. Everyone was on special duty. The group leaders had rehearsed the slogans many, many evenings on Red Square. But the enthusiasm was not feigned. When the columns reached the tribunal, they laughed and shouted cries of joy, gaily waved paper flowers distributed to them and lifted their heads happily toward the small silhouette which from time to time acknowledged their salute by waving its hands. Here and there a child, seated on his father's shoulders, received a store of memorable spectacles when he was raised above the crowd. Some gay dogs who had brought their accordions along could be heard playing their humble music amid the din of loudspeakers vomiting out triumphal hymns.

At the foot of the tomb, foreign diplomats and correspondents craned their necks to look up at the tribune and evaluate the changes that had occurred in the hierarchy.

The most prominent leaders stood at Stalin's left, but the Nineteenth Congress had brought some notable changes among them. Kosygin, who had figured on the tomb regularly since 1946, had disappeared. The Leningrad affair had not finished yielding its deadly fruit, and Kosygin, a regular member of the Politburo, had been brutally demoted to the rank of a candidate.

The Politburo itself,* the most prestigious of the leading organs, had been rebaptized the Presidium. Its membership had been increased from twelve to twenty-five, not counting the eleven candidates. The old stars were still there, but only as a matter of form, since they were already swamped by the influx of new arrivals. The new generation was at hand. Molotov and Mikoyan, whom Stalin had publicly attacked before the Central Committee, could see that their new colleagues had the settled look of heirs.

To show even more clearly that the glorious Politburo was on the way out, that serious matters were handled elsewhere, Stalin had meanwhile reinforced the Secretariat of the Central Committee, which had been his property for the last thirty years. He had added to it newcomers whom he regarded as both able and devoted. One of them found himself for the first time on the top of the tomb at the very end of the row, on the far left. He was not yet forty-six, and beneath his fur cap his face was full, fleshy and florid. His name was Leonid Brezhnev.

He was born in December, 1906, near the Dnieper, the great river of the Ukraine. After the Revolution, Kamenskoye, his native town, became an industrial city and was rebaptized Dneprodzerzhinsk in honor of the founder of the Cheka (Feliks Dzerzhinsky). It is about 930 miles from Leningrad and its white nights. Compared to the pale and silent Kosygin, Brezhnev with his black hair, his ringing laugh, and his rather rich voice was the very picture of the southerner.

He was the son of a metalworker, which was the best possible

* Politburo: Political Bureau of the Central Committee of the Communist Party. It became the Presidium in October, 1952, and again the Politburo in 1966.

origin for a Communist leader. He himself was proud of having had calloused hands when young from having worked as an apprentice at fifteen. Like all or almost all the members of the new elite, he had won his stripes as a technician and engineer, first in a school of agriculture and later in an institute of metallurgy. But he had quickly left the fields and factory to become a party functionary. Having escaped the purges of 1937, he quickly rose high. At thirty-two he was Secretary of the region of Dnepropetrovsk, in other words, already a notable of high rank.

During the war, he scaled, with the same apparent ease, the echelons of the military hierarchy without abandoning his specialty, politics. He was made responsible for the "political direction" of various fronts, and, in May, 1945, young General Brezhnev, his chest covered with decorations, paraded on Red Square. He retained from this period close friends in military circles and a marked taste for armaments.

Strongly built, with a square jaw and the neck of a bull, he looked brutal but was known to be cautious. Beneath enormous eyebrows, his blue eyes were cunning and a trifle ironic. During the Party's interminable meetings, he had learned to control himself and to appear solemn and neutral, by stringing together all the ready-made formulas in long oratorical sentences. In private, he laughed and easily became emotional. He was an expert waltzer and had a passion for hunting. He knew the system inside out, both the machinery and the men; and no one was more skillful than he in wending his way through its complicated administrative labyrinths. A man of endless patience, he was well liked by the departments. From time to time, when he felt that a situation was ripe, he would cut through it with the quick, prompt gesture of a man who is sure of himself. He was fat and heavy, but he moved about briskly. And when he decided to make his big voice heard, one listened.

When Khrushchev was First Secretary in the Ukraine, he had noticed this talented *apparatchik*, who was smart enough not to create problems. It was largely because of him that in this autumn of 1952 Leonid Ilyich Brezhnev had become one of the most powerful men in the Soviet Union. He was not only a candidate member of the former Politburo—the new enlarged Presidium—but a member of the Secretariat, that prestigious group of ten men.

The first of the ten was Joseph Stalin, the Secretary General. Thus, Brezhnev had every reason to pride himself on being at the very center of power. His functions in this group were undoubtedly limited and secondary, and he could not yet hope to equal the "great" secretaries, such as Malenkov or Khrushchev. But he was one of the men who, having scaled the heights, could look down from the top of the tomb and see the crowd beating against the base of the red and brown monument like the waves of the sea.

A month before, in his speech at the Nineteenth Congress, he had glorified at length "the greatest man of our epoch . . . the inspired architect of Communism . . . a man of inexhaustible revolutionary energy . . . the wise leader and teacher . . . our Joseph Vissarionovich Stalin."[1] He had also called him "the liberator of Bessarabia."

Situated between the Dniester and Prut rivers and the delta of the Danube was Bessarabia, a much-coveted, fertile region, for centuries disputed by Hungarian princes, Turkish sultans, and Greek hospodars. In the nineteenth century, the struggle narrowed down to the Romanians and Russians. The Romanians took control in 1918, but the Soviets returned in 1940 and remained after the war.

Bessarabia, now the Soviet Socialist Republic of Moldavia, was Brezhnev's last place of work before Moscow. Sent to Kishinev in 1950 as First Secretary of the Moldavian Party, he ruled for two years in the country of Pan's pipe and impassioned Romanian chants. It is said that this *bon vivant* loved this land of pretty women and good wines.

But, tormented by centrifugal currents, Moldavia is a peripheral region if ever there was one. Ruling for the sake of Russian order was not easy. How did Brezhnev manage? The Moldavians, selling their cherries and grapes for their weight in gold on the kolkhoz markets in Moscow and Leningrad, would whisper discreetly: "Things are not too bad at home."

This man with a double chin was not a frigid ideologue like Suslov, his neighbor on the reviewing stand and his colleague in the Secretariat. He was certainly neither softhearted nor a liberal, but, from time to time, he knew how to be understanding. It was rumored that in Moldavia the purge had been less drastic than in most parts of the Soviet Union.

14

First Among Equals

The assignment of Brezhnev, a man of Russian ancestry and born in the Ukraine, to the Republic of Moldavia had obviously represented a deviation from the much trumpeted "Stalinist policy for the nationalities," which promised to each people in the Soviet Union control and management of its own affairs. But these distortions were so customary that one barely paid any attention to them. According to the Constitution, the sixteen Federated Republics * of the U.S.S.R. all had rights, including the very theoretical right of quitting the Federation. Letts and Turkomans, Moldavians, Azerbaidzhanians, Ukrainians, and Kirgiz each had their own government, parliament, and system of law courts. But Moscow was in charge of everything. The Russians were everywhere.

A formula that could have been written by Orwell summed up the situation: "The Russian People, first among equal peoples." [1] The Soviet hymn, which in 1944 replaced the "International," forgets to speak of the Communist party, but glorifies, in traditional tones, Great Russia, the founder of the Soviet Union.

And for his victory toast, in May, 1945, Stalin raised his glass to the Russian people, "the leading force of the Soviet Union, among all the peoples in our country."

Stalin's strength lay in his ambiguity. Both revolutionary and conservative, he pleased everyone. The old agitator dressed his subjects in uniforms refashioned from the time of the Tsars. The diplomats had theirs, and so did the public prosecutors, as well as the students, male and female; even miners received a suit for their

* A number which since then had been reduced to fifteen, the Karelo-Finnic Republic having been integrated purely and simply into the Republic of Russia.

time off—green cloth with gold braid. The administrative grades were copied from the ranks of yesteryear. The army, no longer called the Red Army, had gone back to Tsarist epaulettes; and the Orthodox Patriarch was decorated with the Order of the Red Banner.

The ambiguity was even greater in regard to the problem of the "nationalities." Stalin, a colonial, became the theoretician of a certain de-colonization, which led Lenin to call him the "miraculous Georgian": In the new community of the Soviet republics, each people of the old Russian empire would be free to enter or leave. That lasted as long as the roses, until the recognition of Finnish independence in 1918. Then Stalin returned to Russian centralism, hiding it under a thick varnish of "multinational" propaganda.

During the war, he was heard invoking Saint Aleksandr Nevsky on the radio. Faced with the advancing Germans, it was a good idea to work up nationalistic emotions. But with the war won, he continued to take pleasure in his role as a Russian patriot. Portraits of Suvorov and Kutuzov continued to hang on the walls of his office. On the Avenue of the Soviets, he replaced the Obelisk of Liberty, erected at Lenin's suggestion, with a statue of Yury Dolgoruki, a feudal Russian prince and the founder of Moscow.

To keep the Soviet Union, this enormous pyramid made up of different peoples and contradictory traditions, from collapsing was an appalling task, and Stalin met the challenge by discarding the equalitarian constructions he had imagined in his youth. With the sly smile of the "realist," he based his power on the strongest and the most numerous. The Russians, who represented about 50 per cent of the population, were called "older brothers," and it mattered little that the Kiev of the Ukrainians or the Samarkand of the Uzbeks, both at least two thousand years old, also had justifiable claims to seniority.

The Russians were patriots. It was their right and duty to be patriots. But national pride among other peoples in the Soviet Union became a slippery slope leading straight to bourgeois nationalism and detestable deviation—great conveyor belts to the concentration camps.

And so one saw Korneichuk, president of the Ukrainian Writers Union, beat his breast. Tormented by diabolical nationalism, Ukrainian critics had neglected to attack a poem entitled "I Love the Ukraine." Even worse, certain critics had praised it. And now another critic dared "to oppose the Ukrainian poet A. Malyshko to the great bard of the Russian people, Vladimir Mayakovsky." [2] Horrors!

Bourgeois nationalist was the opera *Manas*, devoted to the heroes of the old epic tales of the Kirgiz. Also bourgeois nationalist were the Georgian writers Gamsahurdia and Dadiani, who "idealized the

Georgian past" and "incorrectly interpreted the century-long friend-ship between the Russian and Georgian nations." [3] Estonian painters were asked to "study the great Russian painters more," and all of Estonia was asked to sing "songs of greater resonance, which are so numerous among the Russian people." [4]

The official doctrine was that the superiority of the "older brother" did not simply date from the Soviet era. From time immemorial, it was he who had brought light to the underdeveloped peoples of the Russian empire. Thus *Pravda* rehabilitated the conquering Tsars, while blasting the museums of Kazakhstan which concealed "the historic fact that Kazakh people see in their attachment to Russia the means of surmounting their backward character." [5] And it cut to pieces a historian who dared to write that Tsarism chased the population of Dagestan to the foot of the mountains.[6]

It goes without saying that this was not only a matter of museums and literary disputes. Before the Nineteenth Congress, the Parties of the sixteen republics had held their own congresses. The results were chilling. In Turkmenia, a third of the party's delegates were eliminated in one year. In Uzbekistan, four First Secretaries were demoted one after the other by the Tashkent City Party Committee. Everywhere the reason was the same: bourgeois nationalism. The President of the Supreme Soviet of Lithuania, Justas Paleckis, had to perform an act of public self-criticism; he had succumbed to indulgence—read complicity—vis-à-vis certain Lithuanian bourgeois nationalists.

The Baltic countries and the western Ukraine, which had lived for twenty years outside the Soviet orbit, were the most suspect. Several years after the war, a number of anti-Soviet partisans were still hidden in their forests. However, Belorussia, a near cousin, seemed almost immune to the anti-Russian sin. It was simply "economic deficiency" that motivated its purge. Pyotr Abrasimov, a Secretary of the Belorussian Central Committee, was stripped of office for failure to achieve the goals of the Plan. Much later, he would be found in key Soviet diplomatic posts, first in Berlin and then in Paris.

But cases such as this were in sharp contrast with other, more radical purges. In Georgia, the hunt for deviationists among the shepherds and workers in the vineyards was colored in bloody hues. The Republic was still shaken by the Mingrelian affair in which bourgeois nationalism was complicated by pro-Turkish espionage. Beyond the local convulsions, it was Beria's influence which was at stake. Mgeladze, the new First Secretary of the Georgian Party, was supposed to be one of his friends.

On the December, 1949, cover of *Ogonyok,* Stalin replaced the star of Christmas.

Pictures such as this one by Vasilyev, showing an attentive Lenin and the inspired Georgian, magnified out of all proportion Stalin's role during the Revolution.

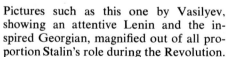

Upper right: Three artists, now forgotten, collaborated to produce this painting entitled "Glory to the Great Stalin."

Lower right: In November, 1952, at a reception celebrating the thirty-fifth anniversary of the October Revolution, Stalin has receded to the second row, behind Beria and Kaganovich, themselves flanked by Malenkov and Khrushchev.

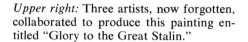

Photograph by I. Rubenchik, Novosti, Moscow, used by permission of Editions Robert Laffont

This statue of Stalin at Yerevan in Armenia was tall enough to be visible to the Turks on the other side of the border.

СПАСИБО
РОДНОМУ СТАЛИНУ
ЗА СЧАСТЛИВОЕ ДЕТСТВО!

The universal godfather—
"Thanks to dear Stalin for our
happy childhood" was the first
motto taught to youth.

*Musée Royal de l'Armée et d'Histoire
Militaire, Brussels, used by permission
of Editions Robert Laffont*

Below: On May 1, 1952, a school-
girl embraces Stalin on the mausoleum.

Agence France-Presse

The theme of this painting, entitled "For the Happiness of the People," is Stalin's "plan for the transformation of nature." Seated are Shvernik, Molotov, Beria, and Malenkov. Bulganin, Mikoyan, and Khrushchev are standing behind Stalin. Kosygin is partially hidden by Voroshilov.

Below: On May Day, 1952, the marshals are to the right of Stalin. To his left are Malenkov, Beria, Molotov, Mikoyan, Kaganovich, Andreyev, Khrushchev, Shvernik, Kosygin, Suslov, Ponomarenko, Shkiryatov.

This is the grave of Nadezhda, Stalin's second wife, at the Novo-Devichi cemetery.

Stalin's son Vasily takes part in an air force review.

In October, 1952, Malenkov presents the report on Party activities to the Nineteenth Congress.

15

A Worker

Pavlusha, a worker in a tractor factory at Kharkov, rubbed his hands with satisfaction. He was about to obtain the thirty-second and last signature he needed to leave on vacation.

For a week, he had spent all his free time waiting patiently in offices for these signatures. First, various officials had to sign his request for vacation. Then, at a second stage, you needed signatures on a special voucher which you had to deliver to the personnel department. You also had to get the warehouse to sign, certifying that you were not carrying off the smallest hammer. Even the librarian had to attest that you had returned all books and newspapers.

Everything was in order; Pavlusha could leave on December 15. To leave was to stay at home. Pavlusha had not received the travel permit, which would have allowed him to go to the factory's "rest house" in the country. Too bad! The food there was not famous, but one could have a pleasant time in the fresh air, playing dominos with comrades. Unfortunately, the factory issued a travel permit to only one worker out of fifteen. And they went first of all to Party members.

Without a travel permit, Pavlusha would spend his annual regulation leave—twenty-four working days—in Kharkov. But there would be plenty to do. He would most likely go to the movies; just then they were showing *The Singer of Leningrad* with a good tenor, and *The Vow,* in which Gelovani was breathtaking as Comrade Stalin. And eventually he would go to the stadium. The ice hockey season was at its height, though tickets were hard to come by. And, of course, there were his friends. He would visit them, and they would visit him, and they would drink tea and play the old phonograph. The evenings would go by quickly.

But first of all, there would be useful occupations. Two shaky stools in his house needed repairing; and, with the boards a pal in the warehouse had put aside for him, he could lengthen his daughter's bed. She was really shooting up fast. He would try to get a new felt lining put in his overcoat, and, above all, help his mother-in-law on the queues.

Pavlusha's wife, daughter and mother-in-law all shared his company-assigned living quarters—ten square yards, and a "community" kitchen shared with three other families in a cascade of shouts and complaints over a dirty stove or a stopped-up sink. His wife was an accountant and, as an office worker, was entitled to only two weeks of vacation each year. She had taken them in October and toured the villages surrounding Kharkov. Thank God, she had brought back a good supply of potatoes. Now it was his job to find what they would need for the holidays at the end of the year. Pavlusha was a good father and a good husband, not one of those who leave the whole of scrounging for food to their wives.

With his mother-in-law's small pension, they brought home about 2,400 rubles a month, a remarkably high income for a family of workers. Pavlusha's family did not hesitate, from time to time, to shop in the kolkhoz market, where everything was expensive but of better quality. Instead of the eternal sausage in the State stores, one could find, at thirty-five rubles a kilo, real meat—which bearded peasants carved with a hatchet—eggs, and vegetables. The Ukraine was rich.

At the price of a discreet present to the salesgirl, grandmother had gotten four pounds of flour for making cake. Pavlusha hunted through the stores looking for pickled herring and a few toys. As for vodka, there was no problem, you could buy all you wanted.

After all, it was good that the factory had granted him his leave only at the end of the year and not in July, as he had hoped. In December, you didn't have time to be bored.

In June, 1946, he was just about to be demobilized when people from Kharkov came to his barracks, recruiting for their factory. "Boys, we offer you good jobs and good pay. You can get prizes for socialist competition if you work hard." Pavlusha, who came from a small town in central Russia, was seduced by Ukrainian dynamism. His heart pounding, he walked through the majestic factory gates with its archway and banners: "Glory to Work. Carry Out the Plan Ahead of Schedule!"

Pavlusha was proud of his work in the glaring heat, the deafening noise of the overhead cranes, the grinders and casting rollers of the foundry. It was a shame that the furnaces were in such bad shape, the tools worn out, the castings so often below par. There was neither time nor desire to do the work properly. The workers were paid by the piece. If they didn't want to lose money, they had to "carry out the Plan." And the Plan was just a matter of quantity. Quality was mentioned favorably in the speeches on holidays, but nobody had ever managed to define it or make it an integral part of their salaries. If Pavlusha had slowed up production out of a desire to be painstaking, his comrades would have jumped on him because he would have caused his brigade to fail to do the job assigned to it. And everyone would make less pay. Therefore, you carried out the Plan, even if not too brilliantly.

Besides, if you had any feelings of morality, the Plan was sacred. Of course, there were all sorts of cheats. How could you carry out the Plan without getting tired? Some work-brigades counted their production twice. With the warehouse men as accomplices, they would take finished products out of the warehouse and put them right back again. Truck and wagon drivers would calmly demand a waybill certifying that they had left fully loaded, even if they had left almost empty. If an engineer frowned, the trucks would break down and the horses go lame. For the drivers, the "Plan" was a combination of miles covered and loads transported.

There was a plethora of engineers with some sort of a diploma, who were often used as simple foremen. But good workers were rare. Pavlusha, conscious of his value, would have liked to work for the steel mill, where the pay and housing were better, or for one of those State "trusts," where resourceful workers actually "exceeded the Plan" and received big bonuses. But his internal passport and his work service book were kept under lock and key by the personnel department, and without them he could not leave. The advantage of the system was that there was no unemployment.

Every day, before starting work, Pavlusha had to listen to the *Pyatiminutki,* the "five minutes" of obligatory political instruction (in fact, the workers were assembled a good half hour before the legal time, to be sure nobody was missing). Last winter, the engineer had read them an article from *Pravda*—the big one, not the Ukrainian edition, entitled "In the City of the Unemployed." It was a description of Detroit, U.S.A. "In the streets of the city from morning till late at night, crowds of people with emaciated, somber, anxious faces roam about. Unemployed, more unemployed, everywhere unemployed. . . ." The article went on to say that those who manage to find a job are forced to work at such furious rates that "many of them cannot maintain the furious speed-up, suffer strokes, or even die from a heart attack right there on the job, on the assembly line." [1] From the bottom of his heart, Pavlusha blessed Soviet power which had spared him all that.

Of course, he did not believe all that he read in the papers. At the end of the war (a wound, two decorations), he spent a few months in Germany. You had to hand it to those Fascists. They must have looted all of Europe to live so luxuriously. Not like us, who help all of the socialist countries and do not even have string and nails. Or paper: All of Pavlusha's engineer's reports were written on wrapping paper.

He had been approached several times by the Party organization in the factory: "You should make a request to enter our ranks. You are a good, serious worker. You are not a tippler. The Party needs Communists like you." Pavlusha knew how to behave. He did not say no. Yes, yes, he would think it over; he would write out his request one of these days. . . . He had let it drag out for two years now. Being in the Party meant, of course, a little more esteem in your own eyes and in those of the management. But it also meant more responsibilities, meetings in the evening. It was the end of one's personal life.

16

The Leaders' Grandeur and Misery

It was the end of the year for the millions of Pavlushas as well as for the powerful managers of the factories enthroned deep in their offices with their double, padded doors. The managers were at once masters and slaves of the ministries which had foreseen everything: the smallest technological operation down to the last millimeter, the wages of the least important worker down to the last ruble.

Everything was determined a year in advance. A manager to whom the plan alloted 5,000 workers could not hire 5,001. And it was not up to him to decide if he would order his screws from Stalingrad or Vladivostok: The Plan bureaus in Moscow knew all that better than he did. Yet he was allowed 1,000 rubles a month (about 120 dollars today) for "miscellaneous purchases." * In a case of extreme need he could buy a few reams of paper and a few pounds of nails without going through the central office.

To keep one's machines running in the midst of this mountain of red tape, one had to cheat a little. So this high personage endowed with both technical and political powers (he was most often a member of the Party's local committee) was in the position of a young kid camouflaging all sorts of disobediences with cunning devices.

Besides, he was watched from all sides. Gigantic control services made sure that each stage of production conformed to the set norms.

* This in a factory which at the time had an output in the hundreds of millions of rubles.

93

He also had to tolerate within his enterprise a permanent antenna of State Security, the "Special Service," which, of course, did not tell him everything. His personnel manager was also recruited by preference from among active or retired members of the police.

On the other hand, the factory manager had all the attributes of power: a long black ZIS, a travel pass for the seaside resorts in the Caucasus, and a comfortable apartment. Sometimes, and this was the height of luxury, his wife could even permit herself not to work. He could draw what he wanted from the canteens of his establishment, which were always better supplied than the city's stores. He was a baron.

His fief existed in a state of extreme autarchy: The factories could build their own buildings, their own roads, railways, canals, even the lodgings of their employees. They manufactured as well as they could a good many of their tools and spare parts and they had their own shoe repair and laundry services. Above all, they had their own police—dozens of armed guards patrolling the walls night and day with dogs to prevent thefts.

Each enterprise had at its disposal a "technical supply corps": ingenious emissaries who scoured the immense hinterland, and stuffed bottles of vodka and other gifts in their capacious briefcases. Their mission was to obtain everything that was lacking, all the deliveries promised for the Plan and never delivered, minerals and wood, as well as screws, electric light bulbs, and rubber tubing. Their weapon was persuasion. . . .

The leading cadres knew no more than the workers what they would earn at the end of the month; whether the factory would stop "carrying out the Plan" and their bonus be lost or whether the bonus might easily represent half of their emoluments. "When we did not fulfill the Plan," Engineer B. M. recalled, "I was even more afraid of my wife's reaction than the Ministry's."

Discipline in this period was rigorous, but it was also full of the unexpected. For having tried to carry off a few pieces of waste sheet iron, a worker was sentenced to two years in prison. On the other hand, a worker found dead drunk during working hours appealed the decision to fire him, sued the factory, and won the case. Instead of him, the engineer was punished for failing to train him and teach him not to drink. He was deprived of his bonus so that he would learn to have better subordinates.

These factories, ponderous and fixed like mammoths in the Siberian ice, worked a great deal for industry but very little for the consumer. Symbolically, heavy industry was "Category A," while light industry was "Category B." A worker in the second category received less pay, poorer housing and generally less esteem than a worker in the first category.

In a country where the forests cover land twenty times the area of France, one still had to turn to the black market to get a plank of wood. But in 1945, Stalin had ordered that steel production be tripled as compared to what existed before the war. And the challenge had been met in fifteen years.

17

Moscow, December, 1952

On December 21, Stalin's seventy-third birthday was greeted rather tamely by the press.

His seventy-second birthday had been marvelous. The whole world had sent gifts, trainloads of them, for which the famous "Museum of Gifts" had to be opened in Moscow. *Pravda* had spent several months printing all the birthday greetings, at the rate of one or two columns a day. At the triumphal soirée at the Bolshoi, all the great figures of world Communism had made ardent speeches for four hours (Stalin had not deigned to open his mouth).

Since then, he had not wished to put his aging on display. His daughter, who visited him at Kuntsevo on his birthday, found him in bad shape. Suffering from high blood pressure and various other ills, he tired quickly. He announced proudly that he had finally managed to give up tobacco, depriving himself of his Dunhill pipes —souvenirs of the great wartime alliance—as well as of his "Kazbek" *papirosy*, cigarettes with long cardboard tips, which he smoked as students do, twisting the tip between his fingers.

He husbanded his strength because he did not think his work was fully accomplished. The world needed him. Moreover, after an outburst of enthusiasm for Malenkov, immediately following the Nineteenth Congress, Soviet papers had progressively reduced their quotations from the "successor."

On this December 21, 1952, page one was devoted to the new Stalin Peace Prize laureates: Yves Farge, Ilya Ehrenburg, Salfuddin Kitchlu, Elisa Branco, Johannes Becher, James Endicott and Paul Robeson.

But the real star was Stalin. The new Bible, his book *The Economic*

Problems of Socialism, had reached 20 million copies three months after publication.

He was also being discussed on the international plane: The *New York Times* published his answers to a questionnaire presented by James Reston. Surprisingly, he raised the possibility of a meeting with Eisenhower to lessen international tension. It was all rather vague and cold. But Western opinion jumped at this hint. A declining Churchill, who wanted to make a grand coup before leaving the stage, clung to the idea of a "summit meeting" in which he could participate and insisted on playing the courier between the new-comer Eisenhower, who was flanked by an intractable John Foster Dulles, and the old beast clothed in mystery.

Inside the country, the year ended on a grim note. On December 24, a *Pravda* editorial by Mikhail A. Suslov, who was firmly in charge of all doctrinal matters, labeled Nikolai Voznesensky's economic theories "anti-Marxist, voluntarist, and subjectivist." This was an eminently restrospective condemnation. More than three long years had passed since Voznesensky had been excluded from the Politburo and his famous work *The War Economy of the U.S.S.R.* and all the other books on economics it had inspired had been cast into the inferno of libraries accessible only to readers with special passes. One wondered with some anxiety whether others who were still untouched were being aimed at through him. Such thoughts would have been even more gloomy if it had been known that Voznesensky was not only disgraced but also dead. Yet very few had been informed of his execution, which dated from September, 1950.

When they were not hurling political curses, the newspapers of this last month of 1952 were denouncing various scandals. From the austere *Izvestia* to the satiric *Krokodil,* one could read about a rich collection of swindlers. In Yaroslavl, a certain Nikolai Pribytkov had earned more than 250,000 rubles—twenty-five times a school teacher's salary—in fraudulent transactions involving timber for construction. A certain Chemadayev, an illegal manufacturer in Moldavia, had been given the very capitalistic nickname "king of perfumes." A speculator in Bashkiria, involved in the theft of horses, had made a sumptuous arrangement with the judges.[1]

Along with this organized fraud, there was small-scale crime. The young people above all were urged to keep an eye on each other, to "expose" the small traders on the black market and the street kids, terrors of the outlying districts.[2] Just at this moment, the Komsomol got a new and energetic First Secretary, Aleksandr N. Shelepin.

And just for good measure, *Pravda,* on December 15, called for denunciations in the bosom of the family: "Here is a family living, as the expression goes, 'beyond its means.' Of course one may admit that the head of the family does not keep his relatives posted on all his shady deals. But do they as Soviet adults reflect on the fact that their husband's or father's salary does not correspond to the extravagant life they lead? . . . They are morally responsible for his acts before Soviet society. In certain cases, it might also be a matter of responsibility before the law. It is not advisable that anyone should forget this."

December brought Moscow wan, fleeting days. By three o'clock, twilight had descended, and a black crowd was moving about on the gray, frozen snow. The padded jackets, felt boots, and even the overcoats and suits were all black. Most of the women wore on their heads the eternal shawl.

Rolling by in Pobedas, the officers' wives, with their high and complicated hairdos, gowns of fine Chinese silks, and their furs, provided a few spots of color.

Stalin had always liked a hierarchical society. At the end of the month in the bureaus, certain high functionaries received not only their salary, but also a "money envelope"—a sheaf of banknotes in a sealed envelope, without a receipt or a signature. Those who refused this exorbitant privilege in the name of old-fashioned Bolshevik purity were viewed askance: "The Party has given you a mark of confidence. You must accept it."

At that time, Moscow was still largely a city built of wood. One could find whole neighborhoods of *izbas*, poetic as Russian fairy tales and dilapidated as hovels, right in the center of town. The overcrowding was frightful. People often lived in cellars ventilated through an opening at street level. Walking by, one would notice a light and see that a whole family was living in a hole.

High above were the towers of the skyscrapers. There were seven of them, all finished or almost finished. This, too, was Stalin's idea. He felt that a capital should be outlined boldly against the horizon, like American cities; and obediently, the architects designed horizons jagged with vertical lines. Unfortunately, the style of the period was uninspired. Following its master, it insisted on the ponderous and the flashy. The skyscrapers were giant hybrids of the mosque and the dungeon, with Gothic bell towers and Grecian colonnades. Large, but looking as though they were crouching, there was something menacing about them. Their only beauty was their stone, which turned golden in the sunlight.

A few prestigious avenues were top-heavy with monumental porticos. The old wooden houses, hidden behind the rows of ponderous new buildings, had granite façades and complicated cornices. Rebuilt Gorky Street was almost sixty yards wide. Two groups of optimistic statues—vigorous workers with their well-nourished children—looked down from the roof tops on the crowds that lined up for every purchase.

Moscow was better supplied with goods than the provinces. People jammed the "chic" food stores. In the old Yeliseyev store, which had become Gastronom No. 1, they shopped among the crystal chandeliers, the gilt ornaments, the whole pastry-shop architecture of Russian turn-of-the-century style. They went to the old Filipov bakery shop, where the bread was baked better and was less stale than elsewhere. But black bread remained the norm. White bread was for the rich.

Vodka was one of the most available products. But it was too expensive for someone who drank every day. This was fortunate because drunkenness was a national sport. On pay days, the areas around the factories were thronged with men staggering along.

Petty crime was the other urban plague. In the public parks or in the back streets, people were robbed, stripped, stabbed, sometimes in full daylight. In the crowded trams, wallets disappeared from clothes artistically slit with a razor. In Leningrad, two steps from the Nevsky Prospect, a black market in gold was functioning almost openly. Crooks were busy getting supplies of precious metals and organizing outlets abroad.

Since Stalin did not sleep, Moscow worked at night. Thousands of functionaries appeared at their offices for a few hours during the day, but what really counted was to return late at night and remain on the job until three or four in the morning. One waited for a telephone call, a summons. The most highly placed persons, ministers or directors, filled these hours of enforced insomnia by having movies shown for them. This was a noble and eminently loyal occupation. Had not Stalin spent a great part of his nights in the Kremlin projection hall? It was well known that he loved Charlie Chaplin and Westerns. To be interested in the cinema was therefore not only a right but a duty. E.R., an English interpreter, earned quite a lot of money going about the ministries at night translating American films.

At the Moskva Hotel, a grandiose, somber fifteen-story building, the restaurant was always full until dawn. People did a lot of drinking but engaged in modest dancing, by preference mazurkas, czar-

das, etc. Jazz was forbidden. Two or three tangos a night, one or
two fox trots were the limits of the permissible. All over town, dancing teachers taught timid bachelors the rudiments of the polka.

Morality was Victorian. At school, the boys and girls were kept
apart from seven to seventeen years of age. On seeing a young student in a sleeveless dress, the directress of an institute fulminated:
"I will not tolerate prostitution in my establishment." The only officially tolerated vice was alcohol.

Two luxuries were considered the height of bad taste: dogs and
privately owned cars. People considered them signs of bourgeois tendencies and an almost anti-Soviet spirit. Concerning an old Bolshevik
who had survived the purges of 1937, I was told: "He no longer fears
anything. He doesn't care what people say: He has a dog and a car."
Despite a very small production, the delays in the delivery of cars
were reasonable and prices were moderate—9,000 rubles, that is,
about $11,880 at current rates of exchange, for a Moskvich, 16,000
rubles for a Pobeda. But nobody bought them because all the
money went for food; also, it was just not done. On the other hand,
official chauffeured cars were displayed with pride and used with few
scruples, for personal needs.

One of the strangest places in Moscow at that time was the Cock-
tail Hall on Gorky Street. It was strange, first of all, because, despite
the wave of chauvinism, it had kept its foreign name. It was also there
that one found what was most unusual in Moscow: a group of semi-
rebellious, semi-"hoolligan" young people who dared to make a point
of openly admiring America. One night, during the last weeks of
1952, a very drunk young man, in homage to the retiring President of
the United States, shouted "Long live Harry Truman!" Ten minutes
later, a group of perfectly sober men burst into the hall, grabbed him
by the shoulders and took him away.

Illuminated fir trees rose 60 to 90 feet high on Moscow's main
square. It was the first of January, an official holiday, that had refur-
bished all the old Russian Christmas folklore: Grandfather Frost, the
fairy godmother *Snegurochka*, etc. Those who really wanted to celebrate Christmas could do so on January 7, according to the old Julian
calendar still followed by the Orthodox Church. But it was best to
be discreet about it. If you had any position at all in society, be it
high or low, it was best not to announce that you were a believer.
Only old, very poor, and very obstinate women, with nothing to gain
or lose, practiced their faith openly.

The Russian Orthodox Church had become marginal and was barely
tolerated. But Stalin covered its leaders with honors. On the great
ceremonial occasions at the Kremlin, the old seminarian Dzhugashvili

would walk to the door of the Hall of St. George to welcome the old Patriarch Alexis.

In return, the clergy did not oppose the cult of Stalin. On the contrary, they prayed and made others pray for "the beloved guide of the people of our great State." [3]

During the war, the guide had understood that the Russians would fight better if they could associate the idea of country with the old religious conditioning. He feverishly reopened some of the churches he had closed, a clever move, which Goebbels, who did not underestimate his adversary, highly praised in his journal.

Why abandon such a good path once the war was over? Stalin had become a Russian patriot, and this church with such a marked national character pleased him. It would serve his plan for Russification. So, in the Ukraine, he installed it in place of the Uniate Catholic clergy, which had been conveniently deported and persecuted.

But it was above all outside the Soviet Union that the services rendered by the Patriarchate were noteworthy. The Metropolitan Nikolai, its majestic, bearded, eloquent spokesman, traveled all over the world, from congress to congress. He harangued the Partisans for Peace, called upon them to acclaim the father of the peoples, denounced bacteriological warfare and the Americans. The Kremlin's spiritual surety bond, he made a fine impression with his staff and large pectoral cross, as he swore that Soviet soldiers had nothing to do with the massacre of Polish officers at Katyn. Due to his efforts, from Paris to Jerusalem a certain number of parishes of the Russian emigré church had agreed to resume their ties with the Moscow hierarchy.

In sum, the Patriarch and the Secretary-General could be happy about their mutual understanding. On the religious side, people applauded the 22,000 churches now open for Orthodox worship as against 4,200 before the war, the 30,000 active priests, and the eight seminaries which had been recently established.[*] On the governmental side, the bureaucrats seemed quite satisfied with this disciplined, correct, and effective ally.

Under these conditions, Stalin considered a Christian who went to Mass less dangerous than a Communist who read Trotsky. He ladled out gentleness and severity accordingly. Besides, it meant nothing to him whether or not someone was a mystic. He didn't understand all that. For him, the Church was an organization, a hierarchy. As a connoisseur, he appreciated its function. What's more, the Orthodox Church was part of his youth, and that counted for something at his age.

[*] These figures diminished considerably during the Khrushchev period, for he closed a great many churches.

Furthermore, he distrusted other religions because they were not Russian. Moslems of Asia or Catholics of Central Asia seemed to him people of another race, centrifugal forces, and therefore dangerous elements. He treated them as such. With docile obstinacy, the Baptists went to rot in the camps.

As for the Jews, it did not matter whether they practiced their religion or not. All sorts of Jews had been persecuted for the last five years. But this was only the beginning. They would be the victims of the coming purge, the sacrifices of the coming winter.

part III
WINTER

18

The Men in White

The lead editorial in *Pravda*—massive and dull as usual—was entitled: "To build quickly, solidly, cheaply." One skipped it and went on.

Below this were a few less banal lines: The night before, at the Bolshoi, Stalin honored with his presence a concert by Polish artists. But it was a headline at the top of the right side of the front page that struck the eye: "MISERABLE SPIES AND ASSASSINS MASKING AS PROFESSORS OF MEDICINE."

"In the U.S.S.R.," the article explained, "the exploiting classes have for a long time been vanquished and liquidated but there still are some survivors . . . some spokesmen for bourgeois opinions and bourgeois customs, LIVING MEN [printing this phrase in large type underlined the intention], hidden enemies of our people."

The style of 1937. The rhetoric of the purges. The old terrors revived.

The affair was summed up on the last page in a communiqué from the Tass agency: "Some time ago the organs of State Security discovered a terrorist group of doctors whose aim was to shorten the lives of leading figures in the Soviet Union by means of harmful treatment."

The victims? First of all, the illustrious Andrei Zhdanov, long considered Stalin's heir, and Aleksandr Shcherbakov, like him, a member of the Politburo and also suffering from heart trouble. Both were dead. And it had been thought that their deaths were natural. But no: By prescribing harmful treatment for them, doctor assassins had shortened their lives.

105

Another target: a series of very important military personalities, among whom were Marshal Vasilevsky, the Minister of War, Marshal Konev, one of the conquerors of Berlin, Marshal Govorov, an admiral, and various generals. All very much alive: With them, the terrorists in white had failed.

And the criminals? "Numbered among the participants in this terrorist group are Professor M. S. Vovsi, general practitioner, Professor V. N. Vinogradov, general practitioner, Professor M. B. Kogan, general practitioner, Professor B. B. Kogan, general practitioner, Professor P. I. Yegorov, general practitioner, Professor A. I. Feldman, ear, nose and throat specialist, Professor A. I. Etinger, general practitioner, Professor A. M. Grinstein, neurologist, and G. I. Maiorov, general practitioner."

Of these nine names, six were immediately identifiable as Jewish. Soviet citizens were expert at this kind of name game.

Buried in the report were two little words: *i drugiye*—"and others." This meant that the list was not complete; there were others under accusation who were not named.

In any event, those who were named were all very important persons. With the exception of Maiorov, they were all full professors, and several were members of the Academy of Medicine. Three were known to their Western colleagues, who had met them at congresses, which was quite rare in this period when scholars, too, were separated by the Iron Curtain.

Another thing they had in common was that they were all "Kremlin doctors," that is to say, doctors to whom important personalities had been entrusted; some of them had treated and saved Maurice Thorez. Why had these men deluged with honors and rubles turned traitor?

"The majority of the terrorist group," the communiqué replied, "were connected with the international Jewish bourgeois nationalist organization, the Joint Board, created by the so-called American intelligence organization to provide material aid to the Jews of other countries. . . . The accused Vovsi has declared to the police examiner that he received the directive to destroy the leadership cadres of the U.S.S.R. from the United States and the Joint Board through the offices of a Moscow doctor named Shimelevich and the well-known bourgeois Jewish nationalist Mikhoels."

Shimelevich was the resident doctor in charge of the large Botkin Hospital. Mikhoels, a close relation of Professor Vovsi, was director and one of the glories of the famous "Moscow Jewish Theater," an inspired actor. Stalin had summoned him several times to recite Shakespeare to him in private and had then had him atrociously murdered, ordering his death camouflaged as an auto accident.

But this went back to January, 1948. Had the conspiracy been going on for five years? What were Soviet intelligence services doing all this time? Was it negligence? Complicity? Already one could distinguish one of the directions the blow would take.

Finally, still according to the communiqué, three of the doctors were "agents of the British Intelligence Service." The contrary would have been a surprise, for Stalin had an almost superstitious respect for the Intelligence Service. His first readings in politics at the end of the last century had left him with a grandiose and terrifying image of England, the country of triumphant capitalism. He had always been less distrustful of Germany, even during the worst moments of the war. Hitler did not figure in the intellectual patterns of his youth.

A great trial had three underlying motivations.

First of all, Stalin believed in and feared conspiracies. When the press spoke of an assassination attempt on the "leading cadres," it was his name which should be read in invisible ink. Of course, this was never written or even formulated: One could not kill God. But the Chekists, who spent their time preventing plots against him, knew what was at stake. The plots were no doubt imaginary, but the Chekists knew that their positions and their own security depended on their zeal toward the boss. For years now, members of the Central Committee, who since the Civil War had had permits to carry arms, had been requested to leave their revolvers in the cloak room when the Secretary-General received them.

Even if he knew that the doctors were in fact innocent, Stalin always harbored a doubt in a corner of his distrustful mind. After all, some of these doctors had also treated him.

Second, a great trial was a signal, a way of initiating a purge, of making it spread out in concentric circles. The preliminary investigation produced suspects in a kind of chain reaction series: Whoever knew an accused was himself a potential accused. And, above all, well-orchestrated revelations created a climate. They reawakened the haunting fear of encirclement and sabotage. The Leningrad affair, the purge of the cadres, and the limited purges of 1949 had been only trial runs. Now, once again, there came a time when the Soviet Union was threatened by an army of innumerable enemies of the people.

And third and last, a great trial permitted the settling of certain family quarrels. Looking from this angle, one could see very well who was being aimed at.

To begin with, there were the directors of the Ministry of Health. "They have not been equal to their task," *Pravda* said. "They never even suspected the terrorist activity and sabotage on the part of these repulsive degenerates." Smirnov, the Minister of Health, dropped out of sight and was quietly replaced by Andrei Tretyakov.

More striking were the accusations brought against police officials. "Some of our Soviet organs * and their directors have lost their vigilance. . . . The organs of State Security have not uncovered plots in time. . . . Yet these organs must be especially vigilant. . . ." Abakumov, the Minister of State Security, had just been replaced for having refused to "unmask" the doctors. And Beria, his protector, now found himself in the line of fire.

Beria's difficulties reflected to some slight degree on his old associate Malenkov (they were sometimes seen out walking arm in arm like good pals). All this could be read on the barometer of newspaper appearances.

By chance or not, Ignatyev, the new chief of State Security— who ferociously hunted down Beria's men—was Khrushchev's man.†

In most trials of this kind, the inquiring magistrates took their time. But in this one, everything proceeded quickly. The accused were beaten, beaten, and beaten again—a sign of impatience. They had to sign confessions quickly. Stalin was in a hurry. He kept personally informed of the interrogations, and, storming and threatening, demanded speed and brutality.

Professor V. H. Vasilenko, one of the anonymous people Tass did not mention, returned from China, where he had been treating an important personage, perhaps Mao Tse-tung himself. He was arrested at the frontier, immediately taken to Moscow, and thrown into Lefortovo prison, where he was beaten terribly. At the end of a few weeks, all of his teeth had been knocked out.

The illustrious Professor Vinogradov, a septuagenarian and a Stalin Prize winner, was bound in chains. Some people thought that it was just what he deserved. In 1938, Vinogradov, called as an expert in the trial of two of his colleagues accused—even then—of having poisoned famous people (Maksim Gorky, Kuibyshev, and Menzhinsky), had blasted them mercilessly.

The accused in the doctors' affair of 1953 would not be shot but hanged. A wartime decree had reinstated this more sinister and ignominious method of execution.

---

* The word "organ" in the U.S.S.R. often refers, in abbreviated fashion, to the political police organization or system.

† For many years, Khrushchev would defend Ignatyev against all attacks. In his speech to the Twentieth Congress, he would try to minimize his protégé's role in the doctors' affair—even though the affair coincided with Ignatyev's arrival at the head of State Security. He would present him as an unlucky man, terrorized by Stalin's threats.

19

In Jerusalem, and Elsewhere

In Jerusalem on the evening of January 13, Rabbi Jacob Kalmans was listening to the news on the radio. When he heard of the arrest of the Soviet doctors, the old man collapsed and died, struck down by a heart attack. The rabbi had been the head of a congregation in Moscow until 1933. His son still lived there. A professor of medicine, he had not answered any letters for the last six months. Many people in Israel interpreted the announcement of this "conspiracy" as a direct threat to their country.

But the Soviet Union had helped to create the new state. Less than five years before, in May, 1948, it had been the first great power to give "de jure" recognition to Israel. In the same year, Golda Meir arrived in Moscow as her country's ambassador and received a triumphal welcome—no doubt too triumphal for the Kremlin, which was somewhat annoyed by the great enthusiasm Soviet Jews lavished on the representative of a foreign state.

Since then, Soviet diplomacy had executed a complete about-face, the immense consequences of which were still far from clear. While betraying tension inside the country, the case of the doctors was obviously part of a foreign policy maneuver. By carrying the anti-Semitic campaign to its highest pitch, after having whipped it up for many months in all the Socialist countries, the U.S.S.R. proved that it had, without the slightest hesitation, now ranged itself on the Arab side. Less than a month later, the opportune explosion of a bomb in the Soviet legation at Tel Aviv would give Moscow the opportunity to sever all diplomatic ties with Israel.

Stalin always killed two birds with one stone.

The machinations of world capitalism, an attack against the land of Socialism—from the very start the "conspiracy of the men in white" had been placed in the realm of the cold war. Thus urged on, Communists the world over had no choice but to go along. When the U.S.S.R. was threatened with encirclement, one did not become too fastidious about details. True militants pulled in their horns and stifled any insidious questions at the back of their minds.

Even the violence of hostile reactions helped. Adversaries took pleasure in comparing Stalin's anti-Semitism to that other fellow's. A headline in the *London Daily Mail:* "STALIN LIKE HITLER!" More subtle but just as vigorous, Raymond Aron commented in *Figaro* on "the surrealism which the police invent." "The poverty of invention," he added, "the mechanical repetition of themes betray a thought which develops all by itself without rational control, as in dreams or the mechanical deliriums of a demented person." For the faithful, if the Right protested like this, it was because Stalin was, as always, right. They never ran out of reassuring explanations: Of course, anti-Zionism has nothing to do with anti-Semitism. And when one condemned a bourgeois nationalist Jew in the U.S.S.R., it was clearly as a nationalist and bourgeois, never as a Jew.

20

Nationality: Jew

Reassuring gestures abroad. Deadly gestures at home. For, as far as Soviet opinion was concerned, Stalin made no attempt at all to minimize the anti-Semitic aspect of the affair. On the contrary, *he exaggerated it.*

Of the fifteen doctors arrested, only six were Jews. But, thanks to the official communiqué, this minority became a top-heavy majority. Tass reported only nine names, of which six were Jewish. Six out of nine! Soviet citizens took the hint; they talked of a "Jewish plot." Spurred on from above, the old pogrom spirit responded without any effort.*

The communiqué had tremendous impact. Frantic patients in the hospitals refused to take their medicine; some even fought with the doctors. On a street in Tambov, a drunk wanted to beat up a bespectacled intellectual. "You miserable bastard, you're the fellow who gives those pills to my children. They are worse now. You Jews are all murderers!" By chance, a colonel who knew the victim was passing by. His respected uniform calmed the drunk and saved the bespectacled intellectual, who was neither a Jew nor a doctor.

From the street, the psychosis invaded the upper levels of society. When the young historian Georges Haupt, a Rumanian studying at the University of Leningrad, became ill, he was sent to a hospital, and, being a foreigner, was placed in a room for "leaders." His roommates were the assistant manager of the immense Kirov factories, a

---

* The *i drugiye*—the six doctors arrested and tortured with the others but not mentioned by the communiqué—were the Professors Vasilenko, Zelenin, Preobrazhensky, Popova (a woman), Zakusov, and Shereshevsky. This was a collection of Russian and Ukrainian names which, if they had been reported to the public, would have greatly "Slavified" the "Jewish plot."

colonel and "Hero of the Soviet Union," and a high Party functionary. Having read the communiqué, these three notables insisted, as one man, that their doctor be changed. He had a suspicious name— a Biblical first name.

Ehrenburg tells this story: "An agronomist, who had conversed with Sartre, spent his vacations in Yalta. He returned sooner than expected and told me that his wife had become frightened: 'Let's leave the sanitarium today. They are going to poison us here.' A woman doctor said: 'Yesterday I had to spend the entire day swallowing pills, powders, dozens of medicines for dozens of patients. They were afraid that I might be a 'conspirator.' . . . At the Tishinsky market, a noisy drunk shouted: 'The Jews tried to assassinate Stalin.' " [1]

At Yaroslavl, a very sick man telephoned for a doctor to visit him at home. The doctor, who happened to be a woman, arrived and spoke about giving him an injection. She was a Jew. The sick man's wife stepped in—not on your life, her husband didn't need any treatment, he had recovered completely.

These great collective fears went back a long way, and the Jews themselves were not immune from accepting them as facts. On January 14, when M., a young, highly cultured poet, met a friend in Moscow, he burst into tears: "We Jews are all bastards. Soviet power has given us everything; and this is how we show our gratitude!"

In Siberia, the rumors, muffled by distance, lost their virulence. The people were stolid. At Kemerovo, the miners joked: "These polyclinics! On top of everything else, they poison you."

The polyclinics were gloomy dispensaries where the sick were received with haughty indolence. Medicine did not enjoy a high priority in the land of Stalin. The medical corps consisted chiefly of a few high-ranking specialists, such as the professors who had been arrested, and poor, underpaid women. A doctor was turned out in four years, and this greatly padded the statistics. But Russia seemed to treat itself largely with home remedies, various medicinal herbs and vodka massages.

Here and there one found heroic souls who refused to believe in the plot. Deeply disturbed by the whole affair of the men in white, S. P. Pisarev, a permanent member of the Party, wrote to Stalin expressing certain doubts about the work of State Security and suggesting that the doctors' guilt should be verified by other investigators. He paid for this letter with two years in a psychiatric hospital.

The rebirth of anti-Semitism did not take place overnight. Already during the war, Soviet propaganda which denounced Nazi crimes so vigorously had proved to be unusually taciturn when it came to the most obvious of these crimes—the slaughter of the Jews. And more than one Jewish officer at the front was astonished to find himself passed over for promotion in favor of his Russian comrades.

In 1948, anti-Semitism became more open. Stalin dissolved the "Jewish Anti-Fascist Committee," which had done such excellent work during the war, arrested or suppressed almost all of its leaders, and liquidated the Moscow Jewish Theater, and most other Jewish cultural institutions. From then on, he purged the Party apparatus and the ministries, at all levels, of Jewish personnel. In certain establishments of higher education, in scientific institutes, and even in many factories, he introduced a quota system.

And important Jewish figures were hustled off to concentration camps or a common grave. An old Lubyanka prisoner recalled that, from 1949 on, he was the only Russian in a cell with six other prisoners. His five cellmates were all Jews.

In 1945, a Balt received a "diploma of honor" from the authorities for having hidden certain Soviet Jews during the German occupation. Four years later, these same authorities threw him into prison for "complicity with the Zionists."

Those who had escaped the German pogroms in the Ukraine and Belorussia found themselves the subjects of another repression. At first concealed and underhanded, it soon became a mass repression.

The intelligentsia was a special target of attack. The renewal of Jewish culture—quite marked in Russia during the first third of the century—was being undermined at its very foundations. A few days after the start of the affair of the men in white, Esther Markish, a writer and translator of many French authors, was deported to Central Asia together with her two children. The reason: "Member of a family of traitors to the country." Her husband, Perets Markish, who, as we know, had been shot with twenty-four other Jewish intellectuals on August 12, was, Manes Sperber tells us, "the best Yiddish poet of our generation. He was just like what an adolescent imagines a poet to be." His wife was still unaware of the fact that she was a widow. The police did not talk.

When his sixteen-year-old daughter had fallen in love with the Jewish movie director Aleksei Kapler, Stalin had been filled with horror and bitterness, and, when a little later she married Grigory Morozov, also a Jew, he refused to meet his son-in-law.

This aversion had a long history. As a young Bolshevik, he had already permitted himself certain unusual jokes about the "Talmudists" who then "filled" the Party. Exasperated by these feverish, bespectacled intellectuals, these Trotskys, Kamenevs, Zinovievs and Radeks, who had for a long time reduced him to the role of dunce—the most dim-witted student in the class—he had destroyed them all with minute precision. Dressed in his boots and peasant blouse, he wanted to personify the revenge of sturdy common sense, the revenge of those who learned little in school but have their feet solidly planted on the ground. Or, even more precisely, the revenge of the Russian middle class, to which he had gained access by entering the seminary. From there, it was not too great a step to the chauvinistic and racist nationalism of his maturity.

Besides, anti-Semitism paid off. The Soviet people were hungry and frightened. It was a good idea to give them a scapegoat and, more precisely, the scapegoat to which they had been long accustomed.

The Generalissimo, the sacred repository of the Russian national past, no longer had any Jews in his immediate entourage, except for Kaganovich, who piously applauded all the anti-Semitic measures. Kaganovich's brother, after being denounced, preferred to commit suicide.*

Among writers of Jewish origin, Ilya Ehrenburg remained afloat and received with compunction the Stalin Peace Prize on January 27. "He has done me a great honor: the right to bear on my chest the image of the man who lives in the hearts of all Soviet citizens." Nevertheless, in his speech he avoided the almost obligatory reference to "the assassins in white," but other Jewish intellectuals accused him of much worse compromises.

Stalin excelled in quietly wiping out all the victories of the Revolution. He robbed the Jews of their dignity, turning them once again into second-class citizens.

For some years now, Jewish "nationality" was no longer held in high regard. In the U.S.S.R., a "multinational" State, one was both a member of the great collectivity and of narrower ethnic group. This was inscribed on two different lines in one's internal passport:

Citizenship: Soviet.

Nationality: . . . .

Beria was a Soviet citizen of Georgian nationality, Mikoyan a Soviet citizen of Armenian nationality, Kosygin a Soviet citizen of Russian nationality, and Kaganovich a Soviet citizen of Jewish nationality.

G.R. was a woman doctor who spent the entire war in front-line

---

* Mekhlis, another dignitary of Jewish origin, would die on February 13, 1953. But he no longer had an important position.

hospitals and had a very good record. When she was demobilized, she was asked: "If you wish, we could put Russian nationality on your passport?"

She replied that she had always been Jewish. A young idealist, she did not realize that they wanted to do her a favor. She regretted it later. After the communiqué on the doctor-assassins, many doctors were dismissed from the large hospitals and sent to treat colds in suburban dispensaries.

Were events tending towards a mass deportation of Jews? Stalin had often severely punished the "small nationalities." The Tatars of the Crimea, the Germans of the Volga, the Kalmyks, Chechens, and Ingushes of the Northern Caucasus, among others, have been collectively wiped off the map, sent to the Great North, Central Asia, or Siberia. Was he planning the same treatment for two and a half million citizens of "Jewish nationality"?

At the end of January, 1953, after ten years of imprisonment, Ignace Szenfeld, a Pole arrested by the Russians, was released from camp as a deportee in the Siberian region of Kazachinskoye. The countryside was inhospitable and the cold deadly. One day, having sold an old pair of shoes, he had enough money to enter a café and to warm himself up with a glass of tea.

A car stopped. A richly dressed man, wearing a fur-lined overcoat and ostentatious riding breeches, got out. He ordered a big dinner and sat down at the table. A little later, another man of the same type showed up. They were both policemen, of a certain rank, one was from the area, the other was from Krasnoyarsk, a provincial capital. Recognizing each other, they started a conversation without noticing the shabby customer eating in a corner.

"What are you doing in this neck of the woods?"

"I'm setting up camps for the Jews. I'm looking for the sort of places we need."

21

The Cosmopolitans

During this period, the hunt was on for Jews in all government services.

Many of them had not declared themselves Jews on their passports, but Russians, Ukrainians, or Belorussians. The new vigilance demanded that they be exposed. Antecedents were explored, people became concerned about aquiline profiles, ears pricked at a slightly nasal accent, and family names were scrutinized along with all first names and patronymics which might reveal a hidden Jew. In certain sectors, special commissions were sent to help the personnel service carry out this task. When these commissions were on the job, a list of discharged persons was posted, and it was politely explained as a cutback in personnel.

Manners could become quite rude in private. A young editor, who had declared himself "Russian" on his passport, was summoned before his boss, who locked the door with a key and demanded that he show him right there and then whether or not he was circumcised.

An obscure functionary named Driesen, who worked at a radio station, felt suspicions gathering threateningly over his head. He was not a Jew but a Baltic baron—Baron von Driesen. He had managed to hide his violently counterrevolutionary origin for more than thirty years. This was quite a feat, since at each stage of his existence—to enter a university, before military service, when he applied for a job, when he changed his place of employment, and whenever the authorities felt it necessary—every Soviet citizen had to fill out a five-page questionnaire. (It was a good idea not to contradict oneself from one questionnaire to the next.) The questions left nothing in the dark: Did you ever live abroad? Do you have any relatives?

Has anyone in your family ever been sent to prison? Under what circumstances? Has anyone in your family ever served in the White Army? Each "yes" would remove you farther from a good position and bring you closer to the worst hardships.

By dint of lapses of memory and astute fuzziness, year after year, Driesen had succeeded in concealing the fact that he was an aristocrat, a class enemy. He was settled in this nice little job, and now he was about to be driven out.

Thinking that he would be discharged anyway, he decided to tell everything. He took his family titles of nobility, documents and coats of arms out of hiding and went to personnel to beat his breast. "I have lied to you. Here's what I really am."

As he spoke, the faces all around him showed signs of relief. One man scolded him on principle, but paternally.

"Oh, so that's it. . . . But why didn't you tell us before? You were just about to have some real trouble."

His mind at rest, the Baron returned to his job.

Official chauvinism went hand in hand with anti-Semitism, and it was almost touching in its childishness. In a classic diversion, Soviet citizens, who were still bandaging their wounds, were urged to go into ecstasies over their own genius. Popov invented everything. Every great discovery had a barely known Russian as its father, whom the press exploited loudly to establish Russian priority in the field. This campaign was not always unfounded: From the incandescent bulb to radio transmission, Russian inventors have shown many signs of genius. What made this campaign absurd was its steamroller tactics. In a *Manual of Radiology and Radiotherapy* published at the time, Roentgen was not even mentioned. It was the self-taught Lomonosov who had foreseen X-rays more than a century and a half before him.

A scientist who dared to praise foreign works was guilty of "obsequiousness and toadyism to bourgeois pseudo-science." In short, "cosmopolitanism." This was extremely serious. For, if research benefited by receiving important credits, it was also sedulously bullied and controlled by the government. When Trofim Lysenko, a hollow-cheeked fanatic, became the great official geneticist, he sent to the concentration camps all "disciples of the monk Mendel," colleagues who dared to doubt the heritability of acquired characteristics.

Sometimes terrorized research workers dared to repeat stories which took revenge on reality by caricaturing it. For example, a physicist was supporting his doctoral thesis. He referred quite frequently to the theories of a certain Odnokamuchin—a Russian name but unknown. Just to be on the safe side, the examiners complimented him. Then, at the end of the examination, one examiner discreetly pulled him aside. "But who is this Odnokamuchin?"

"Who do you think? Einstein." *

The humorous stories invented at such a time were a measure of human courage. The merest wisecrack could be outright suicide. The intelligentsia lived in perpetual fear of informers who listened and reported, of provocateurs who incited you to talk and then denounced you. You could not be sure of anyone. The favorite student, the pleasant errand boy working in a laboratory, the smiling colleague, the respected boss could one day become a stool pigeon out of ambition, a desire to avoid trouble, or out of stupidity, conviction, or political conformism.

This situation was summed up by another story of the period:

A Soviet citizen looked at his image in the mirror. And he murmured, sternly: "One of us is certainly a provocateur."

Responding to the wave of official chauvinism, the language became Russian in the extreme. In the pharmacies "English salts" against constipation became "bitter salts." Bakeries transformed "French bread" into "city bread." On the soccer field, the players talked not of a "penalty" but of "*chirafnoi.*"

"Through the plains of malachite the Khripan River unrolls its silvery ribbon. . . . Beyond the plains, a century-old forest rises up like a bronze wall. In gaps among the pine trees, dachas appear here and there, looking like cottages in a fairy tale."

In contrast to *Pravda*'s habitually austere tone, this flowery exordium announced a *feuilleton* or feature story. The Soviet *feuilleton* was a satire combined with a sermon. It was above all a denunciation in which the villains of the day were singled out for popular obloquy, with their names, titles, and attributes. Corrupt bureaucrats, negligent *apparatchiki*, crooks or "hooligans" and highly placed swindlers were thus exposed to the public. To be attacked in this manner meant at best the end of a career, but generally something much worse. Certain officials committed suicide simply because when they opened the newspaper in the morning they found their name in a *feuilleton*.

In the *feuilleton* just mentioned, the authors—they worked together to write this—denounced the illegal trading that was going on in a cooperative for the construction of villas near Moscow. Created originally to allow deserving workers to rest in the open air, this cooperative was now the domain of speculators.

* Odnokamuchin—literally, "one stone"—is the Russian equivalent of the German name Einstein.

The *feuilleton* described the admission of the new candidate, the technical director of an industrial combine.

"In what way," he was asked, "could you be useful to our cooperatives?"

"My combine," he answered negligently, "makes felt articles, *valenki* . . ."

A hint was all that was needed. The members of the administrative council received forty pairs of felt boots, and on the following Saturday the new member of the cooperative moved into his dacha.

"People hire services, sell and resell from hand to hand," the article continued. "Rooms, landings with their porches, whole villas with their outbuildings are ascribed to one name, and then another. Behind the cooperative's back, a private cabinet of men does business for itself."

The customers thus described were not without interest, but the names involved were even more interesting. For example, the article mentioned a victim, a modest retired man who had waited for years for the dacha to which he was entitled. He had a good old Russian name: Trofim Mikhailovich Klimov. But among the swindlers who tricked him there were a profusion of Kristalls, Galperins, Raisa Khaits, Fabrikants and Levitovas, foreign-sounding names which told the reader: "The Jews again."

This was a constant procedure. During the whole of 1952 and the first part of 1953, the *feuilletons* showed a marked preference for crooks and swindlers with Jewish names.[1]

Thus sustained racial distrust fermented incredible rumors. According to one story, which was firmly believed, the Jewish conspiracy was centered in the Stalin auto factory and its aim was, quite simply, to blow up Moscow.

Such extravagant stories were not picked up by the press, which contented itself with giving rise to them with delicate hypocrisy. The Stalinist press was a precision machine, used to minute work. A few Jewish names scattered through the *feuilletons*, a few hooked noses in the cartoons—that was enough. Sometimes, a play on words, such as a drawing on the cover of *Krokodil* representing the movie director Mikhail Romm absorbed in reading a book by Gide. Gide, in cyrillic characters, was written as *Zhid*, which means Jew, or indeed "kike." That is, as pejorative as you can get.

No point in going too far, devouring a rabbi in each column. Soviet readers had the habit of reading by hints and between the lines.

But foreigners did not really understand all this. Most of the time, those who laboriously deciphered their *Pravda*—and they were rare—

saw nothing but moral lessons in the *feuilletons* and failed to understand the deadly allusions.

Unlike Hitler, Stalin was not a heavy-handed vulgarian who shouted his anti-Semitism from the rooftops. He did so in private. Receiving Djilas in 1948, he said to him with a sarcastic laugh: "In our Central Committee there is not a single Jew. You're an anti-Semite, too, aren't you, Djilas?"

Table talk. In public, he was a person who could announce quite virtuously: "Anti-Semitism, the most extreme form of racial chauvinism, is the most dangerous survival of cannibalism."

Words with a double meaning filtered through the reality and over the closed frontiers; but expressions like "Zionists" and "rootless cosmopolitans," which could be deciphered immediately by any Soviet citizen, were reassuring to certain alarmed Western consciences.

This photo of Stalin was made during his last days.

Stalin lies in state in the Hall of Columns of Moscow's House of Trade Unions. *Wide World Photos*

The funeral procession in Red Square on May 9, 1952: Following the coffin are, from the right, Khrushchev, Beria, and Malenkov. Chou En-lai, the only foreigner in the front row, is between Beria and Malenkov. *Cliché-Editions Robert Laffont*

On March 9, 1952, Pravda carried this picture showing members of the new Party Presidium standing watch at Stalin's bier.

Three disciples stand side by side.

The people's grief was sincere. These women waited in line all day in the cold to view Stalin's remains.

Communist leaders attend funeral rites for Stalin on the stand of the Lenin mausoleum on Red Square, March 9, 1953.

Cliché-Editions Robert Laffont

This is the front page of the French Communist paper *l'Humanité* announcing the death of Stalin.

Right: Malenkov, the new President of the Council of Ministers, speaks to the Supreme Soviet in the Kremlin on March 15, 1953.

This Picasso drawing of Stalin appeared in the March 12, 1953, issue of the French Communist weekly *Les Lettres Françaises*. Both paper and artist were reprimanded by Party leaders, who found the sketch disrespectful.

22

The Wolf and the Peasants

A new star rose in the sky of vigilance: Lidia Timashuk, a woman doctor. It was she who had denounced "the ferocious beasts in human form" and foiled the doctors' plot. *Pravda* told her story.

"Two persons in white smocks met at a patient's bedside. One was a scholar of great renown, with all sorts of titles. The other had no important diplomas, but extensive knowedge and experience from more than twenty years of practical work."

The modest practitioner realized that the eminent professor's diagnosis was false and that the treatment he prescribed was wrong. Such an important doctor could not be so grossly mistaken. Therefore, he was an enemy.

"Yes, she had before her an enemy, and not just one, but a band of wicked, crafty, and well-camouflaged enemies of the Soviet Union.

"The struggle began, a very bitter struggle. For the others, those who had titles, were highly placed and surrounded by their henchmen; but the woman fought as one fights the country's enemies—to the death. Perhaps, during those days, she could see a vision of an airplane in flames and in this plane a Soviet aviator, her only son."

Lidia Timashuk received the Order of Lenin. The press published innumerable letters of support and congratulation, supposedly received from everywhere in the nation. People asked for her picture: "Everyone, whether little or great, framed her picture and put it in a place of honor in the family album." One evening, she heard an unknown, deeply moved voice on the telephone: "Thanks for having restored cleanliness and honor to our white smocks." [1]

Lidia Timashuk was an X-ray technician at the "Kremlin hospital" and a collaborator of the State Security service. Her denunciation of the specialists had probably been carefully prepared.

Two capital sins were given great prominence: carelessness or irresponsibility and daydreaming or taking it easy. Carelessness and daydreaming had made it possible for the enemies to infiltrate.

Everywhere people cried for vigilance, suspicion, denouncements. Children were not neglected. For them, the "Theater of the Young Spectator" revived a classic in the genre: *Pavlik Morozov*, the story of a young boy who, at the time of collectivization, denounced his own father and was then killed by the kulaks. A well-known hero, he was often set before grade school students as an example and had a street named after him in Moscow. If one could believe the newspaper reports, the scene in which Pavel exposes his father was frantically applauded by the boys and girls in the theater.

On February 7 Stalin received the Argentine Ambassador, Leopold Bravo, with whom he spoke about commerce. Ten days later, it was the turn of the Ambassador of India, K. P. R. Menon, and Dr. Kitchlu, the President of the Partisans for Peace in India. The three visitors found the Generalissimo in apparent good health, his mind active, his conversation brilliant. But Ambassador Menon,* a handsome man with a relaxed, serene face, noted with surprise that Stalin continued to draw a series of wolves on a pad. Noticing how intrigued the envoy was by these sketches, Stalin told him that Russian peasants were quite familiar with wolves and knew how to handle them. They exterminated them. The wolves knew this, too, and acted accordingly. With his yellow eyes and his rustic manners, Stalin was at once wolf and peasant.

* Who should not be confused with the famous statesman V. K. Krishna Menon, who was a delegate to the U.N. and later the Minister of War.

23

Looking Through Pravda

January 21, 1953

POEM BY DUDEN

"In everything be more vigilant and more severe,
For the stronger we are, the more wicked is the enemy."

January 24

THE NAÏFS

"We do not doubt that Rogovaya Levitskaya-Kullai will be deservedly punished. Only one thing worries us: Why did the judges not mention in their verdict the foolish ones who have helped this adventurer in his criminal activities? These naïfs must be subjected to harsh and well-deserved sanctions."

January 31

TO EDUCATE THE WORKERS IN A SPIRIT
OF INCREASED POLITICAL VIGILANCE

"The newspaper *Soviet Lithuania* indicates that there have been unmasked in the Republic some unattached cosmopolitans, certain bourgeois nationalist Jews and Lithuanians, vile mercenaries of American imperialism who devote themselves to espionage and sabotage."

GENERAL ASSEMBLY OF THE ACADEMY OF SCIENCES

"In conclusion, Academician Nesmeyanov declared, 'I would like to mention again that the patriotic duty of scholars is always to increase their vigilance in all sectors of their work, to struggle

123

resolutely against naiveté, which has allowed a miserable band
of doctor-saboteurs to remain hidden for so long a time.'"

THE NAÏFS ARE THE ENEMIES' AUXILIARIES

"One cannot explain except by gullibility the fact that at the
Krylov Academy of Leningrad, a professor's chair has for several
years been held by a certain I. G. Khanovich who does not deserve
political trust, who was an admirer of all that was foreign. He has
published many books in which he divulged absolutely secret
information."

February 6

REVOLUTIONARY VIGILANCE

"Some time ago, the organs of State Security arrested a rank
Trotskyist, an agent of foreign intelligence services, S. D. Gurevich.
He was raised in a family of a Menshevik member of the Bund [an
old Jewish Socialist movement in Poland].

". . . Gurevich dragged into this espionage activity the former
collaborator of one of the institutes of the Academy of Sciences
of the U.S.S.R., E. A. Taratuta, whom he set to work obtaining
information on the discoveries of Soviet scholars. Because of the
carelessness and gullibility of some collaborators in the Institute,
Taratuta was able to steal several secret documents."

February 7

Theater Review by V. Frolov

THE ART OF ACCUSING

"The mission of satire is to unmask mercilessly with anger and
hatred the naïfs and all those who protect them.

"S. Mikhalkov has a sensitive feeling for the nature of comic art. . . .
But in his play there is not enough accusing satire, unmasking
dangerous and harmful people."

February 14

THE TERRORIST ACT OF TEL AVIV AND THE DOUBLE GAME OF
ISRAEL'S LEADERS, *by Yury Zhukov*

"The Soviet people will draw the necessary conclusions; it will
consolidate without relaxation its armed forces and the organs of
our State's intelligence services. It will cauterize with a burning
iron the dangerous malady of unconcern, extirpating negligence
from its ranks."

February 20

THE CORRESPONDENCE OF LIDIA TIMASHUK

February 27

A FORMALIST ATTITUDE

"In recent times, the workers of the ministry have spoken a great deal about vigilance, the struggle against naiveté. But what happens at the ministry does not accord with what they say. Documents which are State secrets are put in large heaps on open shelves and cupboards when they are not openly on the tables, radiators and window ledges."

March 1

"The success of the Soviet Union arouses rage and hatred in the imperialist camp. . . . Under these conditions, the workers are asked to reinforce their political vigilance, to extirpate naiveté and carelessness."

24

The Big House

Terror is the rule of people who are themselves terrorized.

—FRIEDRICH ENGELS

In such an atmosphere, the Lubyanka—the MGB, the Ministry of State Security—was overwhelmed with work. From dawn to dusk, through the interminable winter, its windows were always lit up, like the portholes of a giant steamship in the heart of Moscow.

The Lubyanka was the largest institution in the country, and the man who headed it was more powerful than the marshals, with their armored divisions and their atomic toys. Besides, he, too, had the most modern equipment for his own divisions, which ranged from border guards to special troops stationed at sensitive points within the country.

The building occupied by the Lubyanka had been the home of the "Russian Insurance Company" at the end of the century. Now the vast, sumptuous offices were occupied by Ignatyev, the new minister; Ryumin, his assistant, who was personally in charge of the affair of the men in white; and a whole general staff of high functionaries in uniform and civilian clothes, who were busy raising the country to the proper level of vigilance. But all of the occupants knew that at any moment they could end up in certain corridors farther on, in certain cells. The last purge, which resulted in the quiet dismissal of the previous minister, Abakumov, had just ended. There was no profession more honorable than that of a Chekist,*

---

* The political police was first called the Cheka (Ch.K., the initials of the Russian words meaning "Extraordinary Commission"). It was successively rebaptized GPU, OGPU, NKVD, and MGB (and today KGB). But calling its members Chekists is still common usage.

but a Chekist was not exempt from danger. In the camps, inmates had an irritating tendency to disembowel them.

The Lubyanka was a ministry, but it was also a prison, the most famous of the "inner prisons" under the direct control of State Security. It was a closed and secret universe in the very center of the city. All around it, the capital bustled with activity. Only a few hundred yards away was the Maly Theater. The Metropol and the Savoy (today called Hotel Berlin), the famous hotel-restaurants sought out by elegant folk, were also only a few hundred yards away. Kusnetsky Bridge, with its book stores, began a few steps from the Lubyanka, and the Ministry of Foreign Affairs was in a building directly opposite it. Also in the same area were Malaya Lubyanka Street and St. Louis-des-Français, the Catholic church for foreigners passing through Moscow. On all sides, one heard the horns of the cars, the rumble of buses, the low whistle of trams and the sound of pedestrians' feet striking the broad sidewalks. Inside the jail, there was dense silence. Hearing nothing, and without news or visits, the prisoners were cut off from the world as completely as if they lived on Mars.

A heavy, brownish structure with granite foundations, the Lubyanka filled the entire space between Lubyanka Square (rebaptized Dzerzhinsky Square in honor of the founder of the Cheka), and Dzerzhinsky, Kirov, and Furkassovsky streets. Aside from its striking bulk, the entire building looked like an ordinary Soviet administration building, its windows screened with the old-fashioned pleats of large, Italian-style curtains. The heavy building was not isolated; it was rather like the admiral's flagship in the midst of an entire fleet. On nearby streets, ten other large buildings were also occupied by the MGB.

Standing in front of it, if one stepped back a bit and looked up, one could vaguely make out gratings. Sometimes the prisoners took their walk on the roof, unable to see the street and themselves unseen.

Passersby who jammed Lubyanka Square preferred not to look too closely at this large building. It could be dangerous to do so. In 1947, André Pierre, a special correspondent for *Le Monde*, sent to cover a conference in Moscow, intrigued by this majestic façade surmounted by a red flag, stopped to examine it. Worse yet, he consulted an old map of the city he had brought along. No guide to Moscow had been published or sold for a long time—so as to disorient spies. An instant after he stopped in front of the building, the correspondent was asked inside. By a miracle, two of his French colleagues passed at that very moment and heard him expostulating. It was only after a long day of maneuvering that the French Embassy succeeded in having the imprudent correspondent released.

Many of the Lubyanka's prisoners did not even know what their prison looked like. Transferred from some province, they arrived in the dark depths of a police van which entered a discreetly opened carriage gateway on Dzerzhinsky Street and found themselves at the bottom of a small courtyard as deep as a well, stuck between buildings of a dozen stories. They knew this world only from the inside.

One night (almost everything took place at night in this universe), the occupants of a cell saw a new inmate arrive, a large, bewildered man who asked: "Where am I?"

"In the Lubyanka, where do you think!"

"Oh," cried the man as he fainted. When he revived, he explained to them: "What a coincidence! Five days ago in Shanghai I read an article in *Life* discussing the prisons in Moscow. And it actually contained a photo of Dzerzhinsky Square with the Lubyanka in the background."

Valentin Sergeyevich Presyazhnikov, writer and journalist, was one of many Russians living in China. For years he had requested an authorization to return to the Soviet Union.

When he reached Moscow, he was asked to take a seat in a handsome black car and was taken to an office where persons in uniform informed him that he was a known spy.

He was searched, undressed, photographed, and fingerprinted. His head was shaved and he was led to a cell. But the guards were not talkative. Nobody had yet explained to him where he was.

The Lubyanka was the most silent of prisons. In their cells, flooded with electric light, the prisoners had a standing order not to talk loudly. And it was very hard to guess when the guards were coming, since they walked along the corridors with crepe-soled shoes and spoke in whispers.

In the old part of the building, the cells had fine parquet floors. The awful prison soup was served in the remains of an elegant table service; besides insurance companies, the building once housed a hotel, whose equipment was still used. Even the showers were tolerable. Their cleanliness had, nevertheless, a disagreeable overtone. It was said that many people had been shot in them and their blood washed down the drain.

Unfortunately, this convenient prison was overcrowded. The campaign of vigilance had been so successful that new prisoners were kept for several days in a windowless "box" of three or four square yards.

Comfort began in the corridors covered with very soft rugs,

corridors which led to the offices of those preparing one's trial. In each office, a large portrait of Stalin followed the interrogations with a paternal eye.

Was he ever present other than as an effigy? Some years later, an anecdote would make the rounds in circles very close to the top of the government: During a performance of *Swan Lake,* Stalin discreetly left the Bolshoi after the second act, had himself driven to the Lubyanka, and with his own hands shot certain men condemned to death.

In 1953, beatings were rare at the Lubyanka. It was the mother house, so to speak. With the confrontations and interrogations that were held there people were constantly going and coming, and screams of persons being tortured would have had a bad effect. People were beaten more at Lefortovo—the place where the "men in white" were jailed—a massive old prison surrounded by high walls and set in the midst of a lively working-class suburb.

The examining magistrates preferred to take their time. They interrogated and interrogated. The prisoner was systematically deprived of sleep and dragged night after night to the examinations. During the day, sleep was forbidden. Completely worn out, the prisoner usually ended up signing all the required confessions. Tough prisoners who did not sign avoided judgment but not condemnation. The "Special Enclave of the MGB" had the power to deport socially dangerous elements without going through a court.

The much-heralded vigilance had reached its peak.

The police might knock on your door as they do in novels, but they usually preferred more sophisticated methods. One of the most widely used involved sending a man on a mission. The victim would leave on a professional trip and never return. For several days, his friends and relatives would not have the slightest suspicion that anything was wrong. "Pyotr Petrovich is on a mission," they would say. They would talk about him without any sign of concern, and his telephone calls would be answered. Finally, people would realize that Pyotr Petrovich had disappeared. Then, discreetly, and without making a fuss, they would clam up.

"One day," an old male nurse remembered, "my hospital in Tashkent asked me to go to a nearby town. Just as I left my house, I met a very polite man on the street. He asked me if I wouldn't mind going with him to a nearby office to clarify something. It would not take more than five minutes, just five minutes."

The insignificant clarification requested proved to be the following: "At what precise date were you recruited by the British Intelligence

Service?" The old nurse was unable to supply the date since he knew the Intelligence Service only from the movies; so the five minutes stretched into ten years.

In Moscow, Engineer Shishkin was asked by his factory to go to the other end of the capital to get some technical information. While he was waiting for a streetcar, a car stopped.

"Hello, my friend. How are you? Would you like a ride?"

The young engineer did not know these amiable comrades, but he was a sociable, sporty fellow who had many friends. He thought: "I must have met them at the stadium." He got into the car. As they drove along, the car suddenly turned right. An iron door opened. and the engineer found himself at the bottom of the Lubyanka's celebrated, well-shaped courtyard.

"Here you are. You've arrived," his pleasant comrades told him.

No one who entered this jail was ever found innocent. The MGB did not free you. The MGB was never wrong.

The MGB was an empire so enormous that it made your head spin, with its hundreds of thousands of officers in civilian clothes or uniform, its millions of spies, informers, and collaborators, its generals and wardrobe mistresses, its secret agents and barbers' assistants, its engineers, soldiers, prosecutors, its army of bureaucrats and jurists, its high-class whores and its executives. It had networks abroad and representatives in the smallest provincial factories. It was responsible for both counterespionage and economic crimes, and it oversaw the nation's morality, the discretion of its scholars and the good behavior of its ambassadors throughout the world. With its helicopters and speedboats, as well as its army of laborers sifting through the soil of no-man's-land, the MGB locked up the nation's frontiers. It guarded the bridges, supplied the leaders with their cooks and chauffeurs and "purged" waitresses in the National Hotel guilty of serving caviar and borscht to impure foreign delegations. It had under its orders military men with green caps who checked passports at railroad stations and airports, as well as the handsome, blue-capped soldiers who did sentry duty at Lenin's tomb, and the special troops armed with tommy guns who, whenever there was a review on Red Square, swarmed, silent and invisible, into the deserted GUM department store, waiting for God knows what. During this period, the MGB had even taken over the policemen on the street, those fine militiamen with the "pea" whistles who were hard on truck drivers and so patient with drunks.

The MGB had its own stores, specially provided for its personnel. The products on sale there were much superior in quality to those found in ordinary stores. One day, as a reward, M.D., a film-maker, was authorized to buy a suit in one of these special shops. Easily recognized as obtainable only in a MGB store, M.D.'s handsome suit led a policeman to take him for one of them and invite him to a large reception in the Kremlin.

The MGB also controlled the illustrious "Dynamo" Club, perhaps the U.S.S.R.'s most prestigious sports association. Soviet citizens are avid sports fans, and soccer, at this period, was a religion, an official ritual. The Dynamo Club's successes did much to enhance the redoubtable institution's prestige.

The emblem of Stalin's police was the club and the shield. Strike in order to defend. The supreme objective was to defend Stalin, who was considered the target of all counterrevolutionaries.

Any dubious gesture, if it concerned Stalin, was seen as an attempt on his life. In the course of an evening among friends, a slightly sozzled engineer gently banged his glass against a plaster bust of the leader. "To your health, little father." He was denounced, arrested, and sentenced to ten years.

Another engineer who decided to practice with a high-powered air rifle in the garden of his dacha drew a circle on a page from a newspaper for a target, without noticing that there was a photograph of Stalin on the other side. He was denounced, arrested, and sentenced to ten years for a "terroristic attempt." According to all logic, this meant that the little pieces of lead that had pierced the photograph had a homicidal intent. In the country of scientific socialism, the police seemed to believe in sympathetic magic.

Superstitious adoration. We have seen that when the Chekists "discovered" some intrigue against their beloved leader, they never wrote his name in their official report. He became "the leading cadres of the U.S.S.R." To name him could bring down misfortune.

Sympathetic magic, the maleficent power of words. At the end of the 1940s, young Mandel-Korzhavin had written an anti-Stalinist poem. He was discovered, of course, since he made no bones about reading it to his friends. The colonel of State Security who was in charge of the inquiry into the case was so horrified that he did not know how to introduce the *corpus delicti* into his documentary evidence. He *could not* transcribe such a poem. An inquisitor never blasphemed, even by quotation.

Not being able under these circumstances to try the guilty man, they got rid of him by sending him to a lunatic asylum.

25

Stalin's Chips

A large building, not quite as tall as Moscow's skyscrapers, but like them surmounted with a heavy quadrangular, sharply pointed tower, blocked the end of Mayakovsky Square. Some years later, it would become the Peking Hotel, well-known to international tourists because of its "de luxe," richly decorated, uncomfortable suites with their pianos, their Socialist Realist paintings, their profusion of armchairs and pedestal tables, and their hopelessly leaking bathtubs.

But in 1953, the hotel did not as yet have a luminous sign. No traveler in search of a room tried to soften the hearts of the clerks in the lobby. The vast building was wholly set aside for the functionaries and officials of the Ministry of the Interior. All around it stood a series of administrative buildings lodging the services of GULAG—the general headquarters of the concentration camps.

Stalin liked to split up his police force. After the war, the old NKVD, Yezhov's fief and later Beria's, was split into two ministries:

The MGB—the Ministry of State Security.
The MVD—the Ministry of the Interior.

The MGB detected the enemies of the people, imprisoned and sentenced them.

The MVD, which was responsible for the camps, guarded them and made them work. It was the ministry of the camps, the penitentiary labor force. GULAG belonged to it.

Management of the camps involved a flood of documents and red tape. Every day hundreds of pounds of memorandums went out from the MVD to the most distant camps. Instructions on "how to use the straitjacket on prisoners offering physical resistance" occupied all by itself two closely packed pages signed by a deputy minister. Everything was planned: how to place the prisoner's hands behind his back, how to tie them, etc.

It is a shame that the MVD circulars are secret, because, even if one had little flair for administration, the list of those who received these instructions would give one an idea of the immensity of this empire:

"To the head of the general direction of camps (GULAG)."

"To the head of the general direction of forestry camps (GLGMP)."

"To the head of the general direction of mining and metallurgical camps (GLGMP)."

"To the head of the general direction of camps for the construction of railroads (GLZhDS)."

"To the head of the construction of roads and highways (GU-SHOSDOR)."

"To the head of construction in the Far East (DALSTROI)."

"To the head of the general direction of the Volga-Don Canal (Glavgidrovolgodonstroi)."

"To the head of the general direction of the Stalingrad Dam (Glavstalingradgidrostroi)."

"To the head of the general direction of the Kuibyshev Dam (Glavkuibyshevgidrostroi)."

One of the penitentiary bodies, DALSTROI, governed a domain six times larger than France: all of Northeastern Siberia beyond the Lena River, where the thermometer drops to seventy-six degrees below zero. The Soviet Constitution was not in force in this territory. There were no civil authorities, no elections to local or regional soviets. DALSTROI controlled everything. Apart from small indigenous tribes, the population was essentially composed of prisoners (and of old "freed" prisoners released to stay in the area) organized in special work-groups.

DALSTROI was created during the 1930s so as to extract gold from the banks of the Kolyma River. But, by 1953, it had, as the saying goes, greatly diversified its production. It had its own agricultural developments, coal mines, bridges and highways, construction enterprises, State commercial network, and even its own merchant fleet linking the dreadful ports of the Okhotsk Sea to Vladivostok.

All this was in the hands of a general of the MVD and administered by GULAG, with its guards equipped with tommy guns and police dogs.

What Soviet citizens called a "camp" (*lager*) could extend for hundreds of miles. It included dozens of places of incarceration spread over great expanses of tundra, forest, and steppe, and embraced villages, factories, mine shafts, and roads. One of the annexes of the Karaganda camp in the Kazakhstan was about 300 miles from the central camp. Often these concentration camp agglomerations had their own railway systems and their own electrical power plants. The camp which before the war had the task of digging the White Sea-Baltic Sea Canal issued its own money, which was not legal tender in the rest of the U.S.S.R. The traditional image of the camp—an enclosed space surrounded by barbed wire—could be found only in a very inferior administrative subdivision, the *lagpunkt* or "camp area."

The camps were a giant enterprise. They extracted oil, copper, chromium, and nickel; built roads, dams and railroads; manufactured boots for the army and slippers for civilians; and canned meat and fish. They produced a good part of the nation's wood and gold, and hired out prisoners as laborers to the State's factories and farms for good solid cash. It is true, however, that the output of their labor force—these undernourished slaves—was terribly low.

Control and management of these camps were deliberately complicated. The commander of a simple "camp area" was a potentate, but he had to share his authority with the redoubtable "Chekist Section of Operations," controlled not by him but by the MGB—the other ministry. Conflicts of assignments and authority were frequent. Guards were sometimes professionals paid by the penitentiary administration, sometimes young men recruited on the spot. The latter were the most feared, for they were saturated with propaganda. At each change of sentries, they boldly chanted the regulation dialogue:

"Good day, comrade soldiers! What are you doing?"

"We are guarding the enemies of the people."

Trained in this way, they had a quick trigger finger, and it was most persuasive when they shouted each time they escorted a group of prisoners:

"Don't lag behind. Straight ahead, not a step to the right or left! The escort will regard that as an attempt to escape. We will shoot immediately, without warning."

Sometimes an unexpected encounter occurred. At Dubrovlag (Potma), one of these young men recognized his own father, whom he thought had been killed in the war, among the enemies of the people he was guarding. He committed suicide. Another rediscovered his own brother in the same way. Together they planned an escape, fled through the forests of Mordvinia, and, of course, were recaptured.

Despite their economic importance, the camps had an even more important function: to remodel society. It was a question of eliminating undesirable social categories. Hence the successive extremely diverse classes which had populated Siberia and died there: the peasants of 1930, the old Bolsheviks of 1937, and so on.

The affair of the doctors simply announced a new, far-reaching purge. But the alarm had already been sounded by the small purge of 1949 aimed at clearly defined groups such as the young (above all, young intellectuals), the Jews, and the few "prisoners" left from 1937–38 who had been freed after ten years. Within a few months, all of them, without exception, had been sentenced again. In the language of the camps, they were known as the *povtorniki,* "the repeaters," and were often half crazy.

A man was guilty because of his situation, his origins. People were collectively guilty. Some, feeling their arrest imminent, escaped their fate by going to work as volunteers in the depths of Central Asia or Siberia. The MGB did not even look for them. It had, like the factories, quotas to meet, and it simply arrested someone else in the same social category, from the same list of "suspects."

Alongside these collective dramas, all sorts of individual destinies were accidentally swallowed up by the machine. A Soviet woman who had married an American doctor in Germany at the end of the war had, on returning to Russia to visit her parents, disappeared completely. After years of negotiations, her husband finally received a Soviet visa and left the United States to look for her. He arrived in Leningrad in 1951, was immediately arrested, and was sentenced to twenty-five years in a concentration camp for espionage.

The former inmate who told me about this man who had become a prisoner for love remembered that his first name was Mikhail. "He told us about his life in the United States and said that he had his own clinic on the East Coast. He was only forty, but he looked like an old man." Soon after, he lost track of Mikhail, who was transferred to a "special camp."

There were no gas chambers, but for a very long time the camps let the prisoners die from exhaustion, cold, lack of hygiene and proper care, and, above all, from hunger.

In the camps, as in the entire Soviet economy, rations were distributed according to a system of "norms." At the top were the Stakhanovites, who produced more than the "norm" and were entitled to the best rations. At the bottom were those unfitted for physical work, who received the most miserable rations. Between these two were the intermediate categories. Since the 1930s, however, no category had ever received the number of calories necessary to compensate for its output of energy, and, until 1948, mortality in the camps was regularly between ten and twenty per cent a year.

Beginning in 1948, there was a slight improvement in the situation. Rations were to some extent increased, infirmaries were supplied with medicines, and work periods were reduced. Prisoners even began to receive a wage, though withholdings were made by the penitentiary administration for "services rendered" (food, lodging, etc.). Not the least form of withholding was "for sentry duty." You had to pay for being guarded. With all of these withholdings, the prisoners' wages amounted to almost nothing by the time they received them. In the best of cases, all that was left was enough to buy some bread and some sugar at the canteen. Another improvement of the period was the separation of common and political prisoners, intended to make the regime of the second group more severe. In fact, it delivered them from the tyranny of the thugs who ruled the camps with terror, exploiting and hounding them at knife point.

Why this relatively late humanization of the camp system? Had some sort of grace touched the MVD? Each prisoner of this period had memories of a good guard—a man who shut his eyes to a tardiness, who distributed packages without slicing the bread into twenty pieces to search for a message or a hidden knife. Had men returned to the simplicity of animal life?

Some statisticians offer a more cynical explanation: By the end of the 1940s, the flow of prisoners brought about by the collectivization of the land, the great purges, and the population shifts of the war and postwar periods had begun to dry up. Moreover, there was a decrease in the population of the entire country.* Since the penitentiary work force was no longer renewed with the same rapidity, it became more valuable. That is why, say the statisticians, the camp administration quickly began to take better care of it.

Even under improved conditions, a political prisoner knew that he had little chance of returning to normal life. First of all, the duration of the sentence was extravagant. A twenty-five-year sentence was not unusual. And those who had received only ten or fifteen years were often struck with a new sentence before the expiration of the first.

---

* The lack of a labor force, quite apparent at this period in the U.S.S.R.—whether it be a question of free or impressioned labor—was evidently in large part a direct consequence of the war. On the other hand, among young people were some who belonged to the "depleted classes" of the great repression against the peasants in 1930–33.

Once you entered the GULAG universe, it did not want to let you go.

Those who, in spite of everything, were finally freed, generally did not have the right to go back to their town or village. They had to remain on the spot, attached to the penitentiary system as "free workers," often living just as badly as imprisoned workers, or even worse. The Siberian forests were being populated with Russian, Polish, German, or Ukrainian woodcutters, the debris of a hundred races and nations.

Those who came out of prison after so many long years were the strong, the intractable, the metal that nothing can break. Or the hardened and wicked. To survive in this universe, more than one man would allow himself to be persuaded to become a *stukach*, an informer, a stool pigeon. Protected by the security officer or the camp commander, he would live better than the comrades he spied on. Sometimes he would be given a job in the kitchen. But sometimes he would be found in the morning, stiff in his bed, strangled by his fellow prisoners.

All sorts of petty deals flourished; people bartered, bought and sold bread, rations, boots, and packages—anything negotiable. Mixed camps had their prostitutes.

Certain prisoners become addicted to *chaifir*, the jailbird drug made from tea. According to Joseph Berger, a founder of the Communist Party of Palestine, who spent sixteen years in the Soviet camps: "To obtain *chaifir*, you must boil 400 grams of tea in so little water that you get no more than three or four cups. This proportion of tannin is very strong, and its effects astonishing. Those who drink it become drunk or go into a trance and forget all the sufferings they have endured. . . . When it is used in strong doses, *chaifir* can produce the effects of cocaine or opium." [1]

The aristocracy among the prison population was found in the "special prisons" where scholars and highly qualified engineers worked on secret projects under the surveillance of MGB officials. They ate well—better than many free citizens—provided they exhausted themselves working twelve to fourteen hours a day. They found the most recent American scientific publications on their desks, and some of them had the fabulous privilege of a brief meeting with their wives once or twice a year. Apart from that, they were cut off from the world as completely as if they were pouring concrete near the Arctic Circle. The intellectual level of these laboratory prisons was remarkable—this country, so poor in factory foremen, was rich in mathematicians.

In concentration camp slang, an establishment of this kind was called a *sharaga* or *sharashka*. When one got out, it was to pour concrete in the tougher camps, or to become a free man covered with honors. The Academician Korolev, future father of the space program, was for a long time a guest of a famous *sharashka*, "Special Prison No. 4," on Enthusiast's Avenue in Moscow. But his fate changed, and in 1953, Korolev was a respected scholar.

In 1953 the concentration camp structure was still imposing and triumphant. But imperceptible cracks were developing here and there. The war and postwar periods had filled the camps with men trained to fight, accustomed to clandestine existence: Soviet officers who gained fame in the struggle with Germany, anti-Soviet partisans captured in the depths of the forests. Some of them succeeded in organizing networks. In 1948, at Vorkuta, right below the Arctic circle, insurgent prisoners under the leadership of a colonel tried to organize a rebellion in this mining complex, which produces a good part of the U.S.S.R.'s petroleum. Planes had to be called in to massacre them.

"When you cut wood, the chips fly." This is the austere equivalent of "You can't make an omelette without breaking eggs," and it was the proverb that was supposed to justify everything. The chips were the few miserable remnants, the indispensable martyrs of the great Stalinist construction.

How many of Stalin's chips still existed in this glacial winter of 1953? How many were there in the camps of "general regime" and in the camps of "severe regime," in the camps of "penal regime" and in those of *"katorga,"* where the prisoners were put in chains? How many in the "isolators," the prisons, the colonies, the *sharashki?* How many in the mines and forests, the steppes of Central Asia and the fisheries of the Bering Sea, where the polar night reigns and the sun never warms one's bones?

The archives are inaccessible. But, apart from the political prisoners, who represented the vast majority, there were swarms of "ordinary criminals," also victims of peculiarly repressive laws. There were also the old prisoners who stayed on as deportees in the most unhealthy regions, and the families of "traitors to the country" that had been sent into the distant reaches of Asia.

One scrutinized the statistics of production and the Five-Year Plans in an attempt to discover the part played by these ghosts in the country's production. Some prisoners—engineers, scientists—made their own calculations: "With so many prisoners on an average in each *lagpunkt,* with so many *lagpunkty* in each camp, there must be so many prisoners in the region. . . ." But these could only be approximate estimates. How many Soviet citizens were in prison or in camps in 1953? There were few estimates below ten million.

This mass of people was predominantly masculine. Stalin rarely attacked women. It is hard to say whether this was due to scorn for the weaker sex, which he considered politically harmless, or to superstitous respect for the intractable Russian women who held the country at arm's length, sowed and harvested, and kept the factories' assembly lines going while their men were in jail.

26

Engineers of Souls

On February 15, *Pravda* devoted an entire page to a "lead article" demolishing Vasily Grossman's new novel, *For a Just Cause*. The author had been incapable of portraying the heroism of the Soviet soldier. He did not give us the thoughts of the people's true representatives. Besides, and this was the worst that could be said, one felt in him the influence of "the reactionary theory of the Pythagorians." Exit Grossman. A man who for a long time had been one of the most applauded writers in the Soviet Union would be silent until the day of his death. He would leave a posthumous outcry, *Everything Passes,* a black masterpiece written in secret.

"A collaborator of *Pravda*," Ehrenburg has written, "told me that the article was published on Stalin's express instructions." Indeed, it was Stalin's custom to deal personally with the writers who mattered. He believed in the importance of these "engineers of souls." And he prided himself on being an acute, well-informed critic.

The results of this literary solicitude were devastating. It was no longer possible to count the poets killed, like Mandelstam, or reduced to silence, like Pasternak, who managed to live on his translations of Shakespeare. The camps were full of forgotten writers who dug in with tooth and nail in order to survive. Solzhenitsyn, a mathematics professor in love with the Russian language, worked for three years as a mason on a freezing or torrid steppe in Kazakhstan (after having done much more scientific work in a *sharashka* in Moscow). He reached the end of his eight years of imprisonment, which should have transformed him into a "free" deportee. But his entrails had been eaten away by a cancer, which the camp doctors operated on under the worst conditions.

A young writer, introduced to Anna Akhmatova, he expected from the great woman poet some of the brilliant literary insights for which she was famous. But she talked about packages. Her son was a prisoner. This woman, one of the greatest poets of her time, spent her last rubles traveling back and forth between Leningrad and Moscow like a hunted beast. From time to time, spies shadowed her without trying to be too inconspicuous, or walked placidly back and forth in front of the house she stayed at in Moscow.

The exquisite Zoshchenko, a terrorized humanist, was reduced to misery when the Central Committee called him "a trivial and repulsive mind." His friends took up a collection to help him.

On the other hand, the restaurant of the Writers' House, one of Moscow's best, was full of plump essayists and chubby-cheeked novelists. Stalin terrorized with one hand while he corrupted with the other. Nowhere did court poets and moralists in favor of the sanctity of the state ever live better than in Moscow.

One could even find honest people among the prosperous writers. For example, Tvardovsky, who was a fairly intransigent man, was covered with honors by Stalin for depicting the Russian soldier so movingly in his novel *Tyorkin.*

Sholokhov, who was usually drunk, published less and less, appearing chiefly when he wrote long, flat articles glorifying Stalin. In his Cossack village of Veshenskaya, surrounded by a mob of servants, he led the life of a boyar, interrupted by very long, dissipated sojourns in the capital.

Among the composers, Shostakovich and Prokofiev sought forgiveness for their talent as best they could. In February, 1953, Shostakovich composed a cantata celebrating the Nineteenth Congress. Prokofiev, after a long life of invention and courage, received condescendingly good marks; he had managed to overcome the pernicious influence of formalism.[1] Any attempt at innovation could only be "formalist," since Stalin, the man who liked the uniforms of the old regime, detested novelty. He appreciated *A Life for the Tsar* (rebaptized *Ivan Susanin*) because it was a patriotic opera in which the Polish invader is vanquished by the Russians. He sometimes also went to hear *Boris Godunov.* Did he feel somehow a connection with the murderer Tsar, the Tsar-Herod? These dark heroes moved him. He also liked Eisenstein's movie *Ivan the Terrible.*

But Eisenstein's films were no longer shown. *Potemkin, Ten Days That Shook the World*—that was all finished. They were cosmopolitan art. New films were made on the old revolutionary themes, which always gave a becoming role to Stalin—the first, the only one. Many long documentaries told the story of his life and deeds. He was portrayed by actors who looked like him, such as Mikhail Gelovani.

In *The Oath,* Stalin-Gelovani rolled inspired eyes before Lenin's tomb. In *The Fall of Berlin,* he captured the Reich's capital practically singlehanded. There was also a whole series of films—continually shown all over the country—where the leader towered like an apparition above his faithful followers, or descended, like an angel, among his people. It goes without saying that in each regional capital the local theater company also counted among its players an actor who specialized in the role of Stalin.

An avid movie fan, Stalin saw each new production and personally authorized or prohibited its distribution. His judgments were immediate, his motivations summary. For example, one night he was shown a documentary depicting the idyllic life of Siberian natives, since he, Stalin, had pointed out the path to happiness to the Yakuts, Aleuts and Samoyeds. At the end of the screening, he rose without saying a word and left. Upset and agitated, the director questioned Beria.

"Do you want to eat sand?" grunted the man with the pince-nez.

This remark, comparable to our "pushing up daisies," was a permanent part of Beria's repertoire.

A secret service man walked past. Then Beria continued: "Think about it. There's only one sun in the sky, right?"

Leaving the director with this mysterious phrase, Beria also departed.

After three days of looking at the reels and minutely examining each and every frame, the director found it. On the wall of a village in the Great North hung a portrait of Lenin. Lenin alone. The second sun was missing.

Under this regime, the studios became sterile. The best directors, such as Dovzhenko, were in complete disgrace. Even the most servile had difficulty working. Only five full-length pictures in all were released in 1952, as compared with nine in 1951. The void was filled by imports from Czechoslovakia, or by old Soviet police films describing the eternal triumph of the Chekists over the spies. Western films were almost unknown—except, of course, for certain privileged persons who could go to private showings.

27

The Great Candidate

On February 22 and March 1, there took place a new ceremony, the last of the great Stalinist rituals. Elections were held for the local Soviets—those famous "councils" which were supposed to control all public activity, from the whole U.S.S.R. right down to the smallest village. Though the real power eluded all control and the Soviets had no real authority, the fiction was maintained with majestic pomp. People went to vote in the same way they marched on Red Square: following orders but surrounded with grandeur and the ear-splitting roar of imperious slogans.

Even the number of open posts could make one dream: one and a half million. "Vast is my native country," declaimed the most popular of Soviet songs. For each post, a single candidate, so there was no problem of choice. Nevertheless, the women "agitators," that is, the propagandists, were on hand to explain to each elector the good qualities of this obligatory choice, his loyalty to the people, his merits in the eyes of the Party and nation. They could be heard in each house, camping in the "community kitchens" of the period, where five or six housewives coexisted in an atmosphere of simmering exasperation (they even reached the point of putting their utensils under padlocks because of their distrust of the other women). Surrounded by the smell of stewing cabbage soup, the woman agitator recited the candidate's biography. But she talked first of all of "the people's great candidate," Stalin. To show him love and loyalty this vote had to be a powerful demonstration of unanimity.

On voting day, people lined up at six in the morning before the doors of the polling places, which were decorated with streamers, red flags and portraits. Sometimes, big brass bands played stirring fanfares. It was all over by noon, and electoral participation was well

143

beyond ninety-seven per cent. In Moscow, many people left their electoral district—the regulations permitted this—to go and vote in the "Stalin" district. There, Stalin had agreed to be a candidate himself, and one had therefore the honor of electing him directly, personally.

Many of the ballots were covered with phrases of adoration for the wise leader and master, the best friend of all Soviet citizens. One of the preferred formulas was "I wish him long years of life and health."

28

The Day Radio Moscow Went Silent

March 1, 1953, was a Sunday. The following day, *Le Monde*—an important French newspaper—devoted a great deal of space to the oil producers of Iran. For the first time, a country in the Near East had dared to defy the European oil companies by nationalizing its production. Mossadegh, a devil that had jumped out of its box, created an astonishing international stir. Edouard Sablier remarked in his commentary: "Moscow has become the arbiter."

On Tuesday morning, political interest shifted. In the House of Commons, Churchill had tried to set in motion his last great effort: a conference of the "Great Powers." It was an attempt that seemed hopeless, however, since relations between East and West were at their lowest ebb. At the United Nations, Americans and Russians did not greet each other, John Foster Dulles having made it known that he would not be the first to offer his hand to Andrei Vyshinsky.

Yet some people clung to the picture of Ike and Stalin seated at the same table to conjure away the danger of atomic war. The Generalissimo's hidden intentions were scrutinized. People continued to speak of him in the future; they would soon have to speak of him in the past.

That Tuesday evening Moscow was, as usual, late in getting to sleep. Everything was calm and routine. There had been no anomalies in the press of the day. *Pravda* had burned incense to the inspired text of the leader, *The Economic Problems of Socialism in the U.S.S.R.* It had also announced that Comrade Khrushchev had spoken "in recent days" at the plenary session of Obkom, the Party's regional committee in Moscow. Apparently all was in order and everyone was going about his business.

As always, Radio Moscow retransmitted at midnight the Kremlin's noble carillon and then broadcast the even more majestic Soviet hymn:

> The great Lenin has illuminated our path.
> Stalin has formed us. He has inspired us
> With his loyalty to the people, its work and deeds.

It was a night akin to many, many others. But, on Wednesday morning, all programs on Radio Moscow were interrupted.

A world of terror, faith, hatred and adoration; a world of delirious logic, of gigantic, bloody sacrifices; a grandiose and insane world had come to an end.

On the morning of Wednesday, March 4, 800 million men lost their god, their master, their certitude. And all the Communists of the world woke up to find themselves orphans.

29

The Bell Tolls

At eight-thirty, all the radios in Moscow suddenly stopped. Minutes later, a harsh voice was heard stammering:

"The Central Committee of the Communist Party of the Soviet Union and the Council of Ministers of the U.S.S.R. announce the grave misfortune which has been inflicted on our Party and our people: Comrade Stalin's serious illness.

'"During the night, between the first and second of March, Comrade Stalin, while in his apartment in Moscow, was struck by a cerebral hemorrhage which attacked the vital areas of the brain. Comrade Stalin has lost consciousness. His right arm and right leg are paralyzed. He has lost his power of speech. Serious cardiac and respiratory complications have set in."

The communiqué spoke of a "temporary absence from affairs . . . for a more or less long period." But few people were fooled. Besides, the communiqué was followed immediately by a health bulletin that provided more precise information: uneven respiratory rhythm with prolonged pauses; lack of oxygen; pulse, 120 beats per minute with complete irregularity. Between March 1—the date given as that of the stroke—and the morning of March 4, the rupture in the cerebral functions had worsened. Doctors in Vienna, Berlin, and Paris read this and said: "This is the bulletin of a dying man.".

Unhurriedly, Moscow began a new day. The weather was cold but not icy, and sunlight was shining on the expanse of snow. Muscovites on their way to work were a little surprised not to find their papers (publication had been delayed so that the communiqué could be inserted).

But the news ran through the city like a smoldering fuse. All apartments had small loudspeakers connected with the central network which broadcast Radio Moscow's programs. Larger loudspeakers re-transmitted the programs in public parks, factories, courtyards, village squares, and even in concentration camps. Soviet citizens were saturated with well-chosen pieces of music and inspirational propaganda, and it was taken amiss if one did not seem to be listening. Housewives usually left their loudspeakers on from morning to night.

People telephoned friends and knocked on neighbors' doors to tell the incredible news to anyone who might have missed it. When the newspapers finally arrived, hundreds of people lined up in front of the newsstands. But the papers said no more than the communiqués already read over the radio. An anxious silence pervaded the crowds in the subway and the street. Faces were grim. Pedestrians walking past Riding School Square stared fixedly at the Kremlin, imagining the unimaginable, the great man, the immortal man, lying prostrate in his bed behind the thick walls. In a vague way, the communiqué had said that he had been stricken "in Moscow," which reinforced the myth of "Stalin in the Kremlin." According to witnesses, however, it was at his dacha in Kuntsevo that Stalin had suffered his stroke.

Everyone who was present at the time—the guards, officers, generals, servants, doctors, nurses, secretaries and dignitaries—has remained silent except for Khrushchev, Stalin's successor, and Svetlana, his daughter, without whom Stalin's death would have been surrounded by the secrecy he loved. There is no doubt that one cannot accept everything in their accounts at face value; but by speaking out, Khrushchev and Svetlana have at least given us material for historical analysis. What's more, their accounts agree. Here they are: *

On the evening of Saturday, February 28, Stalin invited Malenkov, Beria, Bulganin and Khrushchev, four of his habitual guests, to dinner at his dacha. He was in excellent spirits, and the dinner, in the old tradition of Kuntsevo evenings, was very long, well supplied with drinks, and glittering with pranks and jokes. It lasted until dawn, when the four sodden pals returned to their dachas to get some sleep.

When they awoke, they spent the entire day of March 1 without a sign from Stalin. They were astonished. As a rule, the boss never let a Sunday go by without sending for them or calling them on the phone.

As for Svetlana, she called Kuntsevo that Sunday but failed to reach

* Khrushchev gave his version for the first time in 1959 to Averell Harriman. His various later accounts (notably the one to a minister of General de Gaulle, in 1960) all resemble his first story, as do the memoirs attributed to him.

As for Stalin's daughter, Svetlana Alliluyeva, she published her memoirs for the first time in 1967, after having left the U.S.S.R. Her book appeared in the United States in 1969.

her father. An officer on duty told her: "There's no movement right now," which meant that Stalin had retired to one of his small, bare rooms in the depths of the villa, and that nobody had heard him move about. On such occasions, everyone was forbidden to disturb him. With his habit of reversing night and day and his taste for couches and lying down, he would sleep to all hours.

It was way past nightfall when telephones rang in the dachas of Malenkov, Beria, Bulganin, and Khrushchev. The calls were not from Stalin but from the officer of his guard. Something was wrong. He asked the four guests of the night before to come immediately. All four rushed out of their dachas and returned at full speed over the short, deserted stretch of the "governmental route," the headlights of their cars sweeping the blanket of snow on the silent undergrowth and catching in their beams the pines and bare, white birches that lined the road.

Confusion and uncertainty met them. Stalin had not rung for his dinner that evening. Paralyzed by fear, the Chekists had waited for hours, not daring to enter the master's sacred place. In his savage solitude and distrust, Stalin had taken measures against all threats, except that of a natural death. Instead of stopping assassins, the armored doors and precautions delayed possible rescuers. It would be three in the morning before he would be discovered, still fully dressed, lying on a rug in a deep, abnormal sleep.

Malenkov and the others were as timid as children. What if the boss flew into a rage on finding them there without having been summoned? They sent for his old intimates Voroshilov and Kaganovich. For the moment, Molotov was not informed, perhaps because he was already too far from the sun and sunk in disgrace.

And at long last the doctors arrived—the most reputable doctors after those who had been jailed in January. Their diagnosis was merciless. At best, he had become a hopeless invalid, but it was most probable that he would die.

Svetlana, still unaware of anything, was not told until Monday morning. When she arrived at Kuntsevo, she found her father in a coma, doctors buzzing about, and Khrushchev and Bulganin in tears. Sitting beside the sick man, she took his left hand, the one that still moved, and kissed him. Then she retired to the second floor. In Stalin's Russia, a great personage did not belong to his family but to the State, and Svetlana's father had become almost a stranger to her.

The six members of the Presidium present in the dacha organized guard duty, taking turns two at a time, night and day, both to keep an eye on the doctors—the communiqué emphatically assured the people that "the treatment [had] been placed under the surveillance of the Central Committee"—and also to prepare for the future. That Stalin's heritage was the most onerous in the world could be guessed from the whispers of the inheritors in a room next to the one where he was dying. Two factions had already appeared: Malenkov-Beria on one side, and Khrushchev-Bulganin on the other. Voroshilov and Kaganovich played minor, supporting roles.

Besides, there was the fear of the reactions of the Russian people. Not until two days later was it decided to tell them the news, with pathetic appeals for "unity" and "cohesion"—in short, for loyalty.

For brief spells, Stalin opened his eyes without really regaining consciousness. Everyone rushed to his side, trying to detect some sign of will in the depths of the yellowish-brown pupils that were no longer reflecting anything. At these moments, Beria multiplied his demonstrations of love, but, as soon as the lids closed again and the sick man sank back into his coma, he covered him with jeers and insults. Frightened by this lugubrious cynicism, Khrushchev began turning over various plans in his big head: Certainly, with Stalin dead, Beria would again take charge of the police. How could he be prevented from slaughtering all those he disliked now that the boss was no longer there to protect them? Khrushchev had worked against Beria, undermining his influence and driving his protégés out of State Security. He knew that his head, as well as his share of the power, was at stake during these discreet confabulations in a dacha in the middle of the woods.

On the fourth day, there was the classic "improvement before the end." Stalin regained consciousness, and a nurse got him to drink from a small spoon. He raised his good arm and pointed at the wall to a bad reproduction of a picture of a young girl feeding milk to a lamb. His silent lips tried to trace a smile. He was now the lamb.

Then he went into the death throes. He was suffocating. His face turned almost black and his features became unrecognizable from lack of oxygen. At the last moment, his yellow eyes took in everyone in the room with a furious glance and he raised his hand, as though pointing at something high up, or bringing down a curse. It was all over. Stalin was no more.

Malenkov, Bulganin, Khrushchev, Voroshilov, and Kaganovich wept. Beria, in a loud, triumphant voice, sent someone to get his car and then disappeared, rushing to Lubyanka Square, toward power. So ended the testimony of Khrushchev and Svetlana Stalin.

The communiqué signed by eight professors of medicine said simply: "On March 5 at 21:50, the cardiovascular and respiratory insufficiency became accentuated, and Joseph Vissarionovich Stalin died."

"My brother Vasily was also summoned," Svetlana recalled, "on March 2, 1953. He too spent several hours sitting in the big room that was so crowded with people. But he was drunk, as he often was by then, and he soon left. He went on drinking and raising Cain in the servants' quarters. He gave the doctors hell and shouted that they had killed or were killing our father." [1]

Like so many drunkards, Vasily Stalin had said aloud what the others were thinking to themselves. In less than a month, all sorts of rumors would begin to circulate in Moscow, and people would begin speaking of a crime. Deprived of real information, people had a way of zealously spreading such stories.

Some people said that several members of Stalin's entourage were threatened by the coming purge. Had they taken steps to forestall it? It didn't matter whether death was rapid or slow. Some poisons are very subtle. Other people protested: "You're crazy. They wouldn't have dared. One does not murder God."

Two months later, a group of prisoners in the Siberian district of Kazachinskoye heard an entirely new version through the grapevine. Stalin had convoked the Politburo to inform it of his plan for a massive deportation of Jews. But he ran into opposition from Molotov (who defended his Jewish wife, who had been imprisoned), and perhaps even from Voroshilov and Kaganovich. His amazement and fury at encountering for the first time a rebellion among his own creatures had set off the fatal crisis. Later on, this version, embellished with fanciful variations, would go around the entire world with great success.

Khrushchev and Svetlana did not speak out until much later. Their testimonies are reassuring because they back up the official communiqués and support each other. Is this enough? Khrushchev, one of the four men who shared Stalin's last dinner, had an obvious interest in supporting the version of a natural death. In any hypothesis of a crime, he would have become one of the prime suspects. If he spoke out, it was above all to defend his own reputation.

It is true that Svetlana confirms his statements. But it is known that Khrushchev had some sort of power over her. Hadn't she let herself be impressed by the testimony which the stocky man had, with his customary gift of gab, already put in circulation? And also with all the weight of his authority—for she still was living in Moscow when she wrote her story, and Khrushchev was still the boss.*

* According to statements she herself has made, Svetlana Alliluyeva-Stalin wrote her first book on the outskirts of Moscow, in the village of Zhukovka, "during the summer of 1963." That is, during the Khrushchevian period.

She did not publish it until 1967, after arriving in the United States, but she made a point of emphasizing: "The book remains as it was when it was read by my friends in Moscow." (Author's note to *Twenty Letters to a Friend*.)

[Footnote continues on next page.]

She was undoubtedly present at Kuntsevo. But what had she seen? Hadn't she been kept away from the dying man? Her entire description of the illness is rather hazy, as if hurried, and filled with convenient digressions. One does not feel time passing by. Yet three days watching a man die—and what a man!—means something.

She only regained her descriptive powers when she depicted Stalin's last moments—his gasps in the throes of death—and, above all, when he was actually dead and calm had returned to his face. Until then she was only the shadow of a witness.

Having made these reservations as to the gaps in the testimony, let us return to the basic proposition: Stalin was seventy-three and he was ill. His high blood pressure, his circulatory difficulties could easily have brought about cerebral congestion. Will the partisans of an "aided" death—caused by an entourage anxious about its own security— some day speak openly? Stalin would not have been Stalin if he had not taken some mystery with him to the grave.

But under the first shock of the event, Soviet citizens showed no great desire to weigh the pros and cons. For several days, the event itself, enormous as a sacrilege, plunged the entire country into a state of torpor.

The friends who read the manuscript in Moscow must have been relatively numerous since, still according to the author, "a connoisseur of literature and Russian poetry . . . kept one copy for himself . . . and showed it to anyone he wished, without asking my permission" (*Only One Year*). The Ambassador of India at Moscow also had had a copy in his hands.

One might ask whether Khrushchev's successors, when they granted Svetlana Alliluyeva an exit visa, were completely unaware of a manuscript which had circulated in this manner. At any rate, there was nothing in the description of Stalin's death at the beginning of the book to annoy them. Very soothing and very "respectable," it does not clash with any of the commonplaces about this event.

30

Days of Waiting

The first communiqué had spoken only of the illness. But already, in the streets of Moscow, people were talking in hushed tones, as if they were in the room of a dying man. A young man, K.M., and a friend from the university went into the *shashlychny,* the restaurant on the Arbat that serves *shashlyk,* lamb roasted on skewers. At the threshold, they stopped in amazement. The restaurant, with its usual aroma of grilled meat, its tables covered with small wine bottles, was jammed. But instead of the usual uproar, shouts to waiters, toasts, and noisy conversations, there was a deadly silence. All one heard was the sound of clinking forks. People were eating and drinking—just that—without a word, hunched over their food.

People were afraid. Stalin had been a stern father, but still a father. Without him, what would happen? What plague? What war? What holocaust? The few people who were happy about his death carefully hid their feelings. A student confided to a close friend, who was upset when he had not seen him: "I have been locked in my room, so as not to betray myself. I am so happy! I can just see Beria seated next to his bed, like a snake with spectacles."

People waited. Nothing happened. All through the day of March 4, the radio confined itself to repeating the first bulletin on Stalin's health. On March 5, two other bulletins were broadcast, indicating that his condition had worsened. With an extraordinary wealth of details, they enumerated the treatments he had been given: insufflations of oxygen, medicaments based on camphor, caffeine, strophanthin and glucose, and penicillin—even applications of leeches. It was as if they wanted to make the world see that even the impossible was being attempted to save the sick man.

153

Patriarch Alexis ordered prayers for Stalin's recovery in all the churches, and the Chief Rabbi proclaimed a service and a day of fasting. All the other religious denominations fell into step with them.

Dr. Fritz Heese, a doctor in West Berlin, tells this story: "On the night between the 4th and 5th, my telephone rang. The Soviet military government in Berlin wanted me to come immediately. It involved a consultation about Generalissimo Stalin." Dr. Heese boasted that he had perfected a new treatment for circulatory illnesses.

The Berlin Wall did not yet exist. A car arrived at Dr. Heese's home, which was right in the middle of the American sector. It took him through the Brandenburg Gate and all the way to Karlshorst, the dark, sad district in which General Chuikov's General Headquarters was located. There he was met by doctors who gave him a description of the sick man's condition. Heese replied: "There is nothing more to be done. There's no point in my leaving for Moscow."

The story is interesting but suspect, since Dr. Heese was in general not considered a very serious person by his colleagues. Whenever he heard that an important personage was sick, he would rush and offer his services, whether it was the Pope, the King of Nepal, or the Aga Khan.

In 1953, he was at the peak of his career and was regarded by some people as a miracle doctor. Would General Chuikov, when he heard that his chief was dying, have really turned to him? Did the superstitious respect for German science, which had never lost its power in Russia, this time, too, play a part?

Crushed by debts, Dr. Heese committed suicide in 1959, carrying his secret to the grave. He had vainly bombarded the Kremlin with telegrams demanding payment for his services.

When the first news stories appeared—"Stalin Seriously Ill"—it was a little past midnight in New York. Andrei Vyshinsky, who had just delivered a hard-line speech on Korea at the United Nations, was fast asleep. His collaborators, besieged by journalists, made it quite clear that they dared not wake up the old prosecutor-minister.

In Washington, President Eisenhower was also asleep. His staff waited until he got up at seven in the morning before informing him of the event.

"We know what we are losing, but we do not know what we will get." True to this maxim, the West took little pleasure in learning of its old adversary's disappearance. In the circles farthest from

Marxism, the personal side of the Generalissimo was not judged too harshly. The man with the epaulettes seemed to make people forget the man with the knife clenched between his teeth. Somehow, his seventy-three years were reassuring. Many people liked to see him as an old, sly but wise man, who had a calming effect on the belligerent Malenkov. They considered him a moderate in the midst of a Kremlin erupting with fire and flame.

Truman's estimate in 1948 was quoted: "I like old Uncle Joe Stalin. He is a fine man, but he is the prisoner of the Politburo. You could make an agreement with him, but the other people on the Politburo would not let him keep his word." Also exhumed was an admiring portrait of good Papa Joseph, not by a Communist writer, but from the pen of a former American Ambassador to Moscow, Joseph H. Davies: "The look in his brown eyes was excessively good and loving. I am sure that a child would love to sit on his knees and that a dog would climb up on him."

Summing up the most general opinion, the correspondent of *France-Soir* cabled on March 4: "In the U.S. capital, people fear the recklessness of the successors of the Marshal, who was regarded as a moderating influence." Under the first shock of emotion, this image of a collectively led Kremlin, where Stalin was only the first —and the most cautious—among his peers, cropped up in several commentaries.

More placid, the *Manchester Guardian* observed: "The City expects an easing of the tension." London's stock exchange was firm. There was a vague interest in pre-1917 Russian bonds and a sight climb in the value of certain Polish and Romanian stocks.

Churchill expressed hope for the recovery of his old partner. Vincent Auriol at the Elysée and Georges Bidault at the Quai d'Orsay did likewise. But Eisenhower chose to express his sympathy more for the Soviet citizens than for their leader.

"They are the children of a single God, who is the Father of all peoples. Like all peoples, the millions of Russians share our hopes for a friendly and peaceful world. Whoever their governmental figures may be, Americans will continue to pray that the Almighty watch over the people of this immense country."

Radio Vatican gave the Church's point of view: "This is the moment to see in the head of the Soviet State a soul redeemed by Christ, a soul for which Catholics implore the mercy of God in the universal, supernatural spirit of Christian charity."

L'Humanité, the French Communist paper, devoted an entire page to the meetings of solidarity being held in the outlying, working-class sections of Paris.

"The overwhelming news," *L'Humanité* wrote, "brutally reached the Renault plant at Saint-Ouen just at lunchtime. The workers were in the canteen preparing to eat. One worker came in: 'Comrades, our comrade Stalin is gravely ill.' All faces froze. . . . An old worker chewed angrily on his cigarette.

"Then they all decided to leave, there and then, and hold a meeting. . . . They left their mess-tins, their lunch. . . . There were Communists and others who weren't, but all were swept by the same emotion. A comrade spoke to them. He recalled, simply, the sort of man Stalin was, the leader of the Soviet people.

" 'The leader of the workers of the entire world,' a voice shouted.

"In the sun which burned away the mist, the roughhewn faces looked drawn, contracted. Fists clenched.

" 'He taught us how to fight,' another worker said.

" 'And just recently, he explained to us in *Economic Problems of Socialism in the U.S.S.R.* . . .'

"This evening, from the Renault factory at Saint-Ouen," *L'Humanité* concluded, "a message signed by all the workers will be sent to Stalin."

The editors of the Voice of Peace, the radio station of the French Communist Party, had not lost all hope. After all, Lenin had also suffered a cerebral hemorrhage and afterward had been blessed by a long remission.

Prepared in Paris for French listeners, the two daily programs of the Voice of Peace were broadcast by powerful transmitters in Czechoslovakia, Hungary, and Poland. On the evening of the 5th, the editors in Prague called Paris: "We know from a certain source that Stalin is dead." It was about eight o'clock, that is, ten o'clock in Moscow (the official Soviet communiqué would actually say "at 21:50"). But, for the moment, the news had to remain secret. The Voice of Peace journalists prepared special programs for the next day. Several of them wept.

That night, *L'Humanité* put to press an edition which did not mention the death. But already a special edition, with its first page framed in black, was being prepared.

31

Funeral March

Moscow on March 6, at six o'clock in the morning. With a long, mournful drum roll, followed by the national anthem, the radio resumed its programs. Then Levitan's voice resounded:

"To all members of the Party:

"To all workers in the Soviet Union:

"The heart of Joseph Vissarionovich Stalin, Lenin's comrade-in-arms and inspired continuator of his work, wise leader and educator of the Communist Party and the Soviet people, has stopped beating."

There were twenty-five minutes of slow and solemn reading. First, a long communiqué in which the Central Committee, the government, and the Presidium of the Supreme Soviet in almost anguished terms begged Soviet citizens to show "a unity of steel, a monolithic cohesion," while promising them everything—prosperity, peace, security. Then came the medical bulletin explaining how Stalin had died at exactly ten minutes to ten the night before.

Muscovites, not usually early risers, had gotten up early on this particular morning. They waited and listened. There were few windows that were not lit up, few doors from which a beam of light did not filter. When the reading was over, the lights were switched off. . . . People had gone out to look around and see for themselves.

A few minutes later, in the glacial morning air, a huge crowd was on Red Square walking up and down before the Kremlin. It was not empty. During the night, Stalin's body had been secretly transferred from Kuntsevo to Moscow.

Red flags with black crepe begin to appear at the windows. The entire country was submerged in an immense red and black funeral wreath, the same funeral wreath seen at Moscow in the wan end-of-winter snow, and at Gori, Stalin's native town, where the spring

157

of the Caucasus was already bursting forth in the orchards and the sheep pastures. The same funeral crepe at Magnitogorsk, a great metallurgical complex from which smokestacks rose up densely and stiffly in the icy air of Siberia. And at Vladivostok, where the afternoon had already begun and the sun gleamed brightly on the Sea of Japan.

And music everywhere. Extra loudspeakers had been'installed along the streets. In the apartments, the radios played continuously, without pause. A gigantic, solemn concert inundated the country. All the sad music that sings of dead heroes—Chopin's "Funeral March" and Beethoven's, the last movement of Tchaikovsky's "Symphonie Pathétique," and Berlioz, and then Beethoven again—and hymns and patriotic songs. For four long days. Running short of records and imagination, they would even go on to a few sides of Mozart's "Requiem," not noticing its false ideological note. Accompanied by grave, majestic, or plaintive tones in the streets, in the factories, and in the homes, the strongest nerves began to give way. People cried out of a physical need to cry. "I thought of all the dead relatives I had lost in the war," a woman said. "I cried and cried and cried. . . . It did me good."

In the schools, in many classes, the teacher and the children all cried together.

Sometimes the music over the radio was interrupted by the voice of Levitan or that of one of his imitators, rereading the communiqués, speaking again of the irreparable loss, of the sadness, of unity, of vigilance, even calling upon the citizens—unheard-of words—"to avoid panic and disorder."

The young historian George Haupt, who happened to be convalescing in a sanatorium in the Crimea, discussed the event with a nurse and a patient wounded in the war. The nurse sobbed: "What will become of us without him?" The war veteran said: "Finally, he has left forever." But such explosions of joy were rare, discreet, almost heroic. The wave of tears drowned everything.

In Yerevan, the capital of Soviet Armenia, some women expressed their grief by rolling on the ground. Several cases of suicide were reported.

That very morning, Aleksandr Solzhenitsyn was in Central Asia. He had just been freed after eight years of imprisonment.

"I went out for the first time on the street, free at last, although I was still a deportee," he remembered. "I had gone out because of the insistence of an old deaf woman who had awakened me at an early hour and had asked me to go down into the street to listen to the news which the loudspeakers were broadcasting: It was the death of Stalin."[1]

At Marfino, where Solzhenitsyn had been imprisoned for four years, the prisoners had remained in their dormitories that morning instead of going to work in the laboratories, as was customary. A delicate calculation of probabilities was forming in the heads of these engineers and mathematicians: Would they be shot or wouldn't they? Should they fear a "state of emergency" such as had been proclaimed at the beginning of the war, when there were systematic executions in the prisons and concentration camps? They kept silent.

Some of them, the Communists, who still believed in their good and just leader, wept. But this reaction was extremely rare among the prisoners. Unlike the free population, those in the camps generally associated Stalin with their misfortunes. They understood that with him still alive, the merciless order he had founded would never come to an end.

In the great concentration camp complex of Vorkuta, the prisoner John Nobe, an American citizen who had been arrested in Dresden in 1945, heard the news over a loudspeaker at the bottom of mine shaft No. 16, on the morning of March 6. He saw an old man drop to his knees in the water covering the floor of the mine shaft and begin shouting: "God be praised! There is still someone who thinks of us unfortunates." The German Joseph Scholmer, also at Vorkuta, but at Camp No. 6, also saw old, bearded muzhiks kneel down and pray.[2] "I have been here for nineteen years and this is the first good news I have heard," a Georgian confided, and a Polish Zionist added: "God has saved the Jews. If he had not died, there would have been new pogroms."

The prisoners listened with delight to the sentinels talking feverishly over the telephones, way up there in their watchtowers. They saw free workers running from one office to another, completely at sea, gathering in groups and conferring. On March 6, all work at Vorkuta was interrupted.

That night, in the barracks, several *Zeks* got drunk on joy and vodka. These men who lacked everything had found something to drink.

The next morning, the large portrait of Stalin which had adorned the locomotive that pulled the small tip-trucks of coal at shaft No. 16 was replaced by a portrait of Lenin.

At Colony for Rehabilitation Through Work No. 1 on Shabolovka Street in Moscow, six hundred prisoners stared at guards and free workers crying unrestrainedly. As a rule the "Citizen Chiefs," sheathed in their dignity, never showed their feelings in the presence of the prisoners. Prudently, the prisoners concealed their satisfaction for fear their jailers might pass from sorrow to rage and turn on them.

In the white hell of Kolyma, the poet Varlam Shalamov, arrested in 1937, welcomed the news with glum indifference. He was too busy trying to survive to summon any feelings of hope.

Esther Markish, the wife of the Jewish poet who was shot, learned of Stalin's death just as she reached the bare steppe of Kazakhstan, where she had been deported with her two sons, the younger of whom was thirteen. She was surprised to find in this desert "the best society"—that is, a group of widows of leaders and intellectuals who had been shot. Some of them had been there since 1934.

The announcement of Stalin's death stirred her deeply. But her main concern was finding an oil stove on which to cook the food she may or may not get for her sons and herself.

The prisons did not have loudspeakers. Plunged into a world of silence, some of the prisoners would not know what was happening until several weeks later.

The father of the people was dead but not yet buried. Moscow was caught up in a gigantic homage to his remains.

The results of the autopsy, published with the same wealth of detail as the bulletins on the state of Stalin's health, for the last time tried to show the world that everything possible and impossible had been done for him: "The results of the pathologico-anatomical examination have established the irreversible character of the illness. . . . That is why the treatment's energetic measures could not produce positive results or prevent the fatal outcome."

On March 6, at three o'clock, Stalin's body was put on display at the House of the Trade Unions, a jewel of classic Russian architecture built by Kazakov at the end of the eighteenth century as a clubhouse for the nobility. Against the delicate green façade of the building a huge portrait of Stalin rested on a colossal platform of oak planks framed in black mourning crepe.

Inside, in the vast Hall of Columns, where Lenin's body had lain on display twenty-nine years before, Stalin reposed in state amid a mountain of flowers on a raised bier that, in the Russian tradition, remained uncovered. He was dressed in his military uniform. The old face was peaceful but still imperious. Beneath the thick brown skin, the cheekbones were still prominent; the outstretched hands still seemed ready to clutch and seize.

At four o'clock, the Hall of Columns was opened to the public.

A commission presided over by Khrushchev worked around the

clock to prepare the most stupendous funeral of the century—a funeral that, in every detail, would recall Lenin's, though with an added touch of gigantism.

Any demonstration in the land of Stalin had to be regulated with the precision of a ballet. From the Union of Writers to the smallest factory in the provinces, there was the usual discipline. In thousands upon thousands of meetings, orators with red and black armbands explained in detail what must be done and thought. The factories in Moscow had already elected, with a show of hands and without discussion, the delegations that would carry the flowers to Red Square three days later. On their parade grounds, military regiments were already rehearsing the funeral march. And a search was being made for Vera Kondakova, the little girl who kissed Stalin on May 1, 1952, so that she could meditate before the corpse in the presence of reporters. In principle, nothing could be left to chance. The usual precision machine was functioning in high gear.

But this time, the people added their spontaneity. Of its own accord, the entire population of Moscow flocked to the House of Trade Unions to pay its last respects to the father. The delegations, with their red flags covered with black crepe, filed past side by side with ordinary citizens, fathers of families holding their children by the hand, young girls arm in arm, street kids who wormed their way in. It was cold—several degrees below freezing. In the midst of this crowd, some drunks who had warmed themselves up with vodka sang in thick voices, but they were not chased away. They, too, had the right to see.

Moscow was a wheel whose spokes were fixed in the hub of the Kremlin. The crowd was channeled down a certain number of these spokes, which, after descending a gentle slope, converged at the center. At first swarming and scattered, the crowd then packed together, condensing into enormous columns that filled the entire breadth of the street. A few cars bumped along in the dense tide until they were caught and immobilized. The traffic lights were useless during the passage of this slow avalanche.

That afternoon, A.V., a student, worked his way as far as Trubnaya Square, a crossroads where several human rivers joined to continue their course to the House of the Trade Unions, less than a mile away. The crowd turned into a disorderly mob. The student realized that this would end badly. He gave up the idea of seeing Stalin and somehow managed to get through the police cordon and back to the avenues on the perimeter. Then an unheard-of event occurred. Molotov in person arrived in his car to speak to the crowd. He exhorted them: "Don't push, be patient! Everyone can salute our dear

Joseph Vissarionovich." Nothing helped; the torrent continued forward. At the House of the Trade Unions, Svetlana Stalin heard two completely unnerved generals say that they had lost control of this mass and that it was urgent to "take measures."

Huge trucks with mounted machine guns barred the path of the advancing mutitude. On Gorky Street people started climbing over the barriers. The militiamen * on top of the trucks kept shoving them down again.

All this took place without a single cry, grindingly, with gritted teeth. On Neglinnaya and Pushkinskaya streets, the crowd continued to press forward, but the trucks, jammed one against the other, progressively narrowed the passage, forming a kind of funnel to prevent the mass of people from being crushed in enormous waves against the House of the Trade Unions. The first ranks ran into this bottleneck. Some women were suffocated. Behind them the people forged ahead blindly. Some slipped on the icy surface and were trampled. Others had their spines broken, their rib cages shattered as they were crushed against the iron bars which protected the ground floor windows. Many dead and wounded, all mixed together, poured into Moscow's hospitals.

Yevgeny Yevtushenko recalls the deadly tide of people on Trubnaya Square: "I felt that this blind mass would carry me like a chip of wood tossed about, helpless, on the water. It flung me straight at a lamppost. I had the impression that this metal thing was marching pitilessly towards me.

"Suddenly, a little girl was crushed against the lamppost and screamed with horror. Among the lamentations and gasps, I had not heard her scream but I had seen on her face an unforgettable image of the apocalypse. I felt in my body the breaking of fragile bones and, horrified, I shut my eyes so as not to see any longer the blue gaze of this agonized child.

"When I opened them again, I was already far from the lamppost. Miraculously, the human tide had carried me away from it. The little girl was gone. She had disappeared beneath the mob. Another man struggled in her place, opening his arms like a crucified man and vainly imploring them to let him break loose." [3]

This dogged march would last for three days, three days in the cold snowy wind; and three nights in the livid glare of the searchlights. Several million men and women—some would estimate the crowd at five million—would trample onward in this fashion, hoping to reach the Hall of Columns.

* In the U.S.S.R., the ordinary police, those who patrol the streets, are called the militia.

Beria, once again the great chieftain of all the forces of order, had brought in reinforcements from Leningrad. Detachments of mounted militiamen drove into the crowd, trying to contain it and push it back. Some people were knocked unconscious by the horses' hooves. Moscow was absolutely jammed. Thousands of people from the provinces who had piled into trucks to come and salute the dead god ran into barriers. Those who had taken the train passed through more easily, at least during the first hours. At the railroad stations, there was an atmosphere of sad festivity; many drunks were around, all weeping.

Other policemen were not dealing with the crowd or its problems. When A.V., the student who escaped from Trubnaya Square, sensed the approach of a deadly crush, he managed to reach a quieter district. "All of a sudden," he recalled, "I felt a shock, an intense fright. In the dark street, two steps from Pushkin Square, I saw a dozen parked trucks, with all of their headlights extinguished. They were crammed with soldiers of the MGB in combat dress, with tommy guns slung over their shoulders. These men were not supposed to police the streets. Seated in their trucks, almost invisible in the darkness, they were waiting."

During these days, State Security made hundreds of preventive arrests in the framework of an established "mobilization plan" in case of war or some other serious event. It was on the day of Stalin's death that S. P. Pisarev, the naïve *apparatchik* who had written to Stalin to draw his attention to possible irregularities in the doctors' trial, was arrested.

32

The Heirs

Less than a day after the announcement of Stalin's death, Soviet citizens knew that their new leader was Malenkov and that he had inherited all of Stalin's power. Both President of the Council and First Secretary of the Party,* he appeared to be the universal legatee, as people had expected soon after the Nineteenth Congress. On March 10 *Pravda,* launching the cult of this new personality, published an abominably touched-up photograph from its archives. Thick layers of fog had wiped out many of the figures, leaving only a pensive Stalin and an astonished Mao Tse-tung, both admiring a Malenkov with the look of an eagle and an imperious stance.

Beria, who, with all the fear he inspired, supported Malenkov, contented himself with more modest-appearing functions: Vice-President of the Council and Minister of the Interior. He had just what he wanted: the police. He unified again under his authority the two police empires; the MVD with its camps and the MGB with all the rest were again brought together under his control. He immediately installed himself again on Lubyanka Square, where his portrait would reappear in all the offices, and packed Moscow with special troops.

The Presidium and Secretariat of the Party saw their personnel brutally reduced.† In one blow, most of the newcomers Stalin had brought in six months earlier were ousted. This was the case of Leonid Brezhnev who, again donning a lieutenant-general's uniform, became chief adjutant of the political directorate of the army, an

* However, the appellation "Secretary General," which was Stalin's, disappeared on that very day. It did not reappear until thirteen years later, in 1966.
† The Presidium fell from twenty-five to ten full members.

assignment that was comfortable but unrelated to his previous high position in the Secretariat.

Having gotten rid of the young wolves, the old guard reoccupied in force all the important posts, making sure it was abundantly photographed beside Stalin's corpse and immeasurably praised by the Party's hack writers. Nikita Khrushchev, now the second personage in the Party, was already flexing his muscles in order to rise still higher. Since Beria, that is to say, the police, was Malenkov's support, it was logical that Khrushchev should think of the army.

The boss of the military was Nikolai Bulganin, a well-groomed man with an affable smile, a glacial stare and a goatee, who looked like a bank clerk worn out from a spree. This politician who wore a marshal's kepi was allied with Khrushchev in his fight against Malenkov and his thrust for absolute power, and against Beria's maneuvers behind the scenes.

What's more, many of the real warriors, such as Zhukov, who had been relegated to a mediocre command in the provinces, were tired of being bullied and had nothing but contempt for the general of the police in the Lubyanka. They could help a man who knew how to use them.

Aleksei Kosygin, only recently at the summit, had been seriously downgraded in October after the Nineteenth Congress. And Stalin's disappearance, far from giving him the chance to re-establish himself, only accentuated his descent. On March 6, he was ousted competely from the Party Presidium and stripped of his title as Vice-President of the Council, retaining only his post as Minister of Light Industry and Alimentation. He accepted this reversal of fortune with his customary coldness. Besides, the thankless post was quite suitable to this hard-working man.*

The new nominations were attributed to a "common meeting of the Central Committee, the Council of Ministers, and the Presidium of the Supreme Soviet," an unprecedented procedure. But, more than the manner, it was the rapidity that was surprising. Certainly the urgency was great, certainly the heirs seemed to dread like fire any vacancy in the positions of power. But to transform the entire framework of the Party and the State—and in so radical a fashion—in less than twenty-four hours was amazing for such a slow country!

Some people would later conclude that Stalin did not die on the 5th at ten minutes to ten at night but two or three days earlier,

---

* In accordance with the tendency to concentration which prevailed in March, 1953, the Ministry of Light Industry and Alimentation was the result of the fusion of four specialized ministries.

and that his death had been kept secret until everything was re-organized,* a hypothesis neither verified nor unreasonable.

According to Svetlana Stalin, the dacha at Kuntsevo became empty the day after her father's death. Beria had household equipment, books, furniture, everything carted away and deposited in some MGB warehouse. He had also dispersed all the servants. Two officers of the bodyguard were even shot.

General Poskrebyshev, who was in charge of Stalin's personal secretariat, did not participate in the liquidation as either victim or executioner. This most faithful of the faithful, more devoted than a dog, also wound up being cast out by his master. He retired to his house for a number of months, waiting for the police to come and arrest him. Stalin's death, however, saved him from the worst.

---

* It is understood that, so long as Stalin had even a breath of life, his heirs would not have dared to take any steps as to the succession.

33

Farewell, Father!

Farewell, Father!
That sudden and terrible feeling
of having become an orphan!
—MIKHAIL A. SHOLOKHOV

The entire southern part of the Soviet Union—the Crimea, the Caucasus, and Central Asia—sent flowers. It was impossible to put so many roses and mimosas, poppies, narcissi, dahlias, magnolias and lilies in the Hall of Columns, where Stalin lay in state, so they were lined up outside, creating an astonishing garden on the snow.

Not far from this deified death, a death which is not even mentioned —Sergei Prokofiev, composer of innumerable pieces of music bubbling with life, a good composer and a bad character, passed away. His remains were just across from the Hall of Columns, but, because of the huge crowd blocking traffic and hermetically sealing the streets, his funeral had to delayed. The press did not even report his death, for Moscow could only mourn Stalin.

For sixty hours, the people filed past Stalin's corpse. After a brief interruption at the end of the night, the doors of the hall reopened. The crystal chandeliers were draped in black. Long red flags bordered with black descended the length of Kazakov's graceful neo-classical columns. Funeral music played softly. These men and women who had waited for twelve to fourteen hours in the wind and cold, barely missing being smothered, passed by almost without stopping, borne along by the tide. There was just enough time to etch in one's memory the coffin covered with red silk emerging from the flowers and palms, and the rigid, uniformed shape, its legendary face so close for the first time, humanized by death.

The honor guard around the corpse was constantly being changed. Stakhanovites were followed by writers, "Heroes of Work" were followed by generals, old fighters for Communism who had come running from all over the world were followed by a majestic delegation from the Orthodox Patriarchate. The most notable among these notables stood at attention for a quarter of an hour beside the coffin. Lesser figures were relieved at the end of two or three minutes. The most important, the heirs, headed by Malenkov, returned from time to time throughout the day and night.

On the night of March 8, when the flow of people was brought to an end, when the doors of the Hall of Columns were shut for the last time, the line of people waiting still stretched out for six or seven miles. People could not resign themselves to going home after such a long wait. They remained there in the freezing night, their collars pulled up and the earflaps of their *shapkas* turned down, quietly stamping their feet in their felt *valenki* as they listened to the solemn music from the loudspeakers.

Ten o'clock in the morning. An immense silence covered the country. For three days now life had already been suspended over 8,649,798 square miles. No shows, no concerts, no amusements or pleasures. Even the useless gray posters on Moscow's streets had been scraped off. But on the morning of March 9, everything finally came to a dead stop. All schools were closed, and the entire Soviet Union lived as though muted, in slow motion. Two hundred million people had eyes only for the large square covered with gray paving stones beneath the walls of the Kremlin.

The delegations had been waiting silently, with their black-bordered portraits, since the middle of the night.

In the distance, one could hear Chopin's "Funeral March." A forest of flowers advanced very slowly towards Red Square—twenty-five ranks of marchers bearing giant wreaths and bouquets.

Behind them, six black horses pulled the coffin draped in red and set on a gun carriage. The Generalissimo's visored cap was on top of the coffin, and his decorations were on satin cushions carried by marshals and generals. Behind the gun carriage came all the heirs wearing large red and black armbands, and Chou En-lai, the great ally, who was entitled to a place in the front rank between Malenkov and Beria. Then the family: Svetlana, Vasily, some of the grandchildren. Then everybody else: heads of governments, ministers, ambassadors. The top hats of the Western diplomats formed a strange contrast with the heavy, dark overcoats and fur hats of the Soviet populace.

The cortege came to a halt. The coffin was placed on a catafalque, while the standards of the Moscow regiments and the military academies were dipped. The officials climbed to the top of the tomb. A loud, rather jagged voice with a slightly theatrical enunciation filled the square: Malenkov was speaking. His speech glorifying Stalin, was already post-Stalinist. With noticeable emphasis, he promised bread and peace—above all, peace, Stalin's death had sown dreams and terror with a free hand. The living wished to please.

Around Malenkov on the tomb was the aristocracy of international Communism, but in a disorder that contrasted with the strict alignments of Stalinist times. Ulbricht, with his goatee, rubbed elbows with La Pasionara's black shawl and grand Spanish style. The Czech Gottwald, with his gigantic stature, somewhat dwarfed his neighbor Jacques Duclos. A deceptive burliness: Gottwald would die five days later—and, from all appearances, because of a cold contracted that day while standing on top of the tomb.

Beria, with his heavy accent, spoke after Malenkov. Ears pricked up a bit when the all-powerful chief of police promised Soviet citizens to "protect with constant solicitude their rights as inscribed in the Stalinist Constitution." They remembered the "liberal" Beria of 1938. But they noticed above all his emphatic praise of Malenkov. He seemed to want the world to know that the new boss was truly his pupil.

Molotov, the third orator, was the only one who showed signs of being deeply moved. He really mourned the chief whose death had probably saved him, and he had to break off several times.

Khrushchev, the master of ceremonies, was content to introduce the three orators.

When the speeches were over, Stalin's "comrades-in-arms" lifted the coffin with its glass top onto their shoulders. Aided by robust soldiers, Malenkov, Beria, Molotov, Khrushchev, Voroshilov, Bulganin, Kaganovich and Mikoyan carried Stalin to the bottom of the tomb, into the crypt where Lenin already rested.

The Kremlin clock struck twelve. The cannons roared. The red flag at half-mast was hoisted again to the top of its pole, and the regiments wheeled into position for their last parade before Joseph Stalin.

At noon in Moscow, seven o'clock in the evening in Khabarovsk, and ten o'clock on Kamchatka, for ten minutes, from one end of the Soviet Union to the other, all work and all transportation stopped, all factories, ships, and locomotives silenced their sirens and whistles. From the Gulf of Finland to the Bering Sea, everything stood still.

In Peking, where a human ocean filled the square before the Celestial Gate of Peace, Mao Tse-tung bowed before an immense portrait of Stalin.

In Warsaw, Budapest, Prague and Berlin, all life stopped at the moment that Stalin descended into the tomb. Zealous cameramen had arranged groups, had taught the men how to take off their caps and the women how to bow their heads at the desired angle. The film had to preserve the image of the greatest funeral service of our time.

At the camp of Taishet in Siberia, the prisoner Karlo Stajner, a Yugoslav Communist, was summoned with his comrades to a funeral meeting. The *Zeks* lined up by brigades on the central square of the *lagpunkt*. An MVD officer mounted a table and associated the GULAG universe and its millions of slaves with the national bereavement: "We swear at this sorrowful instant that we will work even more and better." His voice rose, resonant, but a bit muffled by the snow.

With their caps in their hands, the prisoners observed three minutes of silence. Their breath was smoky in the arctic air. Then one of them said:

"Citizen leader, I have in my account a little silver which my wife sent me and which I cannot spend. I would be happy to participate in the purchase of a wreath for our beloved leader. Is it possible?"

The officer thought about it. "You'd better make a request in writing," he said.

In accordance with the Patriarch's instructions, the priests in Moscow's churches prayed for the soul of Joseph Stalin. "May the soul of your servant Joseph rest among the saints, oh Lord." The candles sputtered softly beneath the staring eyes of the icons, and the eternal little old women wrapped in their gray shawls sobbed when they heard the sad chant of the Office for the Dead.

It was all over. Red Square was silent once again. The Spassky tower tolled the hours. People came to see the wreaths piled up by the thousands beneath the walls of the Kremlin, tried to decipher the names written on the ribbons, and went away without saying a word. Stalin's name was already carved on the tomb, just below Lenin's. He must rest there, next to the founder of the Soviet Union, while awaiting the announced construction of a pantheon for all the country's glorious figures.*

Stalin's name was on the tomb, but the public was not yet admitted

* The construction of a pantheon was announced on March 7, but nothing ever came of it.

to see him. The body put on view in the Hall of Columns had received only provisory treatment. It now had to be prepared properly so as to defy the centuries. In 1924, Professor Vorobyev had embalmed Lenin in a very scientific manner (in order to maintain a constant degree of humidity in the tissues, he had installed a small electric pump inside the corpse). Vorobyev was dead, but his assistant Professor Zharsky had inherited his secrets. Stalin had covered him with honors and then arrested him, but with no feeling of rancor, Zharsky dutifully began embalming Stalin's body, a pious task that would take several months.

The tomb would be reopened in November, 1953. Soviet citizens would then see the two glass coffins standing side by side in the cold, reddish-yellow light of the crypt. Lenin austere in his short jacket, Stalin more massive and flamboyant with his huge epaulettes. His eyes were shut and his hands extended. He looked barely asleep, and there was a touch of imperious irony in the heavy aquiline profile.

part IV
AN UNCERTAIN SPRING

34

Forgetting

*Double, triple the guard
around this tomb!
So that Stalin may never
get out, nor the past
with Stalin!*
—YEVGENY YEVTUSHENKO

On March 9, Soviet newsreel cameramen filmed the funeral in all of its details. The results of their labors would never be seen. All of the cameramen's work was consigned to the film archives, where it remains to this day, unavailable for foreign or domestic consumption. For, before the film of the funeral was ready, the wind had changed and it was already time to forget Stalin.

F.L., a literary critic, received an urgent commission from a Moscow magazine to write an essay on Stalin's place in Soviet literature. The entire April issue of the magazine would be devoted to the deceased leader. About two weeks after the assignment, the editor-in-chief telephoned: "No point in continuing. You will be paid for the essay, of course. But the table of contents for April has been changed."

Pravda remained Stalinist-tinged for about thirteen days: From the mourning issue of March 10, which was devoted entirely to the funeral ceremonies, to March 22 inclusive. During this time, Stalin continued to be quoted in many articles. Poems inspired by him still appeared, and his name was still accompanied by glowing superlatives. One also found the themes that had filled the paper before his death: "doctor-assassins," "hidden enemies of our people," "henchmen of the Zionist Jews," as well as the usual appeals for spying on one's neighbors and the usual denunciations of "slackness and naïveté."

With spring, everything changed. The great man's name appeared only two or three times in each issue of the newspaper; sometimes it was completely absent. On April 7, the Constitution of the U.S.S.R. ceased to be "Stalinist Constitution," and became, quite simply, the "Soviet Constitution." On the same day, Yekaterina Furtseva, quoting Stalin's last work, already failed to qualify it as "inspired." [1]

On and after March 23, the word "vigilance" seemed to have been forgotten as all the commentators began discussing the "prosperity of the people." The plots of land given to the workers to grow potatoes became a subject of great concern to the organ of the Central Committee.

At the same time, the articles against Jews ceased. The last big anti-Semitic feature article—one of the most violent published—appeared in the March 20 issue of *Krokodil*. Vasily Ardamatsky, the author of this ill-timed article, would have the unpleasant experience of being shunned by his colleagues and of hearing himself nicknamed Vasya Timashuk, after the woman doctor who had denounced and caused the arrest of the "men in white."

Tears had not yet been dried, but the process of de-Stalinization got under way enthusiastically, and, in the leading circles, one could almost hear an enormous but discreet sigh of relief.

For the old guard, it was a matter of preserving the advantages of succession while eliminating its dangers—of maintaining power but diminishing tensions. After thirty-five years of existence, the Party could flatter itself that it bore, in the eyes of Soviet citizens, the mysterious seal of legitimacy. But now the leaders were going to disassociate the Party from Stalin, even though the habit of identifying it with him had become deeply rooted.*

---

* A convincing example of this can be found by comparing two writings of Mikhail Sholokhov published in *Pravda* at an interval of less than five months. The first was the great funeral chant which appeared on March 8, after Stalin's burial:

> Farewell, father! Farewell, dear father, whom we shall love until our last breath. You will always be with us and with those who are born after us. We hear your voice in the rhythmic rumble of the turbines of the gigantic hydroelectric power plants, and in the crash of the waves of the seas created by your will, and in the cadenced step of the invincible Soviet infantry and in the soft soughing of foliage on the well-timbered plains which stretch to infinity.

The second text, which appeared on July 30, was entitled: "Live eternally, our dear Party." In this article, Sholokhov did not mention Stalin's name even once.

The transition would be difficult. On March 14, Malenkov, who appeared to be the chief heir on March 6, abandoned part of his heritage. Keeping only the presidency of the government, he left the secretariat, and the small wave of adulation which he had enjoyed during those eight days vanished. A month later, a new formula rose on the political horizon: "Collective leadership, supreme principle of the leadership of our Party." [2]

Officially, the collectivity had three heads. Malenkov was actually surrounded by Beria and Molotov, who, besides their titles of first vice-president of the Council, had received, respectively, portfolios as the heads of the Ministry of the Interior and the Ministry of Foreign Affairs. Behind them were other illustrious figures: Bulganin, Kaganovich, and Mikoyan. The West, which was not very sensitive to obscure maneuvers inside the Party, continued to pay little attention to Nikita Khrushchev. Yet it was he who became First Secretary of the Central Committee when Malenkov was "relieved" of his post. Quietly, without a fuss, he began to gather into his hands the real reins of power.

Malenkov, meanwhile, was doing what he could to occupy the front of the stage, to be, if not the boss, at least a bossling. He decided to display his managerial skills. He decided to raise the Soviet standard of living.

The reduction in prices which he had decreed on April 1 was far greater than the reductions announced, ritually, each year under Stalin. To cope with this mass of liberated money, the government feverishly imported consumer goods; it even went so far as to buy 30,000 tons of butter in Denmark, Holland, Australia, and New Zealand. Yet it goes without saying that most of the imports came from the satellite countries, where the U.S.S.R. could have certain quantities of products set aside in advance and could buy at super-preferential prices. The workers of East Berlin, whose production "norms" were greatly increased, would make it clear, with paving stones and Molotov cocktails, that they were not quite ready to foot the bill for raising Soviet citizens' standard of living.

During the summer, Malenkov turned his attention to the peasants. On August 8, he announced that the tax in kind, a scourge for the countryside, was to be greatly reduced, in fact abolished. A witness said: "On that day at the Luzayevka railroad station, I saw kolkhozians weep with joy. When Levitan, the voice he employed for great holidays, began to bellow out the news over the loudspeakers, all the farmers who were there, on the platforms or in the waiting rooms, sitting among their bundles, began feverishly asking each other questions. And when they realized that it was true, that they could now drink the milk their cow produced, raise chickens without the 'inspector of finances' coming and taking everything away, the entire station started laughing and crying. It was a great folk festival."

More consumer goods. In the autumn, the decrees poured down like hail. The airplane factories were ordered to manufacture washing machines, the armament industry shifted to making metal beds. All this bore the marks of haste, of feverish improvisation. In the great feeling of expansiveness that followed Stalin's death, did the people show signs of restlessness so dangerous that they had to be allayed at all costs, even to the point of shaking the edifice of the Plans?

Or was Malenkov trying to win over a specific part of the population—the part that included people with high salaries, the important technicians and managers? Some of his reforms involved the entire population, but the industrial reconversion favored expensive products—refrigerators, motorcycles, the best cloth, Soviet "champagnes"— all things that were in any event beyond the pocketbook of an ordinary worker.

In the offices of the Party, people were a bit nervous. Were they witnessing the dawn of an era of managers and administrators? If so, what would happen to the supremacy of the Party, which was institutional, of the same substance as the regime? Did some vulgar production technicians want to become the equals of the *apparatchiki*, the guardians of the revealed truth?

The military, whose aims, by definition, were linked to those of the people in heavy industry, also had a low opinion of this method of encouraging the appetite for consumer goods.

From the Old Square, headquarters of the Central Committee, Khrushchev, the Party leader, sharply criticized Malenkov's "demagogic" initiatives. Rationing credits to heavy industry in order to produce cameras and watches showed a lack of seriousness. The 1953 grain production was even lower than that of 1913 (in the interval, the population had increased by 30 million); Soviet citizens needed bread, not toys.

What was needed most, Khrushchev continued in his loquacious manner, were tractors and agricultural machines and therefore steel. Thrown out the door, Stalinist industrialism came back through the window.

But Stalin was no longer invoked as an authoritative reference. Before, Olzhegov's *Dictionary of the Russian Language* devoted four lines to the substantive "Stalinist" (*Stalinist: Member of the Communist Party (Bolshevik) of the Soviet Union, faithful disciple of Marxism-Leninism, unshakably devoted to the cause of Lenin-Stalin*). In the 1953 edition, the word and its definition simply vanished. And the most amazing thing of all was the date the dictionary was printed: March 12, 1953. A week after Stalin's death.

35

Malenkov's Bandits

In the camps, the prisoners also waited. On March 7 at Vorkuta, a prisoner asked John Noble: "Who knows? Maybe big Georgy will free us?" Big Georgy was Malenkov.

Such speculation did not last long. On March 28 the Supreme Soviet proclaimed an amnesty.

"As a result of the consolidation of the Soviet regime and the rise in the level of prosperity and culture among the population, together with the rise in the level of consciousness of the citizens and their honest attitude towards the execution of their social duties, legality and the Socialist legal order have been strengthened and criminality has notably diminished in our country.

"Under these conditions, the Presidium of the Supreme Soviet of the U.S.S.R. believes that it is no longer indispensable to continue to confine in the places where they have been kept persons guilty of crimes that do not represent a great danger to the State."

The beneficiaries of the amnesty were the common criminals, who were freed in considerable numbers. Political prisoners were almost completely neglected. But it was they who really constituted the battalions of the *Zeks*, and in the GULAG universe, there was a wave of bitter disappointment. Some exasperated inmates even attacked guards and "brigadiers".

From May to August, great strikes broke out at Norilsk and Vorkuta. Tens of thousands of prisoners crossed their arms for days and weeks at a time, endangering the country's mining production. There were shooting and repressions, but there was also the extraordinary sight of MVD generals negotiating with their slaves, making certain concessions and using patient maneuvers and promises to get them to return to work. Sometimes, the promises would actually be kept. For example, the right of prisoners to correspond with and even receive visits from their families would be greatly increased. A few months earlier, while Stalin was alive, not a single striker would have lived to tell the tale. In Stalin's time, these strikes—more protests than real insurrections—were not even conceivable.

The happy beneficiaries of the amnesty left the prisons of Siberia and the Far North. Among them were many thieves, big and small, crooks and hooligans who flashed knives when they had had too much to drink. These people had a score to settle with the cities— the old score against the order prohibiting ex-convicts from living in certain areas. The crime rate in Moscow rocketed, and Muscovites called the newcomers "Malenkov's bandits."

People barricaded their houses. Women no longer went out at night if they lived on a rather dark street. Terrifying myths surged up from the depths of Russian history. As in the times of the Regent Sophia, people told stories of organized bands which were on their way to Moscow to devastate the city with fire and sword. Overwhelmed, the militia lost no time in returning many of the undesirables to the camps they had come from.

Another fear in this spring of 1953 was economic. Rumors of the ruble's devaluation had begun to circulate, and Muscovites lined up patiently and silently in front of the offices of the *sberkassy*—the savings banks, some to withdraw their money, others to deposit it. For the city was divided by two rumors of equal strength but opposing significance. Some people were saying that the monetary reform would spare the sums deposited in the banks, while others claimed that it would wipe them out. Since in the end nothing happened— neither reform nor devaluation—these gloomy lines eventually diminished and disappeared.* The savings banks again became what they had always been: a cross between a bureau of records, where people came to pay their taxes, and a kind of piggy bank for savers who were putting away a little money for a few purchases.

* However, let us remember that a Draconian monetary reform was put through in Czechoslovakia on May 30 and that this was the root cause of the uprisings in Pilsen and Ostrava.

36

Peace—Really and Truly?

This bewildered country, where authority was imperceptibly wavering, needed peace abroad. The West, at first so worried, quickly sensed which way the wind was blowing. The funeral on Red Square was barely over when John Foster Dulles declared at the U.N.: "Stalin's death increases the hopes for peace."

Three weeks later, the North Koreans proposed resuming armistice negotiations at Panmunjon. Within four months, they would conclude discussions which had been stalled for two years, and the guns would fall silent in Korea.

Apart from this, which was no small matter, there were still great differences. Each side remained faithful to its principles, or its mental reservations, but in a way which caused people slowly, reluctantly, to abandon belief in the inevitability of catastrophe. At the United Nations, a smile relaxed Valerian Zorin's thin lips, while Andrei Vyshinsky and Henry Cabot Lodge joined in a toast to peace.

On April 25, for the first time in ages, *Pravda* devoted almost a whole page to a speech by the President of the United States. Eisenhower's vast "peace plan" was reproduced in its entirety, accompanied by a critical commentary. This was the same *Pravda* which the preceding summer had written: "Drink a glass of cold milk, Ike, and calm your nerves," and which, to top it off, threatened America with an atomic lightning bolt.

Before summer, Tito, "the marshal of the traitors," had been politely requested by Molotov to send an ambassador to Moscow.

Everything seemed to have changed. One Sunday in April, seventeen sailors from the Soviet coal-ship *Kama*, anchored in the port of Le Havre, were authorized by their consul to visit Paris and stroll in a compact group from Montmartre to the wall of the Fédérés. Ten American journalists, who on a visit to Moscow saw old ladies in their shawls jamming the churches on Easter evening, sent a letter of thanks to Malenkov and on their return to the United States were attacked as "the jackasses of the century, the dupes of Communist peace propaganda."

The world was in a questioning mood. Was it really peace? The Soviet army was preparing to explode its first hydrogen bomb, nibbling at American supremacy in the field of armaments. The cruiser *Sverdlov* took part in the naval review organized in England for the coronation of Elizabeth—a gesture of courtesy that partly unveiled a fleet still second in rank but already in full development.

At the beginning of June, uprisings broke out in Czechoslovakia. The workers of East Berlin, Brandenburg, Mecklemburg, Thuringia, and Saxony defied Soviet occupation forces with strikes or uprisings. The immediate reasons for these movements were economic, but the background was political. How far would the new Kremlin carry its tolerance, and what could be extorted from it?

The Kremlin stamped out the uprisings while shouting Fascist provocation, but it continued to allow the tepid wind of a demi-thaw.

Sometimes contradictory moves revealed a certain confusion. At Moscow in this spring of 1953, N. I. Godunov read the galleys of his book dealing with the Resistance in France.[1] This Godunov—whose friends called him Boris, naturally—had been cultural attaché in Paris. An officially certified expert on French politics, charged with supervising radio broadcasts in the French language, he devoted a good part of his book to violent attacks on General de Gaulle. Reverting to Goebbels's accents, he explained that in London "the Gaullist clique" had been entirely subordinated "to the interests of the English ruling class . . . an instrument of British imperialism." Even more: "In order to attain their reactionary objectives, the Gaullists handed over the Resistance fighters to the Nazis." And he explained coldly that de Gaulle lured patriots into traps and then had them massacred by the Nazis, in order to satisfy "his Anglo-American bosses."

At the last moment, somebody realized that after all, de Gaulle was opposed to the European Defense Community, the *bête noire* of Soviet diplomacy. This was the period when Ambassador Vinogradov was sent to Paris, where he would display a discreet but tenacious Gaullism. After publication, the book was attacked by *Pravda*, which amounted to a repudiation, the author being criticized for "inexperience." But, contrary to the custom, Godunov welcomed this redoubtable assault with a serene air. He had been told not to be upset: "It's just for the international context, you understand?"

"Détente" was an expression adopted by Western journalists which it would be hard for the Kremlin to use: that would mean denying the dogma of political continuity and admitting to a reversal. The nationalistic uproar within the U.S.S.R. was still tremendous, so the image the Kremlin intended to give the country was applied only in small strokes—and at first only for foreign consumption.

For many years now, the Foreign Languages Publishing House in Moscow had offered French students a manual entitled *Le Russe* by Nina Potapova. Until Stalin's death, beginners learned from the sixth lesson—and even before reaching the rudiments of the declensions— this basic vocabulary:

"The battle is under way. We advance. The tanks go first, the infantry behind them. We have weapons: rifles, tommy guns, machine guns, mortars. The soldiers shoot. Bullets fly. . . . The artillery is behind. The colonel shouts: 'Fire.'" And so on.

In the editions after Stalin, the sixth lesson was modified, and one learned the following expressions: "It is dawn. The sun rises. The earth is reborn. . . . It is evening. The kolkhozians rest. An accordion plays."

37

Horrible Workers

April 4. A month had passed since the news of Stalin's cerebral congestion had been made public. On the second page of *Pravda,* a "communiqué from the Ministry of the Interior" startled the entire country by announcing that the conspiracy of the men in white had never existed, that the doctor-assassins were innocent and had been rehabilitated.

"It has been established that the depositions of the accused, which supposedly confirmed the accusations hurled at them, were obtained by workers in the investigative service of the former Ministry of State Security by investigative methods rigorously forbidden by Soviet laws."

For the first time, Soviet authorities officially admitted that the police used torture to obtain confessions.

Small groups formed on Gorky Street to read the newspapers that had been pasted on the walls. An old man smiled and said: "There it is!" Nobody answered him. After twenty-five years of silence, the Russians had learned to keep their mouths shut.

At the "Colony of Rehabilitation Through Work No. 1" on Shabolovka Street, the head accountant and the "adjunct jurist" dissected the communiqué. The accountant Pyotr Kuzmich Mnyov was a lieutenant in the Quartermaster Corps. The "jurist" was Leonid Finkelstein, a prisoner who was about to be freed. Something intrigued them in the communiqué. It was divided into two symmetrical sections. First of all, there was a list of the doctors arrested, fifteen names.* After that came the names of the doctors who had been released from prison. If all of the accused had been judged innocent,

---

* This is the complete list. We must remember that only nine names were released to the public on January 13 (see page 106).

the two lists should be exactly the same. But the second list was a trifle shorter.

"Let's work like good accountants," Mnyov said. "We'll put a check next to the names."

The checking was soon over. Professors M. G. Kogan and Etinger figured among the people who had been mistakenly arrested, but they could not be found among those who had been freed.

"Well," said the lieutenant. "Those two went into prison but they did not come out."

With their congenital feeling for the implied unstated, Soviet readers understood what the communiqué had failed to explain: The "inadmissible methods of investigation" utilized "by the workers in the investigative service"—those horrible workers—had transformed two of the accused into corpses.

Right below the communiqué, *Pravda* had run a big article on fruit trees. Looking carefully, a little lower down, attentive readers discovered a very short paragraph announcing that the Supreme Soviet had annulled the decree which conferred the Order of Lenin on Dr. Lidia Timashuk, the woman who had denounced the "assassins in white coats."

The Israeli delegation to the United Nations immediately made it known that it would bring the problem of anti-Semitism in the U.S.S.R. before the international organization. The entire Soviet press had begun to condemn "all propaganda for racial or national discrimination." It rehabilitated, posthumously but with special and warm emphasis, the actor Solomon Mikhoels, "this honest citizen, this great artist of the people of the U.S.S.R." The same person who, just two months before, had been labeled a paid agent of American Zionists.

In the world at large, those who for the last twenty years had denounced the Moscow trials as faked, the confessions extorted, now triumphed. But Communist militants, as a group, did not even flinch. For them, crimes unmasked in the inner circles of the Soviet police were mere accidents. "We belong to an army—and to an encircled army," said an old member of the French Communist Party. "When some lance corporal gets the clap, an entire army should not feel dishonored."

Yet Beria, with his blunt communiqué, had put a crack—still almost invisible—in the principle of infallibility.

Stripped of the Order of Lenin but still on the job, Dr. Timashuk pursued an inglorious career as X-ray technician at the Kremlin Hospital, where she met again the colleagues she had had arrested—at least those who had survived. But not everyone was treated with the same gentleness as she. Ryumin, the former Deputy Minister of State

Security, who had personally directed the investigation of the "men in white," was arrested together with a number of his colleagues. This little man with the look of a pink cherub was actually a frightful torturer. Moreover, it was convenient to make him rather than the former Minister Ignatyev shoulder the heaviest responsibility for the affair. Ignatyev was loyal to Khrushchev, and Khrushchev defended him tooth and nail. So, for the moment, he was only criticized for "political blindness and credulity." He did not follow his ex-subordinate to jail, but he lost his new and prestigious position of Secretary of the Central Committee, to which Khrushchev had just assigned him.

Behind the pompous words, the new scandal fouled up the settlement of accounts. For three months, Ignatyev had given Beria's men in the heart of the security organization some bad moments. Now it was his turn. Furthermore, what most struck the political class about the news of the freeing of the doctors was the signature: "Communiqué of the Ministry of the Interior." In other words, Beria. This sounded like a challenge to the completely new practices of the collective leadership. By mounting all alone this operation from which he gained a certain popularity, the Georgian showed that he could outmaneuver his colleagues. Would he try to get rid of them tomorrow?

To denounce the torturers of yesterday, one had to borrow phrases from their dreadful vocabulary: "Spies and diversionists, bearers of bourgeois ideology, degenerates. . . . Against these true enemies, open and recognized, of the people, these enemies of the Soviet State, it is always necessary to keep our powder dry." [1] Again, the style of the purges. Who would be the "enemies of the people" tomorrow?

38

Death of an Executioner

*She conceived and bore a son, and he
called his name Beriah, because it went
evil with his house.*

—1 Chron. 7:23

On July 4, 1953, the ambassadors of the United States, Great
Britain and France in Moscow held a sort of war council. After ex-
changing information, the three diplomats agreed that it seemed something had happened to Beria, number two man in the new leadership.

A week earlier, on June 27, a great deal of time had been devoted
to looking at the official box at the Bolshoi during the second performance of Yury Shaporin's opera *The Decembrists.* All the regular members of the Presidium were present in a group. Only one was missing:
Beria.

About that time, unusual troop movements were reported in Moscow. Armored cars, which never entered the capital except for parades
and military ceremonies, and columns of tanks had been seen unex-
pectedly rolling up the main streets, sowing panic among the local
traffic cops. "What is happening, Comrade Commander? Would you
please make a detour around the city? You're going to wreck our
streets."

The new American ambassador was Charles "Chip" Bohlen, who
after two months had taken over the post left vacant the previous autumn by the forced departure of George Kennan. According to his
informants, the troops seen in Moscow came from two divisions based
in the Urals and were en route to Germany, theoretically for maneuvers. But there was no justification for their entry into the capital. Louis

Joxe, the French Ambassador, confirmed that one night he was awakened by an unusual sound of traffic beneath the windows of his residence in the Bolshaya Yakimanka—on Great Saint Joachim Street. A *coup d'état* seemed to be in the air.

The three ambassadors informed their governments of their suppositions. But for several days there was no confirmation of anything.

On July 9, the Muscovite engineer V.Ch., bachelor and *bon vivant*, spent the evening drinking with some comrades. He went to bed about four in the morning, very drunk.

He lived in a *kommunalka*, one of those communal apartments shared by several tenants. It was difficult for him to sleep off his vodka in peace. About eight o'clock, half-awakened by the noise of a radio from an adjoining room, he vaguely heard: "Beria . . . enemy of the people . . . excluded from the Central Committee and from the ranks of the Communist Party of the Soviet Union . . . stripped of his post as Minister of the Interior."

"I must absolutely stop drinking," V.Ch. said to himself, very upset. "Beria—an enemy of the people? Soon I'll be seeing pink elephants. Tomorrow I go on the wagon." He dove under the covers again and went back to sleep, feeling very sick.

Two hours later, he woke up again. In the next room, the radio was still screaming: "Beria . . . foreign agent. . . . The criminal activities of Lavrenty Pavlovich Beria have been brought before the Supreme Court of the U.S.S.R."

"Well," our friend thought, reassured, "I wasn't delirious."

In Siberia, it was already afternoon. In a village of about fifty houses, near Kazachinskoye, some deportees were standing in line before the office of the local MVD commander. It was "registration" day. The deportees, let us remember, were not kept in prison like the *Zeks*, but confined to residence here. Once a month, they had to present themselves at the office to prove that they were really here.

The line grew longer. Lithuanians, Estonians, Ukrainians, and Russians, all the nations of the empire and all social conditions, from laborer to man of letters—all of them plunged in the same misery, cutting timber in the sawmills or laying tracks on the railroad.

Suddenly, a deportee ran up, panting. "Brothers, let me go in without standing on line and I swear to you that you will see a show such as you have never seen in your entire life," he shouted.

There was such urgency in his voice that they let him pass through without a word. He went in to the commander, purposely leaving the double door wide open so that his comrades could hear him. On the

wall of the office, which smelled of dust and glue, hung a superb portrait of Beria, looking a good ten years younger than in real life.

"Citizen Commander," said the deportee, "when are you going to
get rid of the portrait of this traitor to his country, this imperialist
spy, this scoundrel Beria?"

The officer thought he hadn't heard him right and made him
repeat his words. Then, putting on his visored cap so as to look more
official:

"Hey, there, two men come here immediately! . . . Deportee B., do
you want to repeat before witnesses what you just said to me?"

The man repeated everything, even adding a few more insulting
epithets.

"Deportee B.," the commander sternly roared, "you are arrested
for insulting Lavrenty Pavlovich Beria, member of the Presidium of
the Central Committee."

"Citizen Commander, don't be stupid. Haven't you been listening to
the radio?"

The deportee spoke with so much conviction that the commander,
seized by a doubt, picked up his telephone and called the radio center
from which the Moscow broadcasts are transmitted to the loudspeakers.

"Petya? How are things? By the way, is there something interesting
in the news just now? . . . Oh! . . . Oh! . . . Ohhh!"

With each successive Oh! his voice became more and more
cavernous.

Sadly putting down the receiver, the commander lifted his fine cap
and announced in a remarkably stifled voice:

"Deportees, for today registration is ended."

A witness of the scene told me twenty years later: "One must live
through such a day to know what real happiness is!"

For an entire week, throughout the U.S.S.R., meetings were held to
heap opprobrium upon the "contemptible, vile Beria, thrice cursed,
rabid enemy of our people." On thousands of platforms, writers, scholars, factory managers, Stakhanovites—all the politico-economic cadres
of the country—paraphrased for hours the communiqués of July 10,
painting over and over again the portrait of the most infamous of the
infamous, the traitor of traitors. This "mercenary of foreign imperialist
forces" had made his first contacts with the British secret service in
1919! A number of years had passed before he could be exposed.

Curiously enough, the official accusations, when their extravagances
were filtered out, left the picture of a semi-liberal. When they
affirmed that this "agent of international imperialism" wished "to

restore capitalism and re-establish the rule of the bourgeoisie," [1] the rhetoric appeared quite obviously delirious. But, in order to bolster more modest accusations, there was mention of certain approaches made in the spring by Beria's secret agents to London and Washington, approaches which, aimed at precipitating a détente, could well have alarmed the orthodox. [*]

When *Pravda* accused Beria of having wanted "to undermine the kolkhozes," one thought of the way he had slowed down the collectivization of the land in Georgia and of his resistance to Khrushchev's "agro-cities." And when it declared that he had tried to "activate bourgeois nationalist elements," one was forced to acknowledge that in fact, from May to June, the imposition of force by the Russians on the outlying regions had somewhat diminished and that Beria had appointed several natives to important local posts.

Had this man covered with blood, this great boss of the repressive apparatus, played the liberal? Why not? It was indeed he who, on the day of Stalin's funeral, had made the unexpected reference to the "rights inscribed in the Constitution." He had also freed the doctors, without fear of accusations against his own police.

There was not a sign of inner conviction in all this. Nobody had ever attempted to endow this pallid executioner with a sense of morality. On the other hand, it was known that he wanted to be popular. It was also known that he was a "realist" with all the skepticism of an old policeman. In short, he was capable of anything and everything, even a show of tolerance.

In order to win, he would have had to act less like a dilettante and devote less time to pleasure and more to hard work. He had undoubtedly underestimated the vigilant alarm of his peers, who were very aware of the danger he held for them—the danger of being thrown out of power, the danger of a bullet in the back of the neck.

The official communiqués repeated incessantly that Beria had wanted "to put the Ministry of the Interior above the Party and the government." There was really no need for this insistence. Everyone understood that it was a struggle for power and, without a doubt, for life.

After a week of ferocious ranting, the Beria affair subsided and then sank into the depths of silence. Much later, at the end of the year, it would be announced that the investigation had ended and that Beria had been judged in a secret trial and executed on the spot, on December 23, with six of his accomplices, nearly all Georgians and all high-ranking police officials. As though to emphasize even more strongly

[*] Several observers mentioned these approaches, notably Joseph Alsop in the New York *Herald Tribune*.

that this crushing of the police was the work of the army, the announcement added that the special tribunal which handed down the sentence was presided over by Marshal Konev.

But were there really a tribunal and a sentence? Could those concerned have waited six months before killing the most powerful man in the U.S.S.R., or have found walls thick enough to make sure that he didn't escape? In short, had Beria really survived his arrest until December?

Some people thought so. In September, 1953, it was rumored in circles close to the army that Beria was still alive and was being kept in prison by reliable military men. The same source added that they had been careless enough to let him keep his pince-nez, that he had used it to sever his veins, and that they were in fact still treating him.

The popular story depicted Beria stalking about his cell like a wild animal in its cage and shouting: "A woman! I want a woman! Bring me a woman!"

In 1969, Professor Aleksei Yakushev, a Soviet citizen who escaped to the West, would describe in the *Spiegel* a session of Beria's trial that he and about a hundred carefully screened spectators had personally witnessed. This assertion contradicts the official communiqué, which had carefully stated that the trial had been held behind locked doors.

However, in a series of confidential remarks, above all to Pierre Commin, adjunct Secretary General of the SFIO, to the Italian Communists Negarville and Paietta, and also, it seems, to the Hungarian Communist leader Rakosi—and a number of years later, to Gomulka and Cyrankiewicz—Nikita Khrushchev bluntly denied the existence of any sort of trial. In his remarks to all these different people, there was not the slightest variation on one essential point: Beria was brought to a meeting of the Presidium at the Kremlin and never came out alive. At a signal already agreed upon, marshals and generals waiting in a nearby room burst in to arrest the Minister of the Interior, who was shot then and there.

But, later, Khrushchev contradicted himself wantonly. First, he described Beria strangled in his chair, then he described him struck down by a shot from a revolver held—depending on his inspiration of the moment—by Marshal Zhukov, by General Moskalenko, by Mikoyan, or by Khrushchev himself.

Besides, one can see in Khrushchev's own memoirs, which appeared in the West in 1970, that he kept the story of the ambush at the Kremlin, but suppressed the immediate murder, again replacing it with a trial.

Historians have failed to be logical about this uncertain story. The safest thing to do was to kill Beria right away. But wasn't this terribly frustrating for his captors? Shouldn't they first have tried to extort all the secrets they could from this man who knew everything about everybody? Should he not have been kept alive for questioning—undoubtedly in accordance with the techniques of criminal investigation which he himself had so brilliantly employed?

One fact is certain: Whether his death was summary or after a certain reprieve, Beria was neutralized by June 26, and, at this time, a radical purge whose victims numbered in the hundreds either liquidated or imprisoned his collaborators. A new Minister of the Interior was appointed—Kruglov, a relatively minor personage—as well as a new General Prosecutor, Rudenko, who had been one of the prosecutors at the Nuremburg trial. The collective leadership could breathe a sigh of relief.

According to a version neither more nor less dubious than the others, the members of the Presidium had, by arresting Beria, forestalled in time a coup he had been plotting. He had planned to arrest his rivals on June 27, as they came out of a performance of *The Decembrists* at the Bolshoi; but they had already gotten rid of him.

To tell the truth, the people did not care very much whether Beria was already dead or merely about to die. They had realized by then that the Georgian was in any event about to be swallowed by the trapdoor of history and that, even better, he would be the scapegoat for all the sins of the Stalinist epoch.

The campaign of meetings was not yet over when all sorts of stories began circulating about his orgies, the girls he had kidnapped, the children he had raped, and the "Athenian nights" he had organized in his own private "deer park." It was the most astonishing public washing of dirty linen which this extremely prudish regime had ever indulged in.

To better confirm Beria in his role of scapegoat, incorrigible public gossip immediately discovered that he had Jewish blood. For the moment, official anti-Semitism was lying low, but old habits are not so easily shaken off. It was suddenly remembered that the new enemy of the people was born in the Mingrel, a region where there were some villages clustered around their synagogues. Moreover, a Beriah, son of Ephraim and direct descendant of Abraham, figures in the Old Testament in the First Book of Chronicles. The name, with its lugubrious omen, comes from two Hebrew words that mean "in misfortune."

It goes without saying that if Beria were alive, nobody would have been permitted to spread such ideas.

The military men who contributed their weighty support would be rewarded. That very year, Marshal Zhukov would return to the Central Committee as a full-fledged member and General Moskalenko would begin a brilliant ascent which would eventually make him the commander-in-chief of the rocket section of the army. This was the first example in Soviet history of an open intervention of the high command in a political conflict. But this army which loaned its tanks was not the sort of army that would make a *coup d'état*. The generals could—and they did not limit themselves in this regard—constitute a pressure group. But they were much too much Party men to become the moving spirit behind a group of putschists.

Beria's supporters would pay their master's debts for two long years. Four of them, including Abakumov, the former Minister of State Security, would not be shot until December, 1954. Even later, at the end of 1955, six high police officers would be executed in Georgia "for having actively participated in the anti-Soviet activities of the people's enemy, Beria." This purge had a long memory.

But after that, customs underwent a change. It actually appeared that the worst survivals of the past were concentrated in the person of Beria. Now, the leaders would no longer kill each other. Some were still excommunicated, but, with a touch of courtesy, they were given good pensions, a few lines in the dictionaries, and even a short obituary notice in *Pravda* at the end of their days, instead of the anonymity of a common grave.

Beria and his followers were the last dignitaries to be liquidated in the Stalinist manner: outrage—death—oblivion.

An abyss of oblivion. Twenty years later, the third volume of the *Great Soviet Encyclopedia* runs blithely from BARI to BRACELET, ignoring that a man named Beria ever existed—the same person who occupied a page and a half in its previous editions.

One of the prime concerns from July, 1953, onward was making sure that the many statues of Beria which adorned his native Caucasus would vanish. They were thrown at night into the rivers and streams.

One summer Sunday, a Georgian Chekist in a festive mood took a joyous dive into the Bioni River. He was dragged out half suffocated, half drowned, having swallowed a great gulp of water due to the shock of surprise and fear. As he had plunged into the clear water, he had seen the bronze visage of his former chief staring at him with immense eyes through his pince-nez.

Epilogue

May 3, 1953. Stalin, who had a flair for striking formulas which would be easily remembered, seems to have chosen the date of his death to facilitate the work of future school children.

This last neat trick didn't work. His own people consigned him to oblivion. On June 10, *Pravda* exhumed from a rather obscure page of Karl Marx an expression which soon became very fashionable: "the cult of personality."

"The great leaders of the working class, Marx, Engels, Lenin, *and Stalin*, by emphasizing the determining role of the popular masses in history, have energetically opposed the cult of personality."

And Stalin. Here he was even compelled to participate in his own dethronement.

Vasily, the prodigal son, the brilliant air force general, vanished for a few weeks after his father's death. Then he was abruptly informed of his own swindles, violent acts, and denunciations. On April 29, he was thrown into jail, sentenced to serve eight years in prison. Freed and exiled to Kazan, the son of the great Stalin would die in March, 1962, at the premature age of forty-one, totally riddled with alcohol, after one last binge.

Svetlana, Stalin's favorite child, gave up the burdensome name of Stalin in 1957 and took the name of her mother, who died so tragically —Alliluyeva. A stranger to politics, concerned with her own destiny as a woman, she withdrew and dreamed of escape.

On March 6, 1967, fourteen years after her father's death, she would take advantage of a sojourn in India to request political asylum in the West. She would settle in the United States, where she would marry. The sober irony of history: The last of Joseph Vissarionovich Stalin's grandchildren would be born in California and would be an American citizen.

The Kremlin would be opened to the public rather quickly. People would be admitted to look at the palace. The notables took pleasure in their new security. Symbolically, a change in "the regulation of the day's work in ministries and administrative offices" invited them to leave their offices at six in the afternoon, instead of staying up till dawn in fear and trembling.

In 1956, Khrushchev swept away the shy reticences, the silence. On the night between February 24 and 25, in the course of a session of the Twentieth Congress held behind locked doors, he denounced at length Stalin's misdeeds and crimes. The Soviet press would never admit the existence of this report, but it was read to all the members of the Party, and even, in the course of "enlarged meetings," to the mass of the workers. Within three months, the majority of the active population of the U.S.S.R. knew about it. Prepared for it a long time, they generally accepted without difficulty the death of their god. For certain people, however, it was a terrible blow. There were suicides. And this bitter remark which I heard one night from the mouth of an old militant:

"Stalin? In his time, all the Communists of the world were happy."

In October, 1961, his body was taken out of the tomb and buried beneath the walls of the Kremlin among graves of other well-known leaders, next to a walk bordered with blue spruce trees. At first there was nothing but a simple stone with his name on it. Then, in 1970, there was a small bust which put Stalin on the same plane as Dzerzhinsky, Kalinin, Frunze, and Zhdanov, his neighbors in this small cemetery.

Was Stalin inevitable? Was he useful? What did he represent: a Russian phenomenon? a consequence of the Marxist-Leninist revolution? or an aberrant deviation from Leninism?

Some scholars in the West likened him to Ivan the Terrible and dismissed him with "That's the sort of country it is, what do you expect?" A convenient form of geopolitics.

Others recalled the tensions of the beginning of his reign, the backwardness of the people, the merciless hatreds sharpened by the Civil War, and later, the Nazi threat. Could anyone rule over all that without an iron fist? They also measured the road covered under his rule: a country of fields and forests had become the second most powerful industrial country on the face of the globe, the illiterates had learned how to read, and Hitler was vanquished. They also argued: A barbarian had fought against barbarism.

But can one wipe out the absurd and terrifying side of all this? The country's elite, intellectuals and politicans, officers and engineers, were beheaded. Whole generations were decimated—by repressions, purges, and by the war which Stalin was incapable of preparing for. These were terrible blows which slowed up and impeded the country's development and checked its demographic growth, leaving its immense plains underpopulated in the face of a swarming, tormented Asia.

Can one ignore the fact that Stalin humiliated the spirit, trampled on the weak, set a prosperous and arrogant bureaucracy above the people?

Can one forgive him for having killed not only men but their faith?

Can one absolve him of being the man who crushed and exterminated people until the end of his days, at a time when the real enemies of his revolution had long been defeated and when nothing moved him but the devouring logic of force, the bitter thirst for power?

Appendixes

*Official Communiqués and Medical Bulletins
Concerning Stalin's Illness and Death*

Appendix I

Tass Communiqué Announcing
Joseph Stalin's Illness

The Central Committee of the Communist Party of the Soviet Union and the Council of Ministers of the U.S.S.R. announce the misfortune which has befallen our country and our people—the grave illness of J. V. Stalin.

During the night between March 1 and 2, Comrade Stalin, while in his apartment in Moscow, was struck by a cerebral hemorrhage affecting the vital areas of his brain. Comrade Stalin has lost consciousness. His right arm and right leg have been paralyzed. He has lost the ability to speak. Serious cardiac and respiratory complications have arisen.

The highest medical authorities have been selected to undertake Comrade Stalin's treatment: Professor of Therapy P. E. Lukomsky; the full members of the Academy of Medicine of the U.S.S.R. Professor N. V. Konovalov, neurologist, Professor E. M. Tareyev, therapist, Professor I. N. Filimonov, neurologist, Professor R. A. Tkachev, neurologist; Professor I. S. Glazunov, neurologist; Ivanov-Nezmanov, lecturer in therapy. Comrade Stalin's treatment is being carried out under the direction of the Minister of Public Health of the U.S.S.R., A. F. Tretyakov, and the head of the Kremlin's health service, I. I. Kuperin.

Comrade Stalin's treatment has been placed under the constant surveillance of the Central Committee of the Communist Party of the U.S.S.R. and the Soviet government.

Due to the gravity of Comrade Stalin's condition, the Central Committee of the Communist Party and the government of the U.S.S.R. have considered it indispensable to publish from today on medical bulletins on Joseph Vissarionovich Stalin's state of health.

The Central Committee of the Communist Party of the Soviet Union and the Council of Ministers of the U.S.S.R., as well as our Party and the entire Soviet people, have full awareness of the fact that Comrade Stalin's grave illness will entail his nonparticipation in the direction of affairs for some time.

The Central Committee and the Council of Ministers have taken into consideration, with all necessary seriousness, the direction of the Party and the country, and all the circumstances relating to the provisional withdrawal of Comrade Stalin from the activities of the direction of the Party and the State.

The Central Committee and the Council of Ministers express the conviction that during these grave days our Party and the entire Soviet people will give proof of the greatest unity, cohesion, force of character and vigilance, will redouble their energy for the establishment of Communism in our country, and will gather even more tightly around the Central Committee and the government of the U.S.S.R.

Appendix II

Final Medical Communiqué on the Illness and Death of Joseph Stalin

During the night between March 1 and 2, Joseph Vassarionovich Stalin was stricken by a hemorrhage in the left cerebral hemisphere, because of high blood pressure and arteriosclerosis, which caused a paralysis of the right side of his body and a loss of consciousness which remained constant.

From the first day of his illness, there were noticeable signs of respiratory difficulties resulting from the disturbance of the functions of the nerve centers.

These difficulties increased from day to day. They had the character of so-called periodic respiration, with long pauses (Cheyne-Stokes respiration).

During the night between March 2 and 3, the respiratory difficulties at moments assumed a threatening nature. Since the beginning of the illness, there had also been observed notable changes affecting the cardiovascular system, that is, elevated arterial tension, an acceleration and irregular rhythm of the pulse, a vacillating arhythmia and dilation of the heart.

In connection with the accentuation of the respiratory and circulatory difficulties, signs of oxygen insufficiency appeared on March 3. From the first days of the illness, his temperature was high and observation was made of a very marked leucocytosis, indicating that centers of inflammation had developed in the lungs.

The last day of the illness was marked by a brusque over-all aggravation of his general state and by a repeated increase in heightened cardiovascular insufficiency (collapse).

An electrocardiogram showed a grave disturbance in the circulation of the blood in the blood vessels of the heart together with the appearance of inflammatory lesions in the cardiac muscle.

During the second half of March 5, the state of the patient worsened with great speed. His respiration became superficial, light, and extremely fast. His pulse beat went up to 140–50 a minute; the pulse became very weak.

At 9:50 at night, the cardiovascular and respiratory insufficiencies were accentuated and Joseph Vissarionovich Stalin passed away.

Signed: Tretyakov, Minister of Health of the U.S.S.R.; Kuperin, head of the Kremlin's health service; Professor Lukomsky, head of the therapeutic services of the Ministry of Health; Professors Konovalov, Myasnikov, and Tareyev, members of the Academy of Medicine of the U.S.S.R.; Professor Filimonov, corresponding member of the Academy of Medicine; Professors Glazunov and Tkachev; Lecturer Ivanov-Nezmanov.

Appendix III

*Official Communiqué Announcing
the Death of Stalin*

In the name of the Central Committee
of the Communist Party of the Soviet Union
In the name of the Council of Ministers of the U.S.S.R.
and the Presidium of the Supreme Soviet of the U.S.S.R.

To all the Members of the Party,
To all the Workers in the Soviet Union.

Dear Comrades and Friends,

It is with a feeling of profound grief that the Central Committee of
the Communist Party of the Soviet Union, the Council of Ministers of
the U.S.S.R., and the Presidium of the Supreme Soviet of the U.S.S.R.
announce to the Party and all the workers of the Soviet Union that
Joseph Vissarionovich Stalin, President of the Council of Ministers of
the U.S.S.R. and Secretary-General of the Central Committee of the
Communist Party of the Soviet Union, passed away on March 5 at
9:50 at night after a grave illness.

The heart of Joseph Vissarionovich Stalin, Lenin's comrade-in-arms
and the inspired continuator of his work, wise leader and teacher of
the Communist Party and the Soviet people, has stopped beating.

Stalin's name is infinitely dear to our Party, to the Soviet people,
and to the workers of the entire world. With Lenin, Comrade Stalin
created the powerful Communist Party, trained and hardened it; with
Lenin, Comrade Stalin was the inspiration and guide of the Great
October Socialist Revolution, the founder of the world's first Socialist State. Continuing the immortal work of Lenin, Comrade Stalin
led the Soviet people to the historic victory and worldwide influence
of Socialism in our country. Comrade Stalin led our country to victory

205

over Fascism in World War II, a victory which radically changed the international situation. Comrade Stalin armed the Party and the entire Soviet People with the great and luminous program of building Communism in the U.S.S.R.

The death of Comrade Stalin, who with abnegation put his whole life at the service of the great cause of Communism, is a cruel loss for our Party, for the workers of the country of the Soviets and the entire world.

The report of Comrade Stalin's death will echo sorrowfully in the hearts of workers, kolkhozians, intellectuals, and all the laborers of our nation, in the hearts of the fighters of our valiant army and our valiant navy, in the hearts of millions of workers in all the countries of the world.

During these sad days, all the peoples of our country will unite even more tightly in a great fraternal family, under the tested leadership of the Communist Party created and educated by Lenin and Stalin.

The Soviet people continue to have complete confidence in and ardent love for their beloved Communist Party, for they know that the supreme law of all the Party's activity is to serve the interests of the people.

Laborers, kolkhozians, and Soviet intellectuals, all the workers of our country, will continue unflinchingly the policy elaborated by our Party, which responds to the vital interests of the workers and aims at the continuous strengthening of the power of our Socialist homeland.

The correctness of the Communist Party's policy has been verified by long years of struggle. It has led the workers of the country of the Soviets to the historic victories of Socialism. Inspired by this policy, the peoples of the Soviet Union go forward with assurance, under the leadership of the Party, towards new successes of Communist edification in our country.

The workers of our country know that the continuous improvement of their material well-being in all strata of the population—workers, kolkhozians, and intellectuals—the maximum satisfaction of the ceaselessly growing material and cultural needs of the entire society have always been and still are the object of particular solicitude on the part of the Communist Party and the Soviet government.

The Soviet people know that the defense capability and the power of the Soviet State have grown and are strengthened, that the Party reinforces as much as possible the Soviet army, navy, and intelligence services with the aim of constantly improving our ability to make a lightning-like response to any aggressor.

The foreign policy of the Communist Party and the government of the Soviet Union was and remains an unalterable policy for the maintenance and consolidation of peace, the struggle against the preparation and launching of a new war, a policy of international cooperation and the development of commercial relations with all countries.

Faithful to the flag of the international proletariat, the peoples of the Soviet Union consolidate and develop a fraternal friendship with the great Chinese people and with the workers of all the countries of the people's democracy; they consolidate and develop friendly relations with the workers of the capitalist and colonial countries who struggle for the cause of peace, democracy, and socialism.

Dear Comrades and Friends!

Our Communist Party is the great force which orients and directs the Soviet people in the struggle for the building of Communism. The steel-like unity and monolithic cohesion of the ranks of our Party are the principal conditions of its strength and its power. Our task is to preserve like the apple of one's eye the unity of the Party, to train Communists in carrying out active political struggles for the application of the policy and decisions of the Party, to reinforce even more the bonds which unite the Party to all laborers, workers, kolkhozians, and intellectuals, for in this indissoluble alliance with the people reside our Party's strength and invincibility.

The Party considers one of its essential tasks to be the education of Communists and of all workers in a spirit of great political vigilance, of steadfastness, and of firmness in the struggle against its enemies inside and outside the country.

Speaking in these days of sorrow to the Party and the people, the Central Committee of the Communist Party of the Soviet Union, the Council of Ministers of the U.S.S.R., and the Presidium of the Supreme Soviet of the U.S.S.R. express the firm conviction that the Party and all the workers of our country will gather even more tightly around the Central Committee and the Soviet government and will mobilize all their forces and all their creative energy for the great cause of building Communism in our country.

The immortal name of Stalin will always live in the hearts of the Soviet people and the hearts of all progressive humanity.

Long live the great, all-powerful doctrine of Marx-Engels, Lenin-Stalin!

Long live our powerful Socialist country!

Long live our heroic Soviet people!

Long live the Great Communist Party of the Soviet Union!

The Central Committee	The Council of	The Presidium of
of the Communist Party	Ministers of the	the Supreme Soviet
of the Soviet Union.	U.S.S.R.	of the U.S.S.R.

This communiqué was dated March 5, 1953. Tass began distributing it a little after four o'clock (Moscow time) on the morning of March 6.

Appendix IV

Pathological and Anatomical Examination of the Body of Joseph Stalin

As the result of a pathological and anatomical examination, an important center of hemorrhage was discovered in the region of subcortical centers of the left hemisphere of the brain. This hemorrhage destroyed important areas of the brain and provoked irreversible disturbances of the respiration and circulation. Besides the cerebral hemorrhage, observation was made of a considerable hypertonic disturbance of the left ventricle of the heart, important hemorrhages of the cardiac muscle and in the mucous of the stomach and intestine, and arteriosclerotic modifications of particularly important vessels in the brain's arteries. This process was the result of high blood pressure. The results of the pathological and anatomical examination have entirely confirmed the diagnosis established by the professors of medicine who treated J. V. Stalin.

The facts of the pathologico-anatomical examination have established the irreversible character of J. V. Stalin's illness since the appearance of the cerebral hemorrhage. That is why the energetic measures of the treatment could not produce positive results, nor prevent the fatal outcome.

Signed: A. F. Tretyakov, Minister of Health of the U.S.S.R.; I. L. Kuperin, head of the Kremlin's health service; N. N. Anisimov, president of the Academy of Medicine of the U.S.S.R.; Professor M. A. Skvortsov, member of the Academy of Medicine of the U.S.S.R.; Professor I. I. Strukov, corresponding member of the Academy of Medicine of the U.S.S.R.; Professor S. R. Mardashev, corresponding member of the Academy of Medicine of the U.S.S.R.; Professor B. I. Migunov, pathologist–anatomist-in-chief of the Ministry of Health of the U.S.S.R.; Professor A. V. Rusakov; Deputy Lecturer B. N. Uskov.

Pravda, March 7, 1953

Notes

Chapter 1

1. *Pravda,* May 22, 1935.
2. *Rodina Schastlivykh,* Moscow, Goslitizdat, 1937.

Chapter 2

1. Svetlana Alliluyeva, *Only One Year,* New York, Harper & Row, 1969.
2. *Pravda,* January 16, 1953: "Against subjectivist deformations in the natural sciences," by Yury Zhdanov.

Chapter 3

1. *Pravda,* September 20, 1952.
2. "Can you imagine the advantage we would have gotten from our Black Sea fleet if it could have reached the Volga during the battle of Stalingrad? Such a canal is of the greatest importance." Milovan Djilas, *Conversations with Stalin,* New York, Harcourt Brace Jovanovich, 1962.

Chapter 4

1. "The Siege" by Chakovsky, *Znamya.*
2. *Pravda,* December 1, 1952.

Chapter 6

1. *Pravda,* July 14, 1952. Similar letters also appeared in the newspapers on July 4, 18, 24, and 25, 1952.
2. Smolensk Archives, Instruction P. 6028 of May 6, 1933.
3. Winston Churchill, *The Second World War,* Vol. 4, Boston, Houghton Mifflin, 1950.
4. J. Stalin, *Economic Problems of Socialism in the U.S.S.R.* (October, 1952).

Chapter 7

1. Svetlana Alliluyeva, *Only One Year,* New York, Harper & Row, 1969.

Chapter 9

1. J. V. Stalin, *Dialectical Materialism and Historical Materialism* (in French), Algiers, Éditions Liberté, 1944.

Chapter 12

1. Transcript of the trial sent out by the Czech Press Agency and quoted by *Pravda* on November 21, 1952.
2. Ilya Ehrenberg, *People, Years, Life, Novy Mir,* April, 1965.

Chapter 13

1. *Pravda,* October 8, 1952.

Chapter 14

1. *Pravda,* March 5, 1953.
2. *Literaturnaya Gazeta,* August 2, 1951.
3. *Pravda,* September 20, 1952.
4. *Pravda,* September 21, 1952.
5. *Pravda,* May 29, 1952.
6. *Pravda,* December 12, 1952.

Chapter 15

1. *Pravda,* February 7, 1952.

Chapter 17

1. *Izvestia,* December 2, 1952; *Pravda,* December 10, 1952.
2. *Komsomolskaya Pravda,* December 11, 16, and 18, 1952.
3. *Journal of the Patriarchate of Moscow,* May, 1952.

Chapter 20

1. Ilya Ehrenburg, *People, Years, Life, Novy Mir,* April, 1965.

Chapter 21

1. See chiefly the *Pravdas* of August 4 and 11, 1952, October 27, 1952, November 18, 1952, February 1 and 7, 1953, etc.

Chapter 22

1. *Pravda,* February 20, 1953.

Chapter 25

1. Joseph Berger, *Shipwreck of a Generation,* London, Harvill Press.

Chapter 26

1. *Pravda,* February 5, 1953.

Chapter 29

1. Svetlana Alliluyeva, *Twenty Letters to a Friend,* New York, Harper & Row, 1967.

Chapter 31

1. Pavel Lichko's interview with Solzhenitsyn, published in *Les Droits de l'Écrivain* (Seuil).
2. *La Grève de Vorkouta,* Amiot-Dumont.
3. Yevgeny Yevtushenko, *A Precocious Autobiography,* New York, E. P. Dutton, 1963.

Chapter 34

1. *Pravda,* April 9, 1953.
2. *Pravda,* April 16, 1953.

Chapter 36

1. N. I. Godunov, *The Struggle of the French People Against the Nazi Occupation Army and Its Accomplices* (in Russian), Moscow, Gospolitizdat, 1953.

Chapter 37

1. *Pravda,* April 6, 1953.

Chapter 38

1. *Pravda,* July 10, 1953.

Bibliography

ALLILUYEVA, SVETLANA. *Only One Year* (Harper & Row).

———. *Twenty Letters to a Friend* (Harper & Row).

L'Anneé Politique, volumes 1952 and 1953 (P.U.F.).

ASTIER, EMMANUEL D'. *Les Grands* (N.R.F.).

———. *Sur Staline* (Plon).

BARBUSSE, HENRI. *Staline* (Flammarion).

BARTON, PAUL. *L'Institution Concentrationnaire en Russie* (Plon).

BEK, ALEKSANDR. *Novoye Naznacheniye* (Possev).

BERGER, JOSEPH R. *Shipwreck of a Generation* (Harvill Press).

CHALAMOV, VARLAM. *Récits de Kolyma* (Denoël).

CHURCHILL, WINSTON. *The Second World War*, 6 vols. (Houghton Mifflin).

CONQUEST, ROBERT. *The Great Terror: Stalin's Purge of the Thirties*, rev. ed. (Macmillan).

CONTE, ARTHUR. *Lénine, Staline* (Librairie Académique Perrin).

———. *Yalta ou le Partage du Monde* (Laffont).

CRANKSHAW, EDWARD. *Khrushchev: A Career* (Viking Press).

DE GAULLE, CHARLES. *The Complete War Memoirs of Charles De Gaulle* (Simon & Schuster).

DEDIDJER, VLADIMIR. *Tito Parle* (N.R.F.).

DEUTSCHER, ISAAC. *Stalin: A Political Biography*, 2d ed. (Oxford University Press).

DJILAS, MILOVAN. *Conversations with Stalin* (Harcourt Brace).

DUCLOS, JACQUES. *Mémoires, T.IV* (Fayard).

EHRENBURG, ILYA. *Lyudi, Gody, Zhizn* (*Novy Mir*, May, 1965).

ESTIER, CLAUDE. *Khrouchtchev* (Seghers).

FAINSOD, MERLE. *How Russia Is Ruled* (Harvard University Press).

———. *Smolensk Under Soviet Rule* (Harvard University Press).

FAUVET, JACQUES. *Histoire du Parti Communiste Français* (Fayard).

FEJTÖ, FRANÇOIS. *History of the People's Democracies* (Praeger).

FERON, BERNARD. *L'U.R.S.S. Sans Idoles* (Casterman).

FISCHER, LOUIS. *Vie et Mort de Staline* (Calmann-Lévy).

FONTAINE, ANDRÉ. *History of the Cold War*, Vols. 1 and 2 (Random).

Grande Encyclopédie Soviétique, 1947 and 1970 editions.

GUINZBOURG, EVGUENIA. *Le Vertige* (Seuil).

HARRIMAN, W. AVERILL. *Peace with Russia* (Simon & Schuster).

HINGLEY, RONALD. *The Russian Secret Police* (Simon & Schuster).

Joseph Staline, Brève Biographie (Moscow, Foreign Languages Publishing House).

KERBLAY, BASILE H. *Les Marchés Paysans en U.R.S.S.* (Mouton).

KHRUSHCHEV, NIKITA. *Khrushchev Remembers* (Little, Brown).

————. *Secret Report to the Twentieth Party Congress.*

K.P.S.S. *v Rezolyutsiakh* (Marx-Engels-Lenin Institute, 1953).

LECOEUR, AUGUSTE. *Le Partisan* (Flammarion).

LONDON, ARTHUR. *Confessions* (Morrow).

LUDWIG, EMIL. *Staline* (Deux Rives).

MANDELSTAM, NADEZHDA. *Hope Against Hope: A Memoir* (Atheneum).

MARIE, JEAN-JACQUES. *Staline* (Seuil).

MEDVEDEV, ROY. *De la Démocratie Socialiste* (Grasset).

————. *Fault-il Réhabiliter Staline?* (Seuil).

————. *Let History Judge* (Macmillan).

NEKRITCH, A. *L'Armée Rouge Asssassinée* (Grasset).

NICOLAEVSKI, BORIS. *Des Dirigeants Soviétiques et la Lutte Pour le Pouvoir* (Denoël).

NOBLE, JOHN. *I Was a Slave in Russia* (Devin-Adair).

PINEAU, CHRISTIAN. *Nikita Sergueevitch Khrouchtchev* (Librairie Académique Perrin).

RODER, BERNHARD. *Der Katorgan* (Kiepenheuer und Witsch).

SALISBURY, HARRISON. *Nine Hundred Days: The Siege of Leningrad* (Harper & Row).

SCHAPIRO, LEONARD. *De Lénine à Staline* (N.R.F.).

SCHOLMER, JOSEPH. *La Grève de Vorkouta* (Amiot-Dumont).

SOLJENITSYNE, ALEXANDRE. *Les Droits de l'Écrivain* (Seuil).

SORIA, GEORGES. *Comment Vivent les Russes?* (Editeurs Français Réunis).

SOUVARINE, BORIS, *Stalin: A Critical Survey of Bolshevism* (Octagon).

STAJNER, KARLO. *7,000 Dana u Sibiru* (Globus, Zagreb).

STALIN, JOSEF. *Dialectical and Historical Materialism* (International Publishers).

————. *Foundations of Leninism* (International Publishers).

————. *Marxism and the Problems of Linguistics* (China Books).

STALINE, JOSEPH. *Le Marxisme et la Question Nationale.*

————. *Les Problèmes Économiques du Socialisme en U.R.S.S.*

SULZBERGER, C. A. *Dans le Tourbillon de l'Histoire* (Albin Michel).

TATU, MICHEL. *Le Pouvoir en U.R.S.S.* (Grasset).

THOREZ, MAURICE. *Oeuvres Choisies* (Éditions Sociales).

TILLON, CHARLES. *Un Procès de Moscou à Paris* (Seuil).

TROTSKY, LEON. *Stalin: An Appraisal of the Man and His Influences* (Stein & Day).

VAILLAND, ROGER. *Écrits Intimes* (N.R.F.).

VILLEFOSSE, LOUIS DE. *L'Oeuf de Wyasma* (Julliard).

VILLEMAREST, P. F. DE. *La Marche au Pouvoir en U.R.S.S.* (Fayard).

VLADIMIROV, LEONID. *Rossia bez Prikras i Umolchanii* (Possev).

WALTER, GÉRARD. *Lénine* (Albin Michel).

YAKIR, PYOTR. *Une Enfance Russe* (Grasset).

YEVTUSHENKO, YEVGENY. *A Precocious Autobiography* (Dutton).

Praise for
Lazarus Awakening

"Joanna Weaver has done it again! By revealing the profound love Jesus had for Lazarus and the shocking life-after-death-on-earth He lavished on His friend, she skillfully points the reader to a vibrant choice—*abundant life!* If you long to wake up to God's unrestricted mercy, unconditional love, and supernatural power, read this book!"

—CAROL KENT, speaker and author of *Between a Rock
and a Grace Place*

"I sat down to read *Lazarus Awakening* and quickly realized this wasn't going to be a fluffy read I'd soon forget. I needed a pen and a journal and time to take notes. *Lazarus Awakening* is full of life-changing truth and application. Through Joanna's beautiful teaching, God is calling us all to resurrected life!"

—ANGELA THOMAS, speaker and best-selling author
of *Do You Know Who I Am?*

"*Lazarus Awakening* firmly establishes Joanna Weaver as one of the finest Christian writers of our time. Spiritually insightful, personally compelling, and magnificently written, this is one of the best books I've read in decades. We know she's walking the journey she's inviting us to take. I believe *Lazarus Awakening* will awaken many more believers to this extraordinarily gifted author."

—DONNA PARTOW, speaker and best-selling author
of *Becoming a Vessel God Can Use*

"The word that wouldn't leave me when reading *Lazarus Awakening* is *deep*. Joanna Weaver's words are rooted deep in Scripture, they dove deep into my heart, and they deeply impacted my emotions as I've come to a better understanding that Jesus loves me because of who I am, not what I've done. I cried many tears through these pages as my own questions were tackled, my own fears revealed. In the end I've come away with a deeper understanding of what it means to be loved by God. I am blessed, I am loved, and Jesus means more to me than ever before."

—TRICIA GOYER, author of *Blue Like Play Dough*

"If you worry that you are unworthy of God's favor or you wonder why He doesn't intervene to prevent your pain, *Lazarus Awakening* will take you straight to the heart of His love for you. With warmth, honesty, and rich biblical insights, Joanna Weaver deftly walks you through the agony of the loss and the triumph of resurrection to reveal how friendship with Jesus makes all the difference."

—JENNIFER ROTHSCHILD, author of *Lessons I Learned in the Dark* and *Me, Myself, and Lies* and founder of WomensMinistry.net

"I needed to read this book. You need to read this book. Sometimes we can get stuck in sin-sickness, living a Christian life that is neither glorious nor free. Joanna Weaver reminds us of all that Jesus offers us when we step out of the tomb of our own making into the joyous life He has created us for. *Lazarus Awakening* awakened something in me."

—SUSANNA FOTH AUGHTMON, author of *My Bangs Look Good and Other Lies I Tell Myself*

"Joanna Weaver has given us two insightful books about some of Jesus's closest friends—Martha and Mary. *Lazarus Awakening* completes the trilogy by taking an inspiring look at the life of their brother, Lazarus. A closer look at his story will help you draw closer to Christ as His intimate friend. I recommend it."

—ANN SPANGLER, author of *Praying the Names of God*

Lazarus
Awakening

JOANNA WEAVER

Finding Your Place *in the* Heart *of* God

Lazarus Awakening

WATERBROOK
PRESS

LAZARUS AWAKENING
PUBLISHED BY WATERBROOK PRESS
12265 Oracle Boulevard, Suite 200
Colorado Springs, Colorado 80921

ISBN 978-0-307-44496-7
ISBN 978-0-307-44497-4 (electronic)

Library of Congress Cataloging-in-Publication Data
Weaver, Joanna.
    Lazarus awakening : finding your place in the heart of God / Joanna Weaver. — 1st ed.
        p. cm.
    Includes bibliographical references.
    ISBN 978-0-307-44496-7 — ISBN 978-0-307-44497-4 (electronic)
    1. Lazarus, of Bethany, Saint. 2. Raising of Lazarus (Miracle) 3. Bible. N.T. John XI-XII, 1-11—Criticism, interpretation, etc. 4. God (Christianity)—Love. I. Title.
    BS2460.L3W43 2011
    226.5'06—dc22
                        2010037933

Printed in the United States of America
2011—First Edition

10 9 8 7 6 5 4 3 2 1

To my father, Cliff Gustafson.
Passionate follower and friend of Jesus Christ,
lover of people,
unwinder of graveclothes.

Daddy,
I met Jesus the day I met you.
Thank you for living your life out loud for God.
I'm so honored to be your daughter.

Lord! We entreat you,

make us truly alive.

SERAPION OF THMUIS (FOURTH CENTURY)

Contents

Acknowledgments

I've been told that before starting a musical composition, Johann Sebastian Bach would write two letters at the top of the score: *J.J.,* which stood for *Jesu Juva.* "Jesus, help." Those two words have been my daily prayer, and if this book ministers to you in any way, it is all due to Jesus Christ—my Helper and my Friend. More than ever before, I'm discovering the truth of these words: "Without Him, I can do nothing."

But I'm also grateful to a family who has loved and supported me through the process. To my dear parents, Cliff and Annette Gustafson. Thank you for interceding daily for me and this book and for making your house so much fun that at times Joshua didn't want to leave! To my older kids—Jessica, John Michael, and my precious new daughter-in-love, Kami—thank you for the encouraging text messages and phone prayers that carried me through. And to my husband, John. There just aren't enough words. I can't imagine who I'd be, let alone where I'd be, without you.

To all my dear friends at church and online who have lifted this book in prayer, especially Lorene Masters, Donna Partow, Jodi Detrick, Sherrie Snyder, and Angela Howard, thank you. Along with the others, your intercession literally put words on the page at times. Special thanks to Randy and Kay Creech for your friendship and generous hospitality. And to Shantel Watson and others who dropped off delicious meals and provided play dates for Josh.

To Wendy Lawton, whose insightful words—"It *is* a book"—launched the whole process of writing the story of Lazarus. You have my gratitude for being God's voice to my heart.

Without Laura Barker, Carol Bartley, and the amazing team of people at Water-Brook, this book wouldn't have been possible. Thank you for your extravagant patience and for believing in this book. You have been so gracious. May God richly bless each and every one of you.

To Anne Christian Buchanan. Thank you for helping me prune and shape my ideas and words. A skilled editor is truly a gift to a writer, and what a gift you've been to me. I thank God for you.

Finally, to Janet Kobobel Grant, my agent. Two are better than one, the Bible says, and oh how that's true of this author. Thank you for seeing something in me so many years ago and walking beside me every step of the way. I am blessed to have you in my life.

When Bach finished a piece of music, he would write another set of letters at the bottom of the page: *S.D.G.—Soli Deo Gloria,* which means "glory to God alone."

That is my prayer for this book as well.

Soli Deo Gloria.

Now a man named Lazarus was sick.
He was from Bethany, the village of
Mary and her sister Martha. This Mary,
whose brother Lazarus now lay sick,
was the same one who poured perfume on the Lord
and wiped his feet with her hair.
So the sisters sent word to Jesus, "Lord, the one you love is sick."

JOHN 11:1–3

seem to change what one friend calls an epidemic among Christian women (and many men as well): a barren heart condition I call love-doubt.

"Jesus loves me—this I know, for the Bible tells me so."[1] Many of us have sung the song since we were children. But do we really believe it? Or has Christ's love remained more of a fairy tale than a reality we've experienced for ourselves in the only place we can really know for sure?

Our hearts.

What Kind of Father Do You Have?

So much of our understanding of God's love is shaped by what we've experienced in life. Those who are abused or misused as children often struggle with the thought of God as a loving Parent, and even those raised in healthy homes can have distorted views of their heavenly Father. Which of the following misrepresentations are you most likely to struggle with?

Abusive Father: You never know what you are going to get with this kind of father. Will he be nice when he walks in, or will he hit you upside the head first chance he gets? His love is determined by his moods. You avoid him as much as possible.

But your true Father is "gracious and compassionate, slow to anger and rich in love" (Psalm 145:8).

Neglectful Father: This dad is far too busy (or just too selfish) to be concerned with you. He's got bigger, more important business to attend to than your insignificant needs. While he may be present in your life, he's largely unaccounted for. You have to take care of yourself.

But your true Father says, "Look at the birds of the air; they do not sow or reap or store away in barns, and yet your

Tale of the
Third Follower

I t's amazing that such a little space could make so much difference.
Just eighteen inches, give or take a few—that's all it needs to move. And yet, for many of us, getting God's love from our heads to our hearts may be the most diffi-cult—yet the most important—thing we ever attempt to do.

"I need to talk," Lisa whispered in my ear one day after women's Bible study. A committed Christian with a deep passion for the Lord, my friend had tears pooling in her dark eyes as we found a quiet corner where we could talk.

"I don't know what's wrong with me," she said, shaking her head as she looked down at her feet. "I could go to the worst criminal or a drug addict living on the street, and I could look him in the eye and tell him, 'Jesus loves you!' and mean it from the bottom of my heart.

"But, Joanna," she said, gripping my hand, "I can't seem to look in the mirro and convince myself."

Her words were familiar to me. I'd felt that same terrible disconnect early in m walk with the Lord. Hoping He loved me but never really knowing for sure. Sac I've heard the same lonely detachment echoed by hundreds of women I've talke around the country. Beautiful women. Plain women. Talented and not-so-tale women. Strong Christian women, deep in the Word and active in their churc well as women brand new to their faith. Personal attributes or IQs seem to m little. Whether they were raised in a loving home or an abusive situation, it c

He Loves Me...He Loves Me Not

You would think after accepting Christ at a young age and being raised in a loving Christian home with a loving, gracious father, I would have been convinced from the beginning that my heavenly Father loved me.

Me. With all my faults and failures. My silly stubbornness and pride.

But those very things kept me from really knowing Christ's love for the majority

---

heavenly Father feeds them. Are you not much more valuable than they?" (Matthew 6:26).

Biased Father: You know this father loves you—or at least you think he does. But he seems to shower affection and gifts on all the other kids, leaving you with leftovers and hand-me-downs. Bottom line: he has favorites, and you're not one of them. You had better get used to it.

But your true Father "does not show favoritism" (Romans 2:11).

Demanding Father: Perfect in nearly every way, this father demands that you be perfect as well. No matter how hard you try, it's never enough. While there are moments when he seems proud of you, they are few and far between. Instead, you carry a heavy sense of his disapproval.

But your true Father "has compassion on his children...for he knows how we are formed, he remembers that we are dust" (Psalm 103:13–14).

How great is the love the Father has lavished on us,
that we should be called children of God! And that is what we are!

1 John 3:1

of my early adult life. There was just so much to dislike, so much to disapprove of. How could God possibly love me? Even *I* wasn't that crazy about me.

For some reason, I'd come to see God as distant and somewhat removed. Rather than transposing upon God the model of my earthly father's balanced love—both unconditional yet corrective—I saw my heavenly Father as a stern teacher with a yardstick in His hand, pacing up and down the classroom of my life as He looked for any and all infractions. Measuring me against what sometimes felt like impossible standards and occasionally slapping me when I failed to make the grade.

Yes, He loved me, I supposed. At least that's what I'd been taught. But I didn't always feel God's love. Most of the time I lived in fear of the yardstick. Who knew when His judgment would snap down its disapproval, leaving a nasty mark on my heart as well as my soul?

As a result, I lived the first three decades of my life like an insecure adolescent, forever picking daisies and tearing them apart, never stopping to enjoy their beauty. *He loves me, He loves me not,* I would say subconsciously, plucking a petal as I weighed my behavior and attitudes against what the Bible said I should be.

Powerful church services and sweet altar times. Ah, I felt secure in His love. Real life and less-than-sweet responses? I felt lost and all alone. Unfortunately, all I got from constantly questioning God's love was a fearful heart and a pile of torn, wilted petals. My overzealous self-analysis never brought the peace I longed for.

Because the peace you and I were created for doesn't come from picking daisies. It only comes from a living relationship with a loving God.

THE TALE OF THE THIRD FOLLOWER

I never planned on writing a trilogy about Mary, Martha, and Lazarus, the siblings from Bethany that we meet in Luke's and John's gospels. In fact, when I wrote *Having a Mary Heart in a Martha World,* I was fairly certain it was the one and only book to be found in those verses. But God surprised me six years later, and *Having a Mary Spirit* was born.

The thought that there might be a third book never crossed my mind until I shared an interesting premise with a few friends who are writers. It was a teaching point I'd hoped to fit into *Having a Mary Spirit* but never quite found room.

"We all know Jesus loved Mary," I told my friends. "After all, look how she worshiped. And we can even understand how Jesus loved Martha. Look how she served. But what about those of us who don't know where we fit in the heart of God?"

The question hung in the air before I continued.

"The only thing of significance that Lazarus did was die. And yet when Mary and Martha sent word to Jesus that Lazarus was ill, they said, 'Lord, the one you *love* is sick.' "

Somehow my words seemed to have extra weight as they floated between us. Extra importance. Even I felt their impact.

After a few moments my friend Wendy broke the silence. "That part of the story didn't make it into the book because *it is* a book."

I can't adequately explain what happened when she said those words, except to say it was as though a giant bell began to sound in my soul. Its reverberations sent shock waves through my body as I tried to change the subject.

The thing is, I didn't *want* to write about Lazarus. I wanted to write a different book. I was ready to move on, to explore other subjects.

But God wouldn't let me. And so you hold this book in your hands.

A PLACE TO CALL HOME

We first meet the family from Bethany in Luke 10:38–42. Or rather we meet part of the family—two followers of Jesus named Martha and Mary.

You're probably familiar with the story Luke tells. Jesus was on His way to Jerusalem for one of the great Jewish feasts when Martha came out to meet Him with an invitation to dinner. But while Martha opened her home, it was her sister, Mary, who opened her heart. To put the story in a nutshell: Mary worshiped. Martha complained. Jesus rebuked. And lives were changed.[2]

Strangely, Luke's account never even mentions Mary and Martha's brother, Lazarus. Perhaps he wasn't home when Martha held her dinner party. Perhaps he was away on business. Or perhaps he was there all the time but no one really noticed.

Some people are like that. They have perfected the art of invisibility. Experts at fading into the background, they go out of their way not to attract attention, and when they get noticed, they feel great discomfort.

Of course, I have no way of knowing if this was true of Lazarus. Scripture doesn't give any information as to who he was or what he was like—only that he lived in Bethany and had two sisters. When we finally meet him, in John 11, it is an odd introduction—for it starts with a 911 call that leads to a funeral:

> Now a man named Lazarus was sick. He was from Bethany, the village of
> Mary and her sister Martha. This Mary, whose brother Lazarus now lay sick,
> was the same one who poured perfume on the Lord and wiped his feet with
> her hair. So the sisters sent word to Jesus, "Lord, the one you love is sick."
>
> When he heard this, Jesus said, "This sickness will not end in death. No,
> it is for God's glory so that God's Son may be glorified through it." Jesus
> loved Martha and her sister and Lazarus. Yet when he heard that Lazarus
> was sick, he stayed where he was two more days.
>
> Then he said to his disciples, "Let us go back to Judea."....
>
> On his arrival, Jesus found that Lazarus had already been in the tomb for
> four days....
>
> ..."Where have you laid him?" he asked.
>
> "Come and see, Lord," they replied.
>
> Jesus wept. (John 11:1–7, 17, 34–35)

What a tender story. A story filled with emotion and dramatic tension. The story of two sisters torn by grief and a Savior who loved them yet chose to tarry.

Of course, there is more to it—more truths we'll discover as we walk through the forty-four verses John devotes to this tale. For the story of Lazarus is also the story of Jesus's greatest miracle: that of awakening His friend from the dead. (To read the whole story all at once, see Appendix A: "The Story.")

Have you noticed that when Jesus comes on the scene, what seems to be the end is rarely the end? In fact, it's nearly always a new beginning.

But Mary and Martha didn't know that at the time. And I'm prone to forget it as well.

Questions and disappointments, sorrow and fear tend to block out the bigger picture in situations like the one we see in Bethany. What do we do when God doesn't come through the way we hoped He would? What should we feel when what is dearest to our hearts is suddenly snatched away? How do we reconcile the love of God with the disappointments we face in life?

Such questions don't have easy answers. However, in this story of Jesus's three friends, I believe we can find clues to help us navigate the unknown and the tragic when we encounter them in our own lives. Tips to help us live in the *mean*time— that cruel in-between time when we are waiting for God to act—as well as insights to help us trust Him when He doesn't seem to be doing anything at all.

But most important, I believe the story of Lazarus reveals the scandalous availability of God's love if we will only reach out and accept it. Even when we don't deserve it. Even when life is hard and we don't understand.

For God's ways are higher than our ways, and His thoughts are higher than our thoughts, Isaiah 55:8–9 tells us. He knows what He's doing.

Even when we can't figure out His math.

ALGEBRA AND ME

Arithmetic was always one of my favorite subjects in grade school, one I excelled at. Of course, that was in the last century, before they started introducing algebra in kindergarten. In my post–*Leave It to Beaver*, yet very serene, childhood, the only equations that wrinkled my nine-year-old forehead were fairly straightforward:

$$2 + 2 = 4$$
$$19 - 7 = 12$$

Of course, fourth-grade math was more difficult than that. But the basic addition and subtraction skills I'd learned in first and second grade helped me tackle the multiplication and division problems of third and fourth grade with confidence. By the time I reached sixth grade, I was fairly proficient with complicated columns of sums and had pretty much conquered the mysterious world of fractions. I was amazing—a math whiz.

But then eighth grade dawned and, with it, a very brief introduction to algebra. It all seemed quite silly to me. Who cared what the y factor was? And why on earth would I ever need to know what $x + y + z$ equaled?

When my teacher gave us a high-school placement math exam that spring, I didn't spend a lot of time trying to figure out the answers—mainly because I had no idea how, and when I tried, it made my head hurt. Instead, when I encountered a difficult problem during the test, I did what had always worked for me: I looked for a pattern in the answers.

Allowing my mind to back up a bit and my eyes to go a little fuzzy, I'd stare at all those little ovals I'd so neatly darkened in with my number-two pencil until I could see a pattern. *I haven't filled in a D for a while.* Or, *There were two Bs and then two Cs and one A, so obviously this must be another A.*

I was amazing at this too.

No, really, I was. Several weeks later when we received the results of our testing, I had been placed not in bonehead math, not even in beginning algebra. No, it was accelerated algebra for me, though I hadn't a clue what I was doing.

To this day I still don't. My algebraic cluelessness has followed me through adulthood and on into parenting. My kids can ask an English question, quiz me on history or government, and I can usually give them an answer or at least help them find one. But when it comes to algebra or geometry or calculus or any of those other advanced math classes invented by some sick, twisted Einstein wannabe...well, they'd better go ask their dad.

Advanced mathematics remains a complete mystery to me. The unknown factors seem so haphazard. What if z/y squared doesn't equal nine? What then?

The unknown factors frustrate us in life's story problems as well—and there are plenty of those in John 11. How are we to compute the fact that Jesus stayed where He was rather than rushing to Lazarus's side when He heard His friend was ill? How do we reconcile Jesus's allowing Mary and Martha to walk through so much pain when He could have prevented it in the first place?

Difficult questions, without a doubt. But there is a foundational truth in this passage we must first acknowledge before we can tackle the tougher issues.

"Jesus *loved* Martha and her sister and Lazarus" (John 11:5, emphasis added).

Jesus loves you and me as well. He loves us just as we are—apart from our Martha works and Mary worship. He even loves those of us who come empty-handed, feeling dead inside and perhaps a little bound.

For while it may not add up in our human calculations, the truth of God's love lies at the heart of the gospel. "While we were still sinners," Romans 5:8 tells us, "Christ died for us." We may not be able to do the math ourselves or reason out such amazing grace, but if we'll simply ask, our heavenly Father longs to help us find the bottom line.

THE LAZARUS FACTOR

I've always told my husband, John, that he has to die before I do—mainly because I don't want him remarrying some wonderful woman and finding out what he's missed all these years. But then again, if he were to go first, I'm convinced I'd face financial ruin in two months. It's not because John hasn't taken very good care of us financially but because I absolutely hate balancing checkbooks.

My idea of reconciling my checking account is to call a very nice lady named Rhonda at our bank. She graciously lets me know the bottom line whenever I'm a little leery of where I stand.

Now, I know this isn't a wise way to handle fiscal matters. In fact, you CPAs reading this are about to faint if you haven't already thrown the book across the room. But, hey, it works for me.

Most of the time.

Okay, so there have been a few blips in my system. But I'm coming to believe that while this may not be such a great method in the natural realm, it may be the only way to go in the spiritual.

After spending the greater part of my life trying to make everything add up on my own—that is, trying to make sure my good outweighed my bad so I was never overdrawn but was continually making deposits in my righteousness bank—I finally realized that nothing I did could ever be enough. No matter how hard I tried, I constantly lived under the weight of my own disapproval. Which, of course, instantly mutated into a sense that God was coldly disappointed with me as well.

He loves me not...

Keeping my own spiritual books has never added up to anything but guilt and condemnation and an overwhelming sense of hopelessness. I'm so glad God's math isn't like mine. And oh how I rejoice that He doesn't demand I come up with the correct answer before He makes me His child. Because when I couldn't make it up to Him, Jesus came down to me. And through His precious blood sacrifice, He made a way for me to come not only into His presence but directly into the heart of God.

"All of this is a gift from God," 2 Corinthians 5:18–19 tells us, "who brought

Holding Out for Grace

I appreciate what Bono, the lead singer of the rock group U2, has to say about grace: "It's a mind-blowing concept that the God who created the Universe might be looking for company, a real relationship with people, but the thing that keeps me on my knees is the difference between Grace and Karma."[3]

Bono explains that the idea of karma is central to all religions:

What you put out comes back to you: an eye for an eye, a tooth for a tooth, or in physics—in physical laws—every action is met by an equal or an opposite one. It's clear to me that Karma is at the very heart of the Universe. I'm absolutely sure of it. And yet, along comes this idea called Grace to upend all that "As you reap, so you will sow" stuff. Grace defies reason and logic. Love interrupts, if you like, the consequences of your actions, which in my case is very good news indeed, because I've done a lot of stupid stuff.... It doesn't excuse my mistakes, but I'm holding out for Grace. I'm holding out that Jesus took my sins onto the Cross, because I know who I am, and I hope I don't have to depend on my own religiosity.[4]

> *There is no God like you. You forgive those who are guilty of sin;*
> *you don't look at the sins of your people who are left alive.*
> *You will not stay angry forever, because you enjoy being kind.*
> MICAH 7:18, NCV

us back to himself through Christ.... no longer counting people's sins against them" (NLT).

NO MORE YARDSTICK

I don't think we can begin to imagine how radical Christ's New Testament message of grace sounded to a people who had been living under the Law for thousands of years. The thought that there might be a different way to approach God—a better way—was appealing to some Jews but threatening to many others.

For those who kept stumbling over the rules and regulations set up by the religious elite—never quite measuring up to the yardstick of the Law—the idea that God might love them apart from what they did must have been incredibly liberating.

But for the Jewish hierarchy who had mastered the Law and felt quite proud of it, Jesus's words surely posed a threat. His message pierced their religious facades, revealing the darkness of their hearts and, quite frankly, making them mad. Rather than running to the grace and forgiveness He offered, they kept defaulting to the yardstick—using it to justify themselves one minute, wielding it as a weapon against Jesus the next.*

"You come from Nazareth?" they said, pointing the yardstick. "Nothing good comes from Nazareth." *That's one whack for you.* "You eat with tax collectors and sinners? That's even worse." *Whack, whack.* "You heal on the Sabbath?" they screamed, waving their rules and regulations. *Off with Your head!*

The Sadducees and Pharisees had no room in their religion for freedom. As a result, they had no room for Christ. They were people of the yardstick. Even though Jesus kept insisting He hadn't come to "abolish the Law or the Prophets...but to fulfill them" (Matthew 5:17), they just wouldn't listen. Like little children they plugged their ears and kept singing the same old tune, though a New Song had been sent from heaven.

---

* Please let me tell you how much I love the nation of Israel. I fully believe they are the chosen people of God and a precious family into which I have been adopted. When I speak of the spiritual pride and blindness of the religious hierarchy of Jesus's day, it is not to condemn the Jews. Instead, I see my own tendency—and the tendency of the body of Christ today—to fall into spiritual pride and blindness when we love our "form of godliness" but miss "the power thereof" (2 Timothy 3:5, KJV).

Which is so very sad. Especially when you consider that the very Law they were so zealous for had been intended to *prepare* them for the Messiah rather than *keep* them from acknowledging Him.

After all, God established His original covenant with Abraham long before He gave Moses the Law—430 years before, to be exact (Galatians 3:17). The love the Father extended to Abraham and to all those who came after him had no strings attached. It was based on the recipient's acceptance of grace from beginning to end.

But somehow Israel fell in love with the Law rather than in love with their God. And we are in danger of doing the same thing. Exalting rules as the pathway to heaven. Embracing formulas as our salvation. Worshiping our own willpower rather than allowing the power of God to work in us to transform our lives.[5]

Such self-induced holiness didn't work for the Jews, and it doesn't work for us. That's why Jesus had to come.

The Law had originally been given "to show people their sins," Galatians 3:19 tells us. But it was "designed to last only until the coming of the child who was promised" (NLT). Though the yardstick of the Law helped keep us in line, it was never intended to save us. Only Christ could do that. And oh may I tell you how that comforts my soul?

I'll never forget the day I handed Jesus my yardstick. I had been saved since childhood, but I was almost thirty before the message of grace finally made the trip from my head to my heart, setting me "free from the law of sin and death" (Romans 8:2). As the light of the good news finally penetrated the darkness of my self-condemning mind, the "perfect love" 1 John 4:18 speaks of finally drove out my insecurity, which had always been rooted in fear of punishment.

When I finally laid down my Pharisee pride and admitted that in myself I would never be—could never be—enough, I experienced a breakthrough that has radically changed my life. For as I surrendered my yardstick—the tool of comparison that had caused so much mental torment and a sense of separation from God—Jesus took it from my hands. Then, with a look of great love, He broke it over His knee and turned it into a cross, reminding me that He died so I wouldn't have to.

That the punishment I so fully deserve has already been paid for.

That the way has been made for everyone who will believe in Jesus not only to come to Him but to come back home to the heart of God.

A Place to Lay Our Hearts

From the moment God so kindly exploded the concept of this book in my soul, I've had just one prayer. It is the prayer Paul prayed for all believers in Ephesians 3:17–19:

> And I pray that you, being rooted and established in love, may have power, together with all the saints, to grasp how wide and long and high and deep is the love of Christ, and to know this love that surpasses knowledge—that you may be filled to the measure of all the fullness of God.

I believe that everything we were made for and everything we've ever wanted is found in these three little verses. But in order to appropriate the all-encompassing love of God, we must give up our obsession with formulas and yardsticks. But how do we do that? Paul's prayer reveals an important key: "that you…may have power… to *know* this love that surpasses knowledge" (emphasis added).

The marvelous incongruity of that statement hit me several years ago. "Wait, Lord! How can I know something that surpasses knowledge?" I asked.

His answer came sweet and low to my spirit. *You have to stop trying to understand it and start accepting it, Joanna. Just let Me love you.*

For the reality is, no matter how hard we try, we will never be able to explain or deserve such amazing grace and incredible love. Nor can we escape it.

It's just too *wide,* Ephesians 3:18 tells us. We can't get around it.

It's just too *high.* We can't get over it.

It's so *long* we'll never be able to outrun it.

And it's so *deep* we'll never be able to exhaust it.

Bottom line: You can't get away from God's love no matter how hard you try. Because He's pursuing you, my friend. Maybe it's time to stop running away from love and start running toward it.

Even if, at times, it seems too good to be true.

Choosing Love

I don't know why Jesus chose me to love. Really, I don't. Perhaps you don't understand why He chose you. But He did. Really, He did. Until we get around to accepting His amazing, undeserved favor, I fear we will miss everything a relationship with Christ really means.

When my husband proposed to me so many years ago, I didn't say, "Wait a minute, John. Do you have any idea what you're getting into?" I didn't pull out a list of reasons why he couldn't possibly love me or a rap sheet detailing my inadequacies to prove why he shouldn't—although there were and are many.

No way! I just threw my arms open wide and accepted his love. I would have been a fool to turn down an offer like that.

I wonder what would happen in our lives if we stopped resisting God's love and started receiving it. What if we stopped trying to do the math, stopped striving to earn His favor? What if we just accepted the altogether-too-good-to-be-true news that the yardstick has been broken and the Cross has opened a door to intimacy with our Maker?

For if we are ever to be His beloved, we must be willing to *be* loved.

Simple, huh? And yet oh so hard. Like my friend Lisa, many of us are plagued by love-doubt. We have hidden tombs yet to be opened. Dark secrets that keep us hanging back. Soul-sicknesses that have left us crippled and embittered by our inability to forgive or forget. Graveclothes that keep tripping us up and fears that hold us back from believing the good news could ever be true for people like us.

I wonder…

Maybe it's time to look in the mirror and start witnessing to ourselves.

Maybe it's time we stop living by what we feel and start proclaiming what our spirits already know: "I have been chosen by God. Whether I feel loved or believe I deserve it, from this moment on I choose to be loved."

Say it out loud: "I choose to be loved."

You may have to force yourself to say the words. Today your emotions may not correspond with what you've just declared. It is likely you may have to repeat the same words tomorrow. And do it again the next day. And the next.

But I promise that as you start appropriating what God has already declared as truth, something's going to shift in the heavenly regions. More important, something's going to shift in you.

So say those words as many times as you need to...until the message gets through your thick head to your newly tender heart. Until you finally come to believe what's been true all along.

Shh...listen. Do you hear it?

It's Love.

And He's calling your name.

So the sisters sent word to Jesus,
"Lord, the one you love is sick."
When he heard this, Jesus said,
"This sickness will not end in death.
No, it is for God's glory so that
God's Son may be glorified through it."
Jesus loved Martha and her sister and Lazarus.
Yet when he heard that Lazarus was sick,
he stayed where he was two more days.
Then he said to his disciples, "Let us go back to Judea."....
After he had said this, he went on to tell them,
"Our friend Lazarus has fallen asleep;
but I am going there to wake him up."

JOHN 11:3–7, 11

Lord, the One You Love Is Sick

The message was brief, but as Jesus listened, He must have felt the pain behind the words. His friend Lazarus was sick.

Breathless in his hurry and dusty from the journey, a weary messenger waited before Him. The disciples waited as well. What would Jesus say? More to the point, what would Jesus do? They'd seen amazing things in the years they'd traveled with the man from Galilee. The lame walked. The blind could see. Even lepers were made completely whole. Surely Jesus would act quickly on behalf of this man who was no stranger.

But they were twenty miles from Bethany, across the River Jordan from the land of Judea—a hard day's journey from the family Jesus loved. There were enemies in nearby Jerusalem to consider, even rumors of a death warrant. Still, knowing how Jesus felt about Lazarus, the disciples must have readied themselves to leave immediately. Then Jesus broke the silence with what surely sounded to their ears like incredibly good news.

"This sickness will not end in death," He declared to the men standing around Him. "No, it is for God's glory so that God's Son may be glorified through it" (John 11:4).

It was good news indeed—especially to the messenger, who hurried back to tell the waiting sisters. What a relief to be able to say that their brother wouldn't die. That Jesus would come and all would be well.

But little did the man know that when he arrived back in Bethany, he'd find two grief-stricken sisters and Jesus's friend Lazarus already dead and gone.[1]

WHEN LIFE DOESN'T MAKE SENSE

It wasn't supposed to be this way. Death, grief, and pain were not part of God's original plan. We were created for life, for an eternity of close communion with our Maker. We were not meant to suffer sickness or feel grief's inexplicable loss.

You and I were made for paradise.

But according to Genesis, the arrival of sin changed all that. Adam and Eve's rebellion opened a dark door, and death entered the world like a conqueror, sweeping indiscriminately across humanity. Turning one person against another, striking down one with illness and another with hatred. Sin has spent millenniums ravaging homes and hearts, leaving a trail of brokenness, tears, and sorrow.

Yet of all sin's evil residue, perhaps nothing torments us more than the questions that swirl in our minds.

Why?

Why am I sick?

Why is my marriage broken?

Why can't I find someone to love?

Why did my friend have to die?

I'm sure Martha and Mary struggled with questions as well. Could they have done something more? Perhaps they should have sent word to Jesus as soon as Lazarus's symptoms worsened. Perhaps they should have been more forceful in the wording of their message. It was a little vague, after all: "Lord, the one you love is sick" (John 11:3). Perhaps their friend hadn't understood how serious the situation had become.

But lingering somewhere in their minds, as they do in ours at times like these, two terrible queries must have wrestled for prominence:

Maybe this is punishment for something we've done. Maybe it's our fault our brother died.

Or perhaps, and even more painful to contemplate:

Maybe Jesus doesn't love us as much as we love Him.

Making Sense of Senseless Things

We humans are big on formulas. We need things to add up, so we're always coming up with rationales and reasons for the way the world works. And it's important that we do, for such curiosity helps make sense of things around us, opening doors to discoveries and innovations that would not be made without it.

But, unfortunately, our insistence that life should always add up often results in faulty conclusions. Especially when we're attempting to reconcile the problem of pain and suffering with belief in a loving, caring God.

One of the most damaging misperceptions of many Christians is that if we are walking with God, nothing bad should ever happen to us. While we might not admit it or even see it, "Bless me, bless me" has been much of the church's cry and expectation these past few decades. So much so that I'm afraid we've actually fallen for the lie that a life of ease and obvious blessing is always an indication of God's favor.

If good things are happening to you, it is because you're doing something right. If you're walking through difficulties, it is because you're doing something wrong.

Sounds logical to our human minds. And it sounded good to the people of the Bible as well. When faced with Job's suffering, his friends insisted there had to be a reason for the painful boils, the destruction of his home, and the devastating loss of his family. "Come on, Job," they prodded. "Fess up! You've obviously done something wrong."

We see the same mind-set in the New Testament, for the scribes and Pharisees loved formulas as well. They had created an encyclopedia-sized index of rules and guidelines for gaining God's pleasure and, thus, His goodies. They, too, were prone to believe that an absence of certain goodies indicated an absence of God's pleasure. If for some reason you fell ill, they reasoned only one thing could explain it: either you or your parents had sinned, and thus you deserved your current state.[2]

It's no wonder that in Jesus's day the lame and the leper, the blind and the deaf were relegated to being outcasts and beggars. Because they deserved their fate, the only responsibility society felt was an occasional gift, a couple of alms, as they passed them begging on the streets.

It was a neat and tidy system...unless, of course, you happened to be one of those sick or maimed or afflicted. Someone like Lazarus.

SICK AND TIRED OF BEING SICK AND TIRED

When we're told that Mary and Martha sent word their brother was ill, the Bible uses the Greek word *astheneo*. According to one writer, "This isn't just the word for a virus or flu bug, it was used for a prolonged illness. Lazarus was 'feeble with sickness'. It is the word used of impotence—lack of power—an ongoing illness or weakness."[3]

My friend Renee knows a little of what Lazarus may have gone through. Medication she took many years ago severely damaged her heart, lungs, and nerves, and they continue to deteriorate. Many days Renee is confined to her bed. On a good morning taking a shower requires an hour and leaves her breathless. My friend is doing the best she can—eating right, trying to exercise. However, doctors can do little except treat the symptoms. Unless Jesus intervenes, my friend may die from her disease.

But you would never know it when meeting her. Renee is one of the most vibrant and joyful people I've ever met—sunshine with glasses on. Her conversation rarely circles around any well-deserved health complaint. Instead, when I answer her phone calls, I am greeted with, "Joanna Gloria! How are you today?"

I love that girl! She is a gift to me and to the body of Christ.

Renee gives thanks to God for every day. For each breath. For the life she has. Yet while I marvel at her endurance and especially at the peaceful joy that literally surrounds her, I must confess I sometimes wonder why. Why Renee? Why not someone who actually deserves a painful death sentence such as this?

But then, I suppose that could very well involve me.

For none of us deserves health. None of us deserves this miraculous gift of life. It's all grace, every bit of it. Even the hard parts. Even the parts we don't understand.

I don't believe Lazarus was ill because of sin in his life. And neither is my friend Renee.

Life just isn't as cut-and-dried as many of us want to make it. We can't point at a particular trouble and assign blame. There's too much we can't see and don't understand.

But let me be clear. Just as it would be wrong to assume that all sickness is caused by some failure on the ill person's part, it would also be incorrect to say that sin has no consequences. Or that sickness never has its roots in disobedience.

After healing a paralyzed man by the pool called Bethesda, Jesus later went out of His way to find the man in the temple. "See, you are well again," Jesus told him. "Stop sinning or something worse may happen to you" (John 5:14).

For there is a disease much more damaging to humanity than those commonly diagnosed by doctors. And Jesus knew that. It is the curse that has plagued our hearts from the moment Eve's lips touched the forbidden fruit.

The very sickness He came to cure.

Fallen Ill

Of all the ailments in all the world, no illness has caused as much pain or as much destruction to us humans as the widespread but often misdiagnosed inner plague called *S-I-N*.

In these three little letters, we find the DNA of a supervirus that has destroyed more careers, more marriages, more families, more churches, and more men, women, boys, and girls than all of earth's diseases put together. It has shredded more reputations, shattered more hearts, and destroyed more minds than any pandemic.

Try as we might, we can't get away from it, for it is interwoven in the fabric of our humanity. Passed down through generation after generation of both good men and bad, gentle mothers and raging lunatics, noble kings and evil tyrants. It rests inside me, and it abides in you as well. For it might be said of each of us, "Lord, the one you love is sick."

We might not be ax murderers. Yet the slander that slips so easily off our tongues murders more than we know.

We might not be meth addicts breaking into houses and terrorizing old ladies to get enough money for another high. But our escapist thinking can be just as dangerous—eroding our marriages and our homes, causing us to be physically present in our relationships yet emotionally unavailable.

We might not be scam artists or child abusers, prostitutes or thugs, but the envy and lust and anger and pride that lurk inside us trouble the heart of God just as much as any of our darker pastimes.

Because sin—all sin—destroys. It maims, and it cuts us off from the life we need.

And if we're honest with ourselves, we know it. We feel it. We are, every one of us, sin-sick—there is no other way to describe it. And our transgressions, if not confessed and dealt with, separate us from God, causing the love-doubt that haunts our nights and clouds our days.

But we don't have to live that way. Because if we'll simply agree with the diagnosis, Jesus has already provided the cure.

FOREVER SEARCHING—FOREVER FOUND

Ten years ago while writing *Having a Mary Heart in a Martha World,* I had a strange recurring dream. At least once a week, I would dream of waking in a dark bedroom

What God Does with Our Sins

Rosalind Goforth, a well-known missionary to China, struggled many years with an oppressive burden of guilt and sin that left her feeling like a spiritual failure. Finally, out of desperation, she sat down with her Bible and a concordance, determined to find out how God views the faults of His children. At the top of the paper, she wrote these words: "What God Does with Our Sins." Then she searched the Scriptures, compiling this list of seventeen truths:

1. He lays them on His Son—Jesus Christ (Isaiah 53:6).
2. Christ takes them away (John 1:29).
3. They are removed an immeasurable distance—as far as east is from west (Psalm 103:12).
4. When sought for [they] are not found (Jeremiah 50:20).
5. The Lord forgives them (1 John 1:9; Ephesians 1:7; Psalm 103:3).
6. He cleanses them all away by the blood of His Son (1 John 1:7).
7. He cleanses them as white as snow or wool (Isaiah 1:18; Psalm 51:7).

in a strange yet somewhat familiar house. In my dream I'd wander through a maze of hallways and rooms looking for something I'd lost. Groping in the dark, I'd inch my way through endless corridors.

The frustration of the search was surpassed only by the urgency I felt. I had to find it—whatever "it" was. But I never did, no matter how many times I had the dream or how diligently I searched. When I'd waken, the intensity of the dream would follow me throughout the day. It felt so real I'd find myself making a mental note to go to that house (wherever it was) and find the treasure I'd somehow misplaced.

Odd dream. And one I didn't fully understand until nearly a year after that first book was published. The illumination finally came in the form of a letter from a reader, a representative of a ministry that we had asked to consider recommending the book.

---

 8. He abundantly pardons them (Isaiah 55:7).

 9. He tramples them underfoot (Micah 7:19).

10. He remembers them no more (Hebrews 10:17; Ezekiel 33:16).

11. He casts them behind His back (Isaiah 38:17).

12. He casts them into the depths of the sea (Micah 7:19).

13. He will not impute [or charge] us with sins (Romans 4:8).

14. He covers them (Romans 4:7).

15. He blots them out (Isaiah 43:25).

16. He blots them out [like] a thick cloud (Isaiah 44:22).

17. He blots out even the proof against us, nailing it to His Son's cross (Colossians 2:14).[4]

Blessed is he whose transgressions are forgiven,

whose sins are covered.

PSALM 32:1

The letter writer was very kind in her comments about the book, but she informed me gently that the ministry she represented would be unable to carry the title on their book tables. Their policy required all recommended books to include a clear plan of salvation. And mine, while written well for established Christians, had not done that.

"You see, Joanna," she wrote, "I was forty-two years old before I was told I could have a personal relationship with Christ. Though I'd gone to church since I was a child, no one had told me how to accept Jesus as my own personal Savior. That's why it's so important to tell people that simply believing in God isn't enough—we must accept the gift Christ offers."

And she was right. The Bible clearly teaches that belief in God's existence doesn't save our souls. "Even the demons believe—and tremble!" (James 2:19, NKJV). If we are ever to find the intimate and personal relationship God longs to have with us, there is only one way. One truth and one life (John 14:6).

You see, the treasure I'd searched for in my dream is found in only one place: in the Person of the God-Man, Jesus Christ. He is much more than an *anecdote*—a heartwarming story portraying a spiritual truth. He is the *antidote* to the poison of sin and the singular cure for the sin-sickness that has infected humanity since that fateful day in the garden.

For only Jesus can provide a Lazarus awakening for the soul-sleep that plagues us all.

AWAKE, SLEEPER!

Two days had passed since they'd heard about Lazarus's sickness. The disciples must have wondered why Jesus waited so long to go to Bethany or if He would go at all. There were plenty of reasons not to, including a death warrant. But then the Master gathered them and said, "Let us go back to Judea" (John 11:7).

The disciples tried to dissuade Him, bringing up the religious mob that had attempted to stone Him just weeks before. But Jesus was unmoved by their argument, telling them, "Our friend Lazarus has fallen asleep; but I am going there to wake him up" (John 11:11).

Stop a moment and reread that last sentence.

"He has fallen asleep, but I'm going to *wake him up.*" Oh how those words speak to me.

Throughout the Bible sleep is synonymous with death. Ironically, as with Snow White, a poisoned fruit caused Adam and Eve to fall into a spiritual unconsciousness that still affects you and me today. When God told the first couple not to eat from the forbidden tree, when He said, "You will surely die" (Genesis 2:17), He wasn't kidding. The moment they disobeyed, the center of their beings fell asleep.

The Invitation

There is no more important question than the one asked by a Philippian jailer over two thousand years ago: "What must I do to be saved?" (Acts 16:30).

Jesus answered that question once and for all by taking the punishment for our sins upon Himself. We simply have to accept the free gift of salvation He offers. How do we do that? The Billy Graham Evangelistic Association outlines four steps for receiving Christ:

- Admit your need. (I am a sinner.)
- Be willing to turn from your sins (repent).
- Believe that Jesus Christ died for you on the cross and rose from the grave.
- Pray a prayer like this: Dear Lord Jesus, I know that I am a sinner, and I ask for Your forgiveness. I believe You died for my sins and rose from the dead. I turn from my sins and invite You to come into my heart and life. I want to trust and follow You as my Lord and Savior. In Your Name, amen.[5]

Yet to all who received him, to those who believed in his name,
he gave the right to become children of God.

JOHN 1:12

The part of them that had communed best with their Creator—that is, their spirits—died.[6]

Likewise, our spirits remain locked in death-sleep until we meet Jesus Christ as our personal Savior. Until the Prince of Peace wakens our slumbering hearts with a tender kiss and the sprinkling of His shed blood, the most important part of our beings will remain lifeless and dead. Only Christ can perform the spiritual CPR we so desperately need.

But it's important to realize that even after we commit our lives to Jesus, the danger of spiritual slumber is never far away. Even though we are no longer dead in our spirits, it's still possible for us to be lulled back to sleep in our souls. Suffering from a type of spiritual narcolepsy and sleepwalking through life, we remain loved by Jesus—just as Lazarus was—but in desperate need of being awakened by an encounter with the living God.

How is it possible that Christians could fall into such slumber? In most cases it doesn't happen suddenly. Nodding off to the things of God is usually an incremental process. A slow numbing of the heart, along with a diminished ability to hear the Spirit's voice. A drifting and dreaming of our souls as they follow other pursuits.

In my case such seemingly innocent naps have often started with a lullaby. A compromising tune hummed by the Deceiver one day. A long ballad of self-pity sung by Satan the next. To think that Lucifer might use his unholy hymns to soothe us into spiritual oblivion makes sense to me. After all, he seems to have quite a musical repertoire.

It's no big deal, he serenaded King David as the man after God's own heart began to chase after another man's wife (2 Samuel 11:2–4).

Everyone's doing it, he hummed softly to Samson as he lured the strongest man who ever lived to trade the secret of his strength for another night in the arms of a Philistine beauty (Judges 16:15–17).

Nobody cares about you, he crooned to a tired prophet as Elijah sat under a broom tree of discouragement (1 Kings 19:3–4).

Satanic songs every one of them, and there are as many different lyrics as there are listening ears. Music to make us doubt God's love. Tunes to make us cease to care. Lullabies intended to lull us bye-bye to the point where we're blind to the Enemy's devices and deaf to the Spirit's voice.

Fast asleep. Drifting farther away from the God we serve and the love we need. And deeply, desperately in need of waking up.

Years ago I was staying at a hotel in Houston, Texas. When I called the front desk to schedule a wake-up call, they promised to do just that and more.

"If you don't answer the phone, we'll knock at the door," the man on the line said. "If you don't answer the door, we will come in and shake you until you get up."

Now that's what I call service! A bit unsettling but, still, service!

I believe God would love to do the same for us if we'd just give Him permission. He knows how easily we sleep through spiritual alarm clocks. He's watched us consistently shrug off His stirrings when He's tried to revive us. But our heavenly Father is willing to go through all that and more if we will only listen and respond to Him.

We're asleep, Lord Jesus. Wake us up! should be our daily prayer. *Wake us up to Your loving mercy. Wake us up to Your goodness and Your power to save.* Even though, like Mary and Martha, we sometimes wonder, *Maybe this sickness is punishment for my sins.* Or, *Maybe Jesus doesn't love me as much as I love Him.*

Wake us up, Lord Jesus, to the thorough trustworthiness of Your ways, for only You can take what was meant for evil and turn it into good (Genesis 50:20).

OUR GREAT REDEEMER

Of all the titles of Jesus, I've come to appreciate most that He is my Redeemer. After walking so many years with the Lord, through both good times and bad, I can declare along with Job, "I know that my Redeemer lives" (Job 19:25). For He takes the worthless and makes it precious when we trust His loving hands.

When God interrupted humanity's downward spiral by sending His own Son, Jesus came into a culture that expected the Messiah to set up a kingdom free from problems, sorrow, and pain. Even His own disciples expected He would topple Rome and set up a new regime complete with corner offices and special perks reserved just for them.

Those looking forward to the Promised One had always believed He would reinvent the world.

Instead, God chose to redeem it.

Which means sin is still present and Satan is still active. Murder and violent wars cover the earth. Sickness ravages bodies and minds and hearts. Too often the innocent die young. Surely, we think, there has to be a better way.

After all, God could have pushed the reset button long ago, at the beginning of time. He could have taken one look at the mess we humans had made—our rebellion, our hatred, our immorality and idolatry—and decided to delete it all. With one push of a button, God could have rebooted and started over.

Instead, He became a man. And on the cross He took the weight of our mistakes. All my failures, all your hurts, all our devastation. With a final breath He redeemed it all.

"It is finished," Jesus said just before He died (John 19:30). And it was. For with those words came the great exchange. His death became ours so that our lives could become His. And three days later tragedy turned into triumph as the Lamb came bursting forth from the tomb like a Lion. Silencing hell's laughter, Jesus snatched the keys of death and the grave and shattered Satan's schemes, redeeming you and me and causing all the destruction the Enemy had perpetrated against us to boomerang back on his deceiving, thieving, troublemaking head.

Christ still does the same recycling work today, taking the garbage of people's lives and fashioning masterpieces of grace. Reclaiming prostitutes and murderers, lepers and beggars, greedy executives and desperate housewives and transforming them all into life-size trophies of His love.

This is the power of the gospel. This is the centerpiece of the good news!

"Christ did not come to make bad men good," Ravi Zacharias points out, "but to make dead men alive."[7] For our heavenly Father knew we needed more than a renovation. We needed a resurrection. And that's what Jesus came to bring.

"This sickness will not end in death," Jesus reassured the disciples in John 11:4, and He whispers the same hope to you and me today.

Go ahead and fill in the blank with your situation. "Lord, the one you love is _____." Diagnosed with cancer, facing bankruptcy, losing a marriage— the list can go on and on. But not one of those problems is too big for God.

This sickness, this heartache, this life-altering situation will not end in death, Jesus promises. Instead, if we'll respond to His invitation and leave the tombs of our sin and even our doubt, our lives will declare the truth of His next statement: "It is for God's glory."

Because, as Saint Irenaeus once said, "The glory of God is man fully alive."[8]

So cure my spiritual narcolepsy, Lord. Rouse me from my slumber. Shake me, if necessary, until I respond. But whatever You do, dear Jesus, don't leave me the same.

For good things come to those who wake!

Then he said to his disciples, "Let us go to back to Judea."....
After he had said this, he went on to tell them,
"Our friend Lazarus has fallen asleep."

JOHN 11:7, 11

Our Friend Lazarus

Ah, the indescribable joy of being loved!
I am currently in the enviable position of having two men absolutely gaga over me.

The first one, my wonderful husband, isn't quite as enthusiastic as the second, though John shows me love a hundred ways every day. But the second guy—well, this little Romeo can't seem to do enough to show how much he adores me. His attentions come complete with dandelions and stick-figure cards…and lots and lots of verbal declarations.

It's not just the words that make my heart go pitter-patter, for I've been blessed to hear "I love you" many times throughout my life. What makes Josh's words so delicious is the *way* he says them. As though he really means them.

He doesn't throw them flippantly over his shoulder as he goes outside to play. Nor does he use his affection to win his own way. Not yet, anyway. For now, at least, his professions of love are just pure adoration. And lately, for whatever reason, Josh infuses these three syllables with such ardor and emotion they take my breath away.

"Mom," he says a bit solemnly, pausing a moment until he has my complete attention. Then, in a slow, sweet drawl marked by his speech impediment, he draws out the middle word to give it extra emphasis. "I wuuuuv you."

Suddenly all is right with my world. And more than right—it's wonderful. Joshua throws himself into my arms, and I return his love, holding him as if I could hold him forever.

Of course, after a bit—sometimes longer if I'm lucky—Josh disengages. He gives me an extra-big squeeze, and then with a jelly-smeared kiss, he hops off my lap and goes back to play.

But before he does, while we're still wrapped in each other's arms, my heart captures a snapshot with a scribbled caption describing the joy of being loved. Not for what I've done, not even for who I am. But simply because the mere sight of me causes such intense emotion that words are required—not just once but several times a day.

I know it's just a phase. I know Joshua will grow up and become enamored with much more than me. Oh, he'll still express his love—that's just the kind of guy he is—but he won't do it as often or as intensely. So for now I'm determined to enjoy every minute. Whenever Josh flings himself my way, I stop what I'm doing to drink in the treasured sweetness. There is an indescribable joy to being loved like that, and I don't want to miss it.

Why am I telling you this? To make you wish you'd had an unexpected pregnancy at age forty that resulted in an amazing little boy like mine?

No, though I could wish no greater gift for anyone.

I'm telling you this because Joshua is teaching me about the kind of relationship Christ longs to have with me. The love affair I'm enjoying with my six-year-old is the kind of love affair God wants to enjoy with all His children. The intermingling of hearts He has longed for since the foundation of the world.

THE LONELINESS OF GOD

That God was lonely had never occurred to the angels. All powerful, all knowing, the eternal Beginning and eternal End, the three-in-one Godhead—how could the Almighty feel any lack?

And yet there'd been a quiet restlessness about Yahweh for some time. A far-off look now and then revealed a yearning, a longing. Almost a sadness. Perhaps, then, it wasn't such a surprise when the Uncreated declared His desire to create.

After witnessing five days of extraordinary work, watching God drop a small blue-green orb into created space, then fill it with one marvelous invention after another, the angels must have stood on tiptoe to see what God would do next.

"Let us make man in our image," said the Creator, stooping down to fill His hands with dust. With great care the Eternal One shaped His work. Then, bending over, He gently breathed into the lifeless clay, and a man was created...then a woman. The two were handsome enough, the angels thought, though a bit ordinary, especially when measured against all they'd seen. Yet God seemed quite pleased.

Perhaps, the angels pondered, this creation had some special talent they were unaware of, some unique quality that would make them useful to the kingdom. So they waited to see these humans perform.

But soon it became evident that all God's previous work—the soaring mountains, the lush green valleys, the glorious sunrises, and watercolor sunsets—had been made for the pleasure and delight of man and woman, His last created works.

But not just for their pleasure. It was for something else as well. The shimmering world, the angels soon realized, was simply a backdrop. A stage upon which they would watch creation's true purpose unfold.

For all of it had been made to facilitate God's passionate pursuit of relationship with humankind.

WHAT WE'RE MADE FOR

Perhaps you've never considered how much your heavenly Father longs to know you and be known by you. We've been told that we were born with a God-shaped hole— a spiritual vacuum that can't be filled by anything or anyone except God Himself. But have you ever considered that God might have a *you*-shaped hole, an emptiness that only you can fill?

That's the overarching implication of the biblical message. From the book of Genesis to the Song of Solomon, from Ecclesiastes to Malachi, from Matthew to Revelation, the entire Bible records an epic story of the ever-reaching, always-pursuing, tenaciously tender love of God. I appreciate the way The Message expresses Ephesians 1:4–6:

> Long before he laid down earth's foundations, [God] had us in mind, had
> settled on us as the focus of his love, to be made whole and holy by his love.

Long, long ago he decided to adopt us into his family through Jesus Christ. (What pleasure he took in planning this!) He wanted us to enter into the celebration of his lavish gift-giving by the hand of his beloved Son.

See what I mean? The Bible is clear. We have a God who is gaga about us. The question is, are we gaga about Him?

I want to be head over heels in love with God, but the problem is I don't always know how to go about it. I'm learning a lot about gaga love from my little son, however, and I'm learning better how to love Jesus from a man in the Bible whose words aren't even recorded. While we don't have a lot of background information from which to speculate and no physical description of Lazarus, we still learn some important things about this man from Scripture.

First, Jesus loved Lazarus.

Second, that love translated into a close relationship between the two.

The first point may seem obvious and somewhat unimportant. After all, Jesus loves everyone. And yet the narrator of the biblical account highlights their closeness several times to make sure we know that this was not merely a generic acquaintance.

In John 11:3, for instance, Lazarus's sisters send word: "Lord, the one you *love* is sick."

Later, in verse 5, John reiterates: "Jesus *loved* Martha and her sister and Lazarus."

Even the Jews who later gathered at Lazarus's funeral must have been aware of an extra-special relationship between Christ and the man they mourned, for when they saw Jesus weeping at the tomb, they said, "See how he *loved* him!" (verse 36).

Jesus loved Lazarus. He loved Martha and Mary as well (verse 5). And I believe the three siblings reciprocated that love. Scripture tells us Christ returned often to Bethany. The family must have brought Him great joy and comfort, offering a home where He was welcomed with open arms, accepted, and truly beloved.

Hearing that Lazarus was ill must have grieved Jesus's heart, even though He knew how the story would end. When Jesus arrived in Bethany and saw Mary weeping, John 11:33 tells us "he was deeply moved in spirit and troubled." So troubled, in fact, that He may have literally groaned out loud. The Greek word for "deeply moved," *embrimaomai,* comes from the root word that means "to snort with anger; to have indignation."[1] Jesus didn't take the family's pain lightly. For Lazarus was much more than a follower.

When referring to Mary and Martha's brother, Jesus used a term that seems generic on the surface but is far more intimate than that—not to mention powerful. And it can change our relationship with our Maker if we will seek to be named by it as well.

When talking about Lazarus, Jesus called him "friend" (John 11:11).

FRIEND OF GOD

What does it mean to be a friend of God? I'm talking about an honest-to-goodness, true-blue, when-the-chips-are-down kind of friend of God.

I've felt the Lord challenging me with this very question. I'd like to think Jesus considers me a friend. But am I really? Am I someone He can feel safe with? Is my heart a place with plenty of room for Him to spread out and relax? Is *mi casa* truly His *casa*?

It isn't easy finding a friend like that. Just ask any Hollywood celebrity who is hounded by friends who seem sincere but are really out for what they can get.

In his book on the psychology of fame and the problems of celebrity, author David Giles describes the loneliness that often stalks famous people: "On meeting each new acquaintance, the question becomes not so much, 'Does this person like me for who I am?' but 'Does this person like me for *what* I am?' "[2]

According to Giles, even the Greek philosopher Cicero experienced this. Back in 60 BC he "complained that, despite the 'droves of friends' surrounding him, he was unable to find one with whom he could 'fetch a private sigh.' "[3]

I wonder if God ever feels like that. Does His heart hurt when He realizes most people hang around Him for what they can get?

For the contacts they can make.

For the warm fuzzies they feel.

For the benefits and perks that come with Christianity—peace, joy, provision.

Or for the rewards they expect when they offer God a calculated gift of service. Such a self-centered, results-oriented relationship must grieve the heart of the Almighty. It certainly causes us to miss out on the intimacy He intends.

Help Me Love You More!

In his book *Crazy Love*, Francis Chan invites us to invite God to help us love Him more.

If you merely pretend that you enjoy God or love Him, He knows. You can't fool Him; don't even try.

Instead, tell Him how you feel. Tell Him that He isn't the most important thing in this life to you, and that you're sorry for that. Tell Him that you've been lukewarm, that you've chosen _____ over Him time and again. Tell Him that you want Him to change you, that you long to genuinely enjoy Him. Tell Him how you want to experience true satisfaction and pleasure and joy in your relationship with Him. Tell Him you want to love Him more than anything on this earth. Tell Him you want to treasure the kingdom of heaven so much that you'd willingly sell everything in order to get it. Tell Him what you like about Him, what you appreciate, and what brings you joy.

Jesus, I need to give myself up. I am not strong enough to love You and walk with You on my own. I can't do it, and I need You. I need You deeply and desperately. I believe You are worth it, that You are better than any-thing else I could have in this life or the next. I want You. And when I don't, I want to want You. Be all in me. Take all of me. Have Your way with me.[4]

My heart says of you, "Seek his face!"
Your face, LORD, I will seek.

PSALM 27:8

In *The Divine Romance,* an imaginative retelling of the biblical story of Exodus, Gene Edwards paints a poignant picture of God's heart toward us. One scene in particular stands out in my mind. It depicts God watching as the people brought out of Egypt's bondage vow to serve Him always. Promising to obey Yahweh in everything both big and small, they bring all their treasures and fall on their faces to worship. And yet, as God looks on, "unobserved by all," He is struck by a "deep sadness." Edwards writes:

A long, deep groan of sorrow, unheard by human ears but shattering the tranquility of the entire heavenly host, rose up from his depths.

> *I did not require of you*
> *your wealth nor coins of gold.*
> *What need have I of these?*
> *I did not ask of you*
> *that you serve me.*
> *Do I, the Mighty One,*
> *need to be waited upon?*
> *Neither did I ask of you*
> *your worship nor your prayers*
> *nor even your obedience.*

He paused. Once more a long, mournful groan rose from his breast.

> *I have asked but this of you,*
> *that you love me...*
> *love me...*
> *love me.*[5]

GOD'S LOVE LANGUAGE

I don't believe any of us intend to set aside a true relationship with God in favor of some kind of performance—whether it be practical or even spiritual. The tendency to do so, however, seems hard-wired in the fallen part of our nature. It's as though back in Eden a faulty switch was thrown, replacing the gift of relationship with the curse of works. Which, I suppose, is exactly what happened that long-ago day.

"Because you...ate from the tree about which I commanded you, 'You must not eat of it,' " God told the first humans, "cursed is the ground because of you; through painful toil you will eat of it all the days of your life" (Genesis 3:17).

From the moment Adam and Eve disobeyed God, the couple would have to work for their food. But please note: God never required them to work up a plan to restore their relationship with Him. For that labor had already begun, and it was God's work alone.

"The cross was no accident," Max Lucado writes in his beautiful book *God Came Near*. "...The moment the forbidden fruit touched the lips of Eve, the shadow of a cross appeared on the horizon."⁶

The brilliant plan of redemption was set in motion the moment sin entered the world. And all of it was orchestrated by God. A living, vibrant relationship with our Father was never intended to be the work of our hands no matter how noble our efforts might be.

Gene Edwards's story haunts me. *"I did not ask of you that you serve me,"* God cries out to His beloved. *"Neither did I ask of you your worship nor your prayers."*

Those are powerful statements, because they zero in on the two ways we Christians usually try to get close to God. Through service and through worship, the same methods by which Lazarus's sisters tended to relate to Jesus.

Martha, of course, is the poster child for service—the original Martha Stewart of Israel. Her story in Luke 10:38–42 highlights the difficulties that arise when we get so caught up in good works that we lose sight of our relationship with God. It's easy to become so enamored with the human approval that comes from giving our lives away—volunteering for worthy causes, teaching Sunday school every week, delivering meals to shut-ins, and so on—that we never get around to resting in God's presence, drinking in His life, and pouring out our love.

Though our acts of service are vital to our walk with God and even prove our faith, according to James 2:17, they were meant to be the outflow of a relationship with God—not a replacement for it.

Edwards's story reminds me that while God has chosen to involve us in His work of redeeming the world, He didn't really *need* to do that. In reality, all He had to do was speak—for He is the all-powerful One. Whatever was needed He could have done.

God didn't need us. But oh how He *wanted* us to be His own.

That's the freedom Jesus offered Martha. Freedom from the God she thought He was, forever demanding more, always more, and of a higher quality, always higher. In Christ she found a God who wanted to share her life, not consume it. A Father who wanted her love more than He wanted her busy service.

But what about worship? After all, that's what Mary seemed to offer Jesus, and He commended her for it. Could it be possible that God desires something more from us than that?

Before we delve into that question, it's important to note that Mary knew what true worship was. She knew it had far more to do with nurturing a relationship than coming up with the appropriate response to a message or singing the right combination of praise songs and hymns. She knew Jesus wanted her heart far more than her liturgy, as beautiful as it might be. He wanted to make her His own. That's why she was able to stop striving and simply sit at His feet. Her availability was more precious than any outward form of worship.

I realize it's almost sacrilegious in some areas of today's Christian culture to suggest that God might be looking for more than our praise. We've elevated worship to a place that nearly teeters on idolatry. We've said worship is our highest calling—and important it is.

But listen! The angels already provide God with praise. They surround the throne of God 24/7. You and I were not created to add voices to the angelic choir. We were created to enjoy an intimate relationship with the King of the Universe.

Please know how much I love praising God, how much I need it! There is something beautiful and profound about expressing my love for God through words and song. There is something sacred about lifting my hands, joining my voice with yours, and exalting Jesus with my lips. I can't live without it!

But if that is where my relationship with Jesus ends, I am missing it. Really missing it. Because it is possible to become addicted to praise without really becoming addicted to God. And when that happens, our worship ceases to be worship and turns into just another ritual. Moving and melodic perhaps, but in the end just empty religious words and motions.

Bottom line: If I truly want to be a friend of God, it won't be my service or my praise that brings Him joy. Instead, the kind of relationship I believe Christ longs for most may be exemplified best in the sibling who said and did the least.

In the beautiful acceptance Jesus offered Lazarus and the love Lazarus returned, we discover the good news of the gospel. Freedom from the tyranny of works and the spiritual contortions we often use in an attempt to please and/or appease our God. In the story of Lazarus, we are invited to relax. To simply enjoy hanging out with God.

Because Jesus isn't looking for servants.

He isn't looking for worshiping admirers.

He is looking for friends.

And the more unlikely the friendship, it seems, the better.

GROUPIES OR FRIENDS?

From the world's point of view, Jesus didn't seem very picky about His friendships. He hung out with the lowliest of the low—the despised, the forgotten, and the unnoticed. One of the accusations leveled against our Savior was that He was "a friend of tax collectors and 'sinners' " (Luke 7:34).

For the most part, that accusation was true. Jesus seemed far more interested in the sincerity of a heart than the perfection of a life, and He found many sincere seekers among those the religious elite labeled as "sinners." But it wasn't just the poor and the messed-up that Jesus came to save. He came for ordinary folks and the extraordinary as well.

"To all who received him," John proclaims in his gospel, "to those who believed in his name, he gave the right to become children of God" (John 1:12). You didn't have to perform or measure up to some religious standard to be Jesus's friend. You simply had to accept what He had to offer. However, the depth and type of friendship depended completely on the response of the person to whom it was offered. And it still does today.

As I was praying about this chapter and what the Holy Spirit wanted to say through it, one thing became very clear to me. Surrounded by people who claim His name, Christ still longs for a genuine friend. A real, true-blue, when-the-chips-are-down kind of friend. A friend who cares about what He cares about. A friend who looks to bring joy and comfort to His heart, with no strings attached. No hidden agendas. No secret wish lists.

Interestingly, in the Greek language there are two distinct words for "friend"—*philos* and *hetairos*. It is unfortunate that the English translation for both terms is the same word, for the Greek terms could not be more different.

The first word, *philos,* is the term Jesus used when He called Lazarus "our friend" in John 11:11. It denotes someone "loved, dear, befriended." It is an intimate classification reserved for those close to the heart.

The second term used in the Greek, *hetairos,* can be translated "comrade or companion," but it refers to a darker kind of relationship. According to Spiros Zodhiates,

> *hetaíros* refer[s] to comrades or companions who were mostly followers of a chief. They were not necessarily companions for the sake of helping the chief, but for getting whatever advantage they could.… The verb *hetaíré* basically means to keep company with or to establish and maintain a meretricious, pretentious, ostentatious, deceptive, and misleading friendship.[7]

Sounds a little like our society today, doesn't it? We are encouraged to network, schmooze, and work the angles. Do whatever it takes to succeed, we're told. Be friendly on the surface. Just make sure it furthers your agenda underneath.

"True friendship," on the other hand, as Zodhiates explains, "is expressed by the verb *phileo*…which means to appropriate another person's interests unselfishly."[8]

At its most benign, *hetairos* was used to describe the pupils or disciples of teachers or rabbis. But this wasn't the term Jesus used when speaking of His own disciples in John 15:15 (or anywhere else for that matter). "I no longer call you servants," Jesus told them, "because a servant does not know his master's business. Instead, I have called you friends [*philous*[9]], for everything that I learned from my Father I have made known to you."

Jesus wasn't fostering an arm's-length business relationship with those who followed Him. He sought a sweet communion that would make the disciples actual

partakers of the divine nature (2 Peter 1:4, NKJV). Jesus promised to take everything God had given Him—the wisdom, the authority, the very character of God—
and share it freely with them. What an incredible gift. What an unimaginable
opportunity.

But not everyone appreciated the Lord's generosity. At least one of the disciples
wanted what *he* wanted—human recognition, power, position.

When Judas betrayed Jesus in Gethsemane, hoping to force the Son of God to

What Kind of Friend Am I?

We've all had needy, clinging friends who tended to take more than they
gave to the relationship. Though it might be a little painful, consider
the following qualities of a good friend as they relate to your relationship with God. How do you rate? Mark each characteristic with a 5
(for "Always"), 4 ("Usually"), 3 ("Sometimes"), 2 ("Rarely"), or 1
("Never").

_____   *Good listener:* Interested in how the other person is doing.
Asks good questions. Hears the other person out; doesn't
interrupt. Cares about that person's feelings. Comfortable
with silence.

_____   *Low maintenance:* Isn't overly needy. Secure in self and
friendship, not demanding. Doesn't need constant attention.
Isn't threatened by time apart.

_____   *Not easily offended:* Patient when needs aren't immediately met. Believes the best, not the worst, of the other
person. Doesn't jump to conclusions. Willing to talk
things out.

_____   *Available:* Always there when needed. Willing to set aside
own plans in order to help a friend. Returns calls quickly and
doesn't ignore e-mails.

do his bidding and declare Himself king, Jesus responded with these amazing words: "Friend, do what you came for" (Matthew 26:50).

Friend? That name seems strange for a betrayer. Until you read it in the Greek. Then you realize Jesus was calling Judas exactly what he had proven himself to be.[10]

Hetairos. Selfish comrade. Opportunist. Groupie. Unfaithful, deceptive friend.

Lazarus or Judas? *Philos* or *hetairos*? Which one will we be?

In the end, it's up to us.

_____ **Not jealous:** Doesn't get mad when time is spent with other people or someone gets a nicer birthday gift. Doesn't give the cold shoulder or leave nasty notes when upset.

_____ **Kind:** Quick with genuine words of affection and affirmation. Looks for practical ways to express love. Gentle sweetness creates a haven of safety.

_____ **Trustworthy:** Can be trusted with delicate information and difficult situations. Doesn't participate in gossip. Will not betray a friend—loyal to the point of death.

Now count your points. A score of 29–35 suggests you are well on your way to being a true friend of God; 22–28 means you'd like to be a good friend but need some work; 14–21 means you probably didn't realize you were supposed to be God's friend; 7–13 means you just don't care.

(Note: If you scored low, you may find your human relationships are suffering as well. How we express our love for God directly affects our love for people—and vice versa.)

He who loves a pure heart and whose speech is gracious
will have the king for his friend.
PROVERBS 22:11

LOVING HIM OR LOVING ME?

I wonder. I just wonder.

What if the love-doubt, the chronic detachment, even the *hetairos* tendency that plagues so many of us as Christians could be solved by a simple mind change? an attitude shift? a softening and opening of a heart that's grown cold and hard?

I know of a woman who has never quite gotten around to accepting her husband's love. Because she grew up in a dysfunctional home, she's never felt worthy or very secure. Her husband has done everything he can to convince her of his love, yet nothing is ever enough.

"I just don't feel like he loves me," she whines, listing all the ways he's let her down, though the man works two or three jobs to be able to give her what she wants. She seems almost happy in her misery, because it's become her identity. As for her poor husband—well, he looks tired. Very tired. He won't leave her or their marriage. He loves her far too much. But I see him slowly stepping back rather than stepping up. Shrugging his shoulders at her displeasure with the weariness only hopelessness can bring.

They will stay married, but unless this woman opens her heart to her husband's love, I fear they will increasingly be strangers. Two lonely people sleeping in one bed with enough love to quench both drought-stricken souls if the one would only open her heart to its flow.

Her husband isn't the only one who suffers this person's demanding diatribes. Her heavenly Father receives His share as well. He's loved her long, and He's loved her well, but you wouldn't know it to talk to her. According to her, nothing He does is ever enough.

When one of His other children receives a blessing, she crosses her arms and turns up her nose. "Well, I guess God loves you better than He loves me," she says, pretending her sarcasm is only pretend. When someone else's prayers are answered, she comments cynically, "I guess I better have you pray. He certainly doesn't listen to me."

She isn't always this cynical. Sometimes, especially when (in her view) God is behaving, she's fairly joyous. But when things don't go her way, she's quick to bad-mouth God. She'd never admit it, of course. She believes she's simply stating the facts. But I've heard her bitter resentment, and others have too.

While I know God will never leave her, I can't help but wonder how He feels when He hears her slander His name. Weary, I'm certain. Discouraged perhaps. For God knows He can't force her to let Him love her. He can't demand she return His friendship. It's a choice only she can make.

Unlike her husband, however, God doesn't put up with spoiled, demanding divas. He disciplines them even as He loves them. But they may never come to appreciate His devotion, let alone feel it, if they continue to insist (either consciously or not): "He just doesn't love me the way I need to be loved."

Speaking Well of His Name

Isn't it strange how we humans tend to view God as our servant rather than our Master? Insisting that He do our bidding rather than standing ready to do His? It's no wonder we fail so often in the holy pursuit of being His friend.

"Here is a solemn thought for those who would be friends of God," Charles Haddon Spurgeon once wrote. "A man's friend must show himself friendly, and behave with tender care for his friend."[11]

Let me ask you a question. Do you speak well of God? Is His name safe on your tongue?

More and more I'm hearing Christians bad-mouth God. Rather than recalling what our heavenly Father has done for us in the past—His faithfulness and His goodness—we fixate on the unresolved problems of the present, thrashing about, accusing God of abandonment. Slandering His name rather than calling on it. Pushing away, rather than stepping toward, the love we so desperately need.

I understand how easy that is to do. Spiritual amnesia is a common condition among Christians. We've all suffered an unholy forgetfulness at times that eclipses any answered prayers or kindnesses received in the past. Like the Israelites of old, we tend to be slow to express gratitude when things are good yet quick to complain when things are bad. But if you and I are ever to be true friends of God, dear one, we need to start acting like one.

George Müller, one of the nineteenth century's greatest missionaries, opened hundreds of orphanages, taking in the indigent children of England. It wasn't an easy job. And yet he wrote at the end of his life, "In the greatest difficulties, in the heaviest trials, in the deepest poverty and necessities, [God] has never failed me; but because I was enabled by His grace to trust in Him, He has always appeared for my help. I delight in speaking well of His Name."[12]

Oh how I want that to be true of my life!

Last night, after being gone for a few days to write, I slipped back into town to spend the evening with John and Joshua.

Most kids, especially little kids, tend to make their parents pay for going away. Whether it's conscious or unconscious, they withdraw a bit, wanting you to know they're put out because you left them. Even if you left them with their dad. Even if he did fix them peanut-butter-and-jelly sandwiches every day, take them to the park, and spring for bowling and pizza one night and a video the next.

No, you surely abandoned them. So you must feel their pain.

I am so fortunate. Josh doesn't play games like that. Instead of sulking, he's the first one to meet me at the door.

"Mommy!" he cries as he rounds the corner and lunges into my arms. "I missed you!" Then pulling me into the living room, he tells me all about his day and the pizza and the bowling.

"I wuuuuv you," he says in his sweet, soft drawl, pressing close. As close as he can, until we're just one mushy heart sitting on a couch, sipping the love shared between us.

Josh doesn't greet me with a cold shoulder. He doesn't wait until I reach out for him. He leaps toward me.

That is the relationship, the friendship, Jesus longs to have with every one of us. And because of the Cross, a door has been opened into God's presence that allows us to run straight into His arms, joyfully claiming His gaga love for us. Singing with confidence the words of the wonderful old song:

> Friendship with Jesus,
> Fellowship divine;

Oh, what blessed sweet communion,
Jesus is a friend of mine.[13]

But true friendship must be reciprocated—a give-and-take of love on both sides. Anything less leads only to mere acquaintances.

Though I'm honored and privileged to have Jesus as my friend, my deepest desire is to be His friend as well. Proclaiming how much I love Him and then showing it in practical, visible ways. Laying down my wants and wishes that I might love my Savior with His best interests in mind.

A true *philos*. A genuine friend. Loyal and devoted.

From beginning to end.

Jesus loved Martha and her sister and Lazarus.
Yet when he heard that Lazarus was sick,
he stayed where he was two more days....
On his arrival, Jesus found that Lazarus had already
been in the tomb for four days....
When Martha heard that Jesus was coming,
she went out to meet him, but Mary stayed at home.
"Lord," Martha said to Jesus, "if you had been here,
my brother would not have died.
But I know that even now God will give you whatever you ask."....
"Where have you laid him?" [Jesus] asked.
"Come and see, Lord," they replied.
Jesus wept.

JOHN 11:5–6, 17, 20–22, 34–35

When Love Tarries

I remember how excited I was the morning of my twelfth Christmas. Of all the things I'd asked for, the one thing I really wanted was the one thing I actually needed (an advent of practicality I wouldn't experience again until my late thirties when my only Christmas wish was for a really good office chair).

That year all I wanted was a metronome—a mechanical device that my piano teacher promised would help my rhythm. Although I'd taken piano lessons for six years, I still struggled with one of the most important and fundamental principles of music. Keeping time.

The composition in front of me might call for adagio, which means "slowly." But I tended to play nearly everything allegro—"fast." Really, really fast. Once I got the notes down and my fingers learned their part, I'd attempt to follow the composer's directions at the top of the page. I'd try to interpret his or her vision for the piece. But eventually, no matter what the instructions, I allegroed everything. I just couldn't help it. And while I've improved a lot since my early days, I still tend to anticipate the beat.

In my defense I must say that long-ago Christmas gift wasn't a lot of help. Rather than performing the crisp *tick, tick, tick* its back-and-forth motion was designed to give, my new metronome had a little hitch in it. A hitch that was in direct opposition to the hitch in me. Rather than anticipating the count, the metronome seemed to pause a bit before sounding the next beat. Which really *tick, tick, tick*ed me off!

I had my mother take the metronome back to the store. I even complained to my teacher. But both sources told us the device was fine. Yes, the pause was a little annoying, they agreed, but the beat itself was right on time. I needed to adjust to the metronome, they told me, rather than demand it adjust to me.

That's a fundamental principle of life I'm still trying to learn—and a valuable one. Because, for some reason, God seems awfully fond of pauses. And nowhere is His propensity toward delay more evident than in the story of Lazarus.

The Inconvenient Patience of Love

"Do you see anything yet?" I imagine Martha asking quietly as she joins her sister on the front porch. "Jesus should have been here by now, don't you think?"

But Mary doesn't answer. She can't. Turning away instead to hide her tears, she goes back into the house to check on their brother.

"Where are You, Lord?" Martha whispers as she gazes down the dirt road, looking for shapes on the horizon or, at the very least, a lone figure coming back with news of Jesus's pending arrival. But there is nothing—only one bird calling to another in the distance and the sun beating down on her head.

"Where are You?" Martha groans softly.

Suddenly a loud wail comes from the house behind her, and Martha knows her brother is gone. After a final desperate glance down the road, she rushes to find her sister collapsed at Lazarus's bedside, stroking and kissing his lifeless hand as tears course down her cheeks.

Why? The depth of sorrow in Mary's eyes magnifies Martha's own pain as her sister pleads for help to make sense of it all. "Why didn't Jesus come?" she asks. "Why did Lazarus have to die?"

But there are no answers—none that make sense. So the two sisters find comfort where they can. In each other's arms.

And in their pain we find echoes of our own confusion. As well as questions—so very many questions.

What are we to do when God doesn't behave the way we thought He should, the way we were taught He would? What are we to feel when our Savior seemingly pulls a no-show, leaving us to wrestle with the pain on our own?

These difficult times—these dark nights of the soul[1]—rattle our convictions and shake the foundations of our faith. Author Brian Jones writes about such a crisis in his book *Second Guessing God:*

The year before I graduated from seminary, I lost my faith in God. That's not a smart thing to do, I'll admit. There's not a big job market out there for pastors who are atheists. But I couldn't help it. Life was becoming too painful. Truth had become too open to interpretation.... My doubts seemed to climb on top of one another, clamoring for attention. Before I knew what had happened, the new car smell of my faith had worn off, and I found myself fighting to hang on.[2]

After reading every book he could find on the existence of God and enduring months of sleepless nights, Jones reached the point of panic attacks and deep depression, even thoughts of suicide. One night, frantic, he called a former professor who had been a mentor to him.

"In the last six months doubt has begun to paralyze me," he told the older man. "It's like when the water goes back out to the ocean. [Doubt] is washing away the sand underneath me, and my feet keep sinking lower and lower and lower. If this keeps up, there won't be anything left to stand on."[3]

Rather than reacting with a sermon on the necessity of faith, the wise professor acknowledged Brian's struggle, even sharing his own battle against unbelief. But then he added these final words: "Brian, listen to me when I say this. When the last grain of sand is finally gone, you're going to discover that you're standing on a rock."[4]

"That one sentence saved me," Jones writes. It helped him hold on long enough to eventually rediscover hope.[5]

No, his doubts weren't obliterated overnight, but the professor's words provided Jones enough light to start heading back home. Away from the wilderness of wondering and wandering, back to the only place that's truly safe.

The heart of God.

Does He Love Me?

In John 11:5–6 we see this strange paradox: "Jesus *loved* Martha and her sister and Lazarus. *Yet* when he heard that Lazarus was sick, he *stayed* where he was two more days" (emphasis added).

Jesus loved…yet He stayed where he was.

He loved…but He didn't show up when He was expected.

How can that be? our hearts cry. It just doesn't make sense.

And that is the core of the issue, isn't it? Because most of the love-doubt we feel can be traced back to troubling contradictions not unlike the one in the story of Lazarus. Inconsistencies like the ones Brian Jones experienced. Doubts that eat away at the bedrock of our faith, leaving us floundering, gasping for air as we try to keep our spiritual heads above water.

I'm sure the sorrow Mary and Martha felt must have threatened to swamp all they knew and believed about Jesus. It certainly left them shaken.

John 11:20 tells us, "When Martha heard that Jesus was coming, she went out to meet him, but Mary stayed at home."

Two different responses from two very different sisters—and unexpected ones, at that. Strangely, it was the sister who had once questioned Jesus's love ("Lord, don't you care?" Luke 10:40) who now went running toward Him. While the sister who had sat at the Master's feet in sweet communion remained in the house, paralyzed by grief.

Why do you suppose they reacted so differently?

I have no way of knowing for sure, but I believe it was because Martha had already gone through a testing of faith, while Mary was just entering that crucible process (as eventually all of us do).

As strange as it might sound, it may have been the Lord's denial of what Martha had wanted earlier in their relationship that allowed her to find what her heart needed most on that grief-filled day.

Rather than responding with practical help when she'd demanded more assistance in the kitchen, Jesus had simply replied, "Martha, Martha, you are worried and upset about many things, but only one thing is needed" (Luke 10:41–42). With those words He'd exposed Martha's biggest problem—and her deepest need.

She hadn't needed more help in the kitchen. She'd needed the "one thing"—Jesus Himself. Though His rebuke must have hurt, I believe Martha took His words to heart. As she humbled herself and embraced the Lord's correction, her heart was enabled to embrace His love. No wonder she was the sister who ran down the road to meet Jesus after her brother died.

Somewhere in that earlier time of testing, I believe Martha discovered three marvelous, indomitable truths we all need to know. Three rock-solid facts on which we too can rest our hearts:

1. God is *love*—therefore I am loved.
2. God is *good*—therefore I am safe.
3. God is *faithful*—therefore it's going to be okay. For God is incapable of doing anything less than marvelous things.[6]

Martha chose to trust God's love and His faithful goodness. Because of that, when tough times came, she was able to trust His sovereignty as well—His right to do as He deems best, when and how He wants to do it.

That's why she could run to Jesus, fall at His feet, and pour out her heart with both pain and sweet abandon. "Lord," she cried, "if you had been here, my brother would not have died. But I know that even now God will give you whatever you ask" (John 11:21–22).

Here is the quill of my will, Lord, Martha was saying. You *write the end of the story. For You do all things well.*

Surrendering the quill of my will has always been a difficult process for me. You see, I have such good ideas about how my story, not to mention the stories of the people I love, should be written. Always Daddy's little helper, I'm quick to provide God with lists of alternate ideas in case my Plan A doesn't match up with His. "You don't care for that one, Lord? Well, how about Plans B, C, D, and E? Why, I even have a Plan Z if you'd like more details."

Unfortunately, none of my planning and plotting has ever drawn me closer to God. In fact, it usually does the opposite.

While I'm busy scheming, my Father is apt to move on, leaving me to work the angles on my own. *That wasn't my plan, Joanna,* He gently whispers when I finally call out to Him. *If you want to walk with Me, you have to surrender your itinerary and trust Mine.*

Surrender was the key to Martha's amazing transformation, and it is the key to ours as well. For whenever we choose to give up our agendas and submit to God's plan, we release Him to have His way in our lives. More important, when we choose to pursue the "one thing" of knowing Christ rather than continually choosing to do "our own thing," we discover the great depths of His love just as Martha did.

Unfortunately, these concepts are easy to talk about and much harder to live out. Especially when God's timing runs contrary to our own.

WHO'S FOLLOWING WHOM?

My son Joshua loves music. Every once in a while, I'll catch him bobbing his head or bouncing around in his chair. "Whatcha doing, honey?" I'll ask.

"Oh, I'm just dancing to the music in my head," he'll reply with a sheepish grin.

What an adorable pastime—for a little boy. But it's not such a good practice for a full-grown adult like me. Because, as I've mentioned, the music in my head often proves faulty, especially when it comes to following a beat.

It's been a while since I've played piano with a worship band. It's proven too traumatic for everyone involved, especially the poor drummers. My anticipation of the downbeat tends to turn the most mellow musicians into *tick, tick, tick*ing time bombs of pure frustration. So most of the time, out of a desire not to cause people to sin, I elect to sit out.

But our new church's sound system has nifty headphones that allow the drummer to block out the piano, if need be, and the pianist to turn up the drummer, if she prefers. So these days, with their help I occasionally try playing with the band.

My tendency to anticipate the downbeat is as strong as ever, but I'm learning to play with the tempo, rather than against it, by

- turning up the beat in my headphones,
- relinquishing control to the drummer,
- relaxing into the flow of the music set by him.

Because here's the deal. Joe, our drummer, has rhythm. I do not—unless I choose to follow his lead.

I'm trying to learn that in my Christian walk as well. If I'll move to the beat of the Spirit and relinquish control of my life to Him, I'll be able to dance to the music God has playing in *His* head rather than movin' and agroovin' to the catchy little tunes I've got going in my own. For when I allow the Lord to provide the accompaniment to my life, I discover a richly layered soundtrack more beautiful than anything I could compose myself.

But following God's beat, dancing to His rhythm, trusting in His sovereignty—all that can be hard for a rhythmically challenged, control-loving person like me. Because when it comes right down to it, I'm a headstrong little girl who wants her own way in pretty much every area of life.

Fortunately, I have a Father who loves me in spite of that. But while He loves me as I am, He also loves me too much to leave me that way. So He insists I follow His lead in order to "grow up" in my salvation (1 Peter 2:2). Becoming more like Jesus and less like me.

The Art of Waiting

Have you ever felt the need to rush ahead of God? All through Scripture we are encouraged to develop the all-important—and really difficult—art of waiting. Warren Wiersbe shares three statements in Scripture that have helped him hone prayerful patience in his own life—principles he applies whenever he feels nervous about a situation and is tempted to hurry God:

1. "*Stand still,* and see the salvation of the LORD" (Exodus 14:13, NKJV).
2. "*Sit still*...until you know how the matter will turn out" (Ruth 3:18, NKJV).
3. "*Be still,* and know that I am God" (Psalm 46:10).

"When you wait on the Lord in prayer," Wiersbe writes, "you are not wasting your time; you are investing it. God is preparing both you and your circumstances so that His purposes will be accomplished. However, when the right time arrives for us to act by faith, we dare not delay."[7]

> *But they that wait upon the LORD shall renew their strength;*
> *they shall mount up with wings as eagles;*
> *they shall run, and not be weary;*
> *and they shall walk, and not faint.*
>
> ISAIAH 40:31, KJV

And therein lies another problem. Because growing up, my friend, can be hard to do.

BEING A BIG GIRL

From the moment we're born, we tend to associate love with what others do (or do not do) for us and the speed with which they do it. We learn to feel loved when we get our needs met—quickly.

And that's appropriate...for babies.

Unfortunately, a lot of us never outgrow that view of love. When we cry (or whine creatively, as I like to call it), we expect an immediate response.

The Blessing of Trouble

Of all the hard sayings of the Bible, perhaps none is as difficult to understand as Jesus's response to Lazarus's death in John 11:15. "For your sake I am glad I was not there," He tells the disciples. But then He adds the reason: "so that you may believe." Jesus knows that some of life's greatest gifts come wrapped in disappointments, and faith is often learned best in the crucible of pain. Listen to Charles Haddon Spurgeon's thoughts on this verse:

> If you want to ruin your son, never let him know a hardship. When he is a child carry him in your arms, when he becomes a youth still dandle him, and when he becomes a man still dry-nurse him, and you will succeed in producing an arrant fool. If you want to prevent his being made useful in the world, guard him from every kind of toil. Do not suffer him to struggle. Wipe the sweat from his dainty brow and say, "Dear child, thou shalt never have another task so arduous." Pity him when he ought to be punished; supply all his wishes, avert all disappointments, prevent all troubles, and you will surely tutor him to be a reprobate and to break your heart. But put him where he must work, expose him to difficulties,

"I'm dying of thirst," I tell my destination-focused husband as we travel down the interstate on vacation.

"You're not dying," he says calmly (though after so many years of marriage, you'd think he'd know this isn't the response I'm looking for).

What I want is for John to immediately look for the next exit and the closest minimart. *If he* really *loved me,* I think (and occasionally comment out loud), *he'd phone ahead to make sure they have the diet drink I prefer as well as a four-star rest room to accommodate the last Big Gulp I gulped down.*

Okay, I'm not that bad...usually. But, sadly, I sometimes carry the same childish, demanding spirit into my relationship with God. Not as often as I used to, however, because like my husband, my heavenly Father has proven difficult to manipulate.

purposely throw him into peril, and in this way you shall make him a man, and when he comes to do man's work and to bear man's trial, he shall be fit for either. My Master does not daintily cradle His children when they ought to run alone; and when they begin to run He is not always putting out His finger for them to lean upon, but He lets them tumble down to the cutting of their knees, because then they will walk more carefully by-and-by, and learn to stand upright by the strength which faith confers upon them.

You see, dear friends, that Jesus Christ was glad—glad that His disciples were blessed by trouble. Will you think of this, you who are so troubled this morning, Jesus Christ does sympathize with you, but still He does it wisely, and He says, "I am glad for your sakes that I was not there."[8]

No discipline seems pleasant at the time, but painful.
Later on, however, it produces a harvest of righteousness and peace
for those who have been trained by it.
HEBREWS 12:11

You see, God knows that if He indulged my insatiable desire to have instantaneous help at each and every juncture, I would never grow up. Not really. Instead, I'd be crippled emotionally and unable to stand, let alone walk, on my own.

Growing to maturity means learning to accept delayed gratification. Children and adults alike must learn to

- adapt to less-than-perfect situations,
- wait for the fulfillment of their needs,
- accept not only delays but also denials of what they want.

For anything less results in demanding divas and toddler terrorists.

"When I was a child," Paul writes in 1 Corinthians 13:11, "I talked like a child, I thought like a child, I reasoned like a child. When I became a man, I put childish ways behind me." Part of putting childish ways behind us, spiritually speaking, involves setting aside our misconception that if God loves us, He must act according to our specifications, our scripts, and especially our time lines.

Why is this important? Consider Paul's words in verse 12: "Now we see but a poor reflection as in a mirror; then we shall see face to face. Now I know in part; then I shall know fully, even as I am fully known."

Whether we realize it or not, we see only a small part of a very big picture. God, on the other hand, sees it all. That's why He refuses to operate solely on our recommendations. While we are encouraged to bring our needs and even our creative whining to Him—to "come boldly to the throne of grace" with full assurance that He hears and answers our prayers (Hebrews 4:16, NKJV)—we must leave the responses to our requests up to Him.

For if we are ever to get past our love-doubt, we must accept the reality that God's answers are not always the answers we are looking for. Instead of saying yes to all our requests, like a wise parent, God often chooses to say no.

And sometimes, as in the case of Lazarus, His answer is…wait awhile.

A Long Time to Wait

According to the Bible, when Jesus arrived in Bethany, Lazarus had been dead for four days. Why did Jesus choose to wait so long before resurrecting His friend?

Some scholars say it was to counteract the Jewish belief that the soul hovers over the body for three days before departing.[9] That explains why grieving families often delayed entombment—to avoid the unlikely but tragic possibility of burying someone alive. Within three days the soul might still reenter the body. But four days? Well, four days meant all hope was gone. It was time to let go and move on.

So Jesus's delay makes sense, I suppose. But I confess to wondering if it was really necessary for Jesus to put His friends through all that painful waiting. Couldn't He have done it a different way?

You could ask the same question about a lot of stories in the Bible.

Was it really necessary to leave Joseph rotting in an Egyptian prison cell for such an extended period? Was it vitally important that the Israelites wander in the desert for forty years and Noah drift on a flood for months in a boat that took perhaps a century to build? Were twenty-five years really necessary to get Abraham from the promise to Pampers? Surely there had to be simpler, not to mention faster, methods by which to fulfill God's purposes.

Now, it could be argued that many of the extended delays outlined above were caused by the people themselves. If Joseph hadn't bragged to his brothers and if the Israelites had believed God rather than their doubting eyes and if Abraham hadn't pulled an Ishmael, who knows what the trajectories of their journeys might have looked like? After all, did the ark really require one hundred years of construction, or was Noah just a procrastinator like me with a tendency to view God's mandate as more of a hobby than an actual career?

We just don't know. But the good news I find in all these stories is the astounding truth that no matter what happens, God's plans always eventually succeed. Despite our stumblings and fumblings and even our outright rebellion, our mighty God will accomplish His work one way or another.

Though it seems to me He could find better resources, God consistently chooses to do it through you and me. Whether we follow willingly (though imperfectly) or have to be dragged kicking and screaming to our own personal Nineveh by a proverbial whale, "it is the LORD's purpose that prevails" (Proverbs 19:21).

But please know that while God is committed to His plans, He is not insensitive to our pain. We are not pawns in some celestial chess match. We are His children, "chosen...and dearly loved" (Colossians 3:12).

Loved, in fact, to the point of tears.

Jesus wept, remember, as He stood before Lazarus's tomb (John 11:35).

While theologians disagree about what may have caused Jesus's tears—some attributing it to anger over what sin had done to the world and others to the lack of faith in the people around Him—I believe it was love that made Jesus weep. Though He knew His friend would soon walk out completely well and fully alive, the Lord still mourned along with the family He counted so dear.

He felt their pain, but His own heart broke as well.

Enduring Love

When the writer of John 11:6 tells us that Jesus stayed where He was two days longer, he uses the Greek word *meno*. "This term not only means that he stayed—or tarried—two days more," Jerry Goebel writes, "it also means he *endured* two more days. This adds great meaning to the verse. It tells us how difficult it was for Jesus to hold Himself back from rushing to Lazarus' side."[10]

Ah, the great restraint of God. We rarely think about how hard it must be for a Father who loves us so much to hold back from running constantly to our rescue. Yet in His merciful wisdom He does, because He knows there is a greater good and a higher plan at work.

Jesus Himself consistently resisted pleas to speed up His work, choosing instead to live by heaven's metronome. He refused to be pushed into a miracle by His mother (John 2:4), and He wouldn't be goaded by His brothers into going to Jerusalem before His time (John 7:6–10). Though our Lord eventually did both, He did them according to the timetable given by His Father, not at the prompting of demanding voices around Him.

So when Jesus told the disciples, "Lazarus is dead, and for your sake I am glad I was not there, so that you may believe" (John 11:14–15), He was declaring His purpose as well as His love. It wasn't that He didn't care. He was simply pointing out that there was a whole lot more at stake than His friends knew. The stage was being set for Jesus to be crucified and God to be glorified. And all of it—the tragedy and the triumph, the sorrow and the joy—was part of what would become the foundation of your faith and mine.[11]

For *"at just the right time,"* Paul writes in Romans 5:6, "when we were still powerless, Christ died for the ungodly" (emphasis added). The events leading up to the Cross didn't happen too soon. Nor did they take place too late.

And neither do the events of our lives, no matter how it may feel. If we'll rest in God's goodness and trust His perfect, sovereign timing, we'll be able to say along with David, "My times are in your hands" (Psalm 31:15). Even when the hourglass seems to be running out and waiting proves the most difficult work we do.

For you can't rush a resurrection, nor can you hurry God along. He has His own internal speedometer, and as much as we'd like it, there is no pedal to push when we wish He'd pick up the pace.

However, we can count on this: God is at work. Though it seems we're walking toward a funeral, something marvelous is waiting on the other side.

A brand-new life, four days in the making.

Christ revealed in you and me so that the whole world might see.

MOVING BEYOND WHY

One of the most powerful testimonies I've ever heard came from a man born with cerebral palsy. David Ring is an evangelist and a powerful communicator even though, at first, his words are difficult to understand. When you listen closely, however, you are drawn into a message that is nothing less than transformative.

"Why, Mama?" David used to ask his mother when school kids teased him. "Why did I have to be born this way?" Although exceptionally bright, he was caught in a body that wouldn't do his bidding and constantly tripped up by a stuttering tongue.

God gave that sweet mother incredible wisdom as she taught her son that perhaps *why* wasn't the best question after all.

"Asking why is like going to a well with a bucket and coming up empty every time," Ring's mother told him. Instead, she said, the question should be, "What can I become?"[12]

What a powerful, life-changing concept for all of us, especially when we're trapped and tripped up by the whys of life. Because when it comes right down to it, life is full of questions that don't have adequate answers.

Why are some children born healthy and others are not?

Why do some mothers have to scrounge for food in sub-Saharan Africa, while mothers like me struggle to choose from endless aisles of endless food in grocery stores just around the corner?

Why do good and godly people die slow and painful deaths while others, depraved and careless, enjoy long lives padded with bulging bank accounts and multiple vacation homes?

Why does it sometimes seem that God has forgotten us?

Such questions haunted the writers of the Old Testament. "Why have you forsaken me?" cried the psalmist (Psalm 22:1). "Why does the way of the wicked prosper?" the prophet Jeremiah asked (Jeremiah 12:1). And again, "Why did I ever come out of the womb to see trouble and sorrow and to end my days in shame?" (Jeremiah 20:18).

Those questions haunted my friend Tom as well.[13] Tom was a sweet kid who started coming to our church as an eleven-year-old. His mom, who struggled with addictions, often drank away the rent money, and Tom lived in fear that they would be kicked out on the street. During his teen years he stayed with us from time to time.

Though Tom loved Jesus, he struggled with his own temptations, especially with the whys of his difficult life. But I'll never forget the morning he came bounding upstairs, his sixteen-year-old face smiling as only Tom can smile. "I figured it out, Mama Jo!" he said. "Now I know why my life is the way it is."

With a huge grin he handed me his Bible and pointed to where he'd been reading. It was the story from John 9 where Jesus healed a man who had been born blind. The disciples (and almost everyone else) assumed that sin—either that of the blind man or his parents—was to blame for the man's disability. But Jesus said otherwise, and that's what had Tom so excited.

"Look, Mama," he said, pointing at the verse, then pointing at himself with a smile as we read it together.

"This happened so that the work of God might be displayed in his life" (John 9:3).

Oh that we all might have vision to see beyond the misery of what is to the miracle of what we can become. But that kind of foresight comes only through surrender. Through laying down our wants and wishes so we might live for God's alone.

In the Meantime

Four days is a long time to wait for a resurrection, especially when you feel that all hope is gone. Figuratively, you may be living in those dark 96 hours before dawn, wondering if the 5,760 minutes will ever end. Each of the 345,600 seconds that make up your waiting seems to hold its breath interminably, like my malfunctioning metronome, leaving you suspended between faith and doubt. Wondering if the dissonant chord hanging over your life will ever be resolved.

Four days is a long time to wait. I know. I've endured their incessant length myself.

But believe me, none of it is wasted time.

Although we may be "hard pressed on every side," Paul reminds us in 2 Corinthians 4:8–9, we are not crushed. Though we may feel "perplexed," we are not in despair. Though we are "persecuted," we are not abandoned. Though "struck down," we are not destroyed.

Instead, the apostle—beaten and stoned, shipwrecked three times—reminds us that we "carry around in our body the death of Jesus, so that the life of Jesus may also be revealed in our body" (verse 10).

Don't you love the creative irony of God! Paul is telling us that the very circumstances and events we believe will destroy us, the ones that generate so many of our whys, can actually serve as catalysts for the full manifestation of Christ in our lives— Jesus more accurately revealed in you and me. After all, as 1 Peter 1:7 reminds us, these trials "have come so that your faith—of greater worth than gold, which perishes even though refined by fire—may be proved genuine and may result in praise, glory and honor when *Jesus Christ is revealed*" (emphasis added).

In other words, don't get so caught up in what's happening that you miss what is really going on.[14] For if we'll listen for the beat of a different Drummer and relinquish control of our lives to His loving, sovereign lead, nothing will be wasted.

Not the waiting, not our questions, not even our pain.

For when you can't trace God's hand, you can trust His heart.

On his arrival, Jesus found that Lazarus had already
been in the tomb for four days.
Bethany was less than two miles from Jerusalem,
and many Jews had come to Martha and Mary to comfort
them in the loss of their brother.
When Martha heard that Jesus was coming, she went
out to meet him, but Mary stayed at home.
"Lord," Martha said to Jesus, "if you had been here,
my brother would not have died.
But I know that even now God will give you whatever you ask."....
When Jesus saw [Mary] weeping, and the Jews who had come
along with her also weeping,
he was deeply moved in spirit and troubled.
"Where have you laid him?" [Jesus] asked.
"Come and see, Lord," they replied.
Jesus wept.

JOHN 11:17–22, 33–35

Tomb Dwelling

I 'll never forget my first visit to New Orleans more than a decade ago. It was before the tragedy of Hurricane Katrina, so the city I encountered was full of life. I enjoyed powdered-sugar beignets at the Café Du Monde, browsed quaint antique shops, and listened to street musicians playing every flavor of jazz imaginable. But of all the sights I saw—the antebellum mansions, the horse-drawn carriages, the paddleboats with their giant wheels patiently treading the Mississippi—it is the cemeteries that I remember most.

Because the city is built below sea level, normal burials are impossible in most of New Orleans. "The coffins eventually float to the surface," the tour guide told us as we passed one enormous graveyard. "That's the reason for the above-ground mausoleums, both individual ones and large ones that hold entire families."

Though the tour bus drove by the cemetery quickly, the sight was graphic and a little disturbing. I couldn't get past the loneliness and haunting sadness that seemed to shroud the graveyard like the Spanish moss dripping from the trees. And that was in broad daylight.

I can't begin to imagine what it would be like to visit a place like that at night... let alone live there.

LIVING AMONG TOMBS

One of the things I love most about Jesus is that He seeks us out wherever we may be. He never tires of going out of His way to find us, crossing stormy seas as well as eternity just to make us His own.

Luke 8:22 tells us that "one day Jesus said to his disciples, 'Let's go over to the other side of the lake.' " According to the parallel time line given in Matthew, He had just finished a busy couple of weeks. After preaching the Sermon on the Mount to thousands (Matthew 5–7), Jesus healed a leper, then traveled to Capernaum to heal a suffering paralytic and Peter's fevered mother-in-law (8:1–15). That same evening, according to Matthew, "many who were demon-possessed were brought to him, and he drove out the spirits with a word and healed all the sick" (8:16).

It was after this exhausting schedule that Jesus gave the order to cross to the other side of the lake. But what might appear at first glance to be a weary man's attempt to get away from a demanding crowd was actually nothing of the kind. Jesus wasn't suggesting an escape route. He was simply moving toward the next destination God had logged into the navigational guide of His ministry from the beginning of time.

Though a crowd of needy people remained on one side of the lake, Jesus left them all in order to meet the needs of an individual on the other side. One lonely, tormented soul living on the outskirts of civilization. In a graveyard.

Listen to how Mark 5:2–5 describes the scene:

When Jesus got out of the boat, a man with an evil spirit came from the tombs to meet Him. This man lived in the tombs, and no one could bind him any more, not even with a chain. For he had often been chained hand and foot, but he tore the chains apart and broke the irons on his feet. No one was strong enough to subdue him. Night and day among the tombs and in the hills he would cry out and cut himself with stones.

What a sad, eerie picture of a tormented life. And yet when the man saw Jesus, he ran and fell at His feet. "What do you want with me, Jesus, Son of the Most High God?" he shouted at the top of his voice. "Swear to God that you won't torture me!" (verse 7).

Isn't it amazing how the very thing we need is often the last thing we want? Here was a man who lived surrounded by death. Yet when he encountered the Lord of Life, the one and only One who could deliver him, he didn't call out for help. Instead, self-preservation was his first response. "What do you want with me? Don't torture me!"

Now, I realize it was the demons in the man who spoke these words. Yet I think it's important to note that Satan often uses the same arguments to keep us from surrendering to the work of God in our lives. *It will be too painful,* he hisses. *Why doesn't He just leave you alone? There's no hope for you anyway.*

It's much easier to stay in your bondage, he suggests. *Sure, you roam the graveyard of your past day and night, trying to find answers. Sure, your mind is tormented as you mutilate yourself in an attempt to obliterate the pain. You can't sleep, and at times you cry uncontrollably. But that's a whole lot less painful than what God has in store for you,* the Deceiver insinuates. *Who knows what God might make you do if you allowed Him to set you free?*

Does any of this sound familiar to you? I know it does to me. For many of us have spent more time among the tombs than we'd care to admit.

Caught Between Death and Life

According to scholars it wasn't unusual for tombs around Israel to be inhabited by the poor or the insane. Graveyards were sometimes the only places where outcasts could find shelter.[1]

Dug into hillsides or straight into the ground, many tombs in Jesus's day were made up of two chambers. The first room, sometimes called a vestibule, held a simple stone seat, while the inner chamber featured a carved-out niche (or niches) where the body was laid.[2] After waiting a year for decay to do its work, the bones would be placed in an ossuary, a stone box, thus making the tomb available when another member of the family passed away.[3]

I'm assuming the outcasts must have made their home in the vestibule. It served as a kind of middle ground—protected from the outside elements yet not quite in the place of death.

Unfortunately, this "midchamber" describes the place where many of us live, metaphorically speaking. Suspended halfway between death and life, we've accepted the Lord as our Savior, but we have yet to step out into the fullness of life Christ

Hurts, Hang-ups, and Habits

The Celebrate Recovery program coined the phrase "hurts, hang-ups, and habits" to describe the things that keep us from true freedom. Consider these three categories (the definitions are mine). Ask the Holy Spirit to reveal anything that may be acting as a stronghold in your life.[4]

Hurts
(painful things that have happened to us)

These are events we keep referring back to, situations that have defined us. Whatever has wounded us has the capacity to keep us bound. (Examples: trauma, abuse, abandonment, bereavement, failure)

Hang-ups
(mental blocks and emotional barriers that cause unhealthy attitudes and patterns of behavior)

These affect the ways we respond to experiences and act toward people. They are often motivated by anger or fear. (Examples: passive-aggressiveness, chronic people pleasing, rage, bigotry)

Habits
(addictions and compulsive behaviors we've turned to so often that they've become a part of us)

Whether the habit is primarily *physical* or *emotional,* it has become ingrained through repetition and exerts a control we feel helpless to break. (Examples: alcoholism, drug addiction, eating disorders, overspending, pornography)

"But I will restore you to health and heal your wounds,"
declares the LORD.
JEREMIAH 30:17

came to give. Instead, we're holed up in the dark, held captive by our hurts, our hang-ups, and our habits.[5] The painful memories we just can't shake. The attitudes that keep us bound. The coping mechanisms we continually return to, though they lead us everywhere but to the heart of God.

"Strongholds," the Bible calls them (2 Corinthians 10:4). And it's a good name, for they truly have a strong hold on us.

Which may explain the spiritual inertia many Christians apparently feel. According to the Willow Creek Association's REVEAL survey of churches, over 20 percent of respondents were honest enough to admit they feel "stalled" in their walk with God. While they aren't necessarily stepping back from their faith, they realize they aren't moving forward. And that concerns them. As it should.[6]

Because if we are ever to experience abundant life in Jesus, we must give God access to anything that holds us back, including the skeletons in our closets and the dark corners of our minds. For He wants to help us "demolish strongholds...and every pretension that sets itself up against the knowledge of God" (2 Corinthians 10:4–5).

TOMBS-R-US

It may seem a little strange to think that believers could still be tomb dwellers. But I think we've all felt the intense struggle of shedding our "old self" so that we might experience the "new self" Paul writes about in Ephesians 4:22–24. Strongholds are simply those places in us where sin and the "old self" have established such an immense power base that we feel helpless to escape their control. We love Jesus, but we remain stuck in our midchambers, unable to live free.

So where do you feel stuck in your Christian walk?

What hurt keeps you emotionally bound, frozen at a point of past failure or pain?

What hang-up keeps tripping you up, ensnaring you time and time again?

What habit or behavior controls you, making you feel perpetually defeated and continually undone? (See Appendix E: "Identifying Strongholds.")

I find it interesting that in the Greek, the root of the word for "tombs" means "to recall or remember."[7] For isn't it true that the majority of our strongholds have their origins in our pasts? Whether because of a long-ago experience or a regret from yesterday afternoon, too many of us travel through life with hurt and anger or guilt and condemnation shadowing our every move.

In a sense we're like the tormented man of Mark 5. We live in graveyards filled with memories. Wandering through life in perpetual mourning over the things we have done and the things that have been done to us. We may do our best to outrun the mistakes and regrets, the hurts and disappointments, but apart from God, we find it difficult to escape the cycle of shame and self-hatred that keeps our "sin...ever before" us (Psalm 51:3, KJV). Unfortunately, the coping mechanisms we embrace in order to manage our pain only reinforce the strongholds in our souls.

That's why Paul prayed that we might be sanctified and made holy "through and through"—spirit, soul, and body (1 Thessalonians 5:23). For although Christ has been enthroned in our spirits, there are kingdoms in our souls that have yet to receive the good news. Places in our minds, wills, and emotions that must be brought under His control.

Because any arena in our lives where Satan feels relatively comfortable is a stronghold from which we need to be set free. A tomb God wants to open.

Whether you struggle to escape a grave of your own making or one imposed on you by outside forces, I can tell you that each and every stronghold in your life was originally outsourced by hell itself. It isn't so much that Satan dislikes you personally. He simply despises God. He will go to any lengths to hurt, wound, and grieve the Father's heart. For you, dearly beloved, happen to be the apple of God's eye (Zechariah 2:8). It's your reflection Satan sees every time he looks at the heart of God. No wonder that from the moment you were born, he has studied you to determine— and target—your weak spots.

Are you shy by nature? Well, then, he'll make sure you are humiliated regularly to reinforce your fear of people. Are you prone to worry and anxiety? He'll make sure that it seems everything and everyone is against you. Do you struggle with pride and anger? He'll make sure that people know how to push your buttons—and that they do it with great frequency!

Why would the enemy of your soul go to all that trouble, you ask? As I wrote in a previous book, I'm convinced that Satan isn't nearly as concerned about losing you from *his* kingdom as he is committed to keeping you from being effective in *God's* kingdom. He has as many different methods as there are individuals, but his one goal is to contain and restrain you. To entomb you so he can consume you. To incarcerate you with so many lies, insecurities, and guilt feelings that the gift God intended your life to be remains undiscovered. Tightly wrapped and left forgotten in a corner cell.

How does he do it? Doubt by doubt, insult by insult, Satan puts backward binoculars to our eyes and distorts our worth and potential until we forget to factor in God. Until, like the Israelites, we say, "We seemed like grasshoppers in our own eyes, and we looked the same to [the enemy]" (Numbers 13:33).

Gleefully, the Accuser sews tight seams across our souls in an attempt to redefine us, hemming us in with tiny little stitches that diminish our lives and dismantle our faith.

This is who you are, he hisses as he bites off the thread. *This is all you'll ever be,* he gloats, turning us inside out to hide leftover fabric as he creates our burial shrouds. Doing his best to convince us how very small he says we are.

FIGHTING FOR LIFE

I received a letter not long ago from a concerned reader. While she enjoyed my books, she felt I gave too much credit to the devil. Didn't I know that Jesus had conquered Satan when He rose from the dead?

I wrote back and assured her that, yes, I did. In fact, Jesus's triumph over Satan is a cornerstone of my faith. I believe Christ not only conquered death through His resurrection; He also demolished the works of Satan and thoroughly humiliated him in the process. The Message paraphrase describes the victorious event so beautifully: "[Christ] stripped all the spiritual tyrants in the universe of their sham authority at the Cross and marched them naked through the streets" (Colossians 2:15).

In other words, Satan has absolutely no power over you and me.

But please, dear friend, don't be surprised when he tries to convince you otherwise.

Even though the devil's ultimate destiny and eventual destruction have been predetermined, he's still doing his best to stir up trouble. First Peter 5:8 tells us, "Your enemy the devil prowls around like a roaring lion looking for someone to devour." That lion has been detoothed and declawed by Christ's work on the cross, but he still howls and prowls this earth, looking for ways to intimidate God's children.

Rick Renner describes it like this in his excellent devotional *Sparkling Gems from the Greek.*

> Because of Jesus' death on the Cross and His resurrection from the dead, the forces of hell are *already* defeated. However, even though they have been legally stripped of their authority and power, they continue to roam around this earth, carrying out evil deeds like criminals, bandits, hooligans, and thugs. And just like criminals who refuse to submit to the law, these evil spirits will continue to operate in this world until some believer uses his God-given authority to enforce their defeat![8]

I want to learn how to use that authority. I don't want to live enslaved to a tyrant who no longer has a right to demean and terrorize me, tormenting me with guilt and self-doubt. I'm tired of giving the devil more airtime in my mind than I give the Holy Spirit.

My friend Kathy stopped listening to Satan's lies several years ago, and the change in her life has been amazing to see. Somewhat shy by nature, as a child she had let ridicule from schoolmates convince her she was better off quiet. Really quiet. So much so that Kathy became a professional wallflower. Always on the outside looking in, she hardly spoke and rarely participated at school. Even after she dedicated her life to Christ and became involved in ministry, it was always behind the scenes. She was the worker bee. Someone else could be the queen.

But as Kathy began getting into the Word, the Holy Spirit began illuminating her life, helping her see it differently. She came to realize she'd been living halfway since early childhood, stuck for decades in a midchamber of fear and rejection. As Kathy acknowledged her need for healing, God began to stir a courage within her that created a small strand of hope. Perhaps, just perhaps, there could be life beyond the tomb she'd settled for.

It's been my personal joy to watch my friend emerge from her tomb like a beautiful butterfly from a cocoon. No longer in the shadows, Kathy teaches women's Bible studies and has served as women's ministry director for our former church, coordinating and emceeing several large events.

All because she stopped cooperating with Satan's attempts to hem her in, shut her down, and close her off from the life God intended her to live.

Tomb Living—What's in It for You?

As I write these words, I have a wooden box sitting in front of me. About seven inches high and thirteen inches square, it is stained a rich walnut color, and is actually quite beautiful. Just looking at it reminds me of an epiphany I had while using it at a conference for pastors' wives several years ago.

"Each one of us contains so much potential," I told the women, holding up the box, "so many gifts God wants to share with the world. When we give Him access to every part of our hearts, the Holy Spirit causes our lives to open to all the possibilities God has placed within us." To show that truth, I'd designed the sides of the box to drop down and lie flat. I showed it to the women completely open and available, ready to showcase any treasure placed within.

"But Satan is aware of our potential as well," I added. "He goes out of his way to keep us from opening up. In fact, he'll do whatever it takes to derail God's plans and obscure His purposes for us."

With those words I began to close the box lying open before me.

"Satan wants to hem you in…" I pulled two sides upright. The sound of wood against wood rang sharply across the room.

"He wants to shut you down…" I slapped two more sides into place.

Then taking the matching lid, I slammed it down on top. "And he wants to close you off."

At the force of the lid coming down, a small shudder echoed through the room—and through our hearts as well. Every one of us had felt the impact of Satan's schemes at one time or another.

The sound was especially familiar to me, because I had just walked through a difficult time in ministry. A time marked by painful misunderstandings and feelings of deep betrayal. I knew what it felt like to be closed off and hemmed in, shut inside my tomb.

But later that night, as I looked at the box sitting in my hotel room, I suddenly realized something else.

A part of me *liked* the grave.

I felt safe there, surrounded by walls of self-pity. The lid of offense promised to close me off from everything that had caused me pain. Though I'd battled to forgive and move on, I still had moments when I preferred the shelter of the tomb to the full light of day.

Dethroning Lies

Many of us believe the lie that we are helpless when it comes to finding true freedom. Our bondage seems too strong and the lies too intense. Yet regularly employing these four powerful principles releases the Holy Spirit to release *us*:

Reveal. Ask God to show the area (or areas) in which you are bound. What stronghold is preventing you from experiencing freedom? What lie has exalted itself above the knowledge of God? Don't try to figure this out on your own. Ask for the Spirit's help.

Repent. Ask God to forgive the times you've sought refuge in your stronghold rather than in Him. Ask the Holy Spirit to take your sin and the accompanying lies and remove them from you "as far as the east is from the west" (Psalm 103:12).

Renounce. Prayerfully renounce any authority you may have given to Satan by embracing your stronghold rather than God. Naming

For that's what makes tombs so attractive. They shut out what we don't want to deal with. They insulate and isolate us from pain.

Or so we think.

And so the Deceiver promises, fooling us into believing that our sepulchers offer two vitally important things we cannot live without:

1. *Identity*—an address that defines who we are and what has happened to us

2. *Security*—a sense of protection from outside forces

What nonsense! Any identity or security we might find inside our strongholds is an illusion—and a dangerous one at that. Though it may be frightening to think

each sin aloud, renounce your attachment to the lie or behavior, giving authority in that area back to Jesus Christ.

Replace. Look for scriptures that pertain to your stronghold or the lie you've believed. Write them down and place them where you can read them several times a day. Memorize and quote these verses whenever you feel the lie trying to reassert its power.

Please note that I'm not outlining four easy steps for curing your hurts, hang-ups, and habits. Strongholds may have a physical or spiritual component, so the process of breaking free can be lengthy and complicated. Some (especially addictions) may require significant time to overcome as well as outside help, such as professional counseling, support groups, intercessory prayer, and more.

The weapons we fight with are not the weapons of the world.
On the contrary, they have divine power to demolish strongholds.

2 CORINTHIANS 10:4

about living outside our tombs, if we want the freedom Jesus offers, that's a chance we have to take.

Which brings us back to where we started in this chapter.

To the story of a demon-possessed man living in a graveyard.

What Jesus Can Do with Our Tombs

Aren't you glad Jesus isn't threatened by our tombs? In fact, He seems to go out of His way to find them. Which is exactly what happened when He left the multitude standing on Galilee's shore. After getting in a boat, He and His disciples began crossing the lake that separated them from a man in desperate need.

On the way they encountered a violent storm that threatened their lives. (Isn't it interesting how all hell tries to break loose just before some of God's greatest breakthroughs?) But the same power that calmed the storm would soon calm a tormented man.

Look at what happened when Jesus stepped ashore, for the encounter that followed can teach us a few things about what God is able to do when we give Him access to our tomb-dwelling lives.

The first thing we learn from the gospel account is that the demon-possessed man actually ran out to meet Jesus and "fell at his feet" (Luke 8:28). Though the demons inside him must have been screaming at the man to run away from the Son of God, he still went toward Him. Which is good news indeed. It tells us that while the enemy of our souls may do his best to separate us from Jesus, he is helpless to keep us away if we choose to come.

In fact, we might conclude from this verse that when we bow to Christ, Satan is forced to bow as well. Don't you love it?

Second, this story smashes the myth that our tombs—the strongholds the devil uses to keep us bound—offer anything remotely like our true identity.

When Jesus asked the man, "What is your name?" (Luke 8:30), the demons were the first to speak up, identifying themselves rather than allowing the man to speak. It was as though the poor guy didn't exist.

Isn't that what happens with our strongholds? Somewhere in our bondage we cease being us and become only our problems. Defined solely by our hurts, hang-ups, and habits, we wear a grave marker like a nametag.

Adulterer! it shouts. *Glutton!* it gloats. *Abused and misused, betrayed and abandoned,* it declares.

But over the cacophony of condemning and demeaning voices, please hear what our heavenly Father says about you and about me. "Fear not, for I have redeemed you," says the Lord in Isaiah 43:1. "I have summoned you by *name;* you are mine."

In other words, don't listen to labels. Listen to your God. You are His child. He knows your name by heart: "I will not forget you! See, I have engraved you on the palms of my hands" (Isaiah 49:15–16).

It is not your sin but His love that marks and defines you in His eyes.

And it's not your tomb but the place that God has prepared for you in His heart that offers true security.

The Ultimate Security System

"When you pass through the waters, I will be with you," the Lord promises in Isaiah 43:2, 5. "When you walk through the fire, you will not be burned.... Do not be afraid, for I am with you."

Now that's what I call protection! And that is what we find when we exchange our midchamber existence for a home in the heart of God. Though Satan may huff and puff and try to blow our lives down, he won't succeed. For we dwell "in the shelter of the Most High" God (Psalm 91:1).

According to the Gospels, the tormented man who ran to Jesus hadn't lived a normal life for a long time. Luke tells us he'd stopped wearing clothes and ran naked among the tombs. Mark writes that the man cut himself with stones, cried out day and night, and broke loose from every attempt to confine him with chains.

So much for Satan's brand of security system. Does that sound like safety to you? Of course it doesn't. And yet many of us buy the slick ads of the Enemy that tell us we're better off holing up in our dark, smelly graves rather than trusting God and coming out into the light. Some of us have gotten so used to tomb dwelling that we've gone to great lengths to make our midchambers plush and comfortable.

Installing sixty-inch plasma televisions and high-speed Internet so we can pretend we're not alone.

We can't imagine leaving our strongholds, much less demolishing them. But the longer we stay gravebound, the more stuck we become.

I've counseled enough hurting people to see firsthand the naked wandering and mental torment that happens when we love our tombs more than we desire our freedom. I've also seen the ineffectiveness of relying totally on human effort to chain and contain our pain. For our lower nature inevitably finds a way to overpower all attempts to constrain our self-destructive tendencies. Both our own attempts and those of others.

The truth is, we need more than restraint; we need a resurrection. Not more chains to control our lower natures. Not more lists of dos and don'ts to make us fit into society. Although they might subdue us for a while, what we really need is a true, from-the-top-of-our-heads-to-the-tips-of-our-toes transformation! And for that, we need Jesus. For "if the Son sets you free," John 8:36 promises, "you will be free indeed."

I love how Luke describes the results of the Lord's work that day in the graveyard. After He cast the evil spirits into a herd of suddenly suicidal pigs, people from all around came to see what had happened. They found the man, Luke 8:35 tells us, "sitting at Jesus' feet, dressed and in his right mind."

Isn't that beautiful? The naked, out-of-control man they'd once feared now sat calmly and peacefully at the feet of Jesus, fully clothed. No longer insane and without the slightest desire to continue hanging out with the dead. Wanting, instead, to follow Jesus all the days of his life (verse 38).

That's the kind of life change I want, the kind of identity and security I crave. I want to be so transformed by my Savior that my nakedness is clothed and my mind is made completely whole. I want my life to be a testimony and so filled with Jesus that I'm completely out of place among the tombs.

"Return home," Jesus told the man, "and tell how much God has done for you" (verse 39).

Which is exactly what the once-possessed, now-Christ-obsessed man did! He not only went to his own town but visited Decapolis as well (Mark 5:20), taking the good news of the gospel to a many-citied region of Gentiles far removed from the things of God.

An encounter with Jesus had transformed his tombstone into a standing stone of grace—like the memorial stones the people of Israel set up after crossing the Jordan River (Joshua 4:8–9). A visible witness to God's power to save, heal, and deliver.

That kind of witness can be mine, and yours as well, if we'll simply choose to run toward Jesus rather than holding back and hiding out in our tombs.

COME AND SEE

"Where have you laid him?" Jesus asked Martha and Mary through His tears (John 11:34).

"Come and see, Lord," they replied. Then together they went to Lazarus's tomb.

Oh how I wish we could grasp the immensity and emotion of this tender exchange and what it means for us today.

Where have you laid your pain? Jesus asks us tenderly. *Where do you keep all your shattered hopes and dreams? Where have you laid the part of you that died when you failed or were abandoned, forgotten, betrayed? Where are you entombed and enslaved, hemmed in, shut down, and closed off?*

Come and see, Lord.

That's the only response we need to give. Come and see.

With the invitation, Jesus steps down into our pain and gathers us in His arms. He doesn't chastise us for what we've gone through or insist we explain the death we now mourn. He holds us close and weeps over what sin and death have done to us, His beloved.

He doesn't look down on our wild-eyed nakedness, because Jesus understands. He has walked where we've walked, and He has felt what we've felt.

"For we do not have a high priest who is unable to sympathize with our weaknesses," Hebrews 4:15 tells us. We have a tender Savior with a heart big enough to handle our sorrow and gentle hands able to carry our pain. "A bruised reed he will not break," Matthew 12:20 promises, "and a smoldering wick he will not snuff out."

So we needn't hold back. We can run to Him as the man living among the tombs did. We needn't self-protect or weigh our words. We can be bold—even desperate like Mary and Martha—as we pour out our fear and disappointment before Him. "Come and see, Lord," we can say, knowing with full assurance that He will come and He will see.

And because of that, all hell trembles. Satan and his demons see what we don't see, and they know what we may not yet fully realize: The victory has already been won. The stone has been rolled away, and the tomb is empty—not only Christ's grave, but ours as well. For sin no longer has power over us (Romans 6:14, NKJV).

But we still have to decide where we will live. Will it be the familiarity of the graveyard or a new life in Christ, as scary as that may seem? Will we choose bondage, or will we choose freedom?

In a sense it's up to us. For the resurrection work has already been accomplished. "I am the living one," Jesus declares in Revelation 1:18. "I died, but look—I am alive forever and ever! And I hold the keys of death and the grave" (NLT).

Which means, of course, He has the ability to open your tomb and mine. Even now He stands outside the doors of our strongholds, our dark, lonely midchambers. Calling with a voice like tender thunder as He challenges you and me.

"Lazarus, come forth...and live!"

When Martha heard that Jesus was coming, she went out
to meet him, but Mary stayed at home.
"Lord," Martha said to Jesus, "if you had been here,
my brother would not have died.
But I know that even now God will give you whatever you ask."
Jesus said to her, "Your brother will rise again."
Martha answered, "I know he will rise again in
the resurrection at the last day."
Jesus said to her, "I am the resurrection and the life.
He who believes in me will live, even though he dies;
and whoever lives and believes in me will never die.
Do you believe this?"
"Yes, Lord," she told him. "I believe that you are the Christ,
the Son of God, who was to come into the world."....
Jesus, once more deeply moved, came to the tomb.
It was a cave with a stone laid across the entrance.
"Take away the stone," he said.
"But, Lord," said Martha, the sister of the dead man,
"by this time there is a bad odor, for he has been there four days."
Then Jesus said, "Did I not tell you that if you believed,
you would see the glory of God?"

JOHN 11:20–27, 38–40

Roll Away
the Stone

I can only imagine what it must have been like. Standing there before the tomb, hoping for the best yet fearing the worst, Mary and Martha must have clasped hands and looked at each other with a mixture of fear and wonder.

"Take away the stone," Jesus had ordered (John 11:39). While Martha wanted to obey, her practicality couldn't help but point out a problem with the plan. "By this time there is a bad odor," she said. The King James Version puts it more bluntly: "He stinketh." After four days of Judean heat and the natural decay of the human body—well, opening the tomb didn't promise to be a pleasant experience.

Why would Jesus want to do that? she must have wondered. Perhaps He wanted to pay His last respects. Perhaps He wanted to see His dear friend one last time, even in death.

Earlier that day, when they'd talked on the road, He'd promised that her brother would rise again. But He didn't mean today, did He?

Right now?

But that is exactly what the Lord had in mind in verse 40. "Did I not tell you that if you believed, you would see the glory of God?" Jesus asked Martha, looking intently into her eyes. And in that moment a decision had to be made.

Would Martha obey Jesus?

Or was the risk of revealing what lay behind the stone too much to bear?

Our Part to Play

To obey or not to obey—that's the question we face continually in our Christian walk. Some days it's easy to comply, but other days it feels all but impossible. Especially when God asks us to do something that doesn't make sense to us.

Something like opening a tomb.

Jesus didn't have to wait for those standing around to obey. After all, He was (and is) God Almighty. With just a word He could have shattered the boulder that lay across Lazarus's grave. That would have been dramatic.

"Why not do an instantaneous miracle like that in my life, Lord?" we ask. "That's what I'd prefer."

Better yet, Jesus could have left the stone in place, and then—to really show His power—just waved His hand, and *poof!* Lazarus could have suddenly appeared, standing outside the tomb in brand-new robes, glowing with health. Now, that would have been impressive.

"Do that in me, God!" we cry.

But instead, Jesus left the job of removing the stone to those standing around Him. For the coming miracle hinged, at least partly, on the willingness of the grieving family to give Jesus access to their pain.

And that's true when it comes to our resurrections as well. While only Christ can make dead men live, only we can remove the obstacles that stand between us and our Savior.

All of us, you see, have blockages in our souls that we've allowed and perhaps even nurtured. False beliefs we've internalized as truth, to the point we believe them before we believe God. As a result, many of us have become, as Craig Groeschel puts it, Christian atheists—"believing in God but living as if He doesn't exist."[1]

I've identified three specific "boulders" that I believe many Christians struggle with. Three obstacles we must examine and relinquish so God can do the work He longs to do. For while Lazarus was powerless to roll away the stone that sealed his tomb, we are not. Our choices and attitudes really do make a difference in our ability to accept Christ's offer of freedom.

So what stones must be rolled away?

The first is the stone of unworthiness—the lie that we are unloved and unlovable.

The second is the stone of unforgiveness—the lie that we must hold on to the hurts of the past.

And the third is the stone of unbelief—the lie that God can't or won't help us so we must do everything ourselves.

Unworthiness, unforgiveness, unbelief—they're daunting, intimidating blockages that lock us in and cut us off. But not one of them is impossible to remove. Not when we put our shoulders to our boulders and cry out to God for help.

The Stone of Unworthiness

Remember my friend Lisa, whom you met in chapter 1? The vibrant Christian who stopped me after Bible study and confessed that she could tell other people Jesus loved them but couldn't convince herself she was accepted by God?

As she and I spent time together that day, we asked the Holy Spirit to reveal what was keeping her heart from truly receiving the good news of God's love. After our prayer Lisa began to tell me the story of her conversion—a beautiful story, indeed. But one thing haunted her, Lisa said. A secret she had told no one, not even her husband.

With tears running down her cheeks, she confessed her shame. "I had an abortion in high school. But not just one, Joanna. I had multiple abortions." Sobs shook my friend's body as the immensity of her words overwhelmed her.

"How could God ever forgive me?" she asked, finally voicing the fear-filled unworthiness that had entombed her for the majority of her life. "How could He ever love me after what I've done?"

I held my friend as she cried and poured out her grief—grief not only for her sin but also for the children she'd never known. Her sorrow was deep and heartrending to witness but also transformative. For both of us.

"Don't you know, Lisa?" I whispered against her hair as the revelation hit my heart. "Don't you know that's why Jesus had to come? That's why He had to die."

We've all sinned. We've all fallen short of what is best and good and right. We've all taken shortcuts of convenience, choosing to ignore God's law and invoking the consequences.

My goody-two-shoes past was and is just as dark and sin laced as Lisa's wild years. Her sins may have been outward, but my inward sins were just as damaging. My pride, my insecurity, my idolatry of other people's approval. The driving force to succeed and the need to be well thought of. All of it lay exposed before me that day, just as wrong as any other sin. Just as needful of a Savior.

"He doesn't forgive us because we deserve it," I told her as well as myself. "God forgives us because we so desperately need it."

And that is what makes the good news so very, very good. The price has been paid. We simply have to accept the gift Christ offers. Our sin may be worthy of punishment. It may even have resulted in a type of death—death of hope, death of confidence, death of any future happiness.

But Jesus took it all on the cross.

And in the process He broke the yardstick—the condemnation that has hung over our lives, declaring us unworthy.

His sacrifice has the power to roll away our shame if we will allow it. Because of Christ's death, we have been accepted into the ranks of the righteous. Our track record has nothing to do with it—we need to settle that fact forever. The only thing that saves us is the Cross and nothing but the Cross. We can't add to it, nor can we diminish it. We simply have to embrace it. And when we do, the stone of unworthiness rolls away.

It has been thrilling to watch Lisa resurrect! Though she'd repented of her sin years before, it wasn't until she revealed her secret to someone else, as frightening as that must have been, that she experienced a breakthrough in her relationship with the Lord.

Perhaps that's why the Holy Spirit inspired James, a brother of Jesus, to write, "Confess your sins to each other and pray for each other so that you may be healed" (James 5:16). While it didn't happen overnight, Lisa's healing has come. Today she shares her story with junior-high and high-school students, urging them to commit to sexual purity but also reminding them that there is forgiveness and a fresh start in Jesus Christ.

What once brought Lisa great shame is now being used by God to bring Him great glory. But it all started with a courageous decision to roll away her stone.

THE STONE OF UNFORGIVENESS

Lisa's boulder was a sense of personal unworthiness along with debilitating guilt and shame over what she had done. But for many of us, our spiritual blockages result from what has been done to us—and our attitudes about it. We've been hurt. We've been falsely accused or misunderstood, misused or betrayed. And we can't seem to get past our anger, resentment, or bitterness.

We *want* to forgive—well, most of the time. Trouble is, we aren't sure we can forgive. The hurt has gone so deep that the tendrils of our pain seem to go on forever. How do you let go of something that has such a hold on you?

That was my dilemma several years ago. "I have to get alone with God," I told my husband, John. "I'm in a very bad place."

As I mentioned in the last chapter, we'd walked through a trying time in ministry, and for the most part I'd handled it pretty well. Miraculously well, in fact. A space of grace had opened up for me to walk through the difficulty without feeling the intense need to fix it or change the people involved. (I told you it was miraculous.)

But somewhere near the anniversary of the hurt, I picked up an offense against someone in the situation. Pain-laced memories began to stick in my craw and bother me anew. Opportunities for self-pity had floated through my mind before, but up to that point I hadn't indulged them. Instead, I'd been experiencing the also-miraculous phenomenon of a disciplined mind.

I'd learned that just because a painful recollection came to memory, I didn't have to embrace it—a revolutionary discovery, let me tell you. Instead of nursing and rehearsing the past, with the Holy Spirit's help, I was learning to disperse it, refusing the offense entrance to my heart and, more important, denying it occupancy in my mind.

However, this particular memory had slipped in through a side entrance. At first it was so tiny I hardly noticed it. But as I allowed my hurt a platform to state its woes, it began to grow, and a boulder of unforgiveness began to move across my soul. As a result, almost without knowing it, I began to cut myself off from people—and not just those who had hurt me.

I wasn't rude or dismissive. But I found myself escaping church services as

Disciplining Your Mind

"The battlefield is the mind" when it comes to the Enemy's attempt to derail our Christianity. But the best defense has always been a good offense, so I'm learning to train my mind for battle by disciplining my thought life. I don't always succeed, but I'm far more effective in rolling away my stones when I practice the following disciplines:

1. **Take every thought captive** (2 Corinthians 10:5). Or, as Joyce Meyer puts it, "Think about what you are thinking about."[2] Try not to let your mind wander indiscriminately. Instead, consider where your thoughts could lead you. If the thought takes you away from God, cut it off. (You really can do this!) Consciously bring it to Jesus and leave it there.

2. **Resist vain imaginations** (Romans 1:21, KJV)—you know, those runaway loops of what if, if only, and woulda-coulda-shoulda. When you feel yourself getting caught up in a cycle of fear, worry, or regret, stop! Consciously rein in your imagination, and shift your focus to Christ as the source of your peace (Isaiah 26:3).

3. **Refuse to agree with the devil.** When thoughts of condemnation or fear come to mind, remind yourself that they are lies, that God is bigger than your biggest problem and stronger than your greatest weakness (Philippians 4:13), and that He's taken care of the Accuser's accusations once and for all (Revelation 12:10–11).

4. **Bless those who curse you** (Luke 6:26). If you carry a grudge in your heart, it will consume your mind. When resentment arises against someone, begin praying *for*, not *against*, that person. Ask

quickly as possible, glad to have a small child who needed my attention. Calls to have lunch with friends went unanswered. Conversations became more polite than personal as I withdrew into my safe little world. My dark little tomb.

God to bless and reveal Himself to him or her…and to help you move past your resentment. (It may take some time to actually *feel* forgiving!)

5. **Renew your mind with the Word of God** (Romans 12:2; Ephesians 5:26). Get into the Word daily, and allow it to transform your thinking. Find a scripture that speaks to your particular situation, then memorize it, making it part of your mental arsenal against the lies of the Enemy.

6. **Speak truth to yourself** (John 8:32). Too many of us play and replay demeaning self-talk and other negative ideas that are contrary to what God has said. Consciously counter that tendency by repeating God's truth to yourself. Declare what you know to be greater than what you feel, proclaiming what God says about you and His power to save.

7. **Develop an attitude of gratitude.** Purposefully think about things that are of "good report" (Philippians 4:8, KJV). Make a list if you need to. Don't give voice to negativity—inwardly or outwardly. Instead, declare out loud your thankfulness to God (1 Thessalonians 5:18).

> *And now, dear brothers and sisters, one final thing.*
> *Fix your thoughts on what is true, and honorable, and right,*
> *and pure, and lovely, and admirable.*
> *Think about things that are excellent and worthy of praise.*
> PHILIPPIANS 4:8, NLT

Finally the chill of bitterness sank in so deep I couldn't find the "want to" to forgive. That terrified me.

And so, with John's blessing, I holed up in a friend's cabin and poured out my heart before the Lord. It was slow going at first. My emotions were rock hard, but as I hammered out obedience to forgiveness, the stone slowly began to roll away.

At the Spirit's prompting, I wrote a letter to the person who had hurt me. I didn't measure my words; I just spilled out my pain. It was difficult giving myself permission to vent, for fear I might never stop, but I knew I had to get honest before God about what I was feeling. After all, as someone once said, "Holding onto bitterness is like drinking poison and waiting for the other person to die."

Funny how pain tends to land on a single scapegoat. After laying down my hurt before the Lord, I was suddenly able to see there were other people I'd been holding in the dungeon of my disapproval. People I needed to write to as well.

None of the letters would ever be postmarked, however. I wasn't writing them for anyone but me. My friends may not have felt the stranglehold of my judgment, but I certainly had.

Letter after letter I allowed the toxic pain to drain from infected wounds, ending each note with a declaration of amnesty and love. I would not hold my hurt against them one more day. Finally I wrote a letter to God, relinquishing all rights to resentment and asking Him to bless the people involved.

I was absolutely exhausted when I penned the last note. But with the exhaustion came the beginning of a sweet sense of release.

For with the mind-over-emotion choice to forgive, my stone of unforgiveness started to move. And somewhere in letting go of those who had hurt me, I walked out free.

THE BIGGEST STONE OF ALL

Unworthiness—that's what Lisa wrestled with. The lie that she didn't deserve God's love.

Unforgiveness—that was my issue. The lie that people who had hurt me should be excluded from my love.

Both false beliefs can thwart our growth as Christians, because they prevent us from moving past our failure or pain. But the reason the stones appeared in the first place isn't the issue. What should concern us most is the fact that we don't live free.

Which brings me to the third stone: unbelief. In my mind it is the most destructive boulder of all, because it is the cornerstone on which the other two rest.

If we struggle to believe that what Jesus did on the cross was really enough to cancel our sins, we will battle with unworthiness.

If we continually doubt that God could ever bring anything good out of our terrible circumstances, we will hold on to unforgiveness as our only recourse.

But nothing is more detrimental to our spiritual lives than allowing the stone of unbelief to wedge itself between us and the heart of God. Causing us to believe the Accuser's lie that our Father is powerless to help us—or, worse, that He just doesn't care.

I appreciate the honesty with which my friend Ann Spangler writes of her struggle to truly believe in the love of God. In *The Tender Words of God,* she details her journey to find her place in His heart.

> I have never found it easy to believe in God's love for me, except perhaps in the first days and weeks of my conversion. No matter where I turned in those bright days I found evidence of God's gracious care and steady forgiveness. The stern-browed god of my youth had suddenly and unexpectedly receded, and in his place came Jesus, bearing gifts of love and peace. Nearly every prayer in those days was answered, sometimes wondrously. I remember thinking that the problem with many people was that they expected so little from a God who was prepared to give so much.
>
> But years passed and something happened. It wasn't one thing but many.... It was tests of faith, sometimes passed and sometimes not. It was sins accruing. It was spiritual skirmishes and full-out battles. It was disappointments and difficulties and circumstances beyond comprehending. All these heaped together like a great black mound, casting a shadow over my sense that God still loved me, still cared for me as tenderly as when he had first wooed me and won my heart.[3]

In an attempt to recapture that sense of God's love, Ann went back to the only place that can set our souls at ease—the promises of the Bible—but even then she found herself unable to shake off her love-doubt. "Like many people who tend to be self-critical," she writes, "I find it easier to absorb the harsher sounding passages in the Bible than those that speak of God's compassion. Somehow, the tender words seem to roll right off me, much like water that beads up and rolls off a well-waxed automobile."[4]

But Ann persisted. Over the next year she immersed herself in the Word of God, allowing truth to wash over her until it finally began to stick, until God's love stopped being a concept and started to feel like a reality. It didn't happen immediately, but it did happen, especially when she began to exercise her faith rather than depend solely on her feelings. (See Appendix D: "Who I Am in Christ.")

But the real change came when Ann began to apply something she'd learned in a conversation with her friend Joan. When she'd asked Joan how she finally became convinced of God's love, Ann had expected a dramatic story—something about how God had spared her friend from tragedy or brought her through a dark time. Instead, Joan described a simple decision "to set aside one month in which to act as though God loved her." All that month "whenever she was tempted to doubt his love, she simply shifted her thoughts and then put the full force of her mind behind believing that God loved her. And that settled it for her—for good."[5]

Act as though God loves you.

Put the *full force of your mind* behind your faith.

Roll aside the stone of unbelief by *replacing lies* with God's eternal truth.

What powerful concepts—concepts that echo throughout the Old Testament and the New.

"Put your hope in God," the psalmist reminds himself not once but three times when he reflects on his troubles and grows disheartened (Psalms 42:5, 11; 43:5).

"Set your mind on things above, not on earthly things," Paul advises the Colossian believers faced with a new age philosophy that sought to undermine the purity of their doctrine (Colossians 3:2).

"We live by faith, not by sight," Paul adds in 2 Corinthians 5:7, still choosing to believe God though he was in prison and under threat of death.

Over and over, the Bible urges us to engage mind, will, and emotions in the pursuit of truths beyond our human senses. For when we choose to trust God above what we see or what we feel, we roll away the stone of unbelief and discover what real life can be.

Because faith does more than release our imprisoned hearts.

It releases God to work as well.

THE PROBLEM OF UNBELIEF

One of the most disturbing passages in Scripture is Mark 6:5–6. When Jesus returned to Nazareth, the people there were less than welcoming to the hometown boy. They couldn't wrap their minds around the idea that God might use someone so ordinary, someone they'd known from childhood. Sure, Jesus preached well, and they'd heard about His miracles, but rather than being impressed, they were offended.

"They could not explain Him," Kenneth Wuest writes, "so they rejected Him."[6]

As a result, the gospel of Mark tells us, "He could not do any miracles there, except lay his hands on a few sick people and heal them" (verse 5). Notice that it says, "he *could not* do any miracles there." Something held back His power. Jesus was limited by their disdain but even more by their determined unbelief.

Isn't it frightening to think that the people who should know Christ best often trust Him the least? And that, according to these verses, a lack of trust can actually limit God's work in our lives?

Oh how I want my faith to serve as a springboard for the miraculous. While my faith isn't perfect, I want to grow. I don't want to hinder God's work in my life or in the lives of those around me.

"Everything is possible for him who believes," Jesus told the desperate father of a demon-possessed boy. "Immediately the boy's father exclaimed, 'I do believe; help me overcome my unbelief!' " (Mark 9:23–24). Though small and underdeveloped, the man's faith was apparently enough. Jesus spoke the words and did what only He could do: heal the man's son and set him free.

Just as He wants to do for you and for me.

WRESTLING WITH SILENCE

Editors say it's best that authors don't include too much about the writing process of a book. I understand their point. I'd rather read a well-polished work than hear an author whine about how hard it was to pen. And yet for some reason my whining—I mean, my writing process—has made it into most of my books. Suffice it to say, I don't find writing easy. In fact, it's the hardest thing I do.

You'd think it would get simpler over time. I certainly hoped it would. But instead, each book has offered a fresh set of difficulties.

Writing *Having a Mary Heart in a Martha World* involved a yearlong bout with insomnia and living twenty-four hours a day in a wind tunnel filled with words and ideas.

Having a Mary Spirit was like wrestling a beast. The idea of cooperating with sanctification was such a huge topic it was all I could do to get my arms around the message, let alone fully grasp it in my heart.

But *Lazarus Awakening* has been completely different. Writing it has felt more like trying to hold on to water or to grasp fine sand—the concepts have seemed so ethereal and shifting. But even worse has been the disturbing quietness of my mind. For months on end I've felt entombed, locked down, and shut up without a breath of an idea to assure me that this book would ever live.

When I missed my book deadline six months into the contract, I had the bare tracings of three chapters. It was a far cry from the ten I'd promised to deliver.

"I feel like I'm holding a pregnancy test stick, and it says I'm expecting a book," I told my publisher, "but I have absolutely no symptoms. No movement, not even a tummy bump to tell me it will be born."

The only assurance I felt was that this book was God's idea and not my own. Though the echoes were distant, the bell that had sounded in my soul years before still reverberated. More important, I could hear God challenging me to believe, no matter what the situation looked like.

So it appears impossible? I felt the Holy Spirit whisper to my spirit. *So it looks like you'll never finish this project?*

"Did I not tell you that if you believed, you would see the glory of God?" Jesus asked Martha at the door of her brother's tomb (John 11:40). Standing at the threshold of my impossibility, I've heard that same question every day for the past twenty-four months.

Four days is a long time to wait for a resurrection. Two years feels like an eternity to write a book.

But if you'll believe, Joanna, you will see.

"Lean not on your own understanding," Proverbs 3:5–6 reminds us. "In all your ways acknowledge Him, and He shall direct your paths" (NKJV).

Don't look at how far you have to go, God seems to whisper each day as I sit down to write. *Instead, look for Me on the journey. Acknowledge My presence even in the middle of this emptiness. Don't try to work up faith for the outcome. Just believe in Me. Then you will see.*

So that's what I've attempted to do. Right here, right now, just barely past the middle of the book. Exercising my faith rather than giving in to my fear. And I'm finally putting words on a page—something that at times has felt literally impossible.

While the fear of failure is never far away, I'm determined to "contend earnestly for the faith" (Jude 3, NKJV). And while my confidence in myself wavers regularly, I will not "cast away [my] confidence" in Him (Hebrews 10:35, NKJV).

For greater is He that is in me than me that is in me (1 John 4:4, Weaver paraphrase).

And so with Martha and that little boy's father and everyone else who has ever struggled to believe in the face of overwhelming odds, I cry:

"Lord, I do believe! Help me overcome my unbelief."

CLEARING AWAY THE BLOCKAGES

I don't think any of us set out deliberately to block ourselves off with stones of unworthiness, unforgiveness, and/or unbelief. But life is hard, and boulders often roll across the doors of our hearts unnoticed, gradually and imperceptibly cutting off the light. Other times they crash down suddenly, unexpected and unasked for, like the landslide that blocked Montana Highway 93 many years ago.

I'll never forget reading about the incident in our local paper. After two years of heavy snowfall and successive wet springs, part of the hillside next to the highway suddenly gave way, scattering massive boulders across the road and shutting off both lanes of traffic.

Miraculously, no one was hurt. But it took crews several days, working around the clock, to open the road to travel. Which wasn't necessarily a big deal unless you happened to live or work on that side of Flathead Lake. For those who did, a detour was required. A two-hour, eighty-six-mile detour around the largest freshwater lake west of the Mississippi.

Faith That Rolls Away Stones

Jesus said, "If you have faith as small as a mustard seed, you can say to this mountain, 'Move'...and it will move. Nothing will be impossible for you" (Matthew 17:20). Imagine what that kind of faith could do when it comes to rolling away our stones! Not a faith in formulas or a faith in our faith, but a heart-focused trust in our God. I'm asking the Lord to help me overcome my unbelief and replace it with three powerful types of faith.

An "even if" kind of faith...

I want a Shadrach-Meshach-and-Abednego faith that refuses to bow to other gods or bend to the fear of other people's displeasure, even though refusing could result in death.

> If we are thrown into the blazing furnace, the God we serve is able to
> save us from it... But even if he does not, we want you to know, O king,
> that we will not serve your gods or worship the image of gold you have
> set up. (Daniel 3:17–18)

An "even though" kind of faith...

I want a faith that isn't dependent on circumstances or rattled by hardship—the kind of faith that chooses to praise even in the midst of unrelenting difficulties.

All because a pile of stones got in the way.

Tombstones. Roadblocks. What is barricading your life today? What's cutting you off, shutting you down, causing endless detours and chronic disconnects in the free flow of your relationship with God?

Perhaps it's time to get out the heavy equipment and, with the Holy Spirit's help, begin removing the blockage in your soul.

For Lisa, the lie of her unworthiness required the blasting cap of confession.

Even though the fig trees have no blossoms, and there are no grapes on the vines; even though the olive crop fails, and the fields lie empty and barren; even though the flocks die in the fields, and the cattle barns are empty, yet I will rejoice in the LORD! I will be joyful in the God of my salvation! (Habakkuk 3:17–18, NLT)

A *"nevertheless"* kind of faith...

I want the kind of faith Jesus displayed in the Garden of Gethsemane. A faith that says, "Here's what I'd like to happen..." but in the end wants what God wants most of all.

O My Father, if it is possible, let this cup pass from Me; nevertheless, not as I will, but as you will. (Matthew 26:39, NKJV)

And without faith it is impossible to
please God, because anyone who comes to him
must believe that he exists and that he rewards those
who earnestly seek him.
HEBREWS 11:6

Before she could live free, she had to reveal the dark secret that had kept her spiritually gagged and emotionally bound for most of her adult life.

For me, a jackhammer of forgiveness was needed to break the rock of resentment that had lodged against my heart. I had to face my pain but then relinquish my right to be offended so that I might choose instead to forgive.

For Ann, the rock of unbelief required a large dose of the *dunamis*—or dynamite[7]—of God's Word. Once she chose to exalt His truth over her feelings, the lie that she was unloved could finally be removed.

"Take away the stone," Jesus commanded those standing around Lazarus's tomb on that long-ago day in Bethany (John 11:39). Though Martha was clearly uncomfortable with the idea of rolling away the only thing that stood between her and the death she mourned, she chose to obey. Though she didn't fully understand why Jesus asked what He asked, she did what she could so Jesus could do the rest.

And in a sense, that's all Christ asks of you and me.

Roll away the stone, beloved. Do what only you can do. Choose to receive My love... choose to forgive...choose to trust in Me no matter what. Then watch what I will do.

For if you believe, our Savior promises, *then you will see...*

the glory of God released in your life and mine to bring us out of our tombs...

fully alive and completely set free.

After he had said this, he went on to tell them,
"Our friend Lazarus has fallen asleep;
but I am going there to wake him up."....
So they took away the stone. Then Jesus looked up and said,
"Father, I thank you that you have heard me.
I knew that you always hear me,
but I said this for the benefit of the people standing here,
that they may believe that you sent me."
When he had said this, Jesus called in a loud voice,
"Lazarus, come out!"

JOHN 11:11, 41–43

When Love Calls Your Name

It's a long drive across Montana. Seven hundred miles, to be exact.

As a young wife and mother living on the very eastern edge of the state, I used to make the drive home to western Montana several times a year. Fastening my first-born in the backseat, I'd place John Michael where I could tickle his toes or hand him a toy for entertainment until he fell asleep. Then, hoping to make time pass more quickly, I'd turn on the radio. But just as towns are few and far between on Montana's eastern plains, so are the radio stations.

Instead of receiving a clear signal, I'd usually get lots of white noise—long strands of static broken now and then by fractured music as I passed over a station. Fortunately, the highway stretched straight and wide before me, so I could concentrate on slowly turning the radio dial, trying to home in on a signal. Until finally, out of all the static, a voice could be heard clear and strong.

I'm coming to believe that it takes that same kind of concentration to break though the white noise of this world and hear the voice of God. A purposeful tuning of our hearts to the voice of His Spirit.

For until we learn to truly listen, we may never hear Love call our name.

COME FORTH!

I wonder what it was like for Lazarus when he heard Jesus's voice from inside his tomb. Was it a far-off echo he first heard? A familiar yet distant voice calling him back from the holding cell of death?

I wonder what happened in Lazarus's body at the sound of his name. Did his heart suddenly start beating again? Was there a great intake of air as he drew his first breath in days? Did he awaken slowly, or did energy come like a lightning bolt, sitting him up straight before propelling him out of the tomb?

Either way, once he was fully conscious, Lazarus was faced with a choice. Just as we are. To go back to sleep and remain where he was or to get up from the grave and walk out into new life.

Because when Love calls our name, we can ignore His voice, or we can respond. We can pull back into the dark familiarity of what we've known, or we can step out into the light, tentatively perhaps and with eyes blinking to adjust, but ready to embrace what God has waiting for us. Though His voice may seem faint and distant, He is calling us out of our tombs just as surely as He called Lazarus.

So what should we do when we hear Him speak?

Only one response has helped me, and I offer it to you as well: choose to move closer. Answer His cry with your own. Shuffle toward the light, and you'll find the Light becoming brighter. His voice growing louder. His words becoming clearer.

All because you've chosen to listen and respond, tuning your heart[1] to the voice of your Savior.

LEARNING TO LISTEN

I remember being offended as a young adult Christian when people talked about hearing the voice of God. "God told me this…," they'd say, or "God told me that…"

"Oh yeah?" I wanted to respond. "Just who do you think you are? How do you *know* that was God talking and not a figment of your imagination? Or the guacamole you just ate?"

After all, I was a twenty-eight-year-old pastor's wife. I'd been raised in the church and had loved Jesus since I was a little girl. But I'd never actually heard God's voice—or so I thought.

I've come to realize, however, that although I have yet to hear God speak audibly, it would be untrue to say I haven't heard His voice. In fact, I believe the Lord is speaking to me more often than I know. The problem is, I'm not always listening. And when I do, the Enemy does his best to convince me that what I'm hearing is anything but the voice of God.

Priscilla Shirer describes this problem in her excellent book *Discerning the Voice of God*:

> If God wants us to hear His voice, the Father of Lies is going to do everything he can to make us think that we *aren't* hearing it. When we hear from God, we call it intuition, coincidence, or even luck—anything but what it is: the voice of God. We're so used to dismissing His voice that we've convinced ourselves that He no longer speaks to His children. But the Bible says over and over that God *does* speak to us. We *are* hearing from Him. We just may not know it's Him.[2]

Some people have come to the conclusion that God speaks only through the Bible. They say that to assume He speaks outside of holy writ is not only presumptuous but dangerous. I understand their concerns. After all, claiming to hear the voice of God has been the excuse for a lot of insanity and outright evil over the centuries— murderous crusades launched under Christian banners, mentally ill mothers drowning their children, and lunatic preachers poisoning their flocks, to mention just a few.

But to conclude from such instances of misuse and abuse that God *doesn't* speak today would be to miss a precious part of our walk with Him and a necessary key to our freedom.

For if we don't hear God speak, we won't be able to obey.

And if we don't obey, we'll never escape our tombs.

DISCERNING HIS VOICE

Have you ever wished God would speak a little louder? Or, better yet, that He would sit next to you with skin on so you could really hear what He said? Could you listen better then?

Don't be so sure!

In the Old Testament, God spoke so loudly at times that His voice made mountains shake and people tremble. But instead of drawing the children of Israel closer, His audible voice made them step back—back to the perceived safety of their tents and a more comfortable, arm's-length relationship with their God.

"Speak to us yourself and we will listen," the children of Israel told Moses in Exodus 20:19. "But do not have God speak to us or we will die."

Though Moses did his best to translate God's heart to the people, familiarity does tend to breed contempt. While they heard the voice of God and feared it, Philip Yancey writes, they also "soon learned to ignore it."[3] So completely, it seems, they hardly noticed when that Voice fell silent for more than four hundred years.

In the New Testament, God's voice sounded once again—first in a baby's cry and later through an altogether approachable man named Jesus Christ. His voice sounded like our own, but He spoke with an authority and wisdom never heard before. His voice could be tender and soft with children and adulterous women, demanding and hard with hypocrites and the spiritually proud. Yet even though

The Art of Listening

"Before we can hear God speaking through the everyday moments of our lives, our heart has to be prepared to listen," Ken Gire writes in his *Reflections on Your Life Journal*. "Which is more art than science. At least it has been that way for me." According to Gire, preparing our hearts in the "art of listening" involves several things:

> *First,* there must be a sense of anticipation that God wants to speak to us and that He *will* speak. This anticipation stems from the belief that God is love and that it is the nature of love to express itself. The form of that expression, though, is remarkably varied. Sometimes love is expressed through words. Other times it is expressed through pictures or gestures or a variety of other ways, often very subtle ways that only the beloved might recognize. That is the nature of intimate communication. It is clear to the beloved but often cryptic to everyone else.
>
> *Second,* there must be a humility of heart, for where we are willing to look and what we are willing to hear will largely determine how many

Jesus lived with us on earth, up close and personal, the very proximity that wooed us allowed us to crucify Him as well.

You see, history proves it isn't a louder voice we need. Nor is it a voice physically embodied and sitting beside us. What we need most is to learn how to listen. Perhaps that is why Jesus said over and over again—fourteen times in the New Testament:

"He who has ears, let him hear" (see, for example, Matthew 11:15).

FINDING EARS TO HEAR

How does this work? you may wonder. If God isn't going to speak audibly, and if He's not physically present as a human who speaks our language, how are we supposed to understand what He's saying? How do we *get* those ears to hear?

---

of those moments we will catch. This posture of the heart stems from a belief that words from God characteristically come swaddled in the most lowly of appearances, and that if we're not willing to stoop, we'll likely miss God among the stench of the stable and the sweetness of the straw.

Third, there must be a responsiveness to what is heard. A willingness to follow where we are being led, wherever that may be. A readiness to admit where we are wrong and to align ourselves with what is right and good and true. An eagerness to enter into the joy of the moment. Or into the sorrow of the moment, if that's the case. It is this responsiveness of the heart that makes us susceptible to the grace of the moment. And it is what prepares us to receive whatever grace is offered to us in the next.[4]

Go near to listen... Do not be quick with your mouth,
do not be hasty in your heart to utter anything before God.
God is in heaven and you are on earth, so let your words be few.
ECCLESIASTES 5:1–2

The disciples must have wondered the same thing when Jesus told them He was leaving to return to His Father. What would they do without the God-with-skin-on they'd experienced daily for the past three years? Without Jesus beside them, telling them what to do, how would they survive, let alone carry out the mission He'd given them to do?

But the Lord reassured them that He wouldn't leave them alone or stop communicating with them. "The Counselor, the Holy Spirit, whom the Father will send in my name, will teach you all things and will remind you of everything I have said to you" (John 14:26).

And that's exactly what happened ten days after Jesus ascended to heaven. The Spirit came, the fire fell, and the trembling, fearful people who had felt so lost after Jesus died were now suddenly filled with power (Acts 1–2). More important, they were filled with Christ Himself.

For Emmanuel—"God *with* us"—had sent the Holy Spirit to be "God *in* us." And nothing would ever be the same. Not for them. Not for you and me.

The Spirit of God now dwells in the heart of every believer. Filling us, if we'll allow Him, with everything we need for this life and the one to come. Leading and guiding us into all truth (John 16:13). Confirming that we are, indeed, children of God and deeply loved (Romans 8:15–16).

And, yes, speaking to us—though not always in the ways we might expect.

"Listen to your heart," Henri Nouwen writes. "It's there that Jesus speaks most intimately to you.... He doesn't shout. He doesn't thrust himself upon you. His voice is an unassuming voice, very nearly a whisper, the voice of a gentle love."[5]

It's a voice that's easy to grieve and, unfortunately, even easier to miss or dismiss—unless we listen intently and train our spiritual ears to hear.

Tuned In to Love

I wish I could outline "Ten Easy Steps to Hear God Speak—Guaranteed!" That would appeal to our human craving for formulas. But God's communication is far more individualized and intimate than anything a self-help bestseller could teach.

Our heavenly Father knows the best kind of communication flows out of relationship. Anything less is just an exchange of information. Since intimacy with us has always been God's goal, it makes sense that hearing His voice would be linked to that very thing. The better we get to know Him, in other words, the better we hear Him.

Perhaps that's one reason God keeps the voice of His Spirit quiet and subtle—so we'll lean in and listen carefully. And perhaps that's why He doesn't converse with us every moment of every day—so we'll treasure the times when He does.

For the Lord wants to accomplish more than just telling us where to go, what to do, and when to do it. He wants to take us by the hand and lead us out of our tombs. Wooing us out of our fear with His tender love. Calling us to higher purposes and deeper places in our walk with Him. All as we respond to His voice.

I'm no expert on hearing God speak. In many ways I'm still a learner. However, I truly believe God wants to draw close to me and speak truth tailored to my specific needs. But in order to have ears to hear, I must open my heart to His voice. And that happens best when I

- prayerfully invite Him into my everyday life,
- fill my heart and mind with His Word,
- remain alert to different ways He may speak to me,
- respond with obedience.

TUNING OUR HEARTS THROUGH PRAYER

If we "lack wisdom," James 1:5 tells us we should "ask God, who gives generously to all without finding fault." Instead of worrying about our problems, we should "in everything, by prayer and petition, with thanksgiving, present [our] requests to God" (Philippians 4:6).

What incredible invitations! We have a Father who longs to meet our needs. But even more, we have a God who truly listens to the cries of our hearts.

Standing outside Lazarus's tomb, Jesus prayed these amazing words: "Father, I thank you that you have heard me. I [know] that you always hear me" (John 11:41–42). We can pray with that same kind of faith—all because of what Jesus did on the cross (Matthew 27:51). We can come boldly into His presence, not just believing, but *knowing* that we too have a Father who hears our prayers and cares about our needs. Including our need to hear His voice.

Like Jesus, we initiate conversation with God through prayer. As I've learned to "practice the presence of God"—the well-known phrase used of Brother Lawrence[6]—inviting Jesus into my daily life each morning and conversing with Him as I go through my day, I've discovered a little more of what Paul must have meant when he said, "Pray without ceasing" (1 Thessalonians 5:17, NKJV).

I'd always thought that meant spending hours on my knees, but instead it has proven to be more like an ongoing conversation with a friend. Talking to the Lord as I drive down the road or wash the dishes. Commenting on the beauty He's created. Thanking Him for a house to call a home. Sharing my concerns as well as my joys. Just talking to my Savior on a daily, hourly, and even moment-by-moment basis. And all the while listening in case He wants to speak.

That kind of free-flowing, honest, heart-to-heart prayer has done more than anything else to open the door of my communication with God. But journaling my prayers during my regular quiet time has also been extremely helpful. For me, writing down what's on my heart helps me get a glimpse of His. Journaling seems to peel back all my facades so that I get honest before Him and with myself. I've also found that recording my prayer requests—and God's answers—helps me nurture a spirit of thankfulness. Because if I don't, by the time an answer comes, I've often forgotten what I asked for![7]

Sometimes, I must admit, the dialogue of prayer can feel a bit one-sided, consisting mostly of me pouring out my concerns. But I'm learning to take a little time to give God a chance to speak before I present my requests, because I want to pray according to His will and not mine. Afterward, I also attempt to still my heart and wait, listening for any wisdom He might want to give in response.

To be honest, the answers to my requests and the wisdom I need rarely come immediately but instead unfold over a period of time. And more often than not, they come from the Bible.

Tuning Our Hearts to (and Through!) God's Word

"I have hidden your word in my heart that I might not sin against you," David wrote in Psalm 119:11. If we want to *know* and *do* God's will, there is no better place to go than to His Word. And if we want to hear Him speak, storing up the truth of what He has already said in Scripture is an important place to start.

When Jesus told the disciples He would send the Holy Spirit to "remind you of everything I have said to you" (John 14:26), He was speaking of the same work the Holy Spirit wants to do for us today. But how can He bring to remembrance things we have never learned?

Studying the Bible regularly, memorizing Scripture, and taking every opportunity to hear the Bible taught and preached—all have increased my spiritual vocabulary exponentially and have helped me better understand God's ways. They have also provided an invaluable knowledge base from which the Holy Spirit can draw when I have a specific problem or when God wants to address an issue in my life.

I can't tell you how often I've received guidance through a verse I once heard or memorized. Without my consciously seeking it, a "God thought" will pop into my head at just the right moment—clearly a word from the Lord. But God has also used the power of His Word to speak to me directly in my quiet time with life-changing, tomb-shattering results.

In my early years of parenting, for instance, I struggled with a stronghold of anger. There's nothing like having headstrong, stubborn three- and five-year-olds to bring out the headstrong stubbornness in a mom! I did my best to change my angry ways, but it just wasn't working. I couldn't seem to stop lashing out at my children. Even worse, I found myself rationalizing my behavior as common and almost expected.

But then one morning the Bible dismantled all my excuses as the Holy Spirit spoke clearly to me through James 1:20. "For the wrath of man," I read, "does not produce the righteousness of God" (NKJV).

I still remember sitting there, staring at the words as the Spirit spoke to my heart. *Your anger might scare your kids into behaving,* He gently whispered, *but it isn't accomplishing the righteousness God desires. Not in them. And definitely not in you.*

That rebuke was the beginning of my healing. As I allowed the Lord to chasten my heart so I could truly repent—truly hate my sin and turn from it—He began to rewire my soul.

Though it took some time, I can honestly say that anger in parenting is no longer a stronghold for me. I'm eternally grateful for that, because it's allowed me to relax and enjoy Josh, our little caboose. But also it's helping me parent my adult children more gracefully (I hope!) and with less need to control.

Tuning Our Hearts by Recognizing His Ways

While Scripture is the main way God speaks to me, it's not the only way. In fact, as I've grown in my walk with the Lord, I've been amazed at His creativity and the variety of experiences He uses to communicate with me. I'm learning to watch as well as listen for the following four methods the Spirit seems to often use:

- *Repeated themes.* Like every wise parent, God repeats Himself when we don't listen the first time![8] So I've learned to be on the lookout for similar messages on similar topics coming from different sources. If the same topic keeps coming up, God is usually trying to tell me something. (Around the time the Spirit revealed my problem with anger, I encountered two sermons, several articles, and a conversation among friends on the very same topic!)

- *Impressions.* This wisdom from the Spirit usually involves an inner urge or prodding to do something or to go a certain direction. Sometimes it's very specific—*Call your mother* or *Stop at that store.* To be honest, it's often tricky to tell whether the impulse is God's idea or my own. After I obey the nudge, however, I can often look back and see it really was from God.

- *Confirmations.* This clarification from the Holy Spirit is especially important when I'm uncertain whether I'm hearing God correctly—whether the impression I've felt or the theme I've sensed is really for me at that particular time. Sometimes corroboration comes through Scripture or from other people, but it can also come from a sense of settled peace.

- *Checks.* Sometimes instead of confirmation I may feel a check regarding certain decisions or actions. I can't always explain it, but something doesn't feel right in my spirit. There may be nothing obviously wrong with the action I'm contemplating, nothing that bothers my conscience, but I don't have peace about it. In those moments I remember my mother's words: "When in doubt, don't." Later I may (or may not) come to understand what the Spirit was warning against, but that isn't as important as the fact I've obeyed.

Regardless of which of these methods God uses to speak to us, it's important to remember that He will never go against His Word. Therefore, I check any communication I believe I've received from Him against the principles of Scripture. If it fails to measure up with the Bible, I must set it aside, no matter how genuinely I believe I've heard from God.

That is why it is so important that we know the Word—and not just in our heads. "The law of his God is in his heart," the psalmist writes. "His feet do not slip" (Psalm 37:31).

TUNING OUR HEARTS BY OBEYING HIS VOICE

"Pay close attention to what you hear," Jesus tells His followers in Mark 4:24–25. "The closer you listen, the more understanding you will be given—and you will receive even more. To those who listen to my teaching, more understanding will be given" (NLT).

In other words, if I want to hear from God, I must learn to respond to what He says. I can't expect the Holy Spirit to give me further instruction if I'm not willing to obey what He's already shared with me. Obedience opens the ears of my heart and invites further revelation (John 14:15–16). And the quicker I obey, the better. For delayed obedience is just disobedience camouflaged by a promise.

Disobedience in any form is a serious problem because it hardens the conscience—the pathway by which the Holy Spirit often speaks. Like ear wax, our sin can stop up our ears, muffling God's voice. Because our rebellion has distanced us from God, we no longer hear the voice behind us saying, " 'This is the way you should go,' whether to the right or to the left" (Isaiah 30:21, NLT). Instead, we find ourselves drifting farther down the path of compromise and sin. And that is a dangerous place to go.

For if we allow the radio dial of our heart to turn whichever way it wants, we'll end up with white noise and fractured bits of worldly wisdom instead of the sound counsel of God. Inevitably we'll end up way off course, which is why Proverbs 16:25 warns, "There is a way that seems right to a man, but in the end it leads to death."

But, praise God, we don't have to end up there! A change of mind, heart, and direction can be ours if we'll just stop what we're doing and truly confess our sins. Repenting of our apathy toward the things we know God has already said to us through His Word and in our spirits. Allowing the Father to cleanse our hearts and wash out our ears so we can once again hear His voice.

The gentle sound of our Shepherd calling, "Come, follow me."

FOLLOWING HIS VOICE

I used to worry a lot about not hearing God's voice. I was so afraid that when He did speak, I was somehow going to miss it. And scriptures like John 10 only added to my concern.

"My sheep listen to my voice," Jesus says in John 10:27. "I know them, and they follow me." Because I was convinced at the time that I didn't hear God speak, I had to wonder, was I really of His flock? Did I really belong to Him?

But I found the answer to those questions when I took another look at John 10:27. "*I know them,* and they follow me."

You see, it isn't my pursuit of relationship that enables me to hear the Lord. It isn't my diligence in prayer or journaling or Bible reading. It isn't my proficiency at picking up on impressions or the quickness with which I obey. Instead, it is the fact that Jesus loves me and keeps calling my name. I am His chosen lamb. I belong to Him. He's going to do whatever is necessary not only to get through to me but also to help me develop ears to hear. And, surprisingly, He's willing to use even my failures to help me draw closer to Him.

Priscilla Shirer puts it this way: "Do I sometimes make mistakes [in hearing God's voice]? I sure do! But that's how we become spiritually mature—by practicing listening to Him speak and obeying His instructions.... God graciously honors our heart's desire to obey even when we may be a little off base."⁹

The best kind of communication, remember, flows out of relationship. And relationships don't just happen. Intimacy must be nurtured and given time to grow. It's a gradual process.

In a sense, we learn to recognize God's voice the same way a child comes to know the voice of his mother. Nestled inside the womb for nine months, the child lives close to her heart in complete dependence. Then cradled near that same heart for years, he learns to discern her voice above all the rest.

Even in a crowded room filled with distractions and toys, my little Joshua knows when I call his name. And he comes running—well, most of the time.

Let's just say Josh is *learning* to come running.

Just as I am learning to respond to my Father's voice...even when He seems so far away.

The Voice of God in Circumstances

God never speaks to us in startling ways, but in ways that are easy to misunderstand, and we say, "I wonder if that is God's voice?" Isaiah said that the Lord spake to him "with a strong hand," that is, by the pressure of circumstances. Nothing touches our lives but it is God Himself speaking. Do we discern His hand or only mere occurrence?

Get into the habit of saying, "Speak, Lord," and life will become a romance. Every time circumstances press, say, "Speak, Lord"; make time to listen. Chastening is more than a means of discipline, it is meant to get me to the place of saying, "Speak, Lord." Recall the time when God did speak to you. Have you forgotten what He said? Was it Luke 11:13, or was it 1 Thessalonians 5:23? As we listen, our ear gets acute, and, like Jesus, we shall hear God all the time.[10]

—OSWALD CHAMBERS

This is what the LORD says—your Redeemer,
the Holy One of Israel:
"I am the LORD your God,
who teaches you what is best for you,
who directs you in the way you should go."
ISAIAH 48:17

Waiting to Hear

I wish I could say that my life with Christ is now one long uninterrupted conversation. To be honest, my spiritual reception just isn't that good yet. But it's getting there, praise God!

As I spend time in prayer, I develop the habit of conversing with the Lord. As I study His Word, I store up rich principles to be brought back to mind when I need them. And as I attend to the ways the Holy Spirit might want to speak, then obey what I sense He's saying, I'm becoming more attuned to His voice and more apt to hear when He calls.

I must tell you, however, there are times when the conversation still feels more like a monologue than a dialogue. Times when it feels as if my calls aren't getting through. As if there's bad cell-phone reception in heaven.

"Hello? Are you there, God?" I ask. "Can you hear me now?"

Sometimes those glitches in reception stretch out into long, painful periods of silence. Though I'm listening as intently as I can—or at least trying to—I just don't hear a thing.

I'm convinced there are times like that in every Christian's life. Times when Scripture seems to say nothing and all our attempts at prayerful communion seem to bounce off the ceiling and crash to the floor. Times when the darkness of difficulty not only deafens but also blinds us, leaving us to grope in the dark.

At times like these I've come to believe we must go back to what we know about God—not what we're presently experiencing. Because as a friend reminded me during a dark, quiet time of my own, "The teacher is always silent during a test."[11]

So often we equate God's voice with God's favor. When He is talking, we feel His love. When He is silent, we battle fear that we've disappointed Him, or we struggle with love-doubt, wondering if He really cares. It is always important, of course, to check our hearts and make sure sin isn't blocking our relationship. But sin isn't the only reason for silence. There may be more going on than we know.

I've found comfort in a little story I once read—a story about a woman who dreamed she saw three people praying. As they knelt, she watched Jesus draw near and approach the first figure, leaning over her tenderly, smiling and speaking "in accents of purest, sweetest music." Then He proceeded to the next figure and placed a gentle hand on her head and nodded with "loving approval." But what happened next perplexed the dreaming woman:

The third woman He passed almost abruptly without stopping for a word or glance. The woman in her dream said to herself, "How greatly He must love the first one, to the second He gave His approval, but none of the special demonstrations of love He gave the first; and the third must have grieved Him deeply, for He gave her no word at all and not even a passing look.

"I wonder what she has done, and why He made so much difference between them?" As she tried to account for the action of her Lord, He Himself stood by her and said: "O woman! how wrongly hast thou interpreted Me. The first kneeling woman needs all the weight of My tenderness and care to keep her feet in My narrow way. She needs My love, thought and help every moment of the day. Without it she would fail and fall.

"The second has stronger faith and deeper love, and I can trust her to trust Me however things may go and whatever people do.

"The third, whom I seemed not to notice, and even to neglect, has faith and love of the finest quality, and her I am training by quick and drastic processes for the highest and holiest service.

"She knows Me so intimately, and trusts Me so utterly, that she is independent of words or looks or any outward intimation of My approval… because she knows that I am working in her for eternity, and that what I do, though she knows not the explanation now, she will understand hereafter."[12]

Dear friend, don't be afraid of the times when Christ seems "silent in his love" (Zephaniah 3:17, DRA), when He answers "not a word" (Matthew 15:23, KJV). Because God is up to something more in your life and mine than just giving us the comfort of His voice.

He is working in us for eternity. He wants to be able to say of us, "She knows Me so well I can trust her with my silence."

As L. B. Cowman puts it, "The silences of Jesus are as eloquent as His speech and may be a sign, not of His disapproval, but of His approval and of a deep purpose of blessing for you."[13]

So in those times when God is quiet, trust Him and wait. For when the right time comes, you'll hear from Him again.

The very act of waiting, in fact, may help us tune in to His voice better than any other spiritual discipline. Because I've found that God often speaks in the middle of the night. When I'm quiet. When my heart's focused and my ears are ready to hear.

Driving across the dark highways of Montana late at night, I can pick up radio stations from all around the country. Spanish stations from Texas. Financial talk shows from New York. Obscure religious stations from who knows where.

So many voices. So many choices. But if I'll take the time to dial through all the noise, I'll find the one I seek.

Spiritually, that's true as well. For as I consistently tune my heart to the real thing, the counterfeits fade. Until all I hear is the Voice I need.

Love. Calling my name.

And I respond.

Now when He had said these things,
[Jesus] cried with a loud voice,
"Lazarus, come forth!"
And he who had died came out bound hand
and foot with graveclothes,
and his face was wrapped with a cloth.
Jesus said to them, "Loose him, and let him go."

JOHN 11:43–44, NKJV

Unwinding Graveclothes

"Teacher, what must I do to inherit eternal life?" a religious expert asked Jesus one afternoon midway into His ministry (Luke 10:25). Not that the man really cared to hear the answer. He only asked the question to test Jesus. That happened a lot. The religious leaders in Jerusalem were frantic to discredit this upstart prophet from Galilee—the heretic they believed threatened everything they stood for, especially their position and power.

But rather than engaging in debate, Jesus turned the question back to the man. "What is written in the Law? How do you read it?" (verse 26).

I can picture the man gathering his scholarly robes around him as he began to quote scripture in a loud, pious voice. " 'Love the Lord your God with all your heart and with all your soul and with all your strength and with all your mind'; and, 'Love your neighbor as yourself' " (verse 27).

Jesus must have smiled at the man as He said, "You have answered correctly. Do this and you will live" (verse 28).

Not exactly the response the assigned troublemaker was expecting. Suddenly insecure, the expert volleyed back the first argument that came to mind, though it must have sounded weak even to his own ears. "And who is my neighbor?" he asked (verse 29).

In response, Jesus told a story that surely haunted the man and all who heard it, challenging them to go beyond the bigotry and hypocrisy that too often marked their religion.

Just as the story of the good Samaritan challenges Christ-followers today.

For this simple parable shatters many of the excuses and carefully formed arguments we Christians tend to use when attempting to escape God's call to a practical, yet radical, hands-on kind of love.

A Tale of an Unlikely Hero

You're probably familiar with the story. It's found in Luke 10:30–35.

> In reply Jesus said: "A man was going down from Jerusalem to Jericho, when he fell into the hands of robbers. They stripped him of his clothes, beat him and went away, leaving him half dead. A priest happened to be going down the same road, and when he saw the man, he passed by on the other side. So too, a Levite, when he came to the place and saw him, passed by on the other side. But a Samaritan, as he traveled, came where the man was; and when he saw him, he took pity on him. He went to him and bandaged his wounds, pouring on oil and wine. Then he put the man on his own donkey, took him to an inn and took care of him. The next day he took out two silver coins and gave them to the innkeeper. 'Look after him,' he said, 'and when I return, I will reimburse you for any extra expense you may have.' "

What was it about this parable that so unsettled the religious elite of Jesus's day? What is it about this story that captures the imagination of today's gospel-illiterate world?

Perhaps it is the insight into our own human condition that resonates most. For which one of us has not felt at some time stripped naked, beaten, and left for dead? Life is hard and habitually unfair. We can be minding our business one minute and lying comatose, barely breathing, the next. Crumpled at the side of the road in need of help, many of us have felt the cold shadow of indifference as people passed by, noting our condition but doing nothing to relieve it. We may even know what it's like to notice a problem yet feel unable to help. No wonder the story hits a nerve.

But I think what gives the story mythic proportions is its absolute unexpectedness. It highlights the compassion of an unlikely hero—a Samaritan, considered by the Jews of Jesus's day as the lowest of the low—against the heart-wrenching indifference of individuals who, by their very roles, should have cared the most.

"If you see your brother's donkey or his ox fallen on the road," Deuteronomy 22:4 commands, "do not ignore it. Help him get it to its feet." Certainly a wounded man deserved as much care as clumsy cattle. And yet in Jesus's story both the priest and the Levite—God's servants, entrusted with ministry to His people—passed by without stopping.

No doubt they had their reasons. They "were both in a hurry," suggests Henry M. Grout.

They had been a month at Jerusalem, and were expected and wanted at home. Their wives and children were anxiously waiting for them. The sun would soon be down, and this was a lonely road even by daylight. Neither of them understood surgery, and could not bind up a wound to save their lives. Moreover, the poor man, already half dead, would be quite dead in an hour or two, and it was a pity to waste time on a hopeless case. The robbers, too, might be back again. Then, the man might die, and the person found near the body be charged with murder.[1]

Legitimate excuses, every one. But as David O. Mears reminds us: "It is not always *convenient* to be good."[2] Especially when it runs counter to our self-centeredness.

Inconvenient love—that's what we're called to as Christians. To "carry each other's burdens," as Galatians 6:2 tells us, for "in this way you will fulfill the law of Christ."

But such love is rarely easy. In fact, it can be downright messy. Especially when God asks us to unwind graveclothes.

LOOSE HIM, LET HIM GO!

I can't imagine what it must have been like to see Lazarus shuffle out of the darkness of the tomb, wrapped in thin strips of linen according to the custom of the day. His

Kissing Frogs

Transformation has always been the stuff of fairy tales—Cinderella's rags turning into a glistening gown and Beauty's love unlocking the Beast's curse. However, no fairy tale compares to the life-changing love story Jesus longs to live out with us. Strangely, while we are part of that story, we are also called to help write it. Wes Seeliger puts it so well, using a familiar tale to describe the important "unwrapping" work Christ-followers are called to share:

Ever feel like a frog? Frogs feel slow, low, ugly, puffy, drooped, pooped. I know. One told me. The frog feeling comes when you want to be bright but feel dumb, when you want to share but are selfish, when you want to be thankful but feel resentment, when you want to be great but are small, when you want to care but are indifferent.

Yes, at one time or another each of us has found himself on a lily pad floating down the great river of life. Frightened and disgusted, we're too froggish to budge. Once upon a time there was a frog. But he really wasn't a frog. He was a prince who looked and felt like a frog. A wicked witch had cast a spell on him. Only the kiss of a beautiful maiden could save him. But since when do cute chicks kiss frogs? So there he sat, unkissed prince in frog form. But miracles happen. One day a beautiful maiden grabbed him up and gave him a big smack. Crash! Boom! Zap!! There he was, a handsome prince. And you know the rest. They lived happily ever after. So what is the task of the [Christian]? To kiss frogs, of course.[3]

Be completely humble and gentle; be patient,
bearing with one another in love.

EPHESIANS 4:2

arms and legs were probably wrapped individually, which would have allowed some movement. But to say the man was restricted would be an understatement.

The stench of death surely lingered around him. Depending on the original sickness, bloody patches may have marked the burial garment here and there, interspersed with yellow-crusted infection. Though a welcome sight to those who loved him, the resurrected Lazarus might also have been a bit frightening to behold.

I wonder what Mary and Martha thought when Jesus said, "Loose him, and let him go" (John 11:44, NKJV). As happy as I'd be to see my brother alive, I wouldn't want to touch the strips of linen that had clung to his rotting flesh. After all, who knew what lay underneath the bandages? Just how resurrected was he?

Unwinding graveclothes. It's a dirty job. But someone has to do it.

Someone has to do it. And that's one of the factors of Lazarus's story that shocks me most. For while Jesus Christ did what only He could do—bring a dead man back to life—He invited those who stood around watching to help with the process.

"Loose him, and let him go." It's the same command Christ gives the church today.

I love what Jerry Goebel says about this passage of Scripture. "The work of Jesus is to bring life; the work of the congregation is to unbind people from the trappings of death. The words that Christ speaks are so full; he literally tells the 'congregation'; 'Destroy what holds him down. Send him forth free.' "[4]

Unfortunately, most of us would rather observe a resurrection than actually participate in one. Like the priest and Levite who passed by the wounded man, we shy away from actually getting involved in the work of loving someone back to life. Some of us may even prefer the role of cynic, refusing to believe that God has really changed a person or that the change can last.

"All too often, we never unbind those who Christ has resurrected," Goebel says. "We would rather continue to see them with the haughty eyes of the skeptic. We are more excited for them to fail than to change…[saying of their experience], 'Oh yea, well. I know that feeling and it will only last a month.' "[5]

An attitude like that breaks God's heart. And it can actually add another layer of graveclothes to someone who is trying to walk out of the tomb of his or her past. Goebel writes:

We bind people through our attitudes toward them. We bind them when we hold onto their faults instead of lifting up and encouraging their attempts to change. We bind people when we don't forgive them. We bind them when we gossip to others about their faults. Whenever we treat people out of our smallness instead of the Lord's abundance; we keep them bound.

We free them when we are determined to see new life in them. We free them when we praise God. We free them when we forgive them. We free them when we smile and welcome them, saying; "I am so glad you are here; do you have anyone to sit with today?" We free them the most when we seek them in their tombs and, "snorting at death," we command them in the name of Christ to come into new life.

Whenever we treat another out of Christ's greatness and not our smallness; we free them.[6]

That is the work we are called to as brothers and sisters in the Lord—unbinding, through acceptance and love, those whom Jesus has resurrected. However, as I've pointed out, helping people walk out into a new life can be a messy process. Though a person has received Christ as Savior, it may take a lot of time and effort before the outer self catches up with the inward work. None of us is born—or reborn—into this world squeaky clean.

Still, if God isn't threatened by the stink,[7] then why are we?

THE POWER OF LOVE

Unwrapping graveclothes—what an amazing call and privilege. But what does it look like, and how do we do it? Unfortunately, no template, no one-size-fits-all guide, is available. But having had the privilege of being raised by a man who loves Jesus so much that he's passionate about people knowing his Lord, I've had a front-row seat to quite a few resurrections.

One of my father's greatest joys has been ministering at the county jail for the past fifty years. Each Sunday he and a team from his church lead afternoon services for the men and women incarcerated there. Through singing songs and sharing the

Word and personal testimonies, they've witnessed some amazing acts of God in the lives of prisoners who've surrendered their hearts to Him.

However, Dad realized long ago that his responsibility didn't end with seeing someone saved. So he's done his best to disciple new converts, following up at times to the point of helping them find a job, a church, and a place to live after they're released from jail.

Once in a while during my growing-up years, that place was our basement. It wasn't unusual to have people stay with us for a few transitional days or weeks. My sister and I used to call our house "Gustafson's Home for Wayward Boys and Girls."

I suppose such hospitality would be considered too dangerous even to contemplate today. But back then? Well, it seemed almost miraculous.

Unwinding graveclothes—that's what Cliff and Annette Gustafson did on a regular basis. Mom's open arms spoke of acceptance, slowly loosening tight bands of rejection that had bound hearts for years. Dad's passion for the Lord and his commitment to family modeled a way of living some had never seen. It wasn't always a tidy process, but it was a valuable one. While many of the men and women Mom and Dad ministered to left and were never heard from again, others grew and flourished and still flourish today.

But the prisoners and ex-prisoners weren't the only ones who benefited from my parents' work. I did too. Watching them love in an active, hands-on way taught me several lessons that have proven invaluable in my own effort to serve the Lord by serving people.

What did I learn? First, that I'm not responsible for everyone, but I am responsible for the ones God lays upon my heart.

Most of the people Dad ministered to didn't stay in our home, but when he felt impressed to go the extra mile, he'd ask my mother for confirmation. If they were in agreement, they did what they felt God would have them do. Whether it was opening their home, lending their car, or investing financially in the life of another, whatever God asked them to do, they did to the best of their ability.

Second, I learned to lay down my expectations for the people I try to help.

The stories I observed in my parents' ministry didn't always have a happy ending—at least that we knew about. Most people were in and out of our lives within days. Sometimes my parents' generosity was misused or, worse, abused. A few "guests" became angry when my parents felt their job was through. If Mom and Dad had done what they did always expecting to be thanked or appreciated, they would have given up long ago.

Which brings us to the most important lesson I learned by watching these two unwind graveclothes: obey God and His promptings, then leave the outcome to Him.

After visiting the Missionaries of Charity in Calcutta, India, an American politician asked Mother Teresa how she could keep doing what she did without being discouraged. After all, the people the nuns cared for were so ill that the majority died within a few weeks. "God has not called me to be successful," Mother Teresa answered. "God has called me to be faithful."[8]

That is the calling my parents answered nearly fifty years ago—the same calling each of us has as Christians. To love the people He gives us. To minister to them just as we find them, gently peeling away their nasty rags and washing away the grime of the tomb with the truth of God's Word. Strip by strip, unwinding the lies that have shriveled their souls. Then covering their nakedness with our love and acceptance, just as Christ has covered ours.

For when we do it to the least of these, Jesus says, we do it unto Him (Matthew 25:40). Because Jesus loves people. Even people who are bound and still feel half-dead.

THE WALKING DEAD

My friend Sarah[9] knows a little of what it feels like to be resurrected yet still totter around in graveclothes. Her story reads like a soap opera and an exaggerated one at that—family problems, legal battles, loss, betrayal, you name it. When I first heard her tale, I thought that surely no one person could go through so much pain in such a short time. And yet she has.

As a result, Sarah has lived most of the last decade in a tomb of intense confusion and shame. Wrapped tight with sorrow over things she's done. Weighed down with false responsibility for sins committed by others.

When we first met, she had trouble meeting my eyes as we sat in the prayer room. Fearful of yet another betrayal of trust, she kept her head down as she tearfully told me her story. The pain was literally palpable as she spilled out the details of a life that seemed shattered beyond repair.

God had brought us together in a divine way—neither of us could deny that. It was time to step out of the tomb. Love was calling her name. But to unwrap the graveclothes? To open her heart and risk rejection? It terrified us both, I suppose.

As difficult as it was for Sarah to trust me with her story, I must admit I trembled as I listened to her pain. I know my inadequacies—my good intentions and lousy follow-through. What if I let her down? What if she went away more wounded than she came, her graveclothes wrapped even more tightly around her?

"Will I ever be okay again?" she finally asked, allowing her fearful eyes to glance at my face. I reached out and grabbed her hand, assuring her that we have a God who specializes in making all things new (Revelation 21:5). Then, together, she and I took all her confusion to the Lord in prayer. Laying out the story of her life before Jesus. Taking the hurt, the disappointment, and the betrayal to the One who has felt everything she's felt and more. Giving it to the only One who can heal a heart wounded beyond human remedy.

The healing hasn't happened quickly. Sarah would be the first one to tell you it has been a journey of stops and starts. One step forward out of the tomb, then suddenly, almost without warning, two steps back. One layer of graveclothes unwrapped, only to have the next layer pulled tighter. And yet there has been progress. True, measurable progress!

Helping unwrap Sarah's graveclothes has been a great privilege. But in the midst of this process, I'm reminded there are limits to what I am called to do. Because if I try to do more than God is asking, I could actually end up doing harm.

THE CHRYSALIS

In her devotional classic *Springs in the Valley,* Lettie B. Cowman tells the story of a naturalist who spotted a large butterfly fluttering frantically as if in distress. It appeared to be caught on something. The man reached down, took hold of its wings, and set it free. The butterfly flew only a few feet before falling to the ground, dead.

Under a magnifying glass in his lab, the naturalist discovered blood flowing from tiny veins in the lovely creature's wings. He realized that inadvertently he had interrupted something very important. The butterfly's frantic fluttering had really been an attempt to emerge from its chrysalis—a strength-building process designed by God. If allowed to struggle long enough, the butterfly would have come forth ready for long and wide flight. Early release, however, ended that beautiful dream.

So it is with God's children, Mrs. Cowman writes.

How the Father wishes for them wide ranges in experience and truth. He permits us to be fastened to some form of struggle. We would tear ourselves free. We cry out in our distress and sometimes think Him cruel that He does not release us. He permits us to flutter and flutter on. Struggle seems to be His program sometimes.[10]

Perhaps that is why Lazarus had to come out of the tomb of his own volition—why Jesus called him out instead of sending Martha and Mary inside to get him. Resurrection often seems to require a willing response, even a struggle, on the part of the one being resurrected. Tombs can be comfortable, remember. And choosing to live can be hard.

Those of us called to remove others' graveclothes need to understand that struggle. We also need to be clear about what our job actually is—and what it is not. We will be tempted to short-cut the time-consuming and painful-to-watch process of tearing loose from death. But if we insist on interrupting and interfering, no matter how good our intentions might be, we run the risk of derailing God's plan and spiritually handicapping those we're trying to help.

OVERCOMING THE FIXER IN ME

I learned an important truth early in ministry: There is only one Savior. And I am not He.

In fact, I do Christ a great disservice when I attempt to fill a role only He can fill. I also sabotage the process when I do things that the people being resurrected are meant to do.

Ministry can be heady stuff at times. It can be strangely satisfying to be the one a needy person turns to for help and answers. But it can also be dangerous...especially when we buy the lie that it's all up to us. That in some way we are meant to be another person's Messiah.

"If you become a necessity to a soul, you are out of God's order," Oswald Chambers writes.

> As a worker, your great responsibility is to be a friend of the Bridegroom...
> Instead of putting out a hand to prevent the throes [in a person's life], pray
> that they grow ten times stronger until there is no power on earth or in hell
> that can hold that soul away from Jesus Christ. Over and over again, we
> become amateur providences, we come in and prevent God; and say—"This
> and that must not be." Instead of proving friends of the Bridegroom, we put
> our sympathy in the way, and the soul will one day say—"That one was a
> thief, he stole my affections from Jesus, and I lost my vision of Him."[11]

Friends of the Bridegroom—that's what we are called to be. Loyal to Christ and His work in the lives of those we minister to rather than loyal to our opinions of how that work should be done.

For we will inevitably encounter moments when God's timing or methods seem a bit cruel, when situations He allows confound our understanding. But if we'll step back and give God room, we'll discover our Father really does know best.

Because God has always been more interested in shaping the character of His children than simply providing them comfort.

In setting people free rather than just letting them be.

And to that end He calls us to join Him in His work. But, surprisingly, we may do it best, not with our hands, but on our knees.

INVESTING IN FREEDOM

When the good Samaritan saw the wounded man lying beside the road, he not only reacted with compassion, he also did what he could do. He bound up the man's wounds, took him to an inn, and apparently spent the night caring for the stranger. Eventually, he had to leave the wounded man in the innkeeper's care—just as we must entrust the finishing work of healing in people's lives to God and God alone.

But that wasn't the end of the good Samaritan's involvement. Before going on his way, he invested in the invalid's continued care. Leaving money to pay for several days' lodging, the man from Samaria promised to return to settle any extra costs that might be incurred.

Oh how I want to display that kind of sacrificial love and tenacious follow-through when it comes to helping my brothers and sisters experience new life.

I want to see people set free. I'm tired of watching Christians walk out of church just as bound as they were when they walked in. I'm tired of seeing people struggle

---

Lessons from Good Sam

We all want to be used by God to help others. But we don't always know what that should look like. The story of the good Samaritan offers several lessons to help shape our response when we see someone in need:

1. *He not only saw but acted.* Other people passed by and saw the wounded man, but the good Samaritan was "moved" with compassion. He didn't just feel sorry for the man's condition; he *moved* to do something to alleviate his pain (Proverbs 3:27).

2. *He used his oil and his donkey.* Don't underestimate what your involvement can mean to someone in need. Investing your practical resources, your emotional support, and your precious time can make all the difference to a broken soul. A kind note, a warm meal, a listening ear—little is much when God is in it (James 2:16; Galatians 6:2).

3. *He went out of his way to help.* Initial compassion can wear off quickly, especially when helping others is inconvenient. The good Samaritan could have left the man at the inn and gone on his way, but instead he stuck around to do the hard stuff—washing

for years with the same issues, the same bondages and addictions, without realizing victory. I want to see people delivered. Don't you?

According to Scripture, such freedom usually involves a specific—and costly—commitment on my part and yours. For beyond our love and hands-on care, true life change and healing are nearly always preceded by an investment of prayer.

After nearly three decades of ministry, I'm coming to understand the best way to unwind other people's graveclothes is through intercession. But can I be honest? Prayer is often the last place I go. I'm ashamed to admit that I'm much quicker to get my hands on people than to get hold of heaven on people's behalf. No wonder I often end up doing too much or too little.

Reading Frank Peretti's book *Piercing the Darkness* has helped revolutionize how

wounds and staying beside him through a long, painful night (Galatians 6:9).

4. *He left the man in capable hands.* There will be times when a person's needs may be beyond our ability to help—times when a pastor, a godly counselor, or another professional will be required. Connecting needy people to other resources may be the most important thing we do (Proverbs 13:10).

5. *He promised to stay engaged in the process.* Following through to see how the person is doing is important—though at times God may ask us to do more. Whatever is required, never underestimate the importance of intercession—standing in the gap as Ezekiel did (Ezekiel 22:30), fighting for final victory in the lives of those we minister to.

The King will reply, "I tell you the truth, whatever you did for one of the least of these brothers of mine, you did for me."
MATTHEW 25:40

I view prayer. While it is a fictional account, it gives an important insight into the spiritual battle that rages around every single one of us. And it shows the vital role intercession plays in the spiritual realm.

You may wonder, as I have, if prayer really makes a difference. I love the picture Peretti paints in his riveting story. Though a heavy spiritual darkness lay like a thick cloud over the small town, each time a prayer went up, a small hole appeared in the darkness. More prayers, more holes allowing the light of truth and illumination of the Spirit to reach the hearts and minds of those living there.[12]

If we only realized how powerful and mighty our intercession can be, how it releases the power of God over people's lives and influences the spiritual battle being waged around them, we'd pray more.

In fact, I think we'd find ourselves investing in other people's freedom on a daily basis. Following through on our knees for as long as it takes for resurrection to happen and graveclothes to fall to the ground. Lifting people to the throne of grace until they're able to find their own way to the holy of holies. Covering them in the precious blood of Jesus until they learn how to walk and then how to run.

As James 5:16 tells us, the "fervent prayer of a righteous man availeth much" (KJV). Not only in the lives of those for whom we're praying, but in our lives as well. Because intercession tunes our hearts to the Spirit's leading, giving us eyes to see what He sees. And giving us His heart so that we can be His hands.

Unwinding graveclothes in the most unlikely ways and in the most unlikely places.

Led by the Spirit

Author Beth Moore tells of a time when she noticed an old man sitting in a wheelchair at a crowded airport. He was a strange sight, with stringy gray hair hanging down over his shoulders.

Trying not to stare, she focused on the Bible in her lap. But the more she tried to concentrate on the Word, the more she felt drawn to the old man.

"I had walked with God long enough to see the handwriting on the wall," Beth writes. "I've learned that when I begin to feel what God feels, something so contrary to my natural feelings, something dramatic is bound to happen. And it may be embarrassing."

Though she tried to resist the prompting, it only grew stronger. "I don't want you to witness to him," God said clearly. "I want you to brush his hair."

Finally she gave up arguing. She walked over to the man and knelt in front of him.

"Sir?" she asked. "May I have the pleasure of brushing your hair?"

He looked confused. "What'd you say?"

She blurted out her request once again, louder, and immediately felt every eye in the waiting area upon her and the old man. "If you really want to," he said.

With a hairbrush she found in his bag, Beth began gently brushing the old man's hair. It was clean, but tangled and matted. However, mothering two little girls had prepared her well for the task.

"A miraculous thing happened to me as I started brushing...," Beth remembers. "Everybody else in the room disappeared.... I know this sounds so strange but I've never felt that kind of love for another soul in my entire life. I believe with all my heart, I—for that few minutes—felt a portion of the very love of God. That He had overtaken my heart...like someone renting a room and making Himself at home for a short while."

The emotions were still strong when she finished. After replacing the brush in the man's bag, she knelt in front of his chair. "Sir, do you know Jesus?"

"Yes, I do," he said. "I've known Him since I married my bride. She wouldn't marry me until I got to know the Savior." He paused a moment. "You see, the problem is, I haven't seen my bride in months. I've had open-heart surgery, and she's been too ill to come see me. I was sitting here thinking to myself, *What a mess I must be for my bride.*"[13]

His Hand Extended

What an amazing privilege it is to be the very hands of God in someone else's life.

I wonder how many opportunities I've missed. How many wounded strangers I've passed by because I was too busy to stop. How many piles of burial garments

I've avoided, not knowing that a resurrected sister or brother lay inside, struggling to get out. Or how many butterfly metamorphoses I've interrupted because my human compassion assumed that I knew the person's needs better than God did.

I want to participate in the miraculous. I want to be a little bit of God's kingdom come to earth—Christ's hand extended, reaching out in love. But that means I have to slow down, and like Beth Moore I have to listen. I must tune my heart to the prompting of the Holy Spirit so that when He beckons, "Loose him; let him go," I step forward rather than pull back. So that when He prompts, "Wait and pray," I'm willing to intercede rather than interfere. So that whatever I do, I do it with His wisdom and love. (For some practical help on unwinding graveclothes, see Appendix F.)

"Who's my neighbor?" the expert asked Jesus.

As Warren Wiersbe puts it, the answer has less to do with geography and more to do with opportunity.[14] Because the best way to love the Lord with all my heart, soul, mind, and strength is to love the people who happen to be standing next to me.

Even when loving them involves unwinding graveclothes.

Jesus said to [Martha], "I am the resurrection and the life.
He who believes in me will live, even though he dies;
and whoever lives and believes in me will never die.
Do you believe this?"
"Yes, Lord," she told him, "I believe that you are the Christ,
the Son of God, who was to come into the world."....
Jesus called in a loud voice, "Lazarus, come out!"
The dead man came out, his hands
and feet wrapped with strips of linen,
and a cloth around his face.
Jesus said to them, "Take off the grave clothes and let him go."
Therefore many of the Jews who...had seen
what Jesus did put their faith in him.
But some of them went to the Pharisees and told
them what Jesus had done.
Then the chief priests and the Pharisees called
a meeting of the Sanhedrin....
So from that day on they plotted to take his life....
[They] made plans to kill Lazarus as well,
for on account of him many of the Jews were going over to Jesus
and putting their faith in him.
JOHN 11:25–27, 43–47, 53; 12:10–11

Living Resurrected

I shouldn't have done it. Many months behind on this book's deadline, I needed to buckle down to make up lost time, but the invitation to speak at a church event in California stirred something in my heart. When they told me I could stay a few days afterward to write, I agreed to come.

I had no idea the location was Lazarusville.

The host church, birthed out of the 1970s Jesus movement, was filled with resurrection stories. Everywhere I turned, I met yet another person who had been spiritually dead and now lived again. My hostess had been a hippie traveling the highways of America when she encountered Jesus Christ in a powerful way. God told her to go back home and love her parents. She did. Not just in word but also in deed.

So drastic was the change in her that both of her parents accepted the Lord. "I gave birth to my daughter," her dear mama told me, eyes all alight, "and she gave birth to me!"

The event's worship leader, once a dancer and lounge singer, also encountered the amazing love of Christ and now leads thousands of people each week to the throne room of God. The husband of another leader, once full of bigotry toward Jews, now works tirelessly for the Lord, especially in the cause of preserving the nation of Israel.

One woman I met was brought to Jesus through her little boy. After years of looking for love in all the wrong places, Robin finally encountered the love of God through a memory verse her son had learned in Sunday school. "[Cast] all your care upon Him, for He cares for you," the little boy recited to his mother (1 Peter 5:7, NKJV).

"Who's 'Him'?" she asked sarcastically.

"Jesus, Mama," he said solemnly. "Jesus cares for you."

Those four little words broke something hard inside Robin. Though she was too proud to take her son to church that Sunday, she followed the bus and slipped in a side door. There she found the Love she'd been looking for her whole life.

Transformation. It was all around me that weekend. The sound of butterfly wings and souls metamorphosing in the presence of the Lord. Lazaruses and Lazarellas—every one of them.

None of them perfect. Not one of them complete.

But resurrected? Most definitely!

Undeniably so.

BEFORE AND AFTER

When Lazarus came forth from the tomb at Jesus's call, those standing around couldn't deny that a miracle had taken place. After all, they'd just sat shivah—part of the traditional seven days of Jewish mourning—with Mary and Martha. They'd held the two sisters as they wept. They'd reheated casseroles, hoping to get the grieving women to eat. They'd even shared a few chuckles as they reminisced about their friend and talked about how they would miss him.

But now Lazarus stood before them alive again, his eyes shining as the burial cloth was lifted from his face. They heard his first words and witnessed his first steps after the graveclothes were fully unwound. They watched as the man they'd helped lay to rest now ran toward Jesus, along with his sisters, until they met together in one giant embrace.

Some of the crowd immediately put their faith in Jesus because of what had happened. Later, others would do the same. For seeing a man raised from the dead was hard to ignore. It was as undeniable as it was unexplainable. All they had to do was look at Lazarus to know a transformation had taken place.

He had been dead. Completely dead. Dead as a doornail.

Now he was alive. Completely alive. A walking, talking miracle.

No wonder so many who saw the event put their trust in the One who'd made it happen.

A Story to Share

I used to long for a powerful Lazarusville testimony. When you are saved at the age of four, there isn't a whole lot of "before" you can point to in order to validate your "after." Not a lot of transformation that people can ooh and ah about.

Over the years when preachers would say, "Think about the day you were saved and what you were before you met Jesus," I honestly wished I could. It would've been so nice to have a born-again moment I could point to and say, "That's where Jesus came. That was the old. Here's the new."

Dramatic testimonies seemed to be the ones God really used. Which bothered me a lot as a young Christian. What did I have to offer?

Sure, I loved Jesus. But had I been transformed?

Most days I couldn't see any noticeable difference between my life and the lives of those around me, at least from my hypercritical point of view.

I knew *something* had happened when Jesus came into my heart. After all, I didn't want to sin, and I hurt inside when I did. I felt a love in my heart for people and prayed diligently that my life would make a difference for God's kingdom. But I knew His kingdom needed to make a difference in me as well.

So began my lifelong prayer: *Lord, change me.*

And He has done just that. Although I still don't have a dramatic conversion story, every time I've allowed God to get His hands on me, He's given me a testimony—a real before-and-after story to share. Because every time I've given God access to yet another place in my heart, abdicating control and allowing Jesus to rule and reign, I've been changed in some important ways. While I'm not yet what I ought to be, I'm no longer what I was, thank God!

That's the kind of freshly baked, hot-out-of-the-oven testimony the Lord wants to give to every one of us. A testimony of resurrection that's just too good not to share.

The Resurrection and the Life

When Martha met Jesus on the road after her brother had died, a powerful exchange of truth occurred between the two of them.

After pouring out her pain and confusion concerning Lazarus's death, Martha gave Jesus permission to do what He thought best, by saying, "But I know that even now God will give you whatever you ask" (John 11:22).

In response, Jesus made one of His seven great "I Am" declarations, all recorded in the gospel of John. "I am the resurrection and the life," He told Martha. "He who believes in me will live, even though he dies; and whoever lives and believes in me will never die. Do you believe this?" (verses 25–26).

"Yes, Lord, I believe that you are the Christ, the Son of God, who was to come into the world," she replied (verse 27).

And Martha did believe! Unlike some of her fellow Jews, she had faith in an end-time resurrection. She knew her brother would live again, just as she would after she died. And she was also completely convinced her friend Jesus was the Messiah, the long-awaited hope of Israel.

In that faith-filled moment, Martha may have even believed He could speak resurrection life into her brother that very day.

But later, as Martha stood before Lazarus's tomb, her faith faltered. Face to face with her grief-filled reality, she found it difficult to believe that anyone—even Jesus—could bring life out of such obvious death and decay.

It can be just as hard for us to imagine such a transformation in our own lives today.

Yes, Lord, we know we're saved and going to heaven. We know that one day we'll be made truly alive when we see you face to face. But to think we might experience resurrection right here in the middle of our messy, mixed-up existence? *It just doesn't seem possible,* we decide, settling for the midchamber and just hanging on until Jesus comes.

Yet all the while, the Resurrection and the Life stands outside our tombs, calling our names.

"Lazarus…"

"Joanna…"

Put your name on His lips. Then listen as Jesus commands, "Come forth!"

But don't let resurrection be the end of your story. Allow Jesus to do all He desires to do in you—for He may have more in mind than you realize.

You see, Jesus Christ didn't come to earth simply to provide us an example to follow (though He did give us an important glimpse of how life should be lived). He didn't come only to show us the Father's heart and reveal the Father's love (though He did just that and more). He didn't even come for the sole purpose of setting us free from the tyranny of death (though, praise God, He did!).

No, Jesus came and died and rose again. Then He returned to heaven and sent His Holy Spirit for one reason and one reason alone: so that He might live His life within us. All of Him in all of you and me.

That's the testimony each of us can have, no matter what our faith journeys look like. The indwelling Christ living and working inside us. So transforming who and what we used to be that those around us can't help but see the miracle and put their faith in God.

It's the marvelous mystery Paul wrote about in Colossians 1:27—the secret "God has chosen to make known among the Gentiles" and to you and me as well.

What mystery? What secret?

Paul goes on to tell us: it is "Christ in you, the hope of glory."

THE VICTORIOUS SECRET

Over and over in the New Testament, we see this concept of the Lord living His life within us and transforming us from the inside out. The message is so pronounced, it's hard to believe many of us miss it. And yet all too often we do.

Hudson Taylor, the famous missionary to China, didn't understand it for a long time. After struggling to live a holy life in his own strength for more than fifteen years of ministry, he despaired of ever being victorious. But one day he read a letter from a friend, John McCarthy, who told of awakening to this marvelous truth:

> To let my loving Saviour work in me...is what I would live for by His grace. Abiding, not striving nor struggling; looking off unto Him; trusting Him for present power; trusting Him to subdue all inward corruption; resting in the love of an almighty Saviour.... Christ literally all seems to me now the power, the only power for service; the only ground for unchanging joy. May He lead us into the realization of His unfathomable fullness.[1]

But one sentence in the letter stood out among the rest. "But how to get faith strengthened?" his friend asked. "Not by striving after faith, but by resting on the Faithful One."[2]

When Hudson Taylor read those words, something deep within him responded. "I saw it all!" he later wrote to his sister, describing his new awareness of Christ living within. It was the Savior's faithfulness that mattered, not his own.

With that realization Scripture took on new life for him, especially John 15, which describes Jesus as the vine and believers as branches who draw life from the vine. Hudson wrote, "The vine now I see, is not the root merely, but all—root, stem, branches, twigs, leaves, flowers, fruit: and Jesus is not only that: He is soil and sunshine, air and showers, and ten thousand times more than we have ever dreamed, wished for, or needed."[3]

The reality of living and resting in the completed work of Jesus—the "exchanged life," as Hudson Taylor called it[4]—changed his life and ministry forever. A missionary friend wrote of the transformation: "He was a joyous man now, a bright, happy Christian. He had been a toiling, burdened one before, with latterly not much rest of soul. It was resting in Jesus now, and letting Him do the work—which makes all the difference!"[5]

But Hudson Taylor isn't the only Christian who discovered the beautiful mystery and magnificent power of "Christ in you, the hope of glory." Others have written of it as well.

In her book *The Unselfishness of God,* Hannah Whitall Smith writes:

What had come to me now was a discovery, and in no sense an attainment. I had not become a better woman than I was before, but I had found out that Christ was a better Savior than I had thought He was. I was not one bit more able to conquer my temptations than I had been in the past, but I had discovered that He was able and willing to conquer them for me. I had no more wisdom or righteousness of my own than I had ever had, but I had found out that He could really and actually be made unto me, as the Apostle declared He would be, wisdom, and righteousness, and sanctification, and redemption.[6]

Jesus wants to be the same for us today—living His life so fully within us that we join Hudson Taylor and Hannah Whitall Smith and the apostle Paul in proclaiming, "I have been crucified with Christ and I no longer live, but *Christ lives in me*. The life I live in the body, I live by faith in the Son of God, who loved me and gave himself for me" (Galatians 2:20, emphasis added).

Note that phrase "I have been crucified with Christ and I no longer live"—for it is the key. If we want to live resurrected and experience the exchanged life so many heroes of the faith describe, we must first get around to dying. Dying to ourselves until we're dead to the world.

For anything less than that results in a half-baked resurrection.

Don't Settle for Zombie Living

In his obscure 1906 novella, Leonid Andreyev paints a disturbing picture of Lazarus after being raised from the dead. Of the few portrayals of Lazarus in literature, this one certainly isn't flattering. Nor is it anything like the life Christ came to give. Here's a synopsis of the story:

> Sumptuously dressed, [Lazarus] is surrounded by his sisters Mary and
> Martha, other relatives, and friends celebrating his resurrection. His three
> days in the grave have left marks on his body; there is a bluish cast to his
> fingertips and face, and there are cracked and oozing blisters on his skin. The
> deterioration of his body has been interrupted, but the restoration, his return
> to health, is incomplete. His demeanor, too, has changed. He is no longer
> joyous, carefree, and laughing, as he was before death.[7]

Instead, Andreyev's Lazarus walks through life tormented—and tormenting those with whom he comes in contact. Looking too long in his eyes causes madness to the beholder. Rather than bringing life where he goes, a kind of death follows in his wake. He is a decomposing ghoul rather than a man made fully alive.

Sadly, I fear too many Christians accept this zombie-like existence as their fate. We're living resurrected—sort of. But we know our lives should be more joyful.

More peaceful. We know we should be loving, kind, forgiving. But instead, too often we're anxious, selfish, and cruel. The odor of our not-yet-decomposed lower nature seems to hang around our lives continually no matter how many disinfectants we try or room fresheners we plug in.

If you find yourself in this condition, may I ask you a question? Have you ever considered dying? Have you ever considered climbing upon the cross and staying there until Christ's life is able to have its way in you?

Though the Bible is clear that what Jesus did on Calvary was enough to purchase your salvation and mine, a sanctifying work still needs to be done—a holy transaction that requires a kind of death.

"If anyone would come after me," Jesus says in Mark 8:34, "he must deny himself and take up his cross and follow me." But may I submit that it isn't enough just to pick up the cross. We must allow the cross to have its way in us. Continually walking down the Via Dolorosa yet never allowing ourselves to reach Golgotha is not what Jesus meant when He said, "Follow me."

For without a crucifixion, there can be no resurrection.

We have to be willing to die if we want to really live.

Until we "put to death...whatever belongs to [our] earthly nature," as Colossians 3:5 commands, we will never be able to emerge from our tombs and actually "practice resurrection" as Wendell Berry describes it.[8]

Putting our earthly nature to death isn't something we can do apart from God. It isn't meant to be a renovation we attempt on our own or a charade we play at until it becomes reality. Believe me, I've tried it that way, and it just doesn't work.

And yet, while the Holy Spirit wants to help us, we must initiate the act. For in a very real sense, only we can choose to die.

PRACTICING RESURRECTION

The question, of course, is *how*. What does "dying to live" look like on a practical level?

For me, it involves rejecting the influence of anything that is in direct opposition to the rule and reign of Christ in my heart, including...

- my desire to control and direct my own life (and the lives of others),
- my right to be treated fairly at all times (and in all ways),
- my need to be well thought of (and thought of frequently),
- my insatiable appetite for escape (whether it be through food, television, books, or other avenues).

Did you notice that all these are me-centered desires? Which is exactly the problem. In order to facilitate Christ's life-changing invasion of the kingdoms in my heart, I must dethrone my lower nature by dying to self.

Buried in Baptism

To me, there is no better picture of dying to live than baptism. Perhaps that is why the first thing Jesus did before beginning His ministry was ask John to baptize Him (Matthew 3:13–17).

The act of baptism is practiced differently in various churches—some immerse, some pour, some sprinkle. However, I love the symbolism of the complete immersion we practice in my tradition. To us, going down into the waters of baptism symbolizes that we have chosen to die to ourselves, to our wishes and wants. Rising out of the water is a symbol that we have been resurrected to Christ. Our life is now His life. His desires are now ours.

As Romans 6:4 puts it, "We were therefore buried with him through baptism into death in order that, just as Christ was raised from the dead through the glory of the Father, we too may live a new life."

If you haven't been baptized, consider talking to your pastor or priest about following Jesus's example. It is an important part of confessing your allegiance "publicly here on earth" (Matthew 10:32, NLT), announcing to the world that you have died and Christ now lives in you.

Therefore go and make disciples of all nations, baptizing them in the name of the Father and of the Son and of the Holy Spirit.

MATTHEW 28:19

Or, to put it another way, I must crucify my Flesh Woman—that 683-pound sumo-wrestler chick I talk a lot about in *Having a Mary Spirit*.⁹ She's what the New International Version refers to as my "sinful nature" (see Romans 7 and 8). And—get this—she thinks she's in charge.

Sadly, too often she *is* in charge. Though Jesus sits on the throne of my spirit, Flesh Woman still exerts a lot of influence in other areas. When I continually give in and let her have her way, her power increases, limiting God's ability to work in me.

For only I can decide whom I will serve.

"Don't you realize that you become the slave of whatever you choose to obey?" Paul writes in Romans 6:16 (NLT). "You can be a slave to sin, which leads to death, or you can choose to obey God, which leads to righteous living."

While I am not my sin, thank the Lord, only I decide whether or not I will be controlled by it. And only I decide whether Flesh Woman continues her tyrannical reign. That's why it's so important that I keep saying no to my self-centeredness.

And my tendency toward self-protection and self-pity.

And my natural inclination to be self-absorbed and self-promoting, self-actualizing and self-relying.

The list can go on and on. Just put *self* before nearly anything, and we've got a sin-sickness problem that can be cured only by a crucifixion.

But if we'll embrace the process of crucifying our flesh, we'll find the joy that Lazarus found. Because spiritually speaking, nothing frees us more than dying to live.

THE GREAT GIVEAWAY

Though there are many reasons to crucify our sinful natures, I think these may be the best: you can't tempt a dead person—or make one afraid.

Go ahead and try. Prop him up in a corner and parade beautiful women past him, and he won't even steal a glance. Set her on a throne and shower her with jewelry and fine clothes; she won't ask for a mirror. Threaten either one with a knife or a lawsuit, and you won't get a blink. Of all the millions of temptations and anxieties surrounding us today, not one can affect a dead man or woman.

That's why Paul, though faced with persecution and prison, beatings and even the threat of death, could say, "But none of these things move me" (Acts 20:24, NKJV).

How in the world was that possible?

I believe Paul remained unshaken and unmoved because he was already a dead man. He no longer belonged to himself. He no longer relied on *past* accomplishments or the *present* approval of men. Paul was motivated by a *future* hope that centered in Christ and being "found in Him" (Philippians 3:9). Everything else was just a big bag of "rubbish" (verse 8) to this man who had given up so much to give Jesus Christ his all.

That's why Paul could say with such confidence, "None of these things move me," then go on to say, "nor do I count my life dear to myself" (Acts 20:24, NKJV).

How dear is my life to me, I wonder. Too dear, I'm afraid. I tend to cling so tightly to my little life and its treasures that when the Lord tries to take away one of my precious toys, I fight to hold on. And all too often when He bids me come and die, I roll over and play possum.

Jesus didn't fight death. He embraced it, climbing onto the cross willingly. "No one can take my life from me," He said in John 10:18. "I sacrifice it voluntarily" (NLT). Oh that I would do the same. For on the other side of abandonment lies the freedom Paul discovered when he came to the end of himself.

The same kind of joyful freedom Lazarus must have experienced after he faced humanity's worst fear—death—and came out alive on the other side.

THAT'S THE LIFE!

Surely people must have found Lazarus different after his resurrection. Not different in the sense of Andreyev's zombie-like portrayal, but different in the sense of being fully alive and wholly unafraid.

When I think of the man, I imagine a joy-filled peace. A serene absence of fear. A holy carelessness concerning the things he used to worry about and the things he used to crave.

"None of these things moves me," I can almost hear him say.

Perhaps that is why people flocked to see this man, once dead but now alive

(John 12:9). But, unfortunately, what awakened faith in one awakened hatred in another—a hatred birthed in the pit of hell. For nothing is more threatening to the devil than a resurrected man or woman of God.

"So the chief priests made plans to kill Lazarus as well [as Jesus]," John tells us,

Unexplainable and Undeniable

In one of my all-time favorite books, *The Indwelling Life of Christ,* Major Ian Thomas explores the mystery and the power of living resurrected:

> The true Christian life can be explained only in terms of Jesus Christ, and if your life as a Christian can still be explained in terms of you—your personality, your willpower, your gifts, your talents, your money, your courage, your scholarship, your dedication, your sacrifice, or your anything—then although you may have the Christian life, you are not yet living it.
>
> If your life as a Christian can be explained in terms of you, what have you to offer to your neighbor next door? The way he lives his life can already be explained in terms of him, and as far as he is concerned, the only difference between him and you is that you happen to be "religious" while he is not. "Christianity" may be your hobby, but not his, and there is nothing about the way you practice it which strikes him as at all remarkable. There is nothing about you which leaves him guessing, and nothing commendable of which he does not feel himself equally capable without the inconvenience of becoming a Christian.
>
> Only when your quality of life baffles your neighbors are you likely to get their attention. It must become patently obvious to them that the kind of life you are living is not only commendable, but beyond all human explanation.[10]

*When they saw the courage of Peter and John...they were astonished
and they took note that these men had been with Jesus.*

ACTS 4:13

"for on account of him many of the Jews were going over to Jesus and putting their faith in him" (12:10–11).

Wouldn't it be amazing to have a life like that? One that so glorifies God the only way to silence it is to kill it. A life that proclaims the reality of Jesus in a way that's neither harsh nor condemning but so winsomely alive and in love with the Savior that people can't help but want it. A life so filled with integrity and purity that critics struggle to find anything bad to say. A life that isn't shut down by threats of death or the fear of people's disfavor but simply walks forward in courage and joy.

That's the life I want. A life so dead to me and my old way of living that I can't help but live differently. The *exchanged life* on display for the world to see, no matter where I am and no matter where I go.

DYING DAY BY DAY

"Willingness to die is the price you must pay if you want to be raised from the dead to live and work and walk in the power of the third morning," Major Ian Thomas writes. "Once the willingness to die is there for us, there are no more issues to face, only instructions to obey."[11]

Walking in the power of the third morning. Practicing resurrection. More of Jesus and less of me. It all comes down to dying to self—of that, I am convinced. So was George Müller, the man I told you about earlier, whose work in England's orphanages made him famous in the last half of the nineteenth century:

> To one who asked him the secret of his service he said: "There was a day when I died, *utterly died*"; and, as he spoke, he bent lower and lower until he almost touched the floor—"died to George Müller, his opinions, preferences, tastes, and will—died to the world, its approval or censure—died to the approval or blame even of my brethren and friends—and since then I have studied only to show myself 'approved unto God.'"[12]

I don't know what that story does to you, but every time I read it, I feel compelled to hold yet another funeral in my own life…and then another. For while I wish I could tell you my resurrection required only one death and one burial, it wouldn't be true. Instead, my story has many obituaries.

Day by day, sometimes minute by minute, I must make that hard decision to deny myself so that I might obey God. Though Christ died once and for all, denying and dying is a daily exercise for those who would follow Him (1 Corinthians 15:31).

I can tell you this, however: Every day in which I've chosen to truly die, to lay down my wants and my wishes in order that Christ's wants and wishes might be realized in me, a little more of my sinful nature has died. And a little more resurrection has taken place.

However, there is another aspect of dying I'd like us to consider. A type of death we don't necessarily choose but is chosen for us. It involves a stripping away and purging of any excess in our lives. It's painful to endure and hard to understand at times. But it is necessary, because it makes room for Christ's life to grow in us.

Pruned by the Master's Hand

My mother is a master gardener. I wish you could sip iced tea with us as we look over her backyard. Every corner is filled with a beautiful tapestry of color that spills over her carefully edged flower beds. The scents are intoxicating and the fruits of her labor luscious as we eat raspberries just picked from the vine.

None of this beauty happened by accident. It has been carefully planned and tended with a lot of backbreaking work. As we walk through the garden, my mother points out each plant by name.

"This rosebush didn't bloom much last year, so I had to cut it back," she says, cradling a lovely blossom in her hand. "This peony had to be moved to get more sun, and I had to pull out a lot of irises to make room for more corn."

Her eyes glow warmly as she talks about her tasks, but what she describes is a series of seemingly brutal acts. Leafy branches chopped off. Healthy bushes pulled up by their roots. Blooming plants dug up and taken away. Each act is a certain kind of death. But all of it is done with love in the interest of summer bounty.

As I stroll with my mother through her garden, I'm reminded of the times I've questioned the One who tends the garden of my heart.

Especially during those times when His work felt more like death than life.

"I never knew suicide was so slow or so painful," I told my husband one night after falling into bed exhausted from an especially difficult period of battling my lower nature. But it wasn't just the "suicide" I was struggling with. It wasn't just my choosing to die to self. God seemed to be working me over as well.

It was the confusing period I wrote about in *Having a Mary Spirit* when God allowed a painful misunderstanding with friends to strip me of everything I had assumed I needed for life. Their love, their friendship, their kind understanding and support—all that was gone. And nothing I did made the situation better, only worse. The removal of their approval hurt me so deeply I thought I was going to die.

Which was the point, of course. But this wasn't the kind of death I had signed up for. I'd been expecting to close my eyes like Sleeping Beauty, then awaken refreshed and resurrected at the kiss of my handsome Savior Prince.

Instead, the Lord had showed up with sturdy gloves. I could almost see Him in blue jeans and a canvas hat, with a water bottle and a sack lunch protruding from a backpack. Was that a tent I saw? And in His hands—what were those?

A pair of heavy-duty shears.

For the "death" I was experiencing was really a season of pruning—lots and lots of pruning. It felt as though the Gardener was cutting off parts of me, pulling me up by the roots, taking away everything that gave testimony to life. The leafy branches that had once bloomed with color and dripped heavy with fruit had been stripped away, leaving me brown and bare and clinging to the trellis where I'd been tied.

Then came the long winter. And it too felt like death.

A SEASON OF DYING

Perhaps you are in a wintry season right now. Perhaps you feel as though everything you've cared about has been taken away, and you've not found anything to take its place. Perhaps God has called you to lay aside a lifetime of striving so you can experience abiding. But to be honest, the stillness is getting on your nerves. Perhaps He has narrowed you to a place where there is little choice but to be quiet. And listen. And wait.

Winter always seems to last longer than we think it should.

Getting through such times, I've learned, is not for the faint of heart. It's not easy to endure the loss of what we once thought was vital. To shiver in the dark, feeling bereft and confused. To wonder when—or if—this season of dying will ever end in true resurrection.

I understand how you feel. And so does Jesus—more than either of us knows. The One who hung forgotten and forsaken, cut down in the prime of His life and buried deep in the tomb, is so intimately acquainted with our suffering that He alone can remind us what is at stake.

"I tell you the truth," Jesus told His disciples after leaving the miracle of Bethany and beginning the hard walk toward Jerusalem and His death, "unless a kernel of wheat falls to the ground and dies, it remains only a single seed. But if it dies, it produces many seeds. The man who loves his life will lose it, while the man who hates his life in this world will keep it for eternal life" (John 12:24–25).

As strange as it sounds, it is in the dark nights of our souls—in those deathlike, midnight places where nothing seems to be happening—that God often does His best work. Preparing our lives—so barren at the moment—for an even greater outpouring of life.

For winter always precedes spring. And in the law of harvest, death always precedes life. But if we'll trust the Gardener, a harvest of fruit awaits—"much fruit," as John 15:5 calls it. Fruit formed out of the life of Christ released in us by our dying.

Abundant, luscious fruit that will last forever (verse 16).

It's amazing to think that so much life could come out of so much death. Yet that is the secret of living resurrected and the key to the exchanged life we need. Jesus alive in you and me. His power giving us all we need to do all He asks. His love, His joy, His peace and His righteousness being manifested in us. And none of it anything we have to do on our own.

Our only responsibility is to die. Jesus will take care of the rest. For He is not only the resurrection. He is also the life.

THE PROMISE OF NEW LIFE

After the women's conference in Lazarusville—not a real name, if you are wondering—I visited a vineyard just a few miles away. As a cold-climate girl from Montana, I was eager to get a closer look at how grapes are actually grown. It was early March, so the first place we stopped had no signs of life yet. Just ancient trunks protruding from the earth with woody vines trained upon thick wire. They were all brown and lifeless at that particular moment—just as I had felt from time to time during the preceding year.

However, as we drove deeper into the valley, we found another vineyard. This one was showing signs of life. Not much. Just a few touches of green among the brown.

"So how does it work?" I asked my hostess. "Is it like apple trees? Are there grape blossoms that have to be pollinated before the fruit can come?"

"I really don't know," my friend answered, perplexed, as she parked the car next to a row of grapevines.

I got out quickly, eager to look at the small clumps of leaves bursting out here and there along the vine. I had my camera and began to take pictures. But then I noticed something amazing.

Something profound.

There in the whorl of leaves slowly unfolding was a perfectly formed miniature cluster of grapes. Each and every tiny piece clearly defined. An exquisite embryo of promise. A not-yet picture of a one-day reality.

I can't begin to explain what I felt as the Holy Spirit later whispered to my heart, *See, Joanna? It's all there—all the potential, all the harvest that will one day be. The life of Christ was put within you at salvation, and He's just waiting to be fully revealed.*

All your striving isn't as necessary as your abiding, He seemed to say as I began to weep. *If you'll trust the seasons…if you're willing to die so that Jesus might live…it will happen. And the Gardener will get the glory.*

It's a word He may be speaking to you as well. Stop trying to produce fruit on your own, beloved. Let the Resurrection and the Life breathe color and beauty into your brown, barren being. Choose to die and embrace the intimate entangling of His life with yours. For there is a harvest within you that's been prepared in advance by God. A purpose for your life waiting to be revealed (Ephesians 2:10).

A Lazarus or a Lazarella in the making! A life meant to be fully lived, bursting with the fruit of righteousness. The type of life that has no explanation except this:

This person has died, and Christ now lives.

Soli Deo Gloria.

Six days before the Passover, Jesus arrived
at Bethany, where Lazarus lived,
whom Jesus had raised from the dead.
Here a dinner was given in Jesus' honor.
Martha served, while Lazarus was among
those reclining at the table with him.
Then Mary took about a pint of pure nard, an expensive perfume;
she poured it on Jesus' feet and wiped his feet with her hair.
And the house was filled with the fragrance of the perfume.

JOHN 12:1–3

Laughing Lazarus

uring and after the Civil War, Sarah Winchester's husband acquired a fortune by manufacturing and selling the famous Winchester repeater rifles. But after his death in 1881, Sarah found herself tormented by grief over losing him and their infant daughter, who had died years before. Sarah sought out a medium to contact her dead husband. The medium said that her family was being haunted by the spirits of those killed by Winchester guns but that Sarah could appease those spirits if she moved out West and built a great house for them. "As long as you keep building it," the medium promised, "you will never face death."

Sarah believed the spiritualist, so she moved to San Jose, California, bought an unfinished eight-room house, and immediately started to expand it. Workers spent nearly four decades building and rebuilding the home—demolishing one section to build another, adding rooms onto rooms and wings onto wings. Staircases were built that led nowhere. Doors opened to nothing. Hallways doubled back throughout the house, creating a giant maze designed to confuse the spirits.

The project continued until Sarah died at the age of eighty-two. It cost more than five million dollars to build and featured 160 rooms, 13 bathrooms, 2,000 doors, 47 fireplaces, and 10,000 windows.

Today the Winchester house stands on a busy boulevard in San Jose, drawing thousands of visitors each year. But as one writer puts it, the house is "more than a tourist attraction. It is a silent witness to the dread of death."[1] The dread that has held humanity in bondage since the beginning of time.

The Fear of Death

For the majority of history, humanity has been plagued with a fear of dying—and with good reason. For the billions of people who lived before modern medicine, death was a daily reality, striking indiscriminately and often without obvious cause. One day a mother held her laughing child; the next day the child was dead from a mysterious fever. A husband would leave to hunt in the morning, only to be found gored to death by a wild animal in the afternoon. When a wife got pregnant, she faced heavy odds of dying in childbirth. Living to middle adulthood was considered quite an accomplishment.

I don't think those of us living in this century can fully appreciate the magnitude of hope Hebrews 2:14–15 must have brought those who read these words: "[Jesus] too shared in their humanity so that by his death he might destroy him who holds the power of death—that is, the devil—and *free those* who all their lives were *held in slavery by their fear of death*" (emphasis added).

While we're further removed from the constant reminders of our mortality, I think it's fair to say that none of us is looking forward to passing away. Woody Allen's famous quip describes our attitude: "I'm not afraid of dying—I just don't want to be there when it happens!"[2]

Perhaps that's why we spend billions of dollars each year attempting to halt or at least slow the march of time. We resolve to exercise, eat right, and take the proper multivitamins. We buy wonder foods and wonder drugs, scouring the Internet and magazines for the current fountain of youth.

Some people even go to the extreme of cryogenics, paying huge sums to have their bodies frozen just before they die in hopes that one day doctors will discover the secret to eternal life (or at least a cure for the disease about to kill them). A quick injection of serum, a few minutes in the microwave…and voilà! They'll be on the golf course the next day. Or so they hope.

But no matter how hard we try to outrun, outbuy, or outbuild death, in the end we will all breathe a last breath. For the cold, hard fact of life is this: we will all die.

That was true of Lazarus as well. Although Jesus dramatically raised him from the dead the first time, the man was *still* destined to die again. In fact, today you can visit two separate tombs that claim the distinction of having held Mary and

Martha's brother. The first one is in Bethany, now called al-Eizariya.³ The second tomb is found on the island of Cyprus. According to Orthodox tradition, Lazarus served as bishop there for thirty years before passing away a final time.⁴

Although there's some controversy over where Lazarus was finally buried,⁵ the fact remains: the one Jesus loved and gloriously resurrected eventually died a second time. Just as you and I will die one day. .

For there is no escaping death. But be assured of this: Death is not the end. There's more to come.

ENLISTING DEATH

God created us with a primal instinct for life and a violent resistance to death. There is a fight reflex within us that battles to breathe, scratching and clawing to the surface of whatever we're going through in order to survive. And that is as it should be. If we don't have a desire to live, then something is terribly wrong. Something has short-circuited our wiring, both physically and spiritually.

Because death was not part of God's original plan. You and I were made for life—life eternal. An eternity lived in the company of our Maker and each other.

Unfortunately, our great-great-not-so-great grandparents Adam and Eve decided they wanted more than what God had offered. So they bit at the serpent's bait and attempted to seize control as God's equals rather than resting in their role as His beloved children.

Consequently, the Father had to limit their freedom. He banished them from the garden and blocked access to the tree of life so they couldn't eat of it and "live forever" (Genesis 3:22). As a result, humanity's life span was radically reduced. Death was given access to beings who had been created to live forever.

Does that sound harsh? Although God's actions might seem extreme, we must understand that the punishment was birthed out of great mercy.

Just think. Without death, the evicted Adam and Eve—not to mention you and I—would be assigned to an eternity of lonely wandering. A 24/7 life of hopeless toil and meaningless monotony. An empty existence bereft of the constant sense of God's presence Adam and Eve had once enjoyed.

For two people who had once walked and talked with God, I can't imagine a more terrible destiny. Forever condemned to treading staircases leading nowhere. Running down hallways that circle back on themselves. Trying to find their way out of the confusing maze their rebellion had created.

What Will It Be Like?

In his commentary on the book of John, Ray Stedman retells a lovely story concerning death and what it will be like to cross from this life to the next.

> When Peter Marshall was Chaplain to the United States Senate, he told of a twelve-year-old boy who knew he was dying. The boy asked his father, "What is it like to die?" The father hugged his son to himself and said, "Son, do you remember when you were little and you used to come and sit on my lap in the big chair in the living room? I would tell you a story, read you a book, or sing you a song and you would go to sleep in my arms. Later, you would wake up in your own bed. That is what it's like to die. When you wake up from death, you are in a place of security and safety and beauty."

"That, Jesus declares, is what death is like," writes Stedman. "It is merely an introduction to another, greater experience of life. From our limited human perspective, we view death as a final farewell, a leap into mystery and darkness and silence. The death of a loved one leaves us feeling lonely and bereft, wandering alone through life. But Jesus says, 'No, death is [only] sleep.' "[6] There is more to come.

> *Brothers, we do not want you to be ignorant about those who fall*
> *asleep, or to grieve like the rest of men, who have no hope.*
> *We believe that Jesus died and rose again and so we believe*
> *that God will bring with Jesus those who have fallen asleep in him.*
> 1 Thessalonians 4:13–14

Which is a fairly accurate description of the life we live today when we attempt to live apart from God.

But here's the good news! God's mercy and grace marked our lives here on earth with a finish line. And with sweet irony, our loving Father took the very thing we feared the most—the threat of death—and turned it on its head. Transforming tombs into doorways and our endings into new beginnings. Turning hearses into glistening carriages to carry us to glorious mansions being prepared as we speak—the eternal home for which we were made (2 Corinthians 5:1).

And all of it ours if we will simply accept the gift Jesus offers—the gift of eternal life.

"Where, O death, is your victory?" Paul writes in 1 Corinthians 15:55 as he considers our final destination and the vehicle that will get us there. "Where, O death, is your sting?"

Through Jesus Christ, "death has been swallowed up in victory" (verse 54).

CROSSING OVER

Victory over death, however, isn't found only in the future. In a very real sense, for those who've received Christ, eternal life starts now. "If the Spirit of him that raised up Jesus from the dead dwell in you," Paul tells us in Romans 8:11 (KJV), "he...shall also *quicken* your mortal bodies by his Spirit that dwelleth in you" (emphasis added).

I love that old King James Version word *quicken.* It doesn't speak of speed but of coming to life. For you see, Jesus doesn't promise half a resurrection. He offers a fullfledged Holy Spirit CPR. A "get out the paddles because we're gonna quicken this guy" kind of life that crackles at the edges with passionate electricity!

Perhaps that's why Leonid Andreyev's portrait of a half-dead Lazarus doesn't ring true to me. The idea that Jesus would resurrect His friend to make him miserable is nothing like the Savior I know, nor is it anything like the mighty power of God I've experienced working in my life. When He resurrects, He resurrects completely.

Which is what happened to our spirits when we were saved. However, that's not to say there isn't more work to be done. Paul accentuates that point when he writes,

"But if Christ is in you, your body is dead because of sin, yet your spirit is alive because of righteousness" (Romans 8:10).

You see, it takes time—and some struggle—for our bodies and souls to catch up with what has happened in our spirits. Bringing resurrection into every part of life is both the joy and the struggle of our Christian walk. But we don't do it alone. It is a cooperative work with the Holy Spirit from beginning to end. The death in us is being conquered, and life is going to win!

So when I think of Lazarus, I don't picture a zombie walking around mad at the world, half-crazed. I don't picture him causing people to lose their minds when they looked in his eyes. Instead, I imagine him opening their minds to all the possibilities, all the sweet ramifications of a second chance at life.

After all, I can't think of anything more transformative, more freeing than facing the thing you fear most and finding it has no power. Talk about a new perspective!

Lazarus Laughed

In my mind Lazarus resurrected would look more like the man depicted in Eugene O'Neill's play *Lazarus Laughed*. While you can't go to O'Neill for sound doctrine, the character he paints captures my heart and challenges my soul. The wonderful preacher John Claypool describes how the short-lived Broadway production depicted the resurrected Lazarus:

> O'Neill has Lazarus coming out of the tomb laughing. Not a bitter, scornful laughter, but a gentle, tender, all-pervasive kind of sound. After he is untied from the graveclothes, the first word he utters is, "YES!" He doesn't have a faraway look in his eyes, but rather, he seems to see the people closest to him with a new kind of delight and affection.... It is as if everything had taken on a new luster because of what he had learned. There was a kind of peace and serenity about him that was almost tangible....
>
> As the play unfolds, Lazarus embodies what it would mean to be freed of death. His house becomes called the house of laughter. There is music and

dancing there night and day, and as he continues to live in this free and wonderful way, other human beings are caught up in the joyfulness of it. They cease to be afraid. They start being generous and humane with one another. They fall back in love with the wonder of life itself.[7]

What would it be like if you and I could finally shed the fear of death and the grasping, clinging obsession with this world that comes with it? What if, in coming to terms with death, we were enabled to fall back in love with the wonder of life itself?

I'm fairly certain we'd experience more joy and less fear. More faith and less doubt. More love and less selfishness. More life in this life!

If we focused on living in the light of eternity, understanding that there is a glorious lifetime in a perfect world to come, I think we'd learn to hold this one more loosely and the ones we love less possessively. God wouldn't always have to do what you and I think is best. We'd see eternal possibilities in everyday troubles. We'd more easily surrender ourselves and those we love to God's plan rather than our demands.

Most of all I think we'd learn to live with an open hand rather than a clenched fist.

THE JOY OF SURRENDER

When I received word that my mother had suffered a massive heart attack and was being rushed into emergency surgery, I immediately began driving the 150 miles south to be with her. That was fourteen years ago, before I had a cell phone, so I had two hours without any updates, without any word of how the surgery was going. I wasn't even certain my mother was still alive.

But something amazing happened during my mad dash down the interstate. As I prayed and drove and prayed and drove some more, I found myself giving my mother to the Lord. Entrusting her to His care. Believing He would do what was best. And with the surrender came a sweet peace like none I'd ever known before. I knew it was going to be okay.

But please understand, I still didn't know if *she* would be okay. The peace I felt wasn't a promise that my mother would survive the surgery. In fact, I found out later that she actually died on the table for a few minutes. The peace that enfolded me as I drove toward the unknown promised only this:

It would be okay. Whatever *it* turned out to be.

As I opened my hand and surrendered my mom to the God who loved her even more than I did, I felt a quiet joy fill my heart. A sweet underlying sense of okayness that surpassed happiness (which tends to rely heavily on happenings).

The settled peace I felt was a gift from the Lord, not something I could have worked up on my own. Lazarus must have felt that same peace when he walked out of the tomb and back into life—but magnified a hundredfold and tinged with amazing joy.

For he had traveled to the place we humans avoid at all cost and had found God waiting there.

WHEN TOMBS DON'T OPEN

Like Mary and Martha, I was blessed to receive my loved one—my mother—back from the brink of death. Yet I'm painfully aware that you may be among the many who've stood before tombs that haven't opened.

You've prayed desperate prayers that were left unanswered. Perhaps, like Job, you've struggled to reconcile your faith in a loving God with a seemingly less-than-loving outcome. You've lain in bed at night wondering how to keep believing that God is good when everything in your life feels so terribly bad.

Over the past twelve months especially, I've had a glimpse of how that must feel. It's been such a strange year for me. In the midst of writing about the miracle-working power of God to rescue and resurrect, I've attended more funerals and witnessed more tragedies than in the past six years combined. Among my friends there have been two massive heart attacks, one severe stroke, three premature deaths due to cancer, the tragic death of a son, and the suicide of a distraught father—to name a few. In June my own dad had a serious subdural hematoma in his brain and then was diagnosed with renal cancer five months later. Three weeks after that my husband was operated on twice for kidney stones.

Through it all, we've run the gamut of emotions: dancing gratefully in hospital waiting rooms one moment, weeping beside snow-covered graves the next.

And through it all, like you, we've hung onto Jesus when the whys of it all were totally beyond us.

I can't begin to fully explain God's ways or why He allows pain and suffering to coexist beside His intense love for us. But I do wonder if He doesn't want to use all the sorrow I've recently witnessed to balance the message He would have me write in this book.

It is far too easy to preach a Pollyanna gospel—a gospel that says if we're good, nothing bad should ever happen. A formula Christianity that is neat and tidy, suggesting that if we play by the rules, we'll win every time.

The story of Lazarus refutes all that. As does the whole of the Bible. Scripture never shies away from the reality that bad things happen to good people. That God doesn't always come running to the rescue, at least not in the ways and in the timing we expect Him to. Love does tarry at times. And there are moments when Love seems to actually take a step back, allowing things to happen that we'd never dream of allowing ourselves.

Just ask Joseph as he scratches yet another day on the wall of his prison cell, counting the long years since he dreamed God's dream and wondering how and when he lost God's favor.

Just ask Daniel as he wraps his cloak around his shoulders and shivers in the pit, half from the cold and half from fear of the lions breathing hot upon his neck—all because Daniel wouldn't deny his God.

And just ask John, the disciple who told us the most about Lazarus. Years later he's an old man exiled and left to starve on the barren island of Patmos. One by one he's heard about the demise of his friends—martyrdom after brutal martyrdom for the men who had followed Christ. The disciples had proven faithful, following Jesus all the way to their deaths. Would he be next?

In each seemingly hopeless case, however, Love's restraint eventually accomplished God's purposes. Saving Egypt and the known world—not to mention Joseph's brothers!—from starvation in a famine. Exalting God among a pagan nation as the one true God, who is able to shut lions' mouths and turn the hearts of kings. And providing us a glimpse of eternity (the book of Revelation) through the pen of a lonely old man.

The same tender-yet-tough-to-understand divine restraint may be required in your life and mine. But it will also accomplish God's purposes if we'll trust Him. Though we may never know the full story here on earth, we can be certain that nothing in our lives will be wasted by God. Trials and tragedies, even death, can't separate us from His love (Romans 8:39). Especially when we surrender our questions and our need to understand, entrusting all our confusion and fear to His heart and to His hands.

Getting Ready for the Real Thing

I'm starting to wonder if one reason God allows difficulties in our lives is to wean us from this world, to cure our addiction to temporal things that will never satisfy. Because it seems that the times we come face to face with pain and death are the times we're reminded best that this world is just a shadow. A crude drawing and a mere outline of the beauty that awaits us in a world outside this one. An alternate reality so magnificent and incomprehensible that we often forget it's there.

In his marvelous book *Things Unseen*, Mark Buchanan tells the story of a couple who lost their barely born son due to a rare and severe genetic disorder. Three months later their two-year-old daughter died as well. In the wake of devastating loss, Marshall and Susan Shelley wrestled painfully with God. *Why, God?* they kept asking. *Why did You do that? What was all that about?*[8]

Marshall later shared his struggle to understand his son's death in an article he wrote for *Christianity Today*. "Why did God create a child to live two minutes?" he asked before answering:

> He didn't. [And] He didn't create Mandy to live two years. He did not create me to live 40 years (or whatever number he may choose to extend my days in this world).
>
> God created Toby for eternity. He created each of us for eternity, where we may be surprised to find our true calling, which always seemed just out of reach here on earth.[9]

What a powerful thought! We were not created for this earth alone but for an infinite future with God. A destiny beyond the realm of mere time and space. How would our lives change if we really woke up to that reality?

Is it just me, or have we lost this sense of another world awaiting us as Christians? Have we become so attached to this world and its comforts that we've forgotten we are only pilgrims? Aliens as it were—created for another place. This life just a spaceship meant to carry us through this world to our one true home.

I love the way Elisabeth Elliot describes it:

Heaven is not *here*, it's *There*. If we were given all we wanted here, our hearts would settle for this world rather than the next. God is forever luring us up and away from this one, wooing us to Himself and His still invisible Kingdom, where we will certainly find what we so keenly long for.[10]

LONELY FOR HOME

Someone once asked, "Why do we tend to live like eternity lasts eighty years, but this life lasts forever?"

It's an important question, I think. As a young Christian, I realized that if I were to draw a time line of eternity, then attempted to place my lifetime on that continuum, it wouldn't even show up. In reality, these eighty-plus years we're given are only a blip on the screen, a "vapor," as James 4:14 (NKJV) describes it. A mist that quickly fades away.

Some people, even some Christians, don't believe there is anything after this life. From their perspective, we live and then we die. Dust to dust, ashes to ashes. Worm food. They say there's no such thing as resurrection and Jesus isn't coming back. Heaven, if there is a heaven, is found right here on earth.

And in a sense they are partly right. Heaven began on earth when, through Christ, the "kingdom of heaven" came near (Matthew 4:17). For those who have put their full hope in Jesus, eternity has already begun.

But to say this is all there is? I can't think of anything more disappointing or sad. For if the limited taste of heaven we experience here on earth is all we have to look forward to, then why bother?

Living in the Light of Eternity

In light of the fact that there is more to come, how then shall we live? If eternity, not this earth, is our true home, don't you think we should live differently than the world does? I'd like to suggest these principles:

- *Live fully.* Don't waste today regretting the past or fearing the future, for it may be your last day on earth. Make it count for God.
- *Hold things loosely.* Since we can't take our possessions with us, enjoy what you have, but don't cling so tightly to stuff or fall into the trap of always wanting more.
- *Value people highly.* People are the true treasures of life, worth nurturing and investing in, for they are the only thing on this earth we can possibly take with us when we leave.
- *Travel lightly.* Don't carry baggage from past hurts, and don't pick up grudges as you go. Life's too short to be voluntarily miserable.
- *Love completely.* Let God reveal His love for people through you. Be tender-hearted, not hardheaded, patient and quick to forgive, merciful and slow to judge.
- *Give freely.* Don't hoard what you have. Instead, share it with a joyful heart, and you'll be given more. Generosity releases blessings as sowing seed leads to harvest.
- *Look expectantly.* Keep looking up even as you walk here on earth, always ready and waiting for the imminent return of Christ. Be heavenly minded so you can be of earthly good.

So then, dear friends, since you are looking forward
to [Christ's return], make every effort
to be found spotless, blameless and at peace with him.

2 PETER 3:14

The apostle Paul agreed. "If there is no resurrection of the dead, then not even Christ has been raised," he argues in 1 Corinthians 15:13–14. "And if Christ has not been raised, our preaching is useless and so is your faith."

Paul was fully convinced that eternity is what matters—not this puny little life we tend so carefully. In fact, Paul makes an incredibly bold statement that should shake not only the way we think but impact the way we live. "If only for this life we have hope in Christ, we are to be pitied more than all men" (1 Corinthians 15:19).

In other words, if this is all there is, folks, we're in big trouble.

That's why living in the light of eternity is so very important. If we don't cultivate an eternal perspective, we will get bogged down in both the blessings and the troubles of this life. We'll tend to become obsessed about success, possessed by our possessions, and addicted to our appetite for more, more, always more.

We may call Jesus our friend. We may even declare Him our most prized possession, saying that He is more than enough. But if we fail to think eternally, chances are we'll tend to hold tightly to everything we can fit in our overcrowded arms for fear that this is all there is and we had better get what we can get while the getting is good.

But this isn't the life we were made for. In fact, it is not life at all. It's just another tomb. Better wallpapered, perhaps, with finer furnishings. But still just a tomb.

THE LAST LAUGH

Lazarus knew that this earthly life isn't what we were made for. And I think he must have laughed. Because in the experience of dying and being resurrected, Lazarus must have discovered there was so much more to living than what he had known. To his reborn eyes, the life he'd been attached to, the one that had seemed so fraught with difficulty, must have looked like child's play.

From his brief glimpse of eternity, Lazarus could surely discern the counterfeit from the genuine. The cardboard facsimiles we work so hard to build. The papier-mâché dreams that occupy our hearts and minds. The silly games we play. The inconsequential things we inflate until they seem monumental.

The resurrected Lazarus surely saw life differently because he knew there was more to come. If we could only grasp that, Lazarus wouldn't be the only one laughing.

For a day is coming that will cause joy like we've never known to well up within us. A laughter that will be triggered by a trumpet and echoed by a magnificent figure on a great white horse, waving the keys of hell, death, and the grave over his head as He comes riding toward us in triumph (Revelation 1:18).

Christ Himself. Our Savior. Once entombed, now alive. Risen and gone to be with the Father. But returning again. We can be sure of that!

> For the Lord himself will come down from heaven, with a loud command,
> with the voice of the archangel and with the trumpet call of God, and the
> dead in Christ will rise first. After that, we who are still alive and are left will
> be caught up together with them in the clouds to meet the Lord in the air.
> And so we will be with the Lord forever. Therefore encourage each other with
> these words. (1 Thessalonians 4:16–18)

What an amazing day that is going to be! We don't know *when* it will happen, but we can be sure it *will* happen. It's written in black and white all over the Word. But more important, it's been signed and sealed in red—by the precious blood of Jesus Christ.

"Do not let your hearts be troubled," Jesus told the disciples shortly after He had raised Lazarus. "Trust in God; trust also in me. In my Father's house are many rooms.... I am going there to prepare a place for you. And if I go and prepare a place for you, I will come back and take you to be with me that you also may be where I am" (John 14:1–3).

Jesus is coming back. He's coming back for me and you. And what He has prepared for us will rival anything Sarah Winchester could have ever imagined. More rooms, more doors, so many more windows! He's building a mansion—"many mansions," the King James Version of John 14:2 tells us—and all of it for His Bride.

For it is love that compels Him. Love for you and me and everyone else who has ever responded to the sound of His voice. Pulling at our graveclothes as we stumble out of our tombs. Running smack-dab into the tender arms of our Lord. Laughing and crying at the same time as we join Him for the ultimate celebration that is to come.

Your Place at the Table

I wish I could have been there at the dinner Mary and Martha threw for Jesus, the man who had brought their brother back to life. John 12:1–3 describes it like this:

> Six days before the Passover, Jesus arrived at Bethany, where Lazarus lived, whom Jesus had raised from the dead. Here a dinner was given in Jesus' honor. Martha served, while Lazarus was among those reclining at the table with him. Then Mary took about a pint of pure nard, an expensive perfume; she poured it on Jesus' feet and wiped his feet with her hair. And the house was filled with the fragrance of the perfume.

What a tender picture of sweet communion. I can picture Martha bringing in her platters of succulent food but this time lingering to listen while her Master spoke. I can see Mary hanging on His every word but also being stirred in her heart to anoint the Lord with the very best she had to give. I can't help but wonder if John, the beloved disciple, didn't give up his regular seat so that Lazarus could have a chance to lean against Jesus. The beautiful fragrance that filled the house surely came from more than Mary's perfume.

But as lovely as the scene must have been, it was also tense. Death threats against Jesus—and against Lazarus—were circulating in the village. Although many people were putting their faith in the Lord because of the miracle, others feared Jesus's growing influence. Even a few of His followers were uncomfortable with the way things were going.

When Mary poured an entire jar of precious perfume over Jesus's feet, Judas Iscariot may not have been the only one who thought it was a waste. But Jesus commended Mary's extravagant offering. "Leave her alone," He said. "It was intended that she should save this perfume for the day of my burial" (verse 7).

You see, the Lord knew His time on earth was coming to a close. It would be the last meal He shared in Bethany with His dear friends. Tender memories must have filled Jesus's mind as He watched Martha serve and Lazarus recline. When Mary bent to spread the perfume with her hair, her love must have washed over His heart as well as His feet.

The description of this meal is especially significant to me, because it is the last time we find the family from Bethany mentioned in Scripture. After spending more than a decade imagining and writing about their lives, I long to meet Mary and Martha and Lazarus in person.

And someday I will! For when the trumpet sounds, we will all meet Jesus in the air. Then later, in heaven, the family from Bethany and the rest of the family of God will sit down together at a sumptuous feast—the marriage supper of the Lamb (Revelation 19:9).

With that thought in mind, may I ask you a few personal questions?

When you think of that glorious day, where do you see yourself sitting? What do you see yourself doing? Will you kneel adoringly at Jesus's feet…or sit close to talk to Him as you hand Him a plate of food? Will you run to Him like a child and climb up on His lap…or look deep in His eyes before falling to your knees in worship? Just imagine how wonderful that is going to be.

Then let me ask you, are you doing that here?

Are you drawing as close to Jesus as you can possibly get while you live for Him here on earth? Shedding your love-doubt and your fear of the yardstick so you can run to Him daily as a friend runs to meet a friend?

First Corinthians 13:12 (KJV) seems to suggest that we will be known in heaven as we are known on earth. And that, I believe, should have radical implications for how we live our lives each day. I don't want to wait until I get to heaven to know Jesus. I want to snuggle up close to Him today.

I want to lay my head on His chest and hear His heart beat as the disciple John did (John 21:20, KJV).

I want to lay my greatest treasures down at His feet as Mary did.

I want to serve the Lord wholeheartedly yet respond to His rebuke and change as Martha did.

Most of all I want to laugh like Lazarus—laugh aloud with pure wonder that I belong to Jesus and He belongs to me. That nothing, absolutely nothing, will ever separate me from His love. Not the trials of this life nor the trinkets of this world. For I am my Beloved's, and He is mine (Song of Songs 6:3).

In 890 AD, when the supposed tomb of Mary and Martha's brother was discovered on Cyprus, the marble sarcophagus they found was marked with a simple inscription: "Lazarus...friend of Christ."[11]

I can't think of a better way to be defined—in life or in death. Both *here* on earth as well as *there* someday. For this world is not our home. We're just passing through.

So let's keep living as if we're dying, keeping eternity ever in view. Especially when life is hard and we don't understand. When love seems to tarry and we're tempted to doubt God's love and give up hope.

For it's in times like these, my friend, that we must remember...

There's more to come.

The Story

John 11:1–12:11

JOHN 11

[1] Now a man named Lazarus was sick. He was from Bethany, the village of Mary and her sister Martha. [2] This Mary, whose brother Lazarus now lay sick, was the same one who poured perfume on the Lord and wiped his feet with her hair. [3] So the sisters sent word to Jesus, "Lord, the one you love is sick."

[4] When he heard this, Jesus said, "This sickness will not end in death. No, it is for God's glory so that God's Son may be glorified through it." [5] Jesus loved Martha and her sister and Lazarus. [6] Yet when he heard that Lazarus was sick, he stayed where he was two more days.

[7] Then he said to his disciples, "Let us go back to Judea."

[8] "But Rabbi," they said, "a short while ago the Jews tried to stone you, and yet you are going back there?"

[9] Jesus answered, "Are there not twelve hours of daylight? A man who walks by day will not stumble, for he sees by this world's light. [10] It is when he walks by night that he stumbles, for he has no light."

[11] After he had said this, he went on to tell them, "Our friend Lazarus has fallen asleep; but I am going there to wake him up."

[12] His disciples replied, "Lord, if he sleeps, he will get better." [13] Jesus had been speaking of his death, but his disciples thought he meant natural sleep.

[14] So then he told them plainly, "Lazarus is dead, [15] and for your sake I am glad I was not there, so that you may believe. But let us go to him."

[16] Then Thomas (called Didymus) said to the rest of the disciples, "Let us also go, that we may die with him."

[17] On his arrival, Jesus found that Lazarus had already been in the tomb for four days. [18] Bethany was less than two miles from Jerusalem, [19] and many Jews had come to Martha and Mary to comfort them in the loss of their brother. [20] When Martha heard that Jesus was coming, she went out to meet him, but Mary stayed at home.

[21] "Lord," Martha said to Jesus, "if you had been here, my brother would not have died. [22] But I know that even now God will give you whatever you ask."

[23] Jesus said to her, "Your brother will rise again."

[24] Martha answered, "I know he will rise again in the resurrection at the last day."

[25] Jesus said to her, "I am the resurrection and the life. He who believes in me will live, even though he dies; [26] and whoever lives and believes in me will never die. Do you believe this?"

[27] "Yes, Lord," she told him, "I believe that you are the Christ, the Son of God, who was to come into the world."

[28] And after she had said this, she went back and called her sister Mary aside. "The Teacher is here," she said, "and is asking for you." [29] When Mary heard this, she got up quickly and went to him. [30] Now Jesus had not yet entered the village, but was still at the place where Martha had met him. [31] When the Jews who had been with Mary in the house, comforting her, noticed how quickly she got up and went out, they followed her, supposing she was going to the tomb to mourn there.

[32] When Mary reached the place where Jesus was and saw him, she fell at his feet and said, "Lord, if you had been here, my brother would not have died."

[33] When Jesus saw her weeping, and the Jews who had come along with her also weeping, he was deeply moved in spirit and troubled. [34] "Where have you laid him?" he asked.

"Come and see, Lord," they replied.

[35] Jesus wept.

[36] Then the Jews said, "See how he loved him!"

[37] But some of them said, "Could not he who opened the eyes of the blind man have kept this man from dying?"

[38] Jesus, once more deeply moved, came to the tomb. It was a cave with a stone laid across the entrance. [39] "Take away the stone," he said.

"But, Lord," said Martha, the sister of the dead man, "by this time there is a bad odor, for he has been there four days."

[40] Then Jesus said, "Did I not tell you that if you believed, you would see the glory of God?"

[41] So they took away the stone. Then Jesus looked up and said, "Father, I thank you that you have heard me. [42] I knew that you always hear me, but I said this for the benefit of the people standing here, that they may believe that you sent me."

[43] When he had said this, Jesus called in a loud voice, "Lazarus, come out!" [44] The dead man came out, his hands and feet wrapped with strips of linen, and a cloth around his face.

Jesus said to them, "Take off the grave clothes and let him go."

[45] Therefore many of the Jews who had come to visit Mary, and had seen what Jesus did, put their faith in him. [46] But some of them went to the Pharisees and told them what Jesus had done. [47] Then the chief priests and the Pharisees called a meeting of the Sanhedrin.

"What are we accomplishing?" they asked. "Here is this man performing many miraculous signs. [48] If we let him go on like this, everyone will believe in him, and then the Romans will come and take away both our place and our nation."

[49] Then one of them, named Caiaphas, who was high priest that year, spoke up, "You know nothing at all! [50] You do not realize that it is better for you that one man die for the people than that the whole nation perish."

[51] He did not say this on his own, but as high priest that year he prophesied that Jesus would die for the Jewish nation, [52] and not only for that nation but also for the scattered children of God, to bring them together and make them one. [53] So from that day on they plotted to take his life.

[54] Therefore Jesus no longer moved about publicly among the Jews. Instead he withdrew to a region near the desert, to a village called Ephraim, where he stayed with his disciples.

[55] When it was almost time for the Jewish Passover, many went up from the country to Jerusalem for their ceremonial cleansing before the Passover. [56] They kept

looking for Jesus, and as they stood in the temple area they asked one another, "What do you think? Isn't he coming to the Feast at all?" [57] But the chief priests and Pharisees had given orders that if anyone found out where Jesus was, he should report it so that they might arrest him.

JOHN 12

[1] Six days before the Passover, Jesus arrived at Bethany, where Lazarus lived, whom Jesus had raised from the dead. [2] Here a dinner was given in Jesus' honor. Martha served, while Lazarus was among those reclining at the table with him. [3] Then Mary took about a pint of pure nard, an expensive perfume; she poured it on Jesus' feet and wiped his feet with her hair. And the house was filled with the fragrance of the perfume.

[4] But one of his disciples, Judas Iscariot, who was later to betray him, objected, [5] "Why wasn't this perfume sold and the money given to the poor? It was worth a year's wages." [6] He did not say this because he cared about the poor but because he was a thief; as keeper of the money bag, he used to help himself to what was put into it.

[7] "Leave her alone," Jesus replied. "It was intended that she should save this perfume for the day of my burial. [8] You will always have the poor among you, but you will not always have me."

[9] Meanwhile a large crowd of Jews found out that Jesus was there and came, not only because of him but also to see Lazarus, whom he had raised from the dead. [10] So the chief priests made plans to kill Lazarus as well, [11] for on account of him many of the Jews were going over to Jesus and putting their faith in him.

Study Guide

With just a word Jesus called Lazarus from the grave, and His Word can help bring us out of our tombs as well. This ten-week Bible study is designed to help you move toward your own Lazarus awakening. (Group leaders, if an eight-week format works better for you, you'll find directions at the end of this guide for adapting it. Also, check out the downloadable workbook and leader's guide available at www.joannaweaverbooks.com.)

Any translation of the Bible you enjoy and understand will work fine for this study (though I have used the NIV to word my questions). You'll also need a notebook and a pen to record your answers to the questions in this guide. Before each lesson ask the Holy Spirit to increase your understanding as you examine God's Word so that you can apply the truths you discover.

Each lesson starts with questions for individual reflection or group discussion, then moves into a "Going Deeper" study of scriptural principles. At the end of the lesson, you'll have an opportunity to write about or discuss what spoke most to you in that chapter. The stories, quotes, and sidebars within the chapters may provide further opportunities for discussion or reflection.

"I will walk about in freedom, for I have sought out your precepts," Psalm 119:45 tells us. The same freedom awaits each one of us as we set our hearts on knowing God's Word. Prayerfully commit yourself to this study, giving God access to every tomb that keeps you from living resurrected. For Love is calling your name.

Are you ready to "come forth"?

Chapter One: Tale
of the Third Follower

Questions for Discussion or Reflection

1. This chapter mentions my difficulty with algebra in high school. What was your best subject in school? What was your worst?

2. Look at the sidebar titled "What Kind of Father Do You Have?" on page 4. Which (if any) misrepresentation of God as Father have you struggled with? Have you experienced another kind not named? How do you think your connection with your earthly father has affected your relationship with God?

Going Deeper

3. Consider the words of David in Psalm 22:1, echoed by Jesus on the cross. Scripture is filled with people who struggled with love-doubt. What kind of circumstances in your life have caused you to question God's love? What has helped you get God's love from your head to your heart?

4. Read the story of Lazarus found in John 11:1–12:11 (or see Appendix A). Circle or underline key phrases. What stands out to you most in this passage, and why?

5. Put yourself in the sandals of Mary, Martha, or Lazarus. Write a letter to Jesus from that person's perspective. You can choose any point on the time line of the story.

6. What do the following verses reveal about the love God has for us?

   Psalm 86:15 _____

   Romans 8:35–39 _____

   1 John 3:1 _____

7. Write out Ephesians 3:17–19 on an index card, beginning with the words "I pray." Refer to the card frequently over the next few days, memorizing the passage phrase by phrase. Repeat it until it becomes a part of you.

8. What spoke most to you in this chapter?

Chapter Two: Lord, the One You Love Is Sick

Questions for Discussion or Reflection

1. Describe briefly how you came to know Jesus as your personal Savior. (If you haven't yet received the gift He offers, why not do it today? Look at "The Invitation" on page 27.)

2. If you were to send a message to Jesus concerning your current situation and need, how would you fill in the blank: "Lord, the one you love is _____"?

Going Deeper

3. Sin is deadly and separates us from God. Match the downward spiral of sin and its effects listed below to the following scriptures by filling in the appropriate letter in the blank before the phrase: (a) Psalm 106:43; (b) Acts 8:23; (c) James 1:14–15.

   ____ Fills us with bitterness   ____ Enticed by our own evil desires
   ____ Makes us waste away   ____ Holds us captive
   ____ Ends in death   ____ Causes us to rebel against God

4. Read "What God Does with Our Sins" (pages 24–25). Which one of the points listed by Rosalind Goforth speaks most to your heart? Look up the accompanying scripture and then write it out in your own words.

5. How does Satan—not to mention your own lower nature—tend to lull you to sleep spiritually, even though you're a Christian?

6. Consider the following verses. According to these scriptures, why is it so important that we wake up, and what should our awakening involve?

Matthew 25:1–13 _____

Romans 13:11–12 _____

Ephesians 5:11–15 _____

7. "God is not mad at you!" That's the best part of the gospel, someone has said. In fact, instead of holding a grudge, the Lord wants to forgive us and make us His own. Look up the following scriptures and really meditate on them. Under each reference listed below, write down keywords or phrases that reveal God's attitude toward us.

Isaiah 44:21–22   2 Corinthians 5:17–21   Colossians 1:21–23a

8. What spoke most to you in this chapter?

CHAPTER THREE: OUR FRIEND LAZARUS

Questions for Discussion or Reflection

1. Describe a moment—big or small—when you felt especially loved. What were the circumstances, and what people were involved? Why do you think that experience was so special to you?

2. Take the test found in the sidebar titled "What Kind of Friend Am I?" on pages 44–45. What did you discover about your relationship with God? with others? Share one aspect of friendship in which you'd like to grow.

Going Deeper

3. How do you respond to the idea that God is an emotional God, feeling deep loneliness and a need for connection? Do you find that possibility

comforting or frightening? Read Genesis 2:18–3:13. What do you think God felt when Adam and Eve chose to disobey? If He had penned a journal entry that day long ago, what might it have said?

4. Read Hebrews 8:10–12, which describes the new covenant God has made with you and me. If we really understood and responded to His deep desire for fellowship, how would our perspective change toward the following things we do as Christians?

Daily prayer and reading the Bible: _____

Attending church: _____

Living a holy life: _____

5. The statements below describe three famous friends of God: Abraham, Moses, and David. Using Numbers 12:7–8, Acts 13:22, and James 2:21–23 as references, match each characteristic below with one of these friends. Do any of these qualities apply to you, even in a small way?

_____   He was a man after God's own heart.

_____   He was faithful in all God's house.

_____   His faith and actions worked together.

_____   He would do everything God wanted him to do.

_____   He believed God, and it was credited to him as righteousness.

_____   God spoke clearly to him and not in riddles.

6. Read John 15:13–17. Write down what you discover in this passage about being a friend of Jesus.

7. Read "Help Me Love You More!" on page 38. How would you fill in the blank in the sidebar? Write your own prayer to the Lord, asking Him to increase your ability to love Him better and more.

8. What spoke most to you in this chapter?

CHAPTER FOUR: WHEN LOVE TARRIES

Questions for Discussion or Reflection

1. Describe a time in your life when waiting was especially difficult. How did you react to the process, and what did you learn?

2. Delayed gratification is difficult for all of us. Consider the following aspects, and identify which one (or ones) you struggled with most while growing up and which is hardest for you today. If possible, give specific examples.

   • Adapting to less-than-perfect situations
   • Waiting for the fulfillment of our needs or desires
   • Accepting not only delays but also denials of what we want
   • Other: _____

Going Deeper

3. One of the hardest things for many people to understand about God is that He doesn't always interrupt or intervene when we're in trouble. Instead, He specializes in redeeming the situation, using it for our good and His kingdom. Look at the following passages and write down the problem God allowed and the benefit that eventually resulted.

   Acts 7:59–8:3   *Problem:* _____
   Acts 11:19–21   *Result:* _____

   Acts 21:30–36   *Problem:* _____
   Philippians 1:12–14 *Result:* _____

4. We humans tend to love formulas—if we do A and we do B, then God will have to do C. Read Isaiah 55:8–9 and Romans 11:33–36 several times, and allow the heavenly perspective to sink into your heart. Write a response to the Lord concerning the ways you may have tried to control Him through "formulas" rather than simply trusting He knows what is best.

5. Read "The Blessing of Trouble" sidebar on pages 58–59. Think of a time when you asked God for something and *didn't* get what you asked for. How has that experience affected your character and your life? Do you think you grew from the experience? Why or why not?

6. What do the following verses have to say about the benefits of waiting? Circle the benefit that means the most to you.

   Psalm 40:1–3 _____

   Isaiah 64:4 _____

   Lamentations 3:24–27 _____

7. In what area of your life do you need to hand God the "quill of your will"? Read Romans 8:28 and write it back to the Lord as a prayer, replacing "all things" with specific details of your situation. End the prayer with a declaration of your love and commitment to His will.

8. What spoke most to you in this chapter?

Chapter Five: Tomb Dwelling

Questions for Discussion or Reflection

1. An old New Mexico tombstone reads, "Here lies Johnny Yeast. Pardon me for not rising."[1] Another one in Colorado protests, "I told you I was sick!" These are silly epitaphs, but on a more serious note, what would you like your grave marker to say?

2. Consider the "Hurts, Hang-ups, and Habits" sidebar on page 70. Which of these three categories of strongholds tends to trip you up most often in your walk with God? If you feel comfortable sharing, name at least one item you're struggling with (or have given in to!) right now. Privately or as a group, take those things to the Lord in prayer, claiming the promise of James 5:16.

Going Deeper

3. The Bible speaks powerfully to so many issues. Using a concordance, look up a word or assorted words that relate to your particular struggle—lust, anger, pride, fear, lying, whatever you may be facing. (If needed, ask a friend experienced in Bible study to help.) Pick three pertinent verses to write down, then choose one to memorize.

4. We all have lies in our lives that have been internalized as truth. In order to uncover false beliefs, consider the following questions. (Don't discount anything, even seemingly small stuff that has happened or innocent pastimes you tend to turn to for escape.)

   • What failure or trauma from your past still defines you as though it's your *identity*?
   • What coping mechanism do you regularly turn to for *security*?
   • In the words of self-help guru Dr. Phil, "How's that workin' for ya?"

5. According to the following verses, why is it so important for us to acknowledge our need of forgiveness and healing?

   Psalm 66:18–20 _____

   Isaiah 30:15–16 _____

   1 John 1:9–10 _____

6. The book of Isaiah gives us many glimpses into the purpose of Jesus's coming and ministry. Under the corresponding verses, list the things you discover.

   Isaiah 42:1–4   Isaiah 61:1–3

7. One of the most precious aspects of God's work in our lives is His ability to redefine us and change our identities. For the following verses, write down the old name and the new name given and the significance of each. Then consider Revelation 2:17 and its significance to you.

    Genesis 32:24–28   Old name: _____

                                New name: _____

                                Significance:_____

    Matthew 16:13–18   Old name: _____

                                New name: _____

                                Significance:_____

    Revelation 2:17   Significance:_____

8. What spoke most to you in this chapter?

CHAPTER SIX: ROLL AWAY THE STONE

Questions for Discussion or Reflection

1. Rolling away stones can be hard. Physically speaking, what is the hardest thing you've ever done (climbed a mountain, given birth, etc.)? Describe the experience.

2. Without giving unnecessary details, share a time when bringing a secret to light destroyed the power it had exerted over you.

Going Deeper

3. Craig Groeschel says that many of us are *Christian atheists*—"believing in God but living as if He doesn't exist." Can you see signs of this contradiction in your life or in the lives of Christians in general? Give an example (big or little) if you can. What could we do to better fight the tendency toward Christian atheism?

4. Read through Psalm 91 and consider the benefits of making God our shelter and dwelling place rather than choosing to remain in our tombs. List five benefits you appreciate, then pick the one that means the most to you, and write a short paragraph explaining why.

5. God went out of His way to remove the barrier that stood between us and Him. Look up the following passages and fill in the blanks.

   Leviticus 16:2   The barrier: _____

   Matthew 27:50–51   The process: _____

   Hebrews 10:19–22   The result: _____

6. Which one of the following "stones" might be blocking God's access to the places in you that need healing? Look up the corresponding verses, and paraphrase your favorite part back to the Lord as a prayer, asking for help to remove it so that you might be free. Can you think of any other stones— besides these three—that might be keeping you from Him?
   - *Unworthiness* (Romans 4:7–8; 8:1)
   - *Unforgiveness* (Ephesians 4:31–5:2)
   - *Unbelief* (Romans 4:20–22)

7. As you hear Jesus asking you to roll away the boulder blockading your heart, what does His response to Martha mean to you: "Did I not tell you that if you believed, you would see the glory of God?" (John 11:40)? What would it take for you to lay aside unbelief and move forward in your process of healing?

8. What spoke most to you in this chapter?

CHAPTER SEVEN: WHEN LOVE CALLS YOUR NAME

Questions for Discussion or Reflection

1. Did you have a nickname growing up? What did your mom call you when you were in trouble?

2. If you were administered a spiritual hearing test today, what do you think the results would be? (Check one.)

___ Excellent

___ Improving

___ Average

___ Poor

___ Acute deafness

Is hearing from God a personal struggle for you? What do you normally do to improve your hearing?

Going Deeper

3. Read the passage from Priscilla Shirer on page 105. In what ways, past or present, has the Enemy tried to convince you that you can't or don't hear God's voice?

4. Elijah heard from God in 1 Kings 19:11–12, but not in the way he expected. What does this passage of Scripture and Isaiah 30:21 reveal about how God tends to speak to us today? What makes the first part of Psalm 46:10 so important to improving our ability to hear Him?

5. Matthew 7:24–27 highlights the importance of obeying when God speaks and warns what happens when we don't. Record the two different responses to the Lord's words you find in the following verses and the outcome of each.

Matthew 7:24–25   *Response:* _____

                         Result: _____

Matthew 7:26–27   *Response:* _____

                         Result: _____

6. If possible, describe a time when the Holy Spirit used one of the following methods to speak to you—a repeated theme, an impression, a confirmation, a spirit check, or a verse from the Bible. How did you know it was God speaking? (Remember, often it isn't until we've obeyed that we realize it was His voice all along.)

7. What does the statement "The teacher is always silent during a test" mean to you (especially in light of the story of Jesus and the three praying women told on pages 116–17)?

8. What spoke most to you in this chapter?

CHAPTER EIGHT: UNWINDING GRAVECLOTHES

Questions for Discussion or Reflection

1. Read the story of the good Samaritan in Luke 10:30–35. Based on your nature, if you had been on the road that day, which of the following roles might you have played? (I've embellished a bit!)
   - The Priest—saw the bruised and bleeding man but kept moving, too busy to stop.
   - The Levite—looked closer but didn't feel adequate to help so dialed 911 as he went on his way.
   - The Soccer Mom—was distracted by squabbling kids and text messages and didn't even notice.
   - The Samaritan—laid aside his plans and got involved, helping the wounded man.
   - Other: _____

2. Read "Kissing Frogs" on page 124. It has been said that we should love people when they least expect it and least deserve it. Think of a time when someone loved you like that—or a time when you had the privilege of doing that for someone else. Describe the experience.

Going Deeper

3. Read 1 John 3:16–20 and answer the following questions:

   • According to verse 16, who is our example, and what did He do?

   • What warning are we given in verse 17?

   • Instead of offering words and lip service, how are we to love (verse 18)?

   • What amazing benefit (verses 19–20) do we derive from loving like that?

4. Which of the "Lessons from Good Sam" (pages 132–33) speaks most to you? Which seems the most challenging? Why?

5. Do you have a friend or acquaintance who is struggling to escape graveclothes right now? Take a moment to pray for her or him. Ask what God would have you do to help love that person back to life. (It may be as simple as a phone call, a shared meal, or an encouraging note.) Whatever He lays on your heart, do it—knowing that God wants to love that person through you.

6. While we've discussed how we can help others unwind their graveclothes, what does Hebrews 12:1–6 tell us about unwinding our own? List at least five things we should do.

7. Read Isaiah 64:6 and Revelation 3:17. How does our insistence on wearing the "filthy rags" of our own righteousness keep us from experiencing true healing and freedom? According to Revelation 3:18–19, what does God "counsel" us to do?

8. What spoke most to you in this chapter?

Chapter Nine: Living Resurrected

Questions for Discussion or Reflection

1. Have you ever witnessed an amazing transformation in someone's life that was brought about by Christ? Describe it. How did seeing it make you feel?

2. If you were asked to give a testimony of transformation in your life, what would you say? If you can't think of one, is there an attitude or behavior you are currently asking the Lord to change? Describe the difference you believe it will make when this aspect of your life is transformed.

Going Deeper

3. Complete Jesus's seven "I am" sayings listed below. Circle the one that currently means the most to you and explain why.

   John 6:35   "I am the bread of life _____."

   John 8:12   "I am the light of the world _____."

   John 10:9   "I am the gate _____."

   John 10:14–15   "I am the good shepherd _____."

   John 11:25   "I am the resurrection and the life _____."

   John 14:6   "I am the way and the truth and the life _____."

   John 15:5   "I am the vine _____."

4. Knowing the "Great I Am" (Jesus Himself) helps us better understand who we are as well. Look at Appendix D: "Who I Am in Christ." Choose one phrase from each of the three categories, and write out the corresponding verse. Memorize one to include in your Holy Spirit "knowledge base."

5. List three things that currently "move you"—make you overreact or feel upset, worried, and/or fearful. Now describe how counting yourself dead (Romans 6:11) might help change your perspective and enable you to say along with Paul, "nor did I count my life dear to myself" (Acts 20:24, NKJV). If applicable, name a time in your life when your relationship with Christ helped change your lower nature reaction.

6. Meditate on John 15:1–8. Read it several times, and allow the verses to penetrate your heart. Circle or underline phrases that have particular meaning for you. In the context of these verses, what is the difference between striving and abiding? In practical terms, what would choosing to abide actually look like in your life? What would have to change?

7. Read George Müller's secret of service on page 151. Using it as a template, write an obituary for yourself, declaring your decision to die so that Christ might live.

8. What spoke most to you in this chapter?

CHAPTER TEN: LAUGHING LAZARUS

Questions for Discussion or Reflection

1. Have you ever escaped a dangerous, life-threatening situation? Describe it and the emotions you felt after cheating death. If you've never actually experienced this, describe how you think you would feel.

2. Read the "Living in the Light of Eternity" sidebar on page 168. What aspect of living resurrected would you like to begin practicing right now? What single change in your life would help you do this?

Going Deeper

3. If you really believed that this world isn't all there is, how would it affect the way you view the following aspects of your life? (Write your response first, then consider the scripture given.)

Finances: _____

(Matthew 6:19–21)

Worries: _____

(2 Corinthians 4:17–18)

Sickness: _____

(2 Corinthians 12:7–9)

Hardships: _____

(James 1:12)

Persecution: _____

(John 15:18–20)

4. Which of the following myths have you been able to discard as you've studied the story of Lazarus? Place a check mark (✓) by those you've let go of and a question mark (?) by the ones you'd like to let go of. Feel free to add any other myths about God's love you have become aware of.

____ We must earn God's favor.

____ If God loves us, terrible things should never happen to us.

____ Death is the worst thing possible.

____ God is distant when we suffer.

____ God's timing really stinks.

____ Tragedy is just tragedy—nothing good can come of it.

____ Other: _____

5. What do the following verses tell us about Jesus's return and the importance of being ready?

Luke 12:35–37 _____

1 Thessalonians 5:1–6 _____

2 Peter 3:4, 8–14 _____

6. Jesus promised that He would come back to take us to heaven so we could be together with Him (John 14:1–3). In light of that reality, consider the following questions:

- What do you imagine that day will be like?
- How close to Jesus do you hope to be?
- Spiritually, what do you need to begin doing here on earth so that when that day comes, you can be known there as you are known here (1 Corinthians 13:12)?

7. Please don't rush through this last exercise. Take time to allow the truth of the following hymn, "The Love of God," to move from your head to your heart. Read the words slowly, then say or sing them again. Allow the immensity of the Father's love to wash over your heart. Rest in it. Revel in it. Receive it as truth. Then write a prayer asking the Holy Spirit to make God's love real in every corner of your heart.

> The love of God is greater far
> Than tongue or pen can ever tell;
> It goes beyond the highest star,
> And reaches to the lowest hell;
> The guilty pair, bowed down with care,
> God gave His Son to win;
> His erring child He reconciled,
> And pardoned from his sin.
>
> *Refrain:*
> O love of God, how rich and pure!
> How measureless and strong!
> It shall forevermore endure
> The saints' and angels' song.
>
> When years of time shall pass away,
> And earthly thrones and kingdoms fall,
> When men, who here refuse to pray,
> On rocks and hills and mountains call,
> God's love so sure, shall still endure,
> All measureless and strong;
> Redeeming grace to Adam's race—
> The saints' and angels' song.
>
> Could we with ink the ocean fill,
> And were the skies of parchment made,

Were every stalk on earth a quill,

And every man a scribe by trade,

To write the love of God above,

Would drain the ocean dry.

Nor could the scroll contain the whole,

Though stretched from sky to sky.

—Frederick M. Lehman[2]

8. Looking back on your journey through this book, what concept has made the biggest impact on you? In what ways has it changed the way you think or live, especially in the area of love-doubt?

Using This Study in an Eight-Week Format

Because this is a shorter study than the ones in my other two books, it may fit well at the end of a Bible-study year or as a summer study. If ten weeks is too long for what you have in mind, you can adapt it to the number of weeks you need by combining chapters (though I would discourage doing fewer than eight sessions).

While you are free to choose how to combine chapters, I suggest covering chapters 1 and 2 ("Tale of the Third Follower" and "Lord, the One You Love Is Sick") in your opening week and chapters 9 and 10 ("Living Resurrected" and "Laughing Lazarus") in your last week of study. When combining weeks, choose one "For Discussion or Reflection" question from each chapter and three from each "Going Deeper" section. Be sure to assign these selected questions the week before the chapters are to be discussed.

As I mentioned at the beginning of this guide, you'll find even more Bible-study resources on my Web site: www.joannaweaverbooks.com. The "Going Deeper/ Book Study Helps" section features a reproducible study guide in a workbook format and a leader's guide. After you've finished your study, please visit the site again to share creative ideas of what worked well for you. I look forward to hearing them!

Resources for Resurrected Living

Never before have there been so many resources available to help Christians live resurrected, grasp God's love better, and learn to be His friend. While nothing replaces the Word of God, the Holy Spirit often speaks through other avenues as well. Here are some books and resources that have really helped me.

GETTING GOD'S LOVE FROM YOUR HEAD TO YOUR HEART

The Rabbi's Heartbeat by Brennan Manning. Colorado Springs, CO: NavPress, 2003. This truly beautiful devotional offers everyday challenges and encouragement to accept your identity as God's beloved child.

The Tender Words of God: A Daily Guide by Ann Spangler. Grand Rapids: Zondervan, 2008. This very personal devotional uses Scripture to help you develop a deeper sense of being loved by God.

Love Beyond Reason: Moving God's Love from Your Head to Your Heart by John Ortberg. Grand Rapids: Zondervan, 1998. This encouraging book reveals a Father who is head over heels in love with His children and committed to their highest joy.

Waking the Dead: The Glory of a Heart Fully Alive by John Eldredge. Nashville: Thomas Nelson, 2003. Eldredge's powerful book shows how to energize your life by living—really living—from the heart.

What's So Amazing About Grace? by Philip Yancey. Grand Rapids: Zondervan, 2002. This modern classic focuses on the transforming—and love-doubt erasing—power of grace in our lives.

Do You Think I'm Beautiful?: The Question Every Woman Asks by Angela Thomas. Nashville: Thomas Nelson, 2005. This warm, reassuring book invites women to meet the embrace of the One who calls them beautiful.

Crazy Love: Overwhelmed by a Relentless God by Francis Chan. Colorado Springs, CO: David C. Cook, 2008. Chan provides a fresh and compelling exploration of God's radical, relentless, "crazy" love for us—and how we can respond.

Being a Friend of God

My Utmost for His Highest by Oswald Chambers. This Christian classic, originally published in 1935, remains fresh and challenging. My edition is from Barbour Books, but an updated-language version is available from Discovery House. You can also access daily readings of this classic work on the Internet at www .myutmost.org.

Streams in the Desert and *Springs in the Valley* by Lettie B. (Mrs. Charles) Cowman. These inspirational compilations first appeared in 1925 and 1939 respectively and are still popular today. I own them in a combined edition. James Reimann edited updated-language versions, which are available from Zondervan.

The Indwelling Life of Christ: All of Him in All of Me by Major W. Ian Thomas. Colorado Springs, CO: Multnomah Publishers, 2006. This devotional—one of my personal favorites—reminds me that the secret of living a transformed life is letting Jesus do the work!

A Call to Die: A 40 Day Journey of Fasting from the World and Feasting on God by David Nasser. Birmingham, AL: Redemptive Art Publishing, 2000. Complete with daily questions and action plans, this remarkable devotional is basically a hands-on workbook on dying to self.

Jesus Calling: Enjoying Peace in His Presence by Sarah Young. Nashville: Thomas, Nelson, 2004. This devotional—a classic in the making—grew out of Sarah Young's prayer journals. Written as if in the voice of Jesus, it speaks words of peace and comfort with remarkable intimacy and immediacy.

The Pursuit of God by A. W. Tozer. Camp Hill, PA: WingSpread, 1992. First published in 1948 and still in print, this perennial classic explores the in-depth implications of knowing Christ, and it challenges me every time I read it.

Discerning the Voice of God: How to Recognize When God Speaks by Priscilla Shirer. Chicago: Moody, 2007. Using biblical principles and practical insights from saints, both current and past, Shirer helps us tune in to God's voice. (The author's six-week DVD teaching series is also available on the subject: *He Speaks to Me: Preparing to Hear from God.* Nashville: LifeWay, 2005.)

GETTING OUT OF YOUR TOMB

One Day at a Time: The Devotional for Overcomers by Neil T. Anderson, Mike and Julia Quarles. Ventura, CA: Regal, 2000. Based on Dr. Anderson's *Steps to Freedom in Christ* recovery model, this devotional provides daily encouragement for anyone struggling with sin, addiction, obsession, and depression. (For more about Dr. Anderson's Freedom in Christ ministry, see his Web site: www.ficm .org/newsite/index.php.)

Get Out of That Pit: Straight Talk about God's Deliverance by Beth Moore. Nashville: Integrity, 2007. America's favorite Bible teacher offers fresh understanding on the pits—or tombs—we get ourselves into and how to find freedom through Christ.

Praying God's Word: Breaking Free from Spiritual Strongholds by Beth Moore. Nashville: Broadman and Holman, 2000. This prayer guide examines fourteen strongholds that entomb Christians and suggests scriptures to help demolish them through daily prayer.

Breaking Free: Making Liberty in Christ a Reality in Life DVD series and workbook by Beth Moore. Nashville: LifeWay Christian Resources, 2006. All Beth Moore studies are good, but this one is a personal favorite. It includes eleven weeks of DVD teaching for groups and individual Bible study. An updated series is available under the title *Breaking Free: The Journey, The Stories.*

The Search for Significance: Seeing Your True Worth through God's Eyes by Robert S. McGee. Rev. ed. Nashville: W Publishing Group, 2003. "Approval addicts" like me and those hung up on performance, blame, and other "self-disorders" will find help in this classic reminder that our true value is found in Christ.

Lord, I Want to Be Whole: The Power of Prayer and Scripture in Emotional Healing by Stormie Omartian. Nashville: Thomas Nelson, 2000. For those who struggle with anger, guilt, and depression, Stormie Omartian offers seven biblical steps to wholeness.

Lies Women Believe: And the Truth That Sets Them Free by Nancy Leigh DeMoss. Chicago: Moody, 2001. DeMoss exposes areas of deception we commonly fall for—about ourselves, sin, relationships, emotions, and circumstances—and shows how confronting these lies can help set us free.

Celebrate Recovery. Based on eight principles from the Beatitudes, this program was begun at Pastor Rick Warren's Saddleback Church and offers a number of Christ-centered resources to help those struggling with sin and addiction—media, resource kits, conferences, and access to support groups throughout the country. Check out the Web site at www.celebraterecovery.com.

A Hunger for Healing: The Twelve Steps as a Classic Model for Christian Spiritual Growth by J. Keith Miller. New York: HarperOne, 1992. This book, too, has become something of a classic and powerfully applies the Twelve Steps of Alcoholics Anonymous not only to addictions but to growing closer to Christ.

OTHER RESOURCES

Christianity.com (www.christianity.com). This is a one-stop source for Bible study, devotionals, articles, blogs—you name it.

Bible Study Tools: Growing Deeper in the Word (www.biblestudytools.com). This site offers commentaries, Bible study helps, and the like.

Bible Gateway (www.biblegateway.com). The site provides easy access to the most popular (and some obscure) Bible translations and allows searches by verse or keyword.

Christian Classics Ethereal Library (www.ccel.org). Most of the great public-domain Christian classics can be found here and read online or downloaded in several different formats.

Christianity Today International (www.christianitytoday.com). This site hosts a number of excellent magazines, including the online version of *Christianity Today* and the women's magazine *Kyria* (formerly *Today's Christian Woman*).

Focus on the Family (www.focusonthefamily.com). This site provides wonderful resources relating to family, marriage, and spiritual growth.

Who I Am in Christ

Ever since Adam and Eve bit into the forbidden fruit, humanity has struggled with an identity crisis. We've forgotten who we really are—chosen and beloved children of God. Consider the following list of scriptures from the wonderful devotional *One Day at a Time*.[1]

I Am Accepted

John 1:12	I am God's child.
John 15:15	I am Christ's friend.
Romans 5:1	I have been justified.
1 Corinthians 6:17	I am united with the Lord, and I am one spirit with Him.
1 Corinthians 6:20	I have been bought with a price. I belong to God.
1 Corinthians12:27	I am a member of Christ's body.
Ephesians 1:1	I am a saint.
Ephesians 1:5	I have been adopted as God's child.
Ephesians 2:18	I have direct access to God through the Holy Spirit.
Colossians 1:14	I have been redeemed and forgiven of all my sins.
Colossians 2:10	I am complete in Christ.

I Am Secure

Romans 8:1–2	I am free from condemnation.
Romans 8:28	I am assured that all things work together for good.

Romans 8:31–34	I am free from any condemning charges against me.
Romans 8:35–39	I cannot be separated from the love of God.
2 Corinthians 1:21–22	I have been established, anointed, and sealed by God.
Colossians 3:3	I am hidden with Christ in God.
Philippians 1:6	I am confident that the good work God has begun in me will be perfected.
Philippians 3:20	I am a citizen of heaven.
2 Timothy 1:7	I have not been given a spirit of fear but of power, love, and a sound mind.
Hebrews 4:16	I can find grace and mercy to help in time of need.
1 John 5:18	I am born of God, and the evil one cannot touch me.

I AM SIGNIFICANT

Matthew 5:13–14	I am the salt and light of the earth.
John 15:1, 5	I am a branch of the true vine, a channel of His life.
John 15:16	I have been chosen and appointed to bear fruit.
Acts 1:8	I am a personal witness of Christ.
1 Corinthians 3:16	I am God's temple.
2 Corinthians 5:17–21	I am a minister of reconciliation for God.
2 Corinthians 6:1	I am God's co-worker (see 1 Corinthians 3:9).
Ephesians 2:6	I am seated with Christ in the heavenly realm.
Ephesians 2:10	I am God's workmanship.
Ephesians 3:12	I may approach God with freedom and confidence.
Philippians 4:13	I can do all things through Christ, who strengthens me.

Identifying Strongholds

Astronghold, remember, is a hurt, a habit, or a hang-up that keeps us entombed, unable to live freely and fully. Strongholds may involve false beliefs, established attitudes, and compulsive behavior patterns, including addictions. Some are inherently harmful (like smoking), while others may only be a problem if they become entrenched in your life and hold you back from freedom. The following questions may help you recognize tombs that are hemming you in, shutting you down, or closing you off:

1. *Do you struggle with "repeated, unwanted behavior"?*[1] You may find yourself doing things you don't want to do or struggling with negative or destructive thought patterns. This behavior is so engrained it is nearly second nature, though you know it isn't right. It can be anything from anger to chronic laziness, violent reactions to habitual lying—to name just a few.

2. *Do you tend to turn to this behavior or thought pattern when things are difficult or you feel depressed?* It may offer a strong (but false) sense of comfort and initially make you feel better, even though you know it's not good for you. Whether it's compulsive shopping; mental escapism through television, reading, or the Internet; overeating; pornography; alcohol; or something else—your first impulse when troubled is to turn to it rather than to God.

3. *Do you have difficulty understanding why you react to certain things the way you do?* Certain experiences may trigger overreactions that don't fit the situation. The strength of the emotion surprises even you, but you can't seem to help yourself. Watch out for tendencies toward verbal retaliation, extreme anger and defensiveness, paranoia, or self-hatred.

4. *Do you have a secret no one knows?* Shame from your past or "family business" that you've been warned not to talk about can haunt your present life and keep you from connecting with people in meaningful ways. Secrets and shame can lead to emotional paralysis, shyness, isolation, cynicism, or a chameleon tendency to role-play rather than be real.

5. *Do you find yourself stuck somewhere in your past or stalled in the grief process?* You may find yourself longing to go back to a certain point in your life or continually reliving a painful event. You may simmer with anger over a long-ago injustice or feel paralyzed by grief over a significant loss. There's nothing wrong with a bit of nostalgia, and needing time to heal after trauma or loss is normal and necessary. But ongoing and unresolved feelings about the past can eventually harden into strongholds.

6. *Do you have an unsubstantiated and intense dislike of a certain type or group of people*—men, women, liberals or conservatives, corporate types, Muslims, Jews, tattooed Norwegians? Any contact with the group—or simply thinking about them—may inspire deep discomfort, fear, anger, or even hatred. Making sweeping judgments and assumptions about individual members of the group without actually getting to know them is a telltale sign as well.

7. *Do you accept your limitations as your definition?* This could mean you've allowed demeaning words from the past to define you: "I'm not athletic… or talented…" "I probably won't amount to anything." You may frequently use the excuse "That's just the way I am" to deflect blame or responsibility for your behavior or your reactions: "I always lose my temper because I'm Italian/Greek/Irish" or "In our family we just don't do feelings."

8. *Do you get offended when other people point out unhealthy behaviors that you don't (or do!) see in yourself?* Defensiveness is usually a sign that we've come in contact with some kind of truth. If more than one person suggests you have a problem, it makes sense to listen, even if you're sure they're wrong. Don't underestimate the power of denial to keep you in bondage. Ask God to help you see what you need to see.

If you have recognized yourself in any of the questions above, the first step toward finding freedom is to bring the situation before God. Here are some suggestions for how to do that:

- Give God specific permission to shine the spotlight of the Holy Spirit on your soul.
- Follow the Reveal-Repent-Renounce-Replace outline suggested in the "Dethroning Lies" sidebar on pages 76–77.
- Ask God to show you what He would have you do next in order to live free. Don't forget to deal with the lies of unworthiness, unforgiveness, and unbelief that may also play a part in your bondage.
- Allow the Holy Spirit to direct your path as you seek further counseling, prayer support, and perhaps a recovery group that addresses your specific need.

Hints for Unwinding Graveclothes

While only God can resurrect dead people, He specifically calls us to help love them back into life. Although chapter 8 already covered a lot of information about unwinding graveclothes, here are some extra tips I've picked up over the years:

1. *Be available (Matthew 9:36).* Ask for eyes to see what God sees and where He would have you participate in His work. When you recognize a need, ask how He wants you to be involved. Sometimes prayer is our only calling. But when the Holy Spirit prompts you to step forward into the situation, don't shrink back.

2. *Pray specifically about what God is calling you to do (Isaiah 30:21).* Whether it involves taking an hour to listen or a significant ongoing investment of time and resources—whatever you feel called to do, do it. But also check your motives. Keep in mind that the work is God's, and you are simply there to do what He tells you.

3. *Listen to the person's story (Galatians 6:2).* Too often we operate out of faulty assumptions. Ask the person to share his or her story, and insert pertinent questions to help the process along. Often it isn't until we know where people have been that we're able to help them get where they need to be—and the very act of listening brings healing. At the same time, don't allow yourself to get swept into an emotional drama and forget to factor in God.

4. *Be trustworthy (Proverbs 11:13).* When a person tells you something in confidence, don't share it elsewhere without permission—not even in vague prayer requests or in general, unnamed discussions. Be a safe haven in which other people can learn to trust and rest their hearts. (Note: The only exception to the confidentiality rule is in cases of abuse, imminent danger, or suicidal tendencies. These must be reported, but let the person involved know you are going to do so.)

5. *Invite Jesus into the interaction (James 5:16).* You'll want to do this with care and sensitivity, as some have been wounded by religious people in the past. (Sadly, it happens.) Look for ways to bring Jesus and His love into the conversation in nonjudgmental ways. Pray together, taking each and every need to Him. Encourage the development of a personal relationship with God, and gently urge the other person to turn to Him first with his or her needs.

6. *Ask God for wisdom (Colossians 1:9).* Let the Bible be your guide. Don't counsel solely out of your own experience, opinion, or bias, or you may give tainted advice. Ask the Holy Spirit for a gift of faith to see what the person can become so that you minister out of hope, not despair. Find scriptural promises to pray and declare boldly over the person's life. Ask the Lord to lead you to helpful resources you can share.

7. *Speak the truth in love (Ephesians 4:15).* Someone has said, "Love without truth is flattery, but truth without love is cruelty." Ask God to give you a genuine love for the person. Speak words of affirmation often, pointing out good qualities in his or her life and praising the progress made. But don't be afraid to gently point out inconsistencies between the person's life and God's Word. Do it humbly and gently, knowing that truth sets us free.

8. *Make room for others to help (Proverbs 15:22).* We are rarely the only ones God uses in people's lives. God has also appointed certain people—parents, spouses, pastors—to provide both authority and spiritual protection. Honor and support such "coverings" when appropriate. Be willing to decrease so other godly influences can increase. If you sense the other person is becoming overly dependent on you, point it out gently and slowly step back so

God can step in. And don't be offended if your season in someone's life comes to an end sooner than you think it should.

9. *Remember, graveclothes consist of layers (Galatians 6:9–10).* Freedom doesn't come all at once. It is a process of healing you are witnessing, not an event. Don't give way to cynicism or frustration when it seems to take longer than it should or when one problem is dealt with only to reappear in another form. Encourage yourself and the one you minister to that God will be faithful to finish what He has started. We simply have to cooperate—one layer at a time.

10. *Above all, trust God (Hebrews 12:2).* Lasting healing is God's work, and He's good at it. Trust that the Holy Spirit is working in the heart of the one who needs freedom, and let Him have His way in you as well. Be willing to do what God asks when He asks it, then commit the person to His love and His care. Operate out of faith, not fear. Then watch what God will do!

Notes

Epigraph

Quoted in Dan Clendenin, "Ancient Wisdom for the Modern World: My New Year's Resolutions with Help from the Desert Monastics," *Journey with Jesus,* January 1, 2006, www.journeywithjesus.net/Essays/20051226JJ.shtml. Adapted from John Chryssavgis's translation in *In the Heart of the Desert: The Spirituality of the Desert Fathers and Mothers,* rev. ed. (Bloomington, IN: World Wisdom, 2008), 1.

Chapter One: Tale of the Third Follower

1. Anna B. Warner, "Jesus Loves Me," first published in Anna B. Warner and Susan Warner, *Say and Seal* (Philadelphia: Lippincott, 1860), 115–16.
2. For the full story of Martha and Mary and the way they grew in relationship to Jesus, see my books, *Having a Mary Heart in a Martha World: Finding Intimacy with God in the Busyness of Life* (Colorado Springs, CO: WaterBrook, 2000, 2002) and *Having a Mary Spirit: Allowing God to Change Us from the Inside Out* (Colorado Springs, CO: WaterBrook, 2006).
3. Bono, in Michka Assayas, *Bono: In Conversation with Michka Assayas* (New York: Penguin, Berkley, 2006), 225.
4. Bono, in Assayas, *Bono: In Conversation,* 226.
5. For an enlightening discussion of the tendency toward "will worship," see Richard J. Foster, *Celebration of Discipline: The Path to Spiritual Growth,* rev. ed. (1978; repr., San Francisco: HarperSanFrancisco, 1988), 5–6.

Chapter Two: Lord, the One You Love Is Sick

1. Commenting on the time line of Lazarus's sickness, Warren Wiersbe writes: "Jesus was at Bethabara, about twenty miles from Bethany.... If the [messenger] had traveled quickly, without any delay, he could have made the trip in one day. Jesus sent him back the next day... Then Jesus waited two more

days…and by the time He and His disciples arrived, Lazarus had been dead for four days. This means that Lazarus had died *the very day* the messenger left to contact Jesus!" In Warren W. Wiersbe, *Be Alive* (Colorado Springs, CO: David C. Cook, 1981), 132.

2. According to the *NIV Study Bible* notes on John 9:2, "The rabbis had developed the principle that 'There is no death without sin, and there is no suffering without iniquity.' They were even capable of thinking that a child could sin in the womb or that its soul might have sinned in a preexistent state. They also held that terrible punishments came on certain people because of the sin of their parents. As the next verse [John 9:3] shows, Jesus plainly contradicted these beliefs." Kenneth L. Barker, ed., *The NIV Study Bible,* 10th anniversary ed. (Grand Rapids: Zondervan, 1995).

3. Jerry Goebel, "Unbind Him and Let Him Go!" ONEFamily Outreach, March 13, 2005, http://onefamilyoutreach.com/bible/John/jn_11_01-45.htm.

4. Adapted from Rosalind Goforth, *Climbing: Memories of a Missionary's Wife,* 2nd ed. (1940; repr., Elkhart, IN: Bethel, 1996), 80.

5. *Steps to Peace with God* (Charlotte, NC: Billy Graham Evangelistic Association, n.d.), www.billygraham.org/specialsections/steps-to-peace/steps-to-peace.asp.

6. After much study I've come to believe we are three-part beings, as referred to by Paul in 1 Thessalonians 5:23: "May God himself, the God of peace, sanctify you through and through. May your whole spirit, soul and body be kept blameless at the coming of our Lord Jesus Christ." The "body" is the physical shell that houses us; the "soul" is our mind, will, and emotions; and the "spirit" is the place that comes alive when Christ takes up residence within us at salvation. For a deeper discussion on this topic and why I believe the distinction is important, see *Having a Mary Spirit: Allowing God to Change Us from the Inside Out* (beginning with chapter 2).

7. Quoted in Dale Fincher, "A Slice of Infinity: What Do You Expect? Part 5," Ravi Zacharias International Ministries, January 30, 2004, www.rzim.org/resources/read/asliceofinfinity/todaysslice.aspx?aid=8420.

8. Quoted in John Eldredge, *Waking the Dead: The Glory of a Heart Fully Alive* (Nashville: Thomas Nelson, 2003), 75.

Chapter Three: Our Friend Lazarus

1. James Strong, *The New Strong's Exhaustive Concordance of the Bible* (Nashville: Thomas Nelson, 1996), s.v. "#1690."

2. David Giles, *Illusions of Immortality: A Psychology of Fame and Celebrity* (London: Macmillan, 2000), 95.

3. Giles, *Illusions of Immortality*, 95.

4. Francis Chan, *Crazy Love: Overwhelmed by a Relentless God* (Colorado Springs, CO: David C. Cook, 2008), 110–11.

5. Gene Edwards, *The Divine Romance* (1984; repr., Wheaton, IL: Tyndale, 1992), 63–64.

6. Max Lucado, *God Came Near* (1986; repr., Nashville: Thomas Nelson, 2004), 56.

7. Spiros Zodhiates, gen. ed., *The Complete Word Study Dictionary: New Testament,* rev. ed. (Chattanooga, TN: AMG International, 1993), s.v. "#2083."

8. Zodhiates, *Complete Word Study Dictionary,* s.v. "#2083."

9. Zodhiates, *Complete Word Study Dictionary,* s.v. "#2083."

10. Zodhiates, *Complete Word Study Dictionary,* s.v. "#2083."

11. C. H. Spurgeon, "The Friend of God," *The Homiletic Review,* vol. 14, no. 1 (July–December 1887), 157.

12. George Müller to J. Hudson Taylor, in Dr. and Mrs. Howard Taylor, *Hudson Taylor's Spiritual Secret,* Moody Classics ed. (Chicago: Moody, 2009), 152–53.

13. Joseph C. Ludgate, "Friendship with Jesus," in *Hymns of Glorious Praise* (Springfield, MO: Gospel Publishing, 1969), 338.

Chapter Four: When Love Tarries

1. *Dark Night of the Soul* was originally the title of a poem and an accompanying commentary by Spanish mystic and Carmelite friar Saint John of the Cross (1542–1591).

2. Brian Jones, *Second Guessing God: Hanging On When You Can't See His Plan* (Cincinnati, OH: Standard Publishing, 2006), 13.

3. Jones, *Second Guessing God,* 15.

4. Jones, *Second Guessing God,* 15.

5. Jones, *Second Guessing God,* 15.

6. Pastor Don Burleson, "Big T-Truth" (sermon, New Covenant Fellowship, Kalispell, MT, June 8, 2008).

7. Warren Wiersbe, *The Wiersbe Bible Commentary: Old Testament,* 2nd ed. (Colorado Springs, CO: David C. Cook, 2007), 755. Emphasis in scriptures and outline format are mine.

8. Charles H. Spurgeon, "A Mystery! Saints Sorrowing and Jesus Glad!" (sermon no. 585, Metropolitan Tabernacle, Newington, England, August 7, 1864), quoted in *Spurgeon's Sermons,* vol. 10: 1864, Christian Classics Ethereal Library, http://153.106.5.3/ccel/spurgeon/sermons10.xviii.html.

9. According to the *NIV Study Bible* notes on John 11:17, "Many Jews believed that the soul remained near the body for three days after death in the hope of returning to it. If this idea was in the minds of these people, they obviously thought all hope was gone—Lazarus was irrevocably dead." Kenneth L. Barker, ed., *The NIV Study Bible,* 10th anniversary ed. (Grand Rapids: Zondervan, 1995).

10. Jerry Goebel, "Unbind Him and Let Him Go!" ONEFamily Outreach, March 13, 2005, http://onefamilyoutreach.com/bible/John/jn_11_01-45.htm.

11. Perhaps you've wondered, as I have, what Jesus meant when He addressed the disciples' concerns about returning to Bethany by saying, "Are there not twelve hours of daylight?" (John 11:9). Ray Stedman writes, "He is referring to the appointed timetable of God… He was determined to walk in the daylight of God's will. To step out of that timetable—even if doing so would *seem* safer by human reasoning—would be tantamount to walking by night. It would lead to stumbling.… God has appointed a time for each of us, and… there is nothing anyone else can do to shorten it, nor is there anything we can do to lengthen it. Our times are in God's hands." Ray C. Stedman with James D. Denney, *God's Loving Word: Exploring the Gospel of John* (Grand Rapids: Discovery House, 1993), 298.

12. I first heard David's story years ago on a recording from a talk he had given. I have since contacted him personally and received both his confirmation that the material is accurate and his permission to use it. For more on David Ring's Reach Out and Touch ministries, visit his Web site: www.davidring.org.

13. Not his real name

14. Thanks to Martha Tennison for this phrase, which I heard in a sermon delivered in Billings, Montana, September 24, 1999.

Chapter Five: Tomb Dwelling

1. [Matthew] Henry and [Thomas] Scott, *A Commentary upon the Holy Bible, Matthew to Acts* (London: Religious Tract Society, 1835), 54 n. 28.

2. "Bethany: Meeting Place for Friends," Franciscan Cyberspot, http://198.62.75.1/www1/ofm/san/BET09mod.html.

3. "The Ossuary of James," The Nazarene Way, www.thenazareneway.com/ossuary_of_james.htm.

4. While the "hurts, hang-ups, and habits" phrase was coined by Rick Warren and John E. Baker and is used extensively in the Celebrate Recovery organization, the descriptions of the three kinds of strongholds are mine. For more about Celebrate Recovery, which I highly recommend, please see Appendix C: "Resources for Resurrected Living."

5. This description is taken from John Baker, *Celebrate Recovery® Leader's Guide,* updated ed. (Grand Rapids: Zondervan, 2005), 56.

6. This information was collected from a four-year (and ongoing) survey of more than 200 churches conducted by the REVEAL™ research and strategy initiative under the auspices of the Willow Creek Association ministry. See Greg Hawkins and Cally Parkinson, *Follow Me: What's Next for You* (South Barrington, IL: Willow Creek Resources, 2008), 100.

7. Spiros Zodhiates, gen. ed., *The Complete Word Study Dictionary: New Testament,* rev. ed. (Chattanooga, TN: AMG International, 1993), s.v. "#3415" and "#3418."

8. Rick Renner, *Sparkling Gems from the Greek: 365 Greek Word Studies for Every Day of the Year to Sharpen Your Understanding of God's Word* (Tulsa, OK: Teach All Nations, 2003), 74.

Chapter Six: Roll Away the Stone

1. This is actually the subtitle of Groeschel's excellent book *The Christian Atheist: Believing in God but Living As If He Doesn't Exist* (Grand Rapids: Zondervan, 2010).

2. Joyce Meyer, *Battlefield of the Mind: Winning the Battle in Your Mind* (1995; repr., New York: Warner Faith, 2002), 12.

3. Ann Spangler, *The Tender Words of God: A Daily Guide* (Grand Rapids: Zondervan, 2008), 13.

4. Spangler, *Tender Words of God,* 15–16.

5. Spangler, *Tender Words of God,* 14.

6. Kenneth Wuest, *Wuest's Word Studies from the Greek New Testament,* vol. 2 (Grand Rapids: Eerdmans, 1973), 121.

7. The Greek word *dunamis* is used in the Bible to describe God's "miraculous power." (See James Strong, *The New Strong's Exhaustive Concordance of the Bible* (Nashville: Thomas Nelson, 1996), s.v. "1411, dunamis." It is also the root of our English word *dynamite.* (See "Word History," *American Heritage Dictionary of the English Language,* 4th ed., s.v. "dynamite," http://dictionary .reference.com/browse/dynamite.

Chapter Seven: When Love Calls Your Name

1. This phrase is inspired by the great hymn "Come Thou Fount of Every Blessing," whose words were written by Robert Robinson in 1758. For the story of how it was written, see "Come Thou Fount of Every Blessing," Center for Church Music Songs and Hymns, http://songsandhymns.org/hymns/ detail/come-thou-fount-of-every-blessing.

2. Priscilla Shirer, *Discerning the Voice of God: How to Recognize When God Speaks* (Chicago: Moody, 2007), 14.

3. Philip Yancey, *Grace Notes: Daily Readings with a Fellow Pilgrim* (Grand Rapids: Zondervan, 2009), 168.

4. Ken Gire, *Reflections on Your Life Journal: Discerning God's Voice in the Everyday Moments of Life* (Colorado Springs, CO: Chariot Victor, 1998), 11–12.

5. Henri J. M. Nouwen, *Letters to Marc About Jesus: Living a Spiritual Life in a Material World,* trans. Hubert Hoskins (San Francisco: HarperSanFrancisco, 1998), 84.

6. Brother Lawrence (ca. 1614–1691) was a French Carmelite lay brother whose simplicity and great wisdom inspired many during his life. After Lawrence's death, Father Joseph de Beaufort compiled his letters and conversations into a book called *The Practice of the Presence of God,* now considered a Christian classic. See "Biography of Brother Lawrence," Christian Classics Ethereal Library, www.ccel.org/l/Lawrence.

7. For more on journaling, see my book *Having a Mary Heart in a Martha World: Finding Intimacy with God in the Busyness of Life* (Colorado Springs, CO: WaterBrook, 2000), chapter 5 and Appendix D.

8. Special thanks to Marla Campbell, who shared this thought with me many years ago.

9. Shirer, *Discerning the Voice of God,* 184.

10. Oswald Chambers, *My Utmost for His Highest: The Golden Book of Oswald Chambers, Selections for the Year* (1935; repr., Westwood, NJ: Barbour, 1963), January 30.

11. Thanks to Dianne Freitag for this phrase, shared in personal conversation.

12. Mrs. Charles [Lettie B.] Cowman, *Streams in the Desert,* in *Streams in the Desert and Springs in the Valley,* Zondervan Treasures (1925; repr., Grand Rapids: Zondervan, 1996), February 9.

13. Cowman, *Streams in the Desert,* February 9.

Chapter Eight: Unwinding Graveclothes

1. Henry M. Grout, "The Good Samaritan," in The Monday Club, *Sermons on the International Sunday-School Lessons for 1881,* Sixth Series (New York: Thomas Y. Crowell, 1880), 151–2. Note: this passage seems to be a summary of ideas found in Charles H. Spurgeon's sermon "The Good Samaritan," sermon no. 1360 (delivered at the Metropolitan Tabernacle, Newington, England, June 17, 1877), www.spurgeongems.org/vols22-24/chs1360.pdf.

2. David O. Mears, "The Good Samaritan," in The Monday Club, *Sermons on the International Sunday-School Lessons for 1878* (Boston: Henry Hoyt, 1878), 303.

3. Wes Seeliger, *Faith at Work,* February 1972, 13, quoted in Bruce Larson, *Ask Me to Dance* (Waco, TX: Word Books, 1972), 11–12.

4. Jerry Goebel, "Unbind Him and Let Him Go!" ONEFamily Outreach, March 13, 2005, http://onefamilyoutreach.com/bible/John/jn_11_01-45.htm.

5. Goebel, "Unbind Him."

6. Goebel, "Unbind Him."

7. Thanks to Pastor Danny Stephenson for this thought.

8. Kathryn Spink, *Mother Teresa: A Complete Authorized Biography* (San Francisco: HarperSanFrancisco, 1997), 245.

9. Not her real name.

10. Mrs. Charles [Lettie B.] Cowman, *Springs in the Valley,* in *Streams in the Desert and Springs in the Valley,* Zondervan Treasures (1939; repr., Grand Rapids: Zondervan, 1996), February 22.

11. Oswald Chambers, *My Utmost for His Highest: The Golden Book of Oswald Chambers, Selections for the Year* (1935; repr., Westwood, NJ: Barbour, 1963), March 24.

12. Frank E. Peretti, *Piercing the Darkness* (Westchester, IL: Crossway Books, 1989).

13. Beth Moore, *Further Still: A Collection of Poetry and Vignettes* (Nashville: Broadman and Holman, 2004), 99–104.

14. Warren Wiersbe, *The Wiersbe Bible Commentary: New Testament,* 2nd ed. (Colorado Springs, CO: David C. Cook, 2007), 862.

Chapter Nine: Living Resurrected

1. Story told in V. Raymond Edman, *They Found the Secret: Twenty Transformed Lives That Reveal a Touch of Eternity* (1960; repr., Grand Rapids: Zondervan, 1984), 17–22. This particular quote is from page 18.

2. Edman, *They Found the Secret,* 19.

3. Edman, *They Found the Secret,* 19.

4. Edman, *They Found the Secret*, 17.

5. Edman, *They Found the Secret*, 17.

6. Hannah Whitall Smith, *The Unselfishness of God* (1903; repr., Princeton, NJ: Littlebrook, 1987), 193.

7. Julie Thompson, "Lazarus," in Charles May, ed., *Masterplots II: Short Story Series*, rev. ed. (Pasadena, CA: Salem Press, 2004), Enotes.com, 2006, www .enotes.com/lazarus-leonid-andreyev-salem/lazarus-9620000246.

8. Wendell Berry, quoted in Eugene H. Peterson, *Living the Resurrection: The Risen Christ in Everyday Life* (Colorado Springs, CO: NavPress, 2006), 13.

9. See my book *Having a Mary Spirit: Allowing God to Change Us from the Inside Out* (Colorado Springs, CO: WaterBrook, 2006), chapters 3 and 5.

10. W. Ian Thomas, *The Indwelling Life of Christ* (Sisters, OR: Multnomah, 2006), 151–52.

11. Thomas, *Indwelling Life of Christ*, 127.

12. Arthur T. Pierson, *George Müller of Bristol* (1899; repr., Grand Rapids: Hendrickson, 2008), 383 (emphasis added).

Chapter Ten: Laughing Lazarus

1. Mrs. Winchester's story and details about the house are summarized from "Sarah Winchester: Woman of Mystery" and "Winchester Mystery House™: Beautiful But Bizarre," Winchester Mystery House, www.winchester mysteryhouse.com/SarahWinchester.cfm and www.winchestermysteryhouse .com/thehouse.cfm. The quotation at the end of this paragraph is from Vernon Grounds, "An Inevitable Appointment," *Our Daily Bread*, April 2, 1994, http://odb.org/1994/04/02/an-inevitable-appointment/.

2. Woody Allen, "Afraid Quotes," Said What? www.saidwhat.co.uk/key wordquotes/afraid.

3. "Al-Eizariya," Serving History: World History Served Up Daily, www.serving history.com/topics/Al-Eizariya. (Al-Eizariya means "place of Lazarus.")

4. "Church of Ayios, Lazaros Larnaca," Serving History: World History Served Up Daily, www.servinghistory.com/topics/Church_of_Ayios,_Lazaros _Larnaca.

5. Eastern Orthodox tradition holds that after his resurrection Lazarus fled to Cyprus to escape persecution, was ordained by Paul and Barnabas as the first bishop of Kition (now Larnarca), and died there thirty years later. A competing tradition, now more or less debunked, holds that Lazarus fled with his sisters to Provence, became bishop of Marseilles, and was martyred and buried in what is now France. See Demetrios Serfes, "St. Lazarus the Friend of Christ and First Bishop of Kition, Cyprus," Lives of the Saints, www.serfes.org/lives/stlazarus.htm and Léon Clugnet, "St. Lazarus of Bethany," *The Catholic Encyclopedia*, vol. 9 (New York: Robert Appleton Company, 1910), www.newadvent .org/cathen/09097a.htm.

6. Ray C. Stedman with James D. Denney, *God's Loving Word: Exploring the Gospel of John* (Grand Rapids: Discovery House, 1993), 300.

7. John Claypool, "Easter and the Fear of Death" (program #3030, Chicago Sunday Evening Club, April 19, 1987), *30 Good Minutes*, www.csec.org// csec/sermon/claypool_3030.htm.

8. Mark Buchanan, *Things Unseen* (Sisters, OR: Multnomah, 2002), 43.

9. Marshall Shelley, "Two Minutes to Eternity," *Christianity Today*, May 16, 1994, 25–7, quoted in Buchanan, *Things Unseen*, 43–44.

10. Elisabeth Elliot, *Keep a Quiet Heart* (Ann Arbor, MI: Servant, 1995), 28.

11. Demetrios Serfes, "St. Lazarus the Friend of Christ and First Bishop of Kition, Cyprus," Lives of the Saints, www.serfes.org/lives/stlazarus.htm.

Appendix B: Study Guide

1. June Shaputis, "Funny Stones to Tickle Your Funny Bones," www.webpanda .com/ponder/epitaphs.htm.

2. Frederick Lehman, "The Love of God," 1917. Lehman wrote this hymn in Pasadena, California, and it was first published in *Songs That Are Different*, vol. 2 (1919). The lyrics are based on the Jewish poem "Haddamut," written in Aramaic in 1050 by Meir Ben Isaac Nehorai, a cantor in Worms, Germany. They have been translated into at least eighteen languages. See www .cyberhymnal.org/htm/l/o/loveofgo.htm.

Appendix D: Who I Am in Christ

1. From *One Day at a Time: The Devotional for Overcomers* by Neil T. Anderson and Mike and Julia Quarles, copyright 2000. Used by permission of Regal Books, a division of Gospel Light Publications. All rights reserved.

Appendix E: Identifying Strongholds

1. Brian Tome, *Free Book* (Nashville: Thomas Nelson, 2010). Tome's chapter on strongholds served as a springboard for some items on this list, but the specific applications and descriptions are mine.

Dear Reader,

After spending an initial year of mental silence while searching for inspiration for this book, I'm amazed at how many more things my heart wants to say as it comes to a close. I keep discovering new facets of the story of Lazarus—ideas and shades of meaning that, along with the ones in this book, can literally change our lives and help us find our place in the heart of God if we'll allow them to do so.

I pray that the Holy Spirit has taken my limited words and breathed fresh revelation to your heart between every line, shaping an individual message that has met your particular need. Helping you to die to yourself daily so that Jesus in you might live.

I'd love to hear about what God has spoken to you and the resurrection that is taking place in your life as you've chosen to obey. While I can't answer every letter, it would be my honor to pray for you. You can reach me through my Web site contact page at www.joannaweaverbooks.com or write me at

Joanna Weaver

PO Box 607

Hamilton, MT 59840

What an amazing adventure and privilege it is to live for God. I'm so grateful we've had a chance to share this part of our lives together. My prayer for you is that God might finish the work He began in you at salvation (Philippians 1:6)—bringing you out of your tomb, unwinding your graveclothes, and transforming your life with a Lazarus awakening. Enabling you to live free and out loud for Him in such a way that the world stands up and takes notice!

I love you, dear friend. I can't wait to meet you on that day we see Jesus face to face. Until then, let's dedicate ourselves to…

Becoming His,

Joanna